The Signs of the Zodiac

Everyone has all 12 signs of the Zodiac in their birth chart, but only one of them describes the person's sense of self, vitality, and purpose: the Sun ☉ sign. A Sun sign is determined by the position of the Sun on the date of a person's birth. If a person is born at the very beginning or end of a Sun sign, a calculated birth chart might be needed to accurately determine the Sun sign. The dates of birth are shown for each Sun sign. But there's much more to who you are than just your Sun sign, as you'll discover in *The Complete Idiot's Guide to Astrology, Third Edition.*

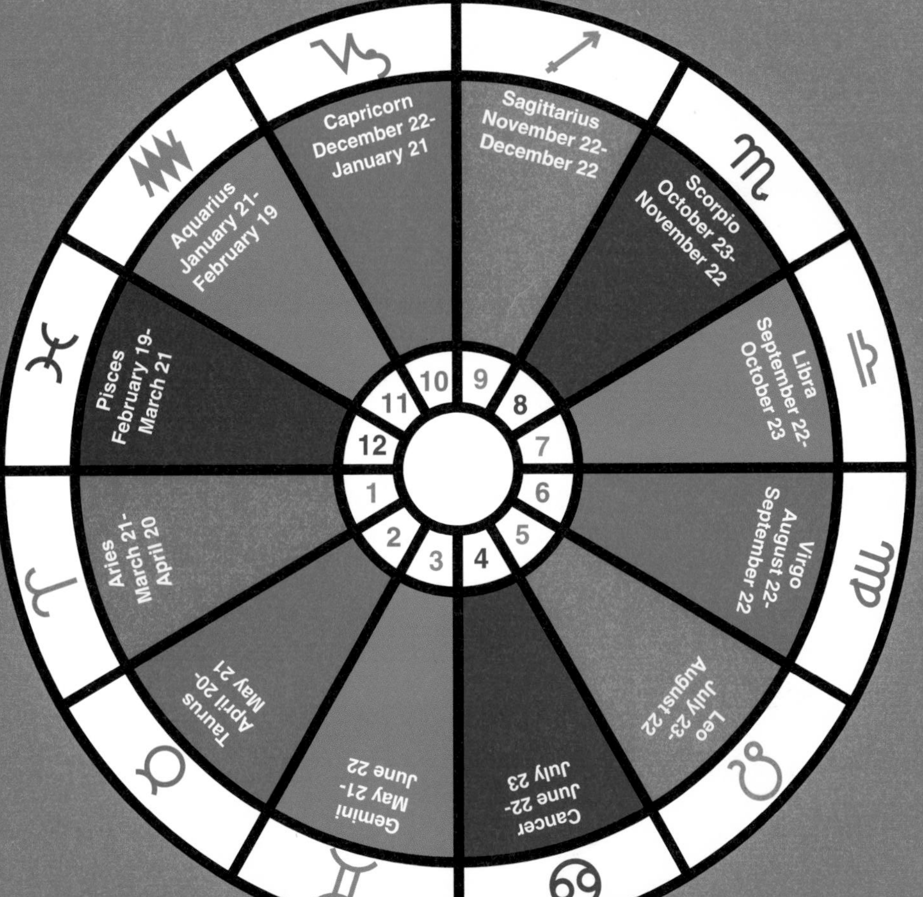

Capricorn
December 22-
January 21

Sagittarius
November 22-
December 22

Aquarius
January 21-
February 19

Scorpio
October 23-
November 22

Pisces
February 19-
March 21

Libra
September 22-
October 23

Aries
March 21-
April 20

Virgo
August 22-
September 22

Taurus
April 20-
May 21

Leo
July 23-
August 22

Gemini
May 21-
June 22

Cancer
June 22-
July 23

11 10 9 8
12   7
1   6
2   3 4 5

ALPHA

The Houses

Each of the 12 houses in a person's birth chart represents a major area of life. Together the houses describe all areas of a person's life, from the physical self to the home, responsibilities, relationships, career, and more. Descriptions for each house, or life area, are shown, and the associated number in each pie slice indicates the name of the house.

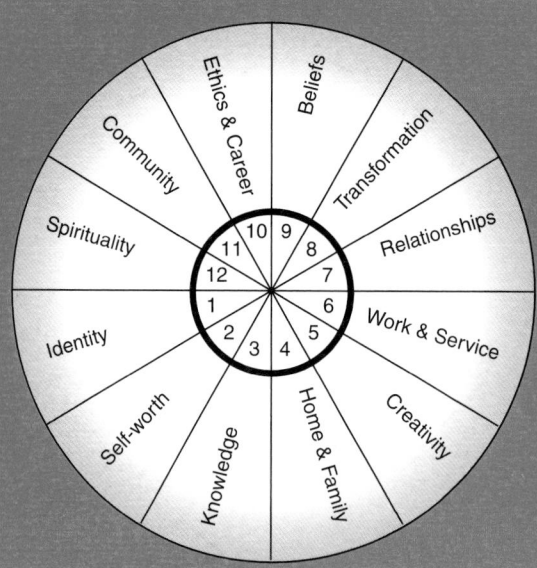

The Planets

Planet	Symbol	Energies
The Luminaries		
Sun	☉	Self, essence, life spirit, creativity, willpower
Moon	☽	Emotions, instincts, unconscious, past memories
The Personal Planets		
Mercury	☿	Mental activities, communication, intelligence
Venus	♀	Love, art, beauty, social graces, harmony, money, resources
Mars	♂	Physical energy, boldness, warrior ways, action, ego
The Social Planets		
Jupiter	♃	Luck, abundance, wisdom, higher education, philosophy
Saturn	♄	Responsibilities, self-discipline, perseverance, limitations
The Transpersonal Planets		
Uranus	♅	Sudden or unexpected change, originality, liberation
Neptune	♆	Idealism, subconscious, spirituality, intuition, clairvoyance
Pluto	♇	Power, regeneration, destruction, rebirth, transformation

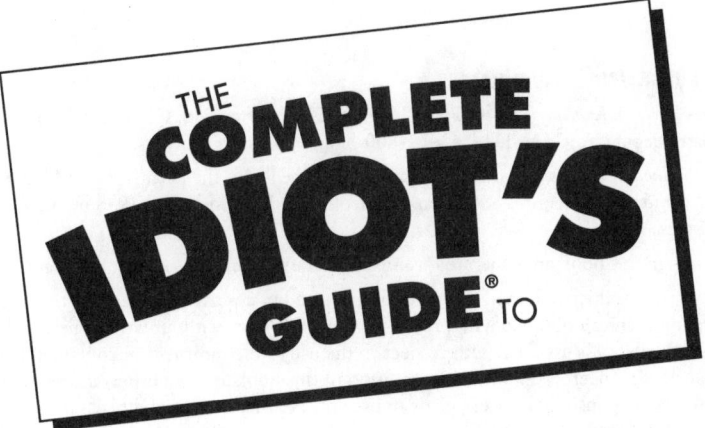

THE COMPLETE IDIOT'S GUIDE® TO

Astrology

Third Edition

by Madeline Gerwick-Brodeur and Lisa Lenard

ALPHA

A member of Penguin Group (USA) Inc.

Publisher: *Marie Butler-Knight*
Product Manager: *Phil Kitchel*
Senior Managing Editor: *Jennifer Chisholm*
Senior Acquisitions Editor: *Mike Sanders*
Book Producer: *Lee Ann Chearney/Amaranth Illuminare*
Development Editor: *Lynn Northrup*
Copy Editor: *Molly W. Schaller*
Illustrator: *Chris Eliopoulos*
Cover/Book Designer: *Trina Wurst*
Indexer: *Tonya Heard*
Layout/Proofreading: *Rebecca Harmon, Mary Hunt*

Contents at a Glance

Part 1:   **All About Astrology**   1

1   What Is Astrology?   3
Even astrology has a history, so let's debunk those myths.

2   Heavenly Revelations   13
Using astrology for love, money, and everything else in your everyday life.

3   Astrology Basics for Your Personal Forecast   25
Your birth chart—and all the mysterious symbols in it.

4   There's More to You Than Just Your Sun ☉ Sign   39
Your ascendant, your planets, your Nodes, and your houses.

Part 2:   **Touring the Zodiac: Sun ☉ Signs and Ascendants**   53

5   Spring Signs: Aries ♈, Taurus ♉, and Gemini ♊   55
The best and worst of the Ram, the Bull, and the Twins.

6   Summer Signs: Cancer ♋, Leo ♌, and Virgo ♍   67
The best and worst of the Crab, the Lion, and the Virgin.

7   Fall Signs: Libra ♎, Scorpio ♏, and Sagittarius ♐   81
The best and worst of the Scales, the Scorpion, and the Archer.

8   Winter Signs: Capricorn ♑, Aquarius ♒, and Pisces ♓   95
The best and worst of the Goat, the Water Bearer, and the Fishes.

9   Ascendants: The Mask You Wear for the World   109
Finding and understanding your rising sign.

Part 3:   **Heavenly Bodies and Your Astrological Birth Chart**   123

10   When the Moon Is in the Seventh House   125
The basics of your planets in their houses.

11   The Inner Planets: *Who Are You?*   135
An in-depth look at your Sun, Moon, Mercury, Venus, and Mars—your personal planets.

12   The Social Planets: You and Your World   153
An in-depth look at your Jupiter and Saturn—the planets that connect you to your world.

13 The Outer Planets and the Nodes: The Bigger Picture   161
    An in-depth look at your Uranus, Neptune, Pluto, and
    Nodes—the planets that connect you to the universe.

14 Retrogrades ℞: One Step Forward and Two Steps Back   175
    Learning about retrograde planets and their energies.

Part 4:   The Twelve Astrological Houses: Unlocking the Mystery of *You*   187

15 Houses in the First Quadrant: Let's Get Personal   189
    A closer look at the first, second, and third houses—where
    you'll find your personality, resources, and surroundings.

16 Houses in the Second Quadrant: Establishing Yourself   205
    A closer look at the fourth, fifth, and sixth houses—where you
    live, work, and create.

17 Houses in the Third Quadrant: Out in the World   219
    A closer look at the seventh, eighth, and ninth houses—those
    places you connect with others.

18 Houses in the Fourth Quadrant: Wishin' and Hopin'   233
    A closer look at the tenth, eleventh, and twelfth houses—
    where you'll find your career, goals, and subconscious.

Part 5:   Getting and Interpreting Your Birth Chart   249

19 Getting Started   251
    The basics for getting your birth chart.

20 Lost in Space: How a Computer Calculates a
    Birth Chart   259
    The math behind calculating your astrological chart.

21 All About Me: Interpreting Your Birth Chart   273
    Beginning your interpretation, plus aspects.

22 Using Astrology to Map Your Life   291
    Transits, progressions, and windows of opportunity.

Part 6:   You've Done Your Chart, Now You Want More   307

23 Relationship Astrology: Love Matches Made in
    Heaven, or in …?   309
    A relationship astrology primer.

24 Other Heavenly Influences: The Asteroids and Chiron   323
    Meet the heavenly bodies that add extra meaning to your
    birth chart.

25 Moon ☽ Phases: Our Unconscious Collective
Mood Monitor   333
Earth-Moon connections go far beyond the tides.

26 The Best Timing for Better Business   341
Using astrology to improve your productivity and profits.

27 Larger Astrological Cycles and the Next 100 Years   351
Using astrology to map the future.

Appendixes

A Online with the Heavens   363

B Resources for the Starry-Eyed: If You Want
to Find Out More   365

C Glossary   373

Index   381

Contents

Part 1: All About Astrology   **1**

1   What Is Astrology?   **3**

Astrology: The First Science 3

Our Calendar Is Based on Astrology 5

Debunking the Myths 6

The Planets Reflect Human Behavior 7

Astrology: An Intuitive Art 7

Astrology and Science Can Peacefully Coexist 8

Smart People Use Astrology 8

Famous Astrologers 9

The Three Wise Men 9

Pythagoras (580?–500? B.C.E.) 10

Nostradamus (1503–1566) 10

Isaac Newton (1642–1727) 10

Steering by the Stars 11

Getting in Touch with Ancient Rhythms 11

An Open Mind, a Curious Nature, and a Sense of Humor 12

2   Heavenly Revelations   **13**

What Astrology Can Reveal in Your Everyday Life 13

The Company You Keep 14

The Signs and Your Career 15

Healthy in Mind and Body 16

Cosmic Investments and Money Management 18

Home Is Where Your Hat Is 19

Horoscope Junkies 19

Can You Believe Everything You Read in the Papers? 20

Free Will vs. Your Daily Forecast 21

Hot Lines: The Best Advice or Costly Rip-Offs? 21

Astrology Is Everywhere: Going Beyond the Stars 22

3   Astrology Basics for Your Personal Forecast   **25**

What Is an Astrological Chart? 26

Your Chart Shows the Position of the Heavens at Your Birth 27

Making Sense of the Symbols 28

Energies, Qualities, and Elements (You Thought This
  Was Gonna Be Easy?) 29
  Energies: Two for the Show *30*
  Qualities: Three to Get Ready *31*
  Elements: Four to Go *33*
Let the Sun Shine 35
  Intuitive Connections *36*
  You and Your Sun ☉ Sign *36*
You Are Unique 38

4 **There's More to You Than Just Your Sun ☉ Sign**   **39**
Ascendants 39
The Sun ☉, the Moon ☽, the Planets, and the Nodes ☊☋ 41
  Every Heavenly Body Tells a Story *42*
  What Are Nodes, Anyway? *43*
  Planetary Rulers *44*
  Planet Power: Where Do You Put Your Energy? *45*
Houses 45
  Each House Is an Area of Your Life *46*
  Knock, Knock, Who's There? Heavenly Bodies in Your Houses *47*
A Tour Beyond the Sun (Sign) 48
  What's Rising? *48*
  The Planets *50*
  Who's in Charge? *51*

Part 2:   **Touring the Zodiac: Sun ☉ Signs and Ascendants**   **53**

5 **Spring Signs: Aries ♈, Taurus ♉, and Gemini ♊**   **55**
Aries ♈, the Ram: Leading the Charge 55
  The Best and Worst of Ram *57*
  Rams in Love *57*
  The Healthy Ram *58*
  Rams at Home *58*
  Rams at Work *58*
  Rams and Their Money *59*
Taurus ♉, the Bull: Keeping the Home Fires Simmering 59
  The Best and Worst of Bull *60*
  Bulls in Love *61*
  The Healthy Bull *61*
  Bulls at Home *62*

Bulls at Work 62
Bulls and Their Money 63
Gemini ♊, the Twins: Quick-Witted, Quicksilver 63
The Best and Worst of Twins 64
Twins in Love 65
Healthy Twins 65
Twins at Home 66
Twins at Work 66
Twins and Their Money 66

6 Summer Signs: Cancer ♋, Leo ♌, and Virgo ♍   67
Cancer ♋, the Crab: Wear Your Heart on Your Sleeve 67
The Best and Worst of Crabs 69
Crabs in Love 69
The Healthy Crab 70
Crabs at Home 70
Crabs at Work 71
Crabs and Their Money 71
Leo ♌, the Lion: King of the Jungle 72
The Best and Worst of Lions 73
Lions in Love 73
The Healthy Lion 74
Lions at Home 74
Lions at Work 75
Lions and Their Money 75
Virgo ♍, the Virgin: Practical Perfection 75
The Best and Worst of Virgins 77
Virgins in Love 78
The Healthy Virgin 78
Virgins at Home 79
Virgins at Work 79
Virgins and Their Money 79

7 Fall Signs: Libra ♎, Scorpio ♏, and Sagittarius ♐   81
Libra ♎, the Scales: A Fine Balance 81
The Best and Worst of Scales 82
Scales in Love 83
Healthy Scales 84
Scales at Home 84
Scales at Work 85
Scales and Their Money 85

Scorpio ♏, the Scorpion: Intense Power 85

The Best and Worst of Scorpions 87

Scorps in Love 88

The Healthy Scorp 88

Scorps at Home 88

Scorps at Work 89

Scorps and Their Money 90

Sagittarius ♐, the Archer: Flying High 90

The Best and Worst of Archers 91

Archers in Love 92

The Healthy Archer 92

Archers at Home 93

Archers at Work 93

Archers and Their Money 93

8 Winter Signs: Capricorn ♑, Aquarius ♒, and Pisces ♓   95

Capricorn ♑, the Goat: Ain't No Mountain High Enough 95

The Best and Worst of Goats 97

Goats in Love 97

The Healthy Goat 98

Goats at Home 98

Goats at Work 99

Goats and Their Money 99

Aquarius ♒, the Water Bearer: The Quiet Revolutionaries 99

The Best and Worst of W-Bs 101

W-Bs in Love 101

The Healthy W-B 102

W-Bs at Home 103

W-Bs at Work 103

W-Bs and Their Money 104

Pisces ♓, the Fishes: How Deep Is the Ocean? 104

The Best and Worst of Fishes 106

Fishes in Love 106

Healthy Fishes 107

Fishes at Home 107

Fishes at Work 108

Fishes and Their Money 108

9 Ascendants: The Mask You Wear for the World   109

What's Rising? 110

Rising Signs 114

Rising Signs of Spring 114
  Ram Rising: The Aries ♈ Ascendant *114*
  Bull Rising: The Taurus ♉ Ascendant *115*
  Twins Rising: The Gemini ♊ Ascendant *115*
The Rising Signs of Summer 116
  Crabs Rising: The Cancer ♋ Ascendant *116*
  Lion Rising: The Leo ♌ Ascendant *117*
  Virgin Rising: The Virgo ♍ Ascendant *117*
The Rising Signs of Fall 118
  Scales Rising: The Libra ♎ Ascendant *118*
  Scorp Rising: The Scorpio ♏ Ascendant *119*
  Archer Rising: The Sagittarius ♐ Ascendant *119*
The Rising Signs of Winter 120
  Goat Rising: The Capricorn ♑ Ascendant *120*
  W-B Rising: The Aquarius ♒ Ascendant *121*
  Fishes Rising: The Pisces ♓ Ascendant *122*

Part 3:   Heavenly Bodies and Your Astrological Birth Chart   123

10   When the Moon Is in the Seventh House   125
The Lessons in Housekeeping 126
  A House Is More Than a Home *126*
  What's Behind Those Doors? *129*
  Star Gazing: Heavenly Bodies in Your Astrological Chart ...*129*
  Where Are the Heavenly Bodies? *130*
The Planets as Landlords 131
When Planets Seem Backward: Retrogrades ℞ 133
Why Neptune ♆ and Pluto ♇ Are Special 133

11   The Inner Planets: *Who Are You?*   135
The Sun ☉: Mr. BIG 136
The Moon ☽: Bewitched, Bothered, and Bewildered 136
Moonshine: The Moon ☽ in Each Zodiac Sign 138
Mercury ☿: Instant Messaging 142
  How You Think: Mercury ☿ in Each Zodiac Sign *142*
Venus ♀: Beauty and the Beast 145
  How You Love: Venus ♀ in Each Zodiac Sign *146*
Mars ♂: War and Peace 148
  How You're Driven: Mars in Each Zodiac Sign *149*

12 The Social Planets: You and Your World 153

Jupiter ♃: Here Comes Santa Claus 154
How You Grow: Jupiter ♃ in Each Zodiac Sign *154*
Saturn ♄: Just the Facts, Ma'am 157
Knowing Your Limits: Saturn ♄ in Each Zodiac Sign *157*

13 The Outer Planets and the Nodes: The Bigger Picture 161

Uranus ♅: Born to Be Wild 162
Your Liberator: Uranus ♅ in Each Zodiac Sign *162*
Neptune ♆: Dream a Little Dream 165
How You're Inspired: Neptune ♆ in Each Zodiac Sign *166*
Pluto ♇: Soul Journey 169
How You're Changing: Pluto ♇ in Each Zodiac Sign *169*
The Nodes ☊☋: Back to the Future 171
Coming and Going: The Nodal Pairs ☊☋ in Each Zodiac Sign *172*

14 Retrogrades ℞: One Step Forward and Two Steps Back 175

A Brief History of Planetary Motion 175
Understanding Retrograde ℞ Planets 176
Personal Retrogrades: Self-Expression *177*
Transiting Retrogrades: Change Is a Fact of Life *178*
Mercury Retrograde: Crossed Wires ☿℞ 179
Personal Mercury Retrograde *179*
Transiting Mercury Retrograde *180*
Venus Retrograde: What's Love Got to Do with It? ♀℞ 180
Personal Venus Retrograde *180*
Transiting Venus Retrograde *181*
Mars Retrograde: Inward Action ♂℞ 181
Personal Mars Retrograde *181*
Transiting Mars Retrograde *181*
Jupiter Retrograde: Stepping Back ♃℞ 182
Personal Jupiter Retrograde *182*
Transiting Jupiter Retrograde *182*
Saturn Retrograde: Restructuring ♄℞ 183
Personal Saturn Retrograde *183*
Transiting Saturn Retrograde *183*
Uranus Retrograde: The Times, They Are A-Changing ♅℞ ..184
Personal Uranus Retrograde *184*
Transiting Uranus Retrograde *184*

Neptune Retrograde: Not Just Blind Faith ΨR 184
Personal Neptune Retrograde *185*
Transiting Neptune Retrograde *185*
Pluto Retrograde: Transformation Time ♇R 185
Personal Pluto Retrograde *186*
Transiting Pluto Retrograde *186*

Part 4: The Twelve Astrological Houses: Unlocking the Mystery of You   187

15   Houses in the First Quadrant: Let's Get Personal   189
Houses Are Where It Is 190
Like Four Points of the Compass 190
The First House: Taking Care of Number 1 192
Heavenly Bodies and Me, Me, Me *193*
The Second House: Are You What You Own? 195
What Do I Have in the House? *196*
The Third House: The Street Where You Live 199
Heavenly Bodies in Your 'Hood *200*

16   Houses in the Second Quadrant: Establishing Yourself   205
The Fourth House: It's a Family Affair 206
Who's Nesting in This House? *207*
The Fifth House: Do What You Wanna Do 209
Getting Creative *210*
The Sixth House: Nine to Five 213
Heavenly Bodies at Work *214*

17   Houses in the Third Quadrant: Out in the World   219
The Seventh House: Forever Yours 219
Heavenly Connections *220*
The Eighth House: Sex, Money, and Other Equally
Important Matters 223
Who's in the Bedroom? *225*
The Ninth House: Don't Know Much About History 228
What's Behind Your Beliefs? *229*

18   Houses in the Fourth Quadrant: Wishin' and Hopin'   233
The Tenth House: They Say the Neon Lights Are Bright 233
Your Supporting Cast *235*

The Eleventh House: When You Wish Upon a Star 238
    Reaching for the Stars *239*
The Twelfth House: Secret Agent 242
    Skeletons in Your Closet *243*

Part 5:   Getting and Interpreting Your Birth Chart   249

19 Getting Started   251
How Easy Is It to Do Your Own Birth Chart? (It's Not) 251
Your Vital Statistics 252
    Your Most Important Day *253*
    The Time of Your Life *254*
    Where Did You Come From? *255*
Resources Your Computer's Replaced (Just to Give
    You an Idea) 255
    Ephemeris *255*
    Table of Houses *256*
    Atlas *256*
    Book of Time Zone Changes *257*
Getting Your Birth Chart Done for You 257

20 Lost in Space: How a Computer Calculates a Birth Chart   259
It's About Time; It's About Space 260
    Working in Base 60 ....*260*
    Converting to GMT *260*
To Boldly Seek Those Planetary Positions 261
    Daily Travel *262*
    What About Retrogrades? *263*
    A Wrinkle in Sidereal, or Star, Time *264*
    Calculating Sidereal Time *265*
    Will the True Local Time Please Stand Up? *265*
    Calculating True Local Time *266*
    Acceleration *267*
    Correction for Place of Birth *268*
Houses, Houses, and More Houses! 269
    Desperately Seeking House Cusps *270*
    The Search for Midheaven *271*
    Calculating the Other Houses *271*
Putting It All Together 272

21 All About Me: Interpreting Your Birth Chart   273

Chart Basics: It's All Greek to Me 273
Aspects: Specifics on Experience 275
  The New Math: From Conjunctions ☌ to Sextiles ⚹ 277
  Getting Along: Venus/Jupiter Aspects 279
  A Harder Row to Hoe: Sun/Saturn Aspects 280
  Aspect Grid 281
Chart Interpretations Even Idiots Can Make 282
  Your Astrological Signature 284
  Sowing or Reaping: Which Lifetime Are You In? 284
A Sample Chart Interpreted, or Let's Be Voyeurs 285
  Here Comes the Sun ☉! 287
  Moon River (a.k.a. Moon ☽ in Scorpio ♏) 288
  And He's Got Personality! 288
  Happy Trails to You! 289
When You Need to Know More: Professional Readings 289

22 Using Astrology to Map Your Life   291

What Transits and Progressions Have to Do with You 291
Progressions, or I Can't Stand Still 292
  Themes for Personal Change 293
  Who, Me? Evolve? 294
  How Your Chart Evolves 294
Transits, or Planetary Triggers 297
  Outer and Social Planet Transits 299
  From the Terrible Twos to the Midlife Crisis and Beyond 300
  Oh, What Fun It Is to Transform Ourselves! 302
  Uranus ♅ and Neptune ♆ and Saturn ♄—Oh My! 302
  Unlocking Personal Transits 303
Astrology Is Your Compass 304
  Windows of Opportunity 304
  Jump or Be Pushed, Your Choice 305
  If You Want to Know More 306

Part 6:   You've Done Your Chart, Now You Want More   **307**

23   Relationship Astrology: Love Matches Made in Heaven, or in ...?   **309**

Relationship Astrology and You 310
Charting Your Relationships 310
   Signposts *312*
   Planet Placings *313*
   House Hunting *314*
   Aspects, Heart to Heart *314*
Stars by the Stars: The Relationship Charts of Michael
   Douglas and Catherine Zeta-Jones 316
Matches Made in Heaven 320

24   Other Heavenly Influences: The Asteroids and Chiron   **323**

Goddesses in Your Everyday Life 324
   Ceres ⚳: Mom, With or Without the Apple Pie *324*
   Juno ⚵: The Queen of All Wives *325*
   Pallas Athene ⚴: Wise Woman and Warrior *326*
   Vesta ⚶: The Importance of Being Devoted *327*
Chiron: Astrology Meets Shamanism 328
   Ancient Art Meets Modern Mastery *328*
   Heal Thyself *329*
But Seriously, Folks: The Asteroids and Chiron in
   Jay Leno's Birth Chart 330

25   Moon ☽ Phases: Our Unconscious Collective Mood Monitor   **333**

What Are Moon Phases? 334
   Flavors of the Day: Every Day Tells a Story *334*
   Void, of Course *335*
   In and Out with the Tide *335*
   Everybody Feels the Pull *336*
How Moon Phases Affect the Way We Do Things 337
   Using Moon Signs to Guide You *338*
   Beginnings and the New Moon ● *338*
   First Quarter Moon: External Challenges ◐ *338*
   Full Moon: The Better to See What's Happening ○ *339*
   Third Quarter Moon: Internal Challenges ◑ *340*

26 The Best Timing for Better Business   341

Working with Cycles, Not Against Them 342
Time Outs: Don't Do It! 342
   Swimming Against the Tide 343
   A Message from the Universe: Relax! 343
Gearing Up and Reaching Out 344
   Listening to Mars ♂ 344
   Warning: Mars Retrograde ♂℞ 345
   What Goes Wrong 345
   And Still More Problems! 346
   What to Do, What Not to Do 346
Communications, Travel, and Computers: Mercury ☿ 346
   Ignoring the Messenger 347
   Don't Rush! 347
   Working with Mercury ☿ 348
Getting to "Yes" and Signing on the Dotted Line 348
   The Venus ♀ Bottom Line 349
   False Starts 349

27 Larger Astrological Cycles and the Next 100 Years   351

How the Heavens Reflect Our Global Experience 352
Where the Heavens Are Now: The Age of Aquarius 352
A Study of Cycles: As Above, So Below 353
Saturn ♄-Jupiter ♃ Challenges and Opportunities 354
   2000 to 2020: Aries ♈ to Pisces ♓ 354
   2020 to 2040: Aries ♈ to Pisces ♓ 356
   2040 to 2060: Aries ♈ to Pisces ♓ 357
   2060 to 2080: Aries ♈ to Pisces ♓ 359
   2080 to 2100: Aries ♈ to Pisces ♓ 360
A New World Awaits 362

Appendixes

A Online with the Heavens   363

B Resources for the Starry-Eyed: If You Want to Find Out More   365

C Glossary   373

Index   381

Foreword

How a Book—Not as Good as This One—Made Me See Stars!!!

I was on a train, going from Grand Central Station in New York City up to New Canaan, Connecticut. I dug into the book I had just bought impulsively—just as you have perhaps bought this one. As far as astrology was concerned—and perhaps brain surgery or fixing electrical appliances—I was at the "idiot level."

I found myself immediately fascinated: There were juicy new power words to learn, ways to say things that sounded a little mysterious but, according to the author, were as clear as the Liberty Bell clanging for my personal freedom, my individuality as a birthright gift from the gods! "I'M A CAPRICORN because the Sun was located in that sign when I was born! I MEAN BUSINESS. I GET THINGS DONE. (I can be pretty melancholic sometimes, but don't tell anyone.) BUT I'M IN THERE FOR THE LONG HAUL. I AGE WELL!"

My brain was racing through the pages to pick up more things about my Capricorn nature. There was something pointed out about my tremendous attraction to any PISCES woman who ever lived. I filed that away (and remembered it regularly throughout 27 years with two Pisces ladies!).

There was a lot about my incompatibility with ARIES people (and I knew that that explained everything about my relationship with my mother, God take her soul!).

Okay. When I finally settled down, I saw that astrology had *reasons* for these generalities, that those reasons were tied to the miracle of creation, to millennia of keen observations by wise people, and that the mysteries of being were easily converted into strategies of becoming—I was hooked!

By the time I had arrived at New Canaan on that hot summer day, I didn't need a cool drink as much as I needed pencil and paper. I was going to follow the guidelines in the book and start to build my horoscope, the portrait of my birth in space and time, the portrait of who I am (the nice stuff, the tough stuff, all of it!).

Books, Lines, and Thinkers: How hooked was I? I studied, studied, studied, and gradually realized that nothing was more interesting to me in the world than astrology—and it probably was also in a previous life, as I was learning. I saw how I could appreciate myself and my purpose in life, and how I could help others to do the same. Time and space now started to mean something more than three meals a day, a raise now and then, college education for the children, and the IRS.

And that book, with the neat lines and the quotes from all the wise men from Ptolemy to Newton to Einstein to J. P. Morgan, was NOWHERE NEAR AS GOOD AS THIS ONE YOU'RE HOLDING RIGHT NOW.

Watch Out! Be warned: Madeline Gerwick-Brodeur has the lines that will hook you, too; she's one of those wise thinkers in astrology who really knows what she's talking about.

And Madeline and her co-author, Lisa Lenard, have STYLE. This book is a breeze. For example (getting back to the Pisces issue, please), their "Fish Facts" talks about the (delightful) character trait to live largely in the world of the imagination, the realm of dreams, where objects and events seem to have no connection to outer reality. (I, the Capricorn warlord of accomplishment, love it!) But then, they tack on the lines that show you the substance within all the fun: "Above all, Fishes (Pisces) are here to give, not just to those like themselves, but to anyone who needs their help, love, attention, or whatever." Isn't that lovely? Isn't that valid? And that's just the beginning. How do all the traits, powers, and interrelationships among the planets within the signs reflect your life, the details of your progress, the outlines of your dreams, the dynamics of your relationships?

Well, my fateful train ride those many years ago took me to write some 24 technical astrological texts of my own, to lecture throughout the world, and to appreciate *this Complete Idiot's Guide* to the field I love. I can tell you for sure that, from now on, when I introduce newcomers to this fascinating world, I will recommend this guide. They, and you, will be thrilled with Madeline Gerwick-Brodeur and Lisa Lenard's introduction to seeing stars. It's expert, it's charming, it's easy.

All aboard!

Noel Tyl
World-renowned astrologer and presiding officer of the Association for Astrological Networking

Introduction

You're probably familiar with Sun sign forecasts, the horoscopes that appear in the daily newspapers. And you probably know your Sun sign, too. But did you know that Sun signs are just the beginning of astrology? Did you know, for example, that all 12 signs appear somewhere in your own birth chart? Or that, in addition to the Sun, the Moon and planets appear in your birth chart, too? Have you ever heard of astrological houses?

Based on the date, place, and time of your birth, the planets and signs in the houses of your birth chart create a metaphor for you. While there are hundreds of astrology books out there, some general and some intricately technical, this book is unique because it's about *you*. It shows you how your planets in their signs and houses can help you understand more about yourself and your life. It explains not only what all those symbols for signs and planets mean, but also how they connect with your everyday life: who you are, who you love (and who you don't!), why you do what you do, feel like you do, live where you live, and work where you work.

Astrology can explain all of that? Yes, it can. Planets are the *what* of astrology, showing the various energies at work in your life. Signs show *how* those energies behave in your birth chart, and houses are *where* the various areas of your life unfold, from relationships to financial concerns. Curious? Read on to find out more about astrology and you.

How to Use This Book

While some of the more advanced material in this book will make more sense if you have a birth chart in front of you, it's not a requirement. We do strongly recommend, though, that you get your birth chart and study it as you read. You can get your birth chart from your local metaphysical bookstore or even online; see Chapter 19 for more details. When getting your chart, be sure to specify Geocentric view, Tropical Zodiac, Placidus house system, and True Node. Charts appearing in this book are generated with Solar Fire software, published by Astrolabe, Inc. Check out their website at www.alabe.com.

The Complete Idiot's Guide to Astrology, Third Edition, is divided into six parts.

Part 1, "All About Astrology," introduces you to astrology: its history, some of its branches, and the basics of exactly what a birth chart is—and what's in one.

Part 2, "Touring the Zodiac: Sun ☉ Signs and Ascendants," takes you through the Sun signs. This is more than just a cursory look; it's an analysis of each sign in love and health, at work, at home, and with money, as well as each sign's best and worst sides. You'll also look at your ascendant, or rising sign.

Part 3, "Heavenly Bodies and Your Astrological Birth Chart," moves through the planets in each sign so that you become more familiar with the potentials for each one. You'll also learn about the effects of retrograde planets.

Part 4, "The Twelve Astrological Houses: Unlocking the Mystery of *You*," explores the signs and planets throughout the houses.

Part 5, "Getting and Interpreting Your Birth Chart," shows you the basics of what a computer does to calculate a birth chart and then moves beyond the basics of a chart to help you understand aspects, transits, and progressions.

Part 6, "You've Done Your Chart, Now You Want More," discusses more ways to use astrology. We'll take a look at relationship astrology. We'll also look at the asteroids, Chiron, Moon phases, and how to time your business decisions wisely. Finally, we'll show you how astrologers look at the future.

Welcome to your past, present, and future. Fasten your seatbelt for an astrological ride—and guide—through your life.

Extras

In addition to helping you understand and learn more about astrology, there's other good information in this book as well, highlighted in sidebars like the following:

Heaven Knows

These astrological tips are just the tip of the iceberg to all that the heavens hold!

StarFacts

Here's where you'll find fascinating bits of information you might not have known that relate to astrology.

Star-Crossed

Take care with these cautionary sidebars; they can help you avoid making astrological errors.

AstroLingo

These sidebars define astrological terms so that you, too, can speak the language.

Acknowledgments

Astrology assumes the interconnectedness of all things, which is called *synchronicity*. And how we came to write this book is a tale of synchronicity: Lee Ann Chearney at Amaranth, our book producer, happened to be in Colorado several years ago, and Lisa happened to meet her there. Then Lisa found Madeline online when Lee Ann approached her about this book. Synchronicity acknowledges that there are meaningful coincidences, and this book is proof that they do exist.

Lisa would like to thank Will Camp, her Spring 1997 Advanced Composition class at Fort Lewis College in Durango, Erika Wilson, for the lightbulb jokes, and her ever-patient family and friends. A special thanks goes to Arlene Tognetti, whose quick astrological insights have come in handy more than once. And most of all, thanks to Madeline, whose voice and passion for astrology come through on every page of this book.

Madeline gives many thanks to David, Aria, and Lee Ann for their support, and to the clients she had to reschedule to meet this book's deadlines. A special thanks also to Harold J. Langseth, her first business client, and to all her friends, peers, and clients for their continued encouragement. Most of all, she gives thanks to Lisa for finding her and for creating a funny, readable book about a complex topic. She dedicates this book to her late brother, James, her family's first author.

Special Thanks to Noel Tyl

Both of us would like to give a very special thanks to world-famous astrologer Noel Tyl, for reviewing and endorsing this book. When we caught up with him he was preparing for a tour of South Africa, guiding 170 correspondent students, writing a book, and, of course, seeing clients! His graciousness in accommodating our special needs was truly tremendous.

Noel Tyl is well known for his more than 24 books on astrology, his frequent talks throughout the world for more than 20 years, and his pioneering work in the connections between psychological need theory and astrology. Mr. Tyl, a graduate of Harvard University, is also an internationally acclaimed opera singer and presiding officer of the Association for Astrological Networking (AFAN). True to his Capricorn nature, Mr. Tyl has distinguished himself in many ways, and we are thrilled to have his endorsement.

Special Thanks to the Technical Reviewers

The Complete Idiot's Guide to Astrology, First Edition, was reviewed by an expert who not only checked its technical accuracy but also added significant insights and suggestions. Our special thanks to Joanne Wickenburg.

Ms. Wickenburg is one of the foremost astrologers in North America. She has conducted classes and workshops throughout the United States and Canada and has designed and teaches an internationally recognized correspondence course in astrology. She is one of the founding Board Members of The Kepler College of Astrological Arts and Sciences, the first-ever liberal arts college in which the complete curriculum is designed around astrology.

Ms. Wickenburg has served as both president and treasurer of the Washington State Astrological Association, who presented her with the Most Inspirational Astrologer award in 1982. She has professional certification through both the WSAA and the American Federation of Astrologers.

A frequent lecturer for numerous national and international astrology conferences, Ms. Wickenburg is the author and co-author of several popular books on astrology.

The second and third editions of *The Complete Idiot's Guide to Astrology* were reviewed by astrologer and Tarot reader Arlene Tognetti, co-author, with Lisa Lenard, of *The Complete Idiot's Guide to Tarot, Second Edition*. We thank Arlene for her attention to technical accuracy and insightfulness, particularly in regard to relationship astrology and selected birth chart interpretations.

Trademarks

All terms mentioned in this book that are known to be or are suspected of being trademarks or service marks have been appropriately capitalized. Alpha Books Penguin Group (USA) Inc. cannot attest to the accuracy of this information. Use of a term in this book should not be regarded as affecting the validity of any trademark or service mark.

Part 1

All About Astrology

What is astrology, anyway? Why are so many people interested in it? Well, for starters, astrology is an intuitive art that smart people use every day. Astrology was the first science, and famous astrologers included the Three Wise Men, Pythagoras, Nostradamus, and Isaac Newton.

Astrology studies the movements of the Sun, Moon, and planets and their connection to everyone and everything on Earth. We like to think of it as a system that uses the outer world as a metaphor for the inner world.

If you're ready to get in touch with ancient rhythms and apply them to your everyday life, pack up your open mind, your curiosity, and your sense of humor and come along for a fascinating tour that takes you beyond your Sun ☉ sign to what astrology reveals about you.

What Is Astrology?

In This Chapter

◆ Astrology was the first science

◆ Astrology is an intuitive art

◆ Astrology and science can coexist

◆ Steering by the stars

Long before physics, chemistry, biology, or any of those other subjects you tried to avoid in high school or college, there was astrology. Astrology, in fact, was the first science. As early as 2900 B.C.E., the Sumerians built temples in the form of ziggurats, or terraced pyramids, to observe the stars and planets. It's a pretty safe assumption that astrology existed even prior to this. In this chapter, we'll explore the scientific origins of astrology.

Astrology: The First Science

From its ancient beginnings, *astrology* soon developed into an incredibly complex practice. By 2000 B.C.E., the magi of Mesopotamia believed that there were no accidents, and that everything in the universe—people, objects, and events—was connected. Not only did the magi (priests trained in astrology and other sacred knowledge) study the stars, they looked for omens in the weather, predicted the future from the livers and intestines of animals, and listened to what they believed to be the words of trees, dogs, cats, and insects to hear what they had to say.

AstroLingo

Astrology began as the study of the "wandering" stars (or planets, as we know them today). It is actually the study of planetary cycles and how the energies of these events relate to their concurrent time on Earth. Put another way, astrology uses the harmony of the universe to observe the possibilities of human behavior and experience. *Astrologers* analyze the position of the planets at the time and place you were born to map not only your strengths and challenges but your soul's purpose as well.

Let's forget about the magi for the time being, and picture our ancestors, standing outside, looking up. What did they see? Well, they saw what we see—stars, and planets, and meteors. They saw the Milky Way, and the sunrise and the sunset, and the Moon in all its phases.

Long before other sciences came along, in fact, astrology was used to explore the relationship between the position of Earth and the positions of these bodies in the heavens. In ancient times, astrology and astronomy were one science, and astrologers were the best educated people: They had to understand astronomy, math, spiritual symbols and mystic meanings, psychology, and human nature.

Heaven Knows

Your birth chart represents *your possibilities*. Knowing if you have a tendency to be direct in matters of business or circumspect in matters of love, for example, can help you determine how to use such strengths and weaknesses to your best advantage. Think of astrology as a way of discovering more about your unique self!

It shouldn't come as a surprise, then, that astrology was taught in the universities until the 1600s, when "rational science" took over. Today, most *astrologers* are still very well educated and often hold college degrees in various fields. They frequently have training in psychology or counseling, and in addition to their in-depth knowledge of astrology have a great deal of spiritual understanding.

Put simply, astrology is based on the relationships between the *planets;* the Sun and the Moon; 12 *zodiac, or Sun, signs;* and 12 areas of a person's life, called *houses.* Even after thousands of years, astrology provides a psychological model that offers explanations for phenomena rational science just can't address.

- **Planets** are the "what" of astrology. They represent the various energies of a person, including one's mental and emotional nature, desires, vitality, soul, will, consciousness, and subconscious, as well as the people in one's life. Throughout this book, we'll include the Sun ☉, Moon ☽, and the North ☊ and South ☋ Nodes, even though they aren't actually planets.

- The **zodiac** is the name of the elliptic pattern the Earth follows in its annual revolution around the Sun. This path is always the same, and always passes through the same 12 signs.

- **Signs** are the "how" of astrology. The signs of the zodiac are: Aries ♈, Taurus ♉, Gemini ♊, Cancer ♋, Leo ♌, Virgo ♍, Libra ♎, Scorpio ♏, Sagittarius ♐, Capricorn ♑, Aquarius ♒, and Pisces ♓. *All zodiac signs appear in every person's chart.* The needs and styles of the planets are shown by the signs, as well as what methods could be used to achieve those needs and styles.

- The **houses** are the "where" of astrology. Each of the 12 houses encompasses a specific arena of life and is the stage where the drama of the planets unfolds.

Our Calendar Is Based on Astrology

You probably didn't know that all common calendar cycles are reflected by the movement in the heavens—and in astrology. A month, for example, is roughly the amount of time between New Moons (about 29 days). And coincidentally, a month is approximately the amount of time it takes for the Sun to move to a new sign in the zodiac.

A year is the amount of time the ancients thought it took for the Sun to travel through the entire zodiac (from the perspective of Earth). Although today we know it's the time it takes Earth to travel around the Sun, this was still a pretty clever deduction for a bunch of guys without computers.

These same clever guys noticed that the Sun was moving through certain constellations at certain times of the year. Each constellation had a specific meaning for the ancients, a meaning reflected when the 12 zodiac signs were named.

> **AstroLingo**
> Your **birth chart** is a unique map of who you are. Using the date, time, and place of your birth, it shows the positions of the planets in the signs and houses. The odds of anyone else having the same birth chart as you are astronomically small!

> ### StarFacts
>
> A week, as you know, has seven days, but you might not have known this is because that's how many planets could be seen by the ancients. In fact, the days of the week are named after the first seven planets (or rather, the first seven discovered celestial bodies, not including Earth):
>
> | | |
> |---|---|
> | Sunday | Sun ☉ |
> | Monday | Moon ☽ |
> | Tuesday (*mardi* in French) | Mars ♂ |
> | Wednesday (*mercredi* in French) | Mercury ☿ |
> | Thursday (*jeudi* in French) | Jupiter ♃ |
> | Friday (*vendredi* in French) | Venus ♀ |
> | Saturday | Saturn ♄ |

The days are named for planets.

Sunday

Monday

Tuesday

Wednesday

Thursday

Friday

Saturday

Debunking the Myths

We modern types like to think that we know better than to believe in astrology, but much of what we think we know about astrology is actually not true at all. For example, astrologers never say that the planets influence human behavior, and, not only is astrology not a "dark art," many smart people, including some well-known physicists, use astrology's ideas as the basis for some far more complex scientific theories. So let's debunk some of those myths about astrology.

The Planets Reflect Human Behavior

The planets do not *cause* things to happen, or *make* people behave in certain ways. It will help if you think of the planets as barometers, metaphors for the energies occurring on Earth—in people, places, in everything. We can watch the planets and use them as indicators of what's happening here, whether in a person or place. To attribute cause or influence to the planets would be like attributing the outside temperature to a thermometer. No one would do that!

Astrology is a symbolic system that appears to work via *synchronicity*, or meaningful coincidences, an idea first proposed by psychoanalysis pioneer Carl Jung. In terms of astrology, this means that what occurs overhead is merely a reflection of what is happening on Earth. In other words, the two are coincident with each other, or synchronous.

AstroLingo

In addition to being the name of a CD by the rock group The Police, **synchronicity** is the idea that everything in the universe is interconnected, a pattern of meaningful coincidences, or, as Jung said, everything that is born or occurs at a particular time has the energies of that time!

Astrology: An Intuitive Art

Astrology is based on three spiritual premises:

◆ The outer reflects the inner, or, to put it another way, our external lives reflect what is happening internally.

◆ Your birth chart shows your soul's purpose.

◆ Each of us is continually evolving spiritually.

Did you know that the Bible is actually filled with astrological information and messages? It's true—but without training no one would ever know it. For example, the 12 disciples of Christ and the 12 tribes or houses of Israel each represented one of the 12 zodiac signs. Christ ushered in the Piscean Age, and the symbol of the fish (Pisces is symbolized by fish) was used as the secret symbol of Christians.

The mystical Jewish text, the Kabbalah, has mystical and astrological meanings as well. One book, for example, the *Zohar*, describes God as containing all of life—and each life containing all of God. In addition, according to the Zohar, an astrological chart was considered an expression of the divine will of God.

Astrology and Science Can Peacefully Coexist

Some physicists now believe that astrology shows the order underneath what we see on the surface. This theory is based on physicist David Bohm's work (Bohm was one of Einstein's right-hand men).

AstroLingo

The four **elements** describe the basic qualities of the signs and of life. There are three signs for each element. The Fire signs are Aries ♈, Leo ♌, and Sagittarius ♐; the Earth signs are Taurus ♉, Virgo ♍, and Capricorn ♑; the Air signs are Gemini ♊, Libra ♎, and Aquarius ♒; and the Water signs are Cancer ♋, Scorpio ♏, and Pisces ♓.

Basically, Bohm explains how energy, matter, and meaning are enfolded together, and he has written formulas that support this, kind of like $E=mc^2$. Bohm's theory explains how inner and outer reality are interwoven, or, as physicist Will Keepin puts it, "The nature of reality is a single undivided wholeness." In other words, we are all part of something, and, like DNA, we each contain the pattern of that something as well.

Keepin explains that for each point in space-time, a unique astrological chart exists. Or to put it another way, when astrologers define an astrological chart, they need a specific point in space plus a specific point in time—and that point is *you!* You don't get much more scientific than that!

Smart People Use Astrology

Carl Jung not only recognized the synchronicity that is the basis of astrology, he once said, "We are born at a given moment, in a given place, and like vintage years of wine, we have the qualities of the year and of the season in which we are born."

T. S. Eliot's epic poem, *The Waste Land*, is filled with astrological references, and four of its sections are named for the astrological elements: Fire, Earth, Air, and Water.

Another well-known user of astrology is Nancy Reagan, who, after the assassination attempt on her husband Ronald Reagan in 1981, used astrology to determine the best times and worst times for Reagan to do everything from sign bills to travel to foreign countries. Although the news media made fun of Mrs. Reagan at the time, it should be noted that Reagan was the first president since Jefferson elected in a year ending in "0" not to die in office. Using astrology can't hurt.

Many other smart people have used astrology, including turn-of-the-century financier J. P. Morgan, who used astrology for business timing to amass his fortune. Morgan might have summed it up best when he said, "Millionaires don't use astrology; *billionaires* do."

Famous Astrologers

Smart people have been using astrology since astrology began, and in fact, there are a lot of historical folks who were astrologers. For example ...

The Three Wise Men

Have you ever wondered why the Three Wise Men were looking for that star over Bethlehem in the first place? The answer is that they were astrologers! It is believed that they learned that the Christ child would be born at the time of a *conjunction* of planets that signaled the arrival of a new age (the Piscean) from their study of the stars.

> **AstroLingo**
>
> A **conjunction** of planets means that the two planets appear in the same place in the sky at the same time. Conjunctions ♂ begin new cycles that reflect the planets involved.

This wasn't quite as easy at it sounds: The two planets involved in the conjunction—Jupiter ♃ and Saturn ♄—were bright, but not something an average person would have noticed. So even though they were trained astrologers, it took the Three Wise Men some time to actually locate Jesus in Bethlehem. But if they hadn't studied the stars, they might not have been looking in the first place.

The Three Wise Men looking for the conjunction of Jupiter and Saturn. Or written in the symbols of astrology: ♃♂♄.

Pythagoras (580?–500? b.c.e.)

Although you might have trouble remembering the Pythagorean theorem (try to remember the Scarecrow reciting it in *The Wizard of Oz*—something about the hypotenuse of a right triangle), we'll bet you won't forget that the mathematician responsible for that leap of logic was also an astrologer.

In addition to the Pythagorean theorem, Pythagoras gave us the musical scale. Pythagoras believed that, similar to musical harmonies, the larger harmony of the universe could be discovered in numbers as well. (It is still believed by many mathematicians that the secret of the universe can be discovered somewhere in *pi*, the ratio of a circle's circumference to its diameter.)

Nostradamus (1503–1566)

This is the guy who supposedly predicted most of the bad stuff that's happened in the twentieth century, like world wars, atomic bombs, and assassinations. Nostradamus's predictions, written in 1555, foretold everything that would happen from that date until the end of the world, which he posted at 3797 c.e. (thank goodness!).

But what did he base those predictions on? You guessed it—astrology. Although Nostradamus predicted many disasters and tough times, he predicted some good stuff, too, including a Golden Age, or 1,000 years of peace, beginning around the millennium (let's hope he's right). After all, in addition to being an astrologer and a seer, Nostradamus was also a practicing physician, so his motto was "Do no harm."

Isaac Newton (1642–1727)

Long before he sat under the proverbial apple tree, Isaac Newton was a practicing astrologer. Like all sixteenth-century scientists, he studied the stars and understood the larger relationship between everything that's since been largely ignored by the rational sciences.

Among Newton's many ponderings were questions about the secret of the universe, the nature of gravity itself (yes, it *exists*—but *why?*), and a belief in the existence of animal spirits in the human body. It's ironic that scientists after Newton would use Newton's Laws to discount any further examination of the more occult sciences he had examined himself!

Steering by the Stars

As you likely learned in grade school, the ancient navigators thought the world was flat. Yet they got into those ships of theirs anyway. How did they steer? Remember, this is before radar and sonar and cell phones (which is probably why it took Odysseus so long to return home after the Trojan War).

You guessed it again: They steered by the stars. Ancient astrologers and astronomers drew maps of the sky, and, just as we notice the Sun ☉ rising and setting in slightly different places at different times of year, those maps showed where certain constellations would be at certain times of year.

Star-Crossed

It's popular to assume that astrology is the same as fate. Not so! Astrology shows potentials, just as a map can show you possible routes. To think of astrology as an absolute is a big mistake. Instead of looking to astrology for answers, look at it for choices. *You* provide the answers—*you* pick the route you want to take.

This was called celestial navigation. Those ancient ship captains could just point toward Orion and sail toward Cairo (or wherever it was they wanted to go). And although celestial navigation, the most ancient way to plot a course, can be limited by the weather (you can't see the stars if it's cloudy, after all), it is still used today.

Of course, our ancestors used the stars for far more than navigation. Planetary placements helped them determine when to sow and when to reap, as well as when to celebrate various holidays. Ancient peoples noticed a regularity to the movements of the planets, and that everything from the seasons to social needs could be predicted by those patterns. Some ancient ruins, such as those at Monte Alban in Oaxaca, Mexico, contain buildings constructed in alignment with heavenly bodies and solar and lunar cycles. Archaeologists believe these structures were used for sacred purposes.

Astrology is a symbolic system from which we can learn the interconnection between external reality and internal reality. Like the smart people we've learned about throughout this chapter, we can use astrology as a map for our own route through life. Like those ancient sailors, we, too, can learn to steer by the stars.

Getting in Touch with Ancient Rhythms

Using *natal* astrology, this book will help you discover your own unique position in the synchronicity of the universe. We'll show you how to find out about your Sun ☉ sign, Moon ☽ sign, *ascendant*, *descendant*, the signs for all your planets, and the houses in which those planets reside. This all adds up to a special portrait of you alone.

AstroLingo

Natal astrology involves the creation of your birth chart based on the position of the planets at the time and place that you were born. It creates a map unique to you and your true self.

Your **ascendant,** or **rising sign,** is the sign that was rising over the horizon at the moment of your birth. Your rising sign represents the "you" that the outside world perceives, as well as your personality traits, needs, and physical characteristics.

Your **descendant,** located on the cusp of your seventh house, represents how you channel your energies through partnerships and relationships.

Getting in touch with the ancient rhythms of astrology involves both being aware of your constantly evolving history, a history that includes both Now and Then, and your unique position within that history. You'll learn more about just *how* unique you are in Chapter 2.

An Open Mind, a Curious Nature, and a Sense of Humor

If you're a Taurus ♉, you might already be wondering what all the fuss is about. That's because Taureans are from Missouri: They're constantly saying, "Show me," and if you can't show 'em, they just won't believe it.

Even if you're a Taurus, or any of the other Doubting Thomases of the zodiac, we hope you'll keep an open mind. Find the Gemini ♊ in your chart, the part of you that's naturally curious, and get in touch with your Sagittarius ♐, where your sense of humor lies. Sure, it's hard to believe in something you can't see, but we're not asking you to believe; we're asking you to come along and see what astrology has to offer you. You *will* be surprised—and you'll be rewarded and shown something about the cycles of your life as well.

The Least You Need to Know

- ◆ Astrology, the first science, is a complex study of planetary cycles and their relationship with energies and events on Earth.

- ◆ Astrology has its own language.

- ◆ Astrology creates a unique birth chart for you, based on the positions of the planets in the sky at the time and place that you were born.

- ◆ Planets are the "what" of astrology.

- ◆ Signs are the "how" of astrology, and reveal your needs and styles.

- ◆ Houses are the "where" of astrology.

2

Heavenly Revelations

In This Chapter

- ◆ What astrology can tell you about your everyday life
- ◆ Astrology and your love life
- ◆ Astrology on the job
- ◆ Astrology and your health
- ◆ Astrology and your money

Whether it's about love, work, family, health, or money, astrology can help you navigate the waters of your daily life. Just as there are specialists in other fields, there are astrological specialists in each of these astrological areas. In this chapter, you'll learn how these well-trained pros can help you chart your own astrological course.

What Astrology Can Reveal in Your Everyday Life

Just like doctors, lawyers, or teachers, astrologers have different areas of expertise, based on their backgrounds and interests. Astrology is used in many different ways, from counseling political and business leaders about strategies, tactics, and timing to learning about personal astrology for health, vocation, relationships, evolutionary paths, strengths, and challenges.

Some astrologers specialize in the stock market or relationships—even in sports. And there are those who specialize in psychological astrology, which gets to the root of why you behave a certain way and explores your mental makeup. So move over brokers, bankers, personal trainers, and therapists—make room for astrologers!

Star-Crossed

Astrological charts can be interpreted and understood on many different levels. The same astrological symbol can represent events in your childhood, people in your life, an internalized psychological complex, or a spiritual lesson. Don't assume that if you know one possible interpretation for a particular item, you understand it completely. To fully understand your chart (or anything in it) takes time, patience, and plenty of study. Remember, there's more to a book than its cover.

In addition to helping you understand various areas of your life, astrology also can predict what you might do next. Part of this stems from the fact that people don't change their behavior very much—predicting that Julia Roberts might get divorced or married again might not be a great stretch, for example. Because there are actually many different ways the same energy or prediction can manifest itself, however, predictions don't limit your scope, but rather, show your direction.

It's also important to remember that the "outer" reflects the "inner," so if you're in complete inner turmoil, that's what's going to manifest itself, not what you *want* to control and *have* happen. We all know someone who always seems to pick the same kind of wrong guy—that's an example of what we mean here.

StarFacts

In many of the countries where marriages are arranged, astrologers are consulted first to determine if the two people are compatible. Only then is the couple approved for marriage by the families.

You *do* have more control than you realize, but much of it is given over to your subconscious and might manifest itself as your fears—or as a replaying of scenes from your childhood to discredit something you learned then. The patterns of our lives are reflected—and revealed—in the patterns of our birth charts.

How much conscious control you have usually depends on how aware you are of your own strengths and challenges. Just remember, what happens is entirely up to you—and what you do with your potential.

The Company You Keep

Your relationships are based on all the planets, signs, and houses in your birth chart—and how they interact with all the planets, signs, and houses in other people's charts.

(And here you thought it was that great new haircut.) *Relationship astrology* studies just how compatible two (or more) people are, taking into account all the different aspects between the people, as well as what type of relationship it is. Here are just a few of the areas relationship astrology can help you with:

♦ Relationship astrology can tell whether two people are emotionally, mentally, or sexually compatible, and whether they would work well together as partners, as boss and employee, or should just be good friends.

♦ Although you can't choose your family, with relationship astrology, at least you'll have fun exploring your family's dys*fun*ction. Who knows, maybe you'll gain some valuable insights.

♦ Relationship astrology also can tell you when one person in a relationship will want to control the other, and in what ways—good-intentioned, devious, bold, steam-rolling, empowering, manipulative, or unconscious.

AstroLingo

Relationship astrology studies people's charts to determine their compatibility (or incompatibility).

♦ Relationship astrology can determine if you have similar or conflicting value systems or beliefs, as well as many other specific issues and strengths.

Relationship astrology can save you a whole lot of heartache and headaches right from the start. So pay attention, okay? In Chapter 23 we'll be taking a closer look at how relationship astrology can help you chart a course in your interpersonal life.

The Signs and Your Career

Vocational astrology assesses your personality traits and needs, your productive resources and capabilities, your special talents, and the paths you have taken up to now, as well as what type of work you will find rewarding in order to recommend the best possibilities for your career. Imagine—all this, just from carefully studying your birth chart.

AstroLingo

Vocational astrology studies your potentials in order to determine your career or path.

What kind of work you will do is related to your Sun ☉ sign, but it's not quite that simple. Let's use the example of a Gemini ♊ Sun, which signals work in communications.

You might be a journalist, teacher, writer, someone who creates websites, or you might work in advertising. Maybe you'll be a manager, negotiate contracts, or work as a partner in a business.

Or you might travel or work with foreign trade, work in publishing or the legal system, or teach at a university. There's obviously a great deal more to choosing your vocation or career than just what your Sun sign can predict.

All these examples deal with communications in some way, right? But they're all very different ways of working in communications. Vocational astrologers *never* look at *just* your Sun ☉ sign—and neither should you.

Healthy in Mind and Body

Nothing is more important to us than our health; without it, we can't do any of the other things that matter so much to our lives—from love to work to where we live. Astrology and health have been connected for a very long time. Hippocrates, the Greek philosopher and physician who lived circa 400 B.C.E. and is considered the father of modern medicine (do the words "Hippocratic Oath" ring a bell?), once said, "A physician without a knowledge of astrology has no right to call himself a physician."

In "the good old days," when people went to the doctor, the first thing that doctor did was draw up their astrological charts. These days, most doctors don't do that, but we can still use what astrology tells us to stay healthy and achieve a sense of well-being.

AstroLingo

Medical astrology uses your chart to determine the best ways for you to stay healthy and achieve a sense of well-being. It also can be used for diagnosis.

Today, there are medical astrologers—and even physicians—who use astrology to discover what isn't always found through the tests commonly used in traditional medicine. *Medical astrology* also can be used for more basic information, such as understanding your metabolic nature, the types of foods that will be helpful or stressful to you, and general areas that need to be monitored in order for you to maintain your optimum health.

From top to toe, each sign of the zodiac is associated with a particular part of the body: The first sign, Aries ♈, is associated with the head, and the last, Pisces ♓, with the feet. You'll find more information on what your Sun sign's health quotient is in Chapters 5 through 8.

The Signs and Their Associated Parts of the Body

Astro Sign	Associated Body Parts
Aries ♈	Head and face
Taurus ♉	Neck and throat
Gemini ♊	Head, arms, shoulders, nervous system, and lungs
Cancer ♋	Stomach and breasts
Leo ♌	Back, spine, and heart
Virgo ♍	Intestines, liver, pancreas, gall bladder, and bowels
Libra ♎	Kidneys, lower back, and adrenal glands
Scorpio ♏	Genitals, and the urinary and reproductive organs
Sagittarius ♐	Liver, hips, and thighs
Capricorn ♑	Bones, teeth, joints, and knees
Aquarius ♒	Ankles and circulation
Pisces ♓	Feet and the immune and hormonal systems

In addition to representing a part of the body, each sign is associated with certain glands, and so has particular dietary and vitamin needs associated with it. Certain foods might be very good for you, while others might send you spinning. Capricorn, for example, represents the bones, joints, knees, and teeth; so naturally, a lot of protein and calcium are going to be useful if you were born under this Sun sign.

Like all of astrology, the connections between the signs and parts of the body are part of the science that holds that the entire cosmos is reflected in the human body. As Shakespeare's Hamlet muses, "What a piece of work is man." Remember, too, that *all* the zodiac signs, not just the Sun sign you are born under, are represented in your astrological chart, and all have a bearing on a healthy you.

When we discuss each Sun sign in Chapters 5 through 8, we'll also discuss what you can do to keep your astrological body parts at their best. Of course, we're not doctors. But if you're in tune with a body/mind approach to health, you'll want to consider looking for a medical doctor (M.D.) who practices integrative medicine, a balance of traditional Western medicine and natural or complementary alternatives, such as massage, meditation, and acupuncture. After all, the human bodymind is not a machine, but a universe in microcosm.

Cosmic Investments and Money Management

Did you ever think that what you do with your money reveals a great deal about how you feel about yourself? In some signs, people may equate themselves with what they own, but others may see money as a means to an end. You might only have a dollar in your pocket like the Bruce Springsteen song, feel as expansive as the Oracle of Omaha Warren Buffett, or admire the simplicity of the Dalai Lama. As with all astrological possibilities, remember that there's nothing *wrong* with your personal style; for those who truly feel their home reflects themselves, it does, just as there are people who simply don't worry about money at all.

The natives of each sign handle their money in different ways: Cancers ♋, for example, tend to hoard their cash, saving it for an unspecified rainy day; Sagittarians ♐ might spend it freely, enjoying what's happening right this very minute.

> **AstroLingo**
>
> **Financial astrology** studies how and when you can best invest your money, as well as the best way for you to manage your finances.

But there are other factors at play in cosmic investment, too, and this is where *financial astrology* comes into play. Financial astrologers study the cycles of planets to determine the best available investment strategies. And they study the cycles of companies, too, so they'll know which ones are on their way up and which ones aren't. Does *your* mutual fund have a financial astrologer on the Board?

Companies have charts, just like people do, based on when they were incorporated or started. When these companies have certain positive astrological connections, their stock goes up. Financial astrologers specialize in investments and the financial markets; many of them put out newsletters to help their clients become successful in the markets.

Astrology also can help determine if you're under good or challenging cycles for financial investments. If you're investing during periods when your financial cycles are challenging, there's a greater likelihood you're going to lose money, or, at best, not make any.

> **StarFacts**
>
> J. P. Morgan, a *very* wealthy American financier at the turn of the century, used astrology for business timing purposes. He financed such companies as the U.S. Steel Corporation and the Great Northern & Pacific Railroad, as well as other ventures, such as the Boer War in South Africa. His use of astrology for business investments made him a billionaire, back in the early part of this century when even a *million* dollars represented a vast fortune.

Home Is Where Your Hat Is

Another branch of astrology can actually determine what kinds of experiences you will have in a particular location. In relocation astrology, your birth chart is done for the same time and day of birth, but for a location other than your birthplace. In this way, your chart changes to show what your life would be like in *that* location. Hmmm … Australia? Tahiti? Paris?

Then there's AstroCartoGraphy. As you might suspect from its name, this type of astrology is basically a map of the world with lines all over it, showing where in the world your planets were rising and setting at the moment of your birth. (If I was born in New Jersey, then why am I strangely drawn to India?)

In the place where you now are, you might be introspective and rarely voice your feelings, but if you moved to a different location, you might be very different; your personality might focus outward rather than inward, and you might be outgoing and direct instead.

Relocation astrology can help you determine in advance what types of experiences you might tend to have in particular places. Depending on the location, you might have very good career circumstances, a wonderful home life, or transformational experiences that totally change your identity—or you could have more challenges than you ever dreamed of. So if you've been daydreaming that a move might make all the difference, consulting a relocation astrologer might be your ticket.

Horoscope Junkies

Do you read your horoscope? (And do you remember it, if you do?) Millions of people in the United States don't leave home without it—without reading it, that is. Are they "horoscope junkies"?

A daily horoscope for a Sun sign might read: "A good day for fishing. And we don't just mean for fish! Pay attention to possible catches, but throw back the little stuff." A horoscope junkie who pays attention to this forecast will pay attention to *anything* that they "catch" that day, from fish to advice— and probably for good reason.

> **StarFacts**
>
> When astrologers write daily Sun ☉ sign forecasts, they look at aspects for that day for each sign. Sun sign forecasts are necessarily general, but if you have a number of planets in the same sign, you'll likely notice just how on target the daily horoscopes provided by a good astrologer can be.

What about the rest of us, who read our horoscopes sometimes or never? Are we heading for possible ruination, or worse? Of course not. But it might not hurt us to check our horoscopes a little more often. After all, you listen to the weather report before you go outside, don't you? C'mon, we know you do.

A sample daily horoscope.

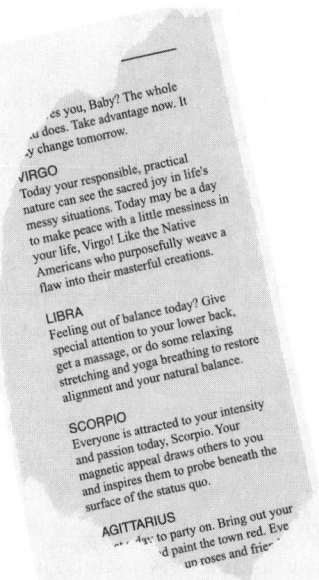

es you, Baby? The whole
u does. Take advantage now. It
y change tomorrow.

VIRGO
Today your responsible, practical
nature can see the sacred joy in life's
messy situations. Today may be a day
to make peace with a little messiness in
your life, Virgo! Like the Native
Americans who purposefully weave a
flaw into their masterful creations.

LIBRA
Feeling out of balance today? Give
special attention to your lower back,
get a massage, or do some relaxing
stretching and yoga breathing to restore
alignment and your natural balance.

SCORPIO
Everyone is attracted to your intensity
and passion today, Scorpio. Your
magnetic appeal draws others to you
and inspires them to probe beneath the
surface of the status quo.

AGITTARIUS
day to party on. Bring out your
d paint the town red. Eve
un roses and frie

Can You Believe Everything You Read in the Papers?

The daily forecasts in the newspapers are *Sun sign horoscopes* only. Your Sun sign may be a dominant feature of your chart, but it's certainly not the only one. The Sun ☉ is just one of at least 40 different elements shown in your astrological birth chart. Yes, a Sun sign reading applies to everyone with that Sun sign, in the same way that every person needs to eat a balanced diet. But each person's individual dietary needs are different because of the infinite ways you can mix and match these 40 elements.

As we've noted, Sun sign forecasts are very general. You can be undergoing severe stress and difficulties because your own personal cycles are at a very challenging point, even though your Sun sign forecast is all cheery and nice for that day. On that same day, however, someone may say something nice to you. It's not going to be enough to overcome the larger crisis, but it *can* make a difference.

So can you believe everything you read in the papers? If your Sun sign forecast is written by a reputable astrologer, *absolutely*. These forecasts are rather general, but astrologers are looking at more than just your Sun sign to make them. They're looking at the planets and their cycles, and the relationship of the planets to your Sun sign. All of this added together *can* color a day in a certain way.

Of course, we can't answer the larger question about believing *everything* you read in the papers: You might want to take some of the things *other* than your daily forecast with a grain of salt.

Free Will vs. Your Daily Forecast

As you may have already come to suspect, astrology connects your outer world to your inner world in order to reveal your potentials. Of course, how you manifest your potentials is where free will comes in.

In Chapter 9 we'll be talking about how your rising sign can reveal the lessons that you need to learn in your life. You may need to realize, for example, when you let others pull your strings and why, and then seek to reclaim that part of yourself. Or if you need to learn a particular lesson, there's nothing that's going to prevent it (except, maybe death), even if your conscious self is completely unaware of it.

Fate and free will are actually two very different things. It's possible to predict, for example, that you're going to have major changes to your home life in a certain time period, based on your present cycles.

Now you could take the bull by the horns, so to speak, and decide you're going to make that move you've been wanting to make for a long time, or you could remodel or make some other changes to your home. Or you could wait to get evicted, or for the house to get hit by a tree or by lightning!

In the first example, you have choices and you make them: This is *free will*. In the second, if you choose to wait for an eviction or catastrophe, it could be called *fate*.

To put it another way, whatever you need to learn, you *are going to learn*, whether your conscious self wants to or not. This also could be called fate.

Madeline believes that in the areas where you have lessons to learn, you really don't have a choice, except whether you're going to cooperate and make it easy on yourself or *not* cooperate and make it hard on yourself. In other words, you *do* have choices (free will) but they're not about whether you can avoid learning your lessons; that's called fate.

Hot Lines: The Best Advice or Costly Rip-Offs?

Ah … hot lines. These are the toll phone numbers you can dial to get your astrological reading for the day. What can we say? Well, for starters, the rates for these hot lines can be very high, usually *well* over what you would pay a *certified astrologer* for a session—as much as 200 percent over that amount. Many hot lines charge $3 per minute, an hourly rate of $180.

There aren't many astrologers who charge *that* much, and if they do, it's often because they're highly experienced and highly skilled, with tremendous knowledge. Hot lines, on the other hand, are often staffed with people who might know *some* astrology, but usually not enough to be actual astrologers.

AstroLingo

A **certified astrologer** is someone who has not only studied astrology, but who also has taken professional tests to become certified. These tests are *tough*. They usually last at least eight hours, and sometimes go for days.

Heaven Knows

Before you decide to spend your money on a hot line, check with your local certified astrologers (see Chapter 19 for information on getting your astrological birth chart and having it interpreted). You could save yourself a whole lot of money—and end up with far better advice.

Whether the hot-line person is actually doing the client's astrological birth chart while on the phone with the client, for example, is unknown. Some of these hot-line hoaxes might not even have the software and computer to do birth charts, and instead might simply look up the client's birth date information in a book, and then answer questions based on that. It might be better than nothing, but this sort of treatment would certainly provide incomplete information.

If, on the other hand, you went to an actual astrologer, not only would you pay far less and get more accurate information, the astrologer would prepare and study your chart and current cycles *before* meeting with you, to get oriented to your needs, challenges, and path.

Because every astrological birth chart is quite different, there is literally a mystery in every chart just waiting to be unlocked and revealed. No telephone hot-line person is going to be prepared enough, either in training or adequate analysis time, to evaluate and unlock these important aspects for you.

To be fair, though, hot lines are convenient and don't require appointments. But it *can* be expensive—and might yield wrong, or inadequate, information. So we say *caveat emptor*. That's Latin for "let the buyer beware."

Astrology Is Everywhere: Going Beyond the Stars

When you realize the connection between you and the rest of the world, you also realize that astrology is everywhere. First of all, it's about *you*—and about everyone else. It's about your relationships, health, career, and money—and it's about why you (and everyone else) behave the way you do. In addition, astrology is about your evolutionary purpose and what your soul came to learn and experience.

Astrology is also about the sky; in fact, some astrologers call the study of natal astrology "the inner sky." When you stand outside at night, beneath a sky filled with stars, planets, comets, and meteorites (and satellites and airplanes and maybe a UFO or two), you're reliving the human-sky connection where astrology began.

Astrology connects *you* with *everything*. You know the saying, "God is in the details." Whatever the God of your understanding, you can appreciate the concept of the universal essence of all things. Remember those physicists, discussing the inner order and the outer order? Both of those concepts are about the same thing, that astrology goes beyond the stars, to the place of each individual in the universe, and the place of the universe in each individual.

We don't yet know for certain what's "out there" beyond the stars, but just the fact that our imaginations take us there again and again should be enough evidence that we are connected with whatever might be there. *Star Trek*, *Star Wars*, or *Harry Potter*, perhaps we intuitively know more than we realize.

> **StarFacts**
>
> Five thousand years ago, Egyptian astrologers saw a comet in the sky, and soon after, the building of the pyramids was begun. When that comet returned to Earth's view recently, we named it Hale-Bopp. Yes, the same comet that helped inspire the pyramids was the one you saw back in the spring of 1997. Small world, isn't it?

When Sigmund Freud first unveiled his theories of the unconscious, they were called revolutionary—by everyone except astrologers, that is. Astrologers had been studying the effects of the hidden self on the visible self for thousands of years; they just didn't call it "the unconscious."

> **StarFacts**
>
> The *Star Wars* films, it seems, will always be with us; and film producers, sociologists, mythologists, and philosophers alike have all sought to explore the reasons for these films' continued popularity. Part of it is the mythic structure of the story itself. But the main thing everyone who studied the *Star Wars* phenomenon found was the universal appeal of The Force. Indeed, The Force *is* with us.

Just as therapy might reveal your childhood traumas, your dreams, and your hidden hostilities and hopes, astrology can reveal things about yourself you might not be aware of. By looking at your birth chart, you could discover that you have a tendency toward secretiveness and why, or what the placement of Saturn ♄ or Pluto ♀ in your astrological birth chart reveals about your power struggles with your father and other authority figures.

Astrologically speaking, your unconscious is not really hidden. Rather, you might say, it is "written." All *you* have to do is "read" what's there.

The Least You Need to Know

- ◆ Relationship astrology reveals who you get along with and who you don't.
- ◆ Vocational astrology helps you find the right job or path.
- ◆ Medical astrology connects your birth chart to your health.
- ◆ Financial astrology helps you manage your money.
- ◆ Relocation astrology explores where you live and its relationship to your behavior.
- ◆ Astrology is everywhere and connects *you* with *everything*.

Astrology Basics for Your Personal Forecast

In This Chapter

- ◆ What is your astrological chart?
- ◆ Your chart shows the position of the heavens at your birth
- ◆ Energies, qualities, and elements
- ◆ The Tarot and astrology
- ◆ Your Sun ☉ sign and you
- ◆ No one else is exactly like you

It looks like a wheel, or a pie, or yet another odd distribution of your taxes by Uncle Sam. But no—it's your astrological chart, a metaphor for *you*, designed for the day and the time and place that you were born. In this chapter, we'll introduce you to the basics for reading your own astrological chart, your own special blueprint.

What Is an Astrological Chart?

Simply put, your *astrological chart* (also called a *birth chart* or *natal chart*) is a map of the heavens for the location, date, and time you were born. Its symbols represent the locations of the planets on that map.

The sample chart is for His Holiness, the Dalai Lama. Each of the 12 sections of the circle is called a house, and the symbols represent the signs and the planets. In this chapter, we will begin to unlock the mysteries of these symbols for you. As we do, we'll return to the Dalai Lama's chart and unlock some of *his* secrets as well.

His Holiness, the Dalai Lama's birth chart with ascendant, descendant, mid-heaven, and lower heaven indicated.

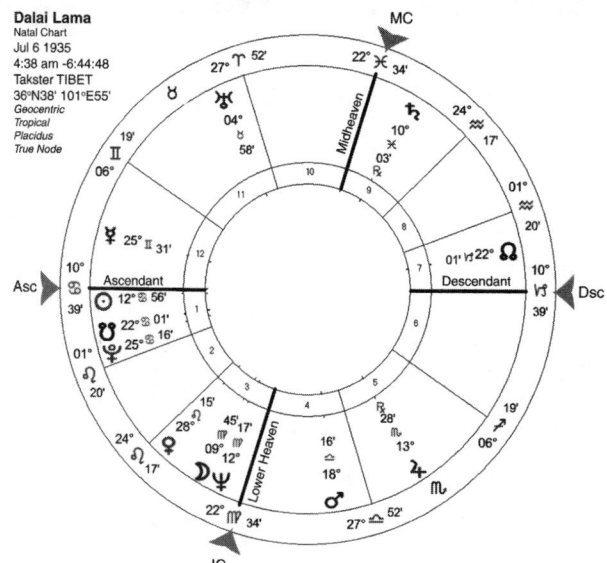

Your Chart Shows the Position of the Heavens at Your Birth

Now take a look at the Dalai Lama's astrological birth chart. First, notice the information in the top left-hand corner: It shows his birth date, birth time, and birthplace: July 6, 1935, 4:38 A.M., Takstar, Tibet. The Dalai Lama's chart is calculated for this date, time, and location. Had he been born at another time, place, or date, the chart would be different from the one shown here.

The symbols in the birth chart represent the location of the planets, and the signs they were in, at the time, date, and place of the Dalai Lama's birth. It might help you to think of the center of the chart as the position of the earth, and the placement of the planets as what's in the sky all around it.

StarFacts

The heavy, horizontal line through the center of the chart is called the horizon, and the sign that was rising in the east over the horizon at your time of birth is called the ascendant. Everything above it was in the visible portion of the sky at the moment you were born, and everything below it wasn't visible. The *left* end of this line is the *east*, not the west, as it is on maps. It helps to visualize this if you imagine yourself standing on top of the world, facing south, at the moment of your birth: east is on your left, right?

Now, the highest point of this chart (the upper, heavy vertical line on the Dalai Lama's chart, marked with an "M.C.") represents the highest point that the Sun ☉ reached on the day of his birth. On the Dalai Lama's chart, this is Pisces ♓. Note, too, the horizon line; this is the heavy horizontal line across the birth chart. Its left is the east horizon (Cancer ♋, on the Dalai Lama's chart), and its right is where the Sun sets in the west (Capricorn ♑, on the Dalai Lama's chart).

AstroLingo

Your **midheaven** or **M.C.** represents your ambition, career, or social role and public image. It's the highest point that the Sun reached on the day of your birth, and is located on the cusp of the tenth house. Your **lower heaven** or **I.C.** is the point on your birth chart that represents your life's foundations and psychological roots. It's found on the exact opposite side of the earth from the midheaven, on the cusp of the fourth house.

Your ascendant, or rising sign—the mask you wear for the world—is the sign at the easternmost end of this line (Cancer ♋ on the Dalai Lama's chart). The lowest point in the chart, or *lower heaven* (the lower, heavy vertical line marked with an "*I.C.*"), would be the exact opposite side of the earth from the *M.C.*, or the *midheaven*, and is in the sign of Virgo ♍ for the Dalai Lama.

Your descendant represents how you relate to others through partnerships and relationships. It's the sign next to the horizon (center line) on the right side of the chart and is Capricorn ♑ on the Dalai Lama's chart.

The Dalai Lama's Pisces midheaven highlights his life's vocation in a role of compassion, universality, and inclusiveness; his Virgo lower heaven reveals his foundation in a role of service to others. Note, too, that one of the archetypes for Pisces is Christ!

Making Sense of the Symbols

The following tables show you which signs and planets are represented by which symbols. Each *planet* represents your different energies, and parts of yourself. Each *sign* manifests those energies in different ways, and all of these things combine to make you who you are.

The Signs and Their Symbols

Astrological Sign	Symbol
Aries	♈
Taurus	♉
Gemini	♊
Cancer	♋
Leo	♌
Virgo	♍
Libra	♎
Scorpio	♏
Sagittarius	♐
Capricorn	♑
Aquarius	♒
Pisces	♓

The Planets and Their Symbols

Planet	Symbol
Sun	☉
Moon	☽
Mercury	☿
Venus	♀
Mars	♂
Jupiter	♃
Saturn	♄
Uranus	♅
Neptune	♆

Planet	Symbol
Pluto	♀
North Node	☊
South Node	☋

Soon, you'll learn that there's more to your astrological birth chart than what you see here. For now, all you need to remember is that your chart shows the position of the heavens at *your* birth—just as the Dalai Lama's shows *his* universe.

Energies, Qualities, and Elements (You Thought This Was Gonna Be Easy?)

Each of the 12 *Sun signs* is categorized in a number of ways. First of all, there are two *energies*, or genders, and each sign is either one or the other. Then there are three *quadruplicities*, called *qualities*, each of which appears in four signs. Last, there are four *triplicities*, each of which appears in three signs; these are called *elements*. Let's take all that a little more slowly.

People born in signs with the same energy, quality, or element will have certain things in common. For example, people born in signs with a *cardinal* (or first) quality are likely to be leaders; and people in signs with an *air* element might always seem to be thinking or communicating.

Now, each *combination* of energy, quality, and element appears in only one sign. Aries ♈, for example, has a *yang* energy, a *cardinal* quality, and the element of *Fire*. This means that after you understand what each of these characteristics represents, you also can begin to understand certain aspects of an Aries personality. See? It's not so hard.

AstroLingo

A **Sun ☉ sign** represents the position of the Sun in the heavens at the moment of your birth. The **energies** represent whether the energy manifested by a Sun sign is *yang* (direct and externally oriented) or *yin* (indirect and internally oriented). **Qualities** represent different types of activities and are related to where in a season a sign falls. **Cardinal** signs begin each season, so they like to begin things; **fixed** signs, in the middle of each season, are preservers, keeping things as they are; and **mutable** signs occur as the season is changing, and so are associated with transitions. The four **elements** describe the basic nature of the signs and of life: *Fire*, *Earth*, *Air*, and *Water*, each representing very distinct temperamental characteristics.

Energies: Two for the Show

Every sign is either direct or indirect, male or female. You'll see the energies called "feminine" and "masculine" in some books, but we prefer to call them *yang* (direct/masculine) and *yin* (indirect/feminine), which avoids all that gender-based nonsense. All fire and air signs are *yang*, while all earth and water signs are *yin*. Each *energy* has certain characteristics that, coupled with the qualities and elements, create a unique picture for each sign.

The ancient symbol for the union of yin *and* yang *energies evokes a heavenly sphere of celestial balance.*

The Signs and Their Energies

Yang	Yin
Aries ♈	Taurus ♉
Gemini ♊	Cancer ♋
Leo ♌	Virgo ♍
Libra ♎	Scorpio ♏
Sagittarius ♐	Capricorn ♑
Aquarius ♒	Pisces ♓

The following table may help you differentiate between *yang* and *yin* more easily.

Yang	Yin
Specific	Holistic
Positive	Negative
Left brain	Right brain

Yang	*Yin*
White	Black
Morning	Evening
Conscious	Unconscious
Heavy	Light
Male	Female

As this table reveals, *yang* signs tend toward direct action rather than waiting for things to come to them, like the bee that pollinates the flower. *Yang* represents the outgoing, the positive electrical charge, an external orientation, and the direct, "male" side of things.

Yin represents the indirect forces and actions, those that understand what is needed to attract and create the desired outcome, like the flower that blooms in order to attract the bee. *Yin* is also called the receptive, the negative electrical charge, an internal orientation, and the "female" side of things.

> **CAUTION**
>
> **Star-Crossed**
>
> If you are a male in a *yin* sign, or a female in a *yang* sign, it doesn't mean you need to research hormone therapy. It simply means your sign has an energy that is one-half of the natural life force of everything that lives. Black/white. Positive/negative. Up/down. Internal/external. Two halves of the same whole. That's all there is to it.

Qualities: Three to Get Ready

The qualities represent different types of activity. Think of the way a season progresses, from its forceful beginning, its fixed middle, and its transitional ending. This is what the *qualities* represent: each season, as it moves through its paces—and its three signs.

As there are 3 qualities and 12 signs, there are 4 signs for each quality. Signs that share a quality share certain characteristics.

The Signs and Their Qualities

Cardinal	Fixed	Mutable
Aries ♈	Taurus ♉	Gemini ♊
Cancer ♋	Leo ♌	Virgo ♍
Libra ♎	Scorpio ♏	Sagittarius ♐
Capricorn ♑	Aquarius ♒	Pisces ♓

Qualities and Their Characteristics

Cardinal	Fixed	Mutable
Independent	Persistent	Adaptable
Impatient	Consistent	Flexible
Go-getting	Reliable	Mercurial

You'll notice on the figure that the qualities in each of the signs form a square; that's one of the reasons they're called quadruplicities (the other reason is that there are four signs for each quality).

The qualities form a square.

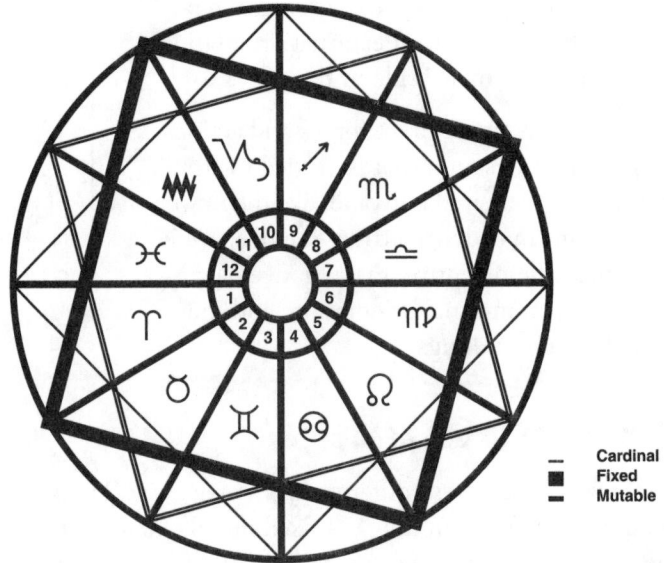

Cardinal
Fixed
Mutable

The first quality, for the first sign in each season—Aries ♈ in spring, Cancer ♋ in summer, Libra ♎ in autumn, and Capricorn ♑ in winter—is called *cardinal*. People with cardinal quality signs are independent. They seek to move ahead and start new things, and they can be proactive and enterprising. They also can be impatient if others don't move as quickly as they do, but they're independent, too—the signs of beginnings. Of course, once they get something started and established, cardinal people tend to lose interest in the project. Instead, they're off to start something else. Remember, it's a certain type of person who likes to start things, and if you've got heavy cardinal influences in your chart, you're just that kind of person.

In the midst of each season, we have what is called the *fixed* quality. People with fixed quality signs—Taurus ♉ in spring, Leo ♌ in summer, Scorpio ♏ in autumn, and Aquarius ♒ in winter—are consistent, reliable, determined, and persistent. They often have great reserves of power, but they also can become stubborn, or set in their ways. These are, after all, characteristics needed to preserve what has already been started. Remember, though, that people with fixed quality signs are the ones who, once cardinal people have started things, take over from there.

The end of each season signifies a time of change, and so the signs in this placement are called *mutable*. People with mutable quality signs—Gemini ♊ in spring, Virgo ♍ in summer, Sagittarius ♐ in autumn, and Pisces ♓ in winter—adapt easily, are flexible and resourceful, are quick to learn, and can see issues from more than one angle. They also can lack perseverance, but this is precisely because they're adaptable and flexible. That's what's needed to make transitions. After all, they've already seen the beginning and the middle of the process.

Elements: Four to Go

Think of the *elements* as tendencies of the temperament: *Fire, Earth, Air, Water*. Everything that exists is composed of these characteristics, and every astrological sign manifests one of them as well. In addition, all Fire and Air signs are *yang*, and all Earth and Water signs are *yin*.

The signs that share an element share certain characteristics, depending on what that element is.

The Signs and Their Elements

Fire	Earth	Air	Water
Aries ♈	Taurus ♉	Gemini ♊	Cancer ♋
Leo ♌	Virgo ♍	Libra ♎	Scorpio ♏
Sagittarius ♐	Capricorn ♑	Aquarius ♒	Pisces ♓

The Elements and Their Characteristics

Fire	Earth	Air	Water
Energetic	Practical	Intellectual	Emotional
Courageous	Skillful	Social	Intuitive
Passionate	Down to earth	Thoughtful	Romantic

You'll notice in the following illustration that the elements in each of the signs form a triangle; that's one of the reasons they're called the triplicities (the other reason is that there are three signs for each element).

The elements form a triangle.

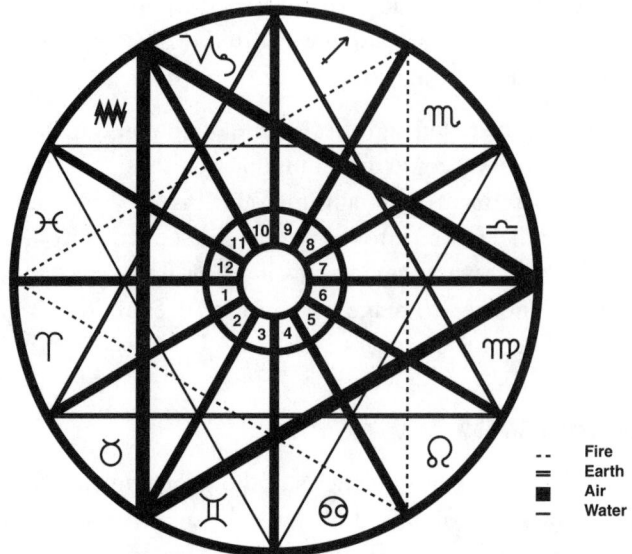

The first element is *Fire*. Fire signs (Aries ♈, Leo ♌, and Sagittarius ♐) are energetic, idealistic, self-assertive, courageous, and often visionary. If you remember that *fire is first*, it might help you to remember that Fire signs are very active, stimulating creative expression, and always passionate. People with lots of Fire planets are often known as "fireballs."

The second element is *Earth*. Earth signs (Taurus ♉, Virgo ♍, and Capricorn ♑) are practical and skillful, good at managing physical assets, financial matters—or any form of matter. Think of Earth signs as *down to earth* and you also will remember their characteristics. People with lots of Earth planets are sometimes called "grounded" or "rooted."

The third element is *Air*. Air signs (Gemini ♊, Libra ♎, and Aquarius ♒) represent social and intellectual abilities: ideas, communications, thinking, and social interrelationships. People with Air signs operate on a mental plane, through air, so to speak, which might help you to remember what Air signs are like. People with lots of Air planets are often known as "airy" or just plain "head in the clouds."

The fourth element is *Water*. Water signs (Cancer ♋, Scorpio ♏, and Pisces ♓) are sensitive and emotional; they think with their feelings, intuitively, and are often romantic. Cancer represents the lake, Scorpio represents the river, and Pisces represents the ocean. If you think of water as emotion, you will remember the characteristics of Water signs. People with lots of Water planets are often known as "water babies" or "in the flow."

Let the Sun Shine

Just as the Sun is the strongest light in our solar system, *your* Sun ☉ sign is the strongest representation of who *you* are. It's not the only one, but it's what you'll notice the most, because it's like the fuel you burn.

Symbolically, the Sun represents your self, your willpower, and your creativity. And mythologically, the Sun represents the Source, the unlimited resources of the universe or the God of your understanding. Remember that the Sun's symbol ☉ is a perfect circle, an endless whole—and many believe that the universe, people, and people's creativity are interconnected.

When you look at the Dalai Lama's chart, you will see that his birth date is July 6, 1935. This means that his Sun ☉ is in Cancer ♋. Now we already know that Cancer has a *yin* energy, a *cardinal* quality, and *Water* as its element. Just for fun, let's try translating this into the beginning of a birth chart reading for His Holiness.

People with *yin* energy signs tend to use a holistic approach, intuiting what needs to be done rather than insisting on specific, ordered steps. Cancer, with Water and *yin*, is intuitive and receptive as well. Add in Cancer's cardinal quality, and you find someone who will be able to use his innate intuitive and holistic nature to take charge and get things done.

That this fourteenth incarnation of the Dalai Lama has a Cancer Sun sign is no surprise to us. Rather than simply *lead* his exiled people, the Dalai Lama has chosen to reach out to the larger world, communicating his ideas through speaking engagements and books that appeal to humanity's need for a more intuitive and holistic approach, sharing a vision that encompasses all of humanity, while never losing his larger vision for the future. His Holiness, the fourteenth Dalai Lama is the recipient of the 1989 Nobel Peace Prize.

Intuitive Connections

Like astrology, the *Tarot* is an intuitive art. Modern readers use this 78-card deck not so much to predict the future as to help us connect with our inner selves. Naturally, Tarot's four *Minor Arcana* suits can be divided into energies and elements as easily as astrology's signs. Tarot's Wands are the suit of enterprise and imagination, Cups are the suit of emotion and creativity, Swords are the suit of action and power, and Pentacles are the suit of wealth and security.

AstroLingo

The **Tarot** is the name for a deck of 78 cards used for tapping the uncon-scious. As the cards are dealt, the images are interpreted by a reader based on the cards' combinations. The 22 **Major Arcana** correlate to the 12 signs and 10 planets of astrology (see Chapters 5 through 9) and represent your destiny. The 56 **Minor Arcana** are divided into four elements, or suits, and represent your free will.

Energies and Elements of the Minor Arcana

Tarot Deck Suit	Common Deck Equivalent	Energy	Element
Wands	Clubs	*Yang*	Fire
Cups	Hearts	*Yin*	Water
Swords	Spades	*Yang*	Air
Pentacles	Diamonds	*Yin*	Earth

As we move through the Sun signs in Chapters 5 through 9, we'll tell you more about the connections between the Tarot and astrology. But you don't have to wait. You can read *The Complete Idiot's Guide to Tarot, Second Edition,* by Arlene Tognetti and Lisa Lenard, and get all the skinny on this easily mastered intuitive art.

You and Your Sun ☉ Sign

Most people know their Sun sign, but not everybody knows just what that means. As we've explained, your Sun sign is probably the strongest representation of who you are. But who decided just where the Sun signs begin and end, and why they are the way they are?

Remember those ancient astronomers, watching the apparent movement of the sky over Earth? Well, they're back! Part of their sky-mapping determined that the Sun went through certain constellations at certain times of the year—and that people born at that time of year seemed to share certain characteristics.

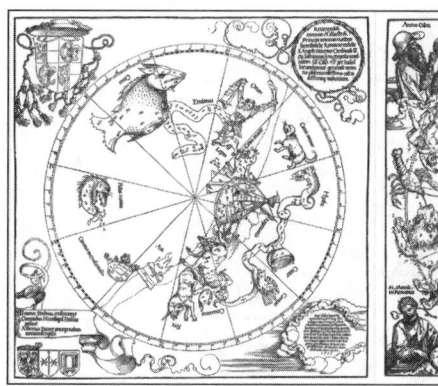 

Albrecht Dürer, a contemporary of the mystic Nostradamus, depicted the skies of the Northern and Southern Hemispheres in 1515, illustrating the blending of science, astronomy, and astrology at this time in human history.

Now this isn't really so mysterious: Scientific evidence corroborates that people born at night might be night-owls, for example, and that people born in the summer might love warm weather. But if you know anything about astronomy, you also know that the constellations are *not* overhead at the times of year the zodiac indicates. So what's going on here?

Star-Crossed _____

If you were born at the beginning or end of a sign, you might need to have your horoscope calculated to determine which Sun sign you have.

A very long time ago, the constellations of the signs *were* in the area of the sky that was named for them. But due to the earth's wobble, and the fact that the earth shifts a tiny bit in space over a long period of time, the constellations have shifted out of those positions. So Western astrology uses the seasons, which don't change over time, as its basis for Sun signs, and has kept the names the same.

So what's the big deal about knowing your Sun ☉ sign? Knowing it means you can …

5. Reveal whether the love of your life is a perfect match or a stupendous dud.

4. Always have something to talk about at parties.

3. Make excuses for your inexcusable behavior.

2. Have the best pick-up line ever.

And …

1. Have the best tattoo ideas.

Use the following illustration to find your Sun sign—the first step in creating the astrological map that reveals your uniqueness.

The zodiac: finding your Sun ☉ sign.

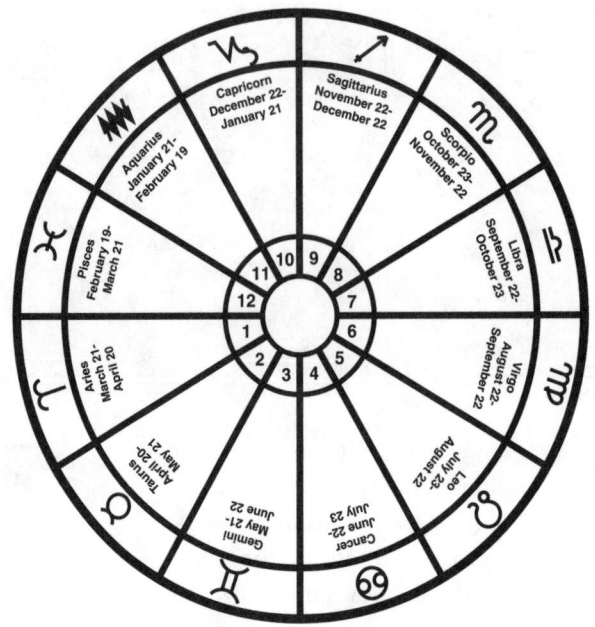

You Are Unique

No one has the same astrological birth chart as you. The odds of that happening are astronomically small. We've seen those odds calculated as high as 10^{312}, a number that would take up this whole book if you wrote it down.

This number also reveals something of the complexity of astrology—and the complexity of people—something no other model about people is able to do, except maybe DNA. No other models can come up with so many different combinations. Translation: You are unique!

The Least You Need to Know

- ◆ Your astrological birth chart shows the position of the heavens at the time and place you were born.

- ◆ A sign is one of two energies: *yin* or *yang;* and three qualities: cardinal, fixed, or mutable.

- ◆ A sign is one of four elements: Fire, Earth, Air, or Water.

- ◆ Like astrology, the Tarot can help you connect with your inner self.

- ◆ Your Sun ☉ sign is the position of the Sun at the time of your birth.

- ◆ No one else has the same astrological birth chart as you.

There's More to You Than Just Your Sun ⊙ Sign

In This Chapter

- ◆ Ascendants, or rising signs: the "you" the world sees
- ◆ Your rising sign: the lessons you'll learn during your life
- ◆ Planet power: Where do you put your energy?
- ◆ Each house is an area of your life
- ◆ A tour beyond the Sun (sign)

Sun ⊙ signs are just the beginning of astrology. Every one of the signs appears somewhere on your birth chart, and every sign is a part of who you are in some way. In this chapter, we'll look in more detail at ascendants, planets, and houses, because there's a whole lot more to you than just your Sun sign.

Ascendants

Your *ascendant*, or rising sign, is the sign that was rising over the horizon at the moment of your birth. This sign is your outward manifestation—the "you" that the outside world perceives. At the same time, your ascendant also is the way you express yourself (which is probably why the outside world perceives you that way). Usually, your Sun sign and ascendant are different, which is why your ascendant is perceived as a "mask"—most of the time, hiding your true self, your Sun sign.

AstroLingo

Your **ascendant** is your rising sign, the sign that was rising over the horizon at the moment of your birth. Your rising sign represents the "you" that the outside world perceives, as well as personality traits and needs, and your physical characteristics.

Star-Crossed

You shouldn't think of your ascendant as an "excuse"; just because you've got Aries ♈ rising, for example, doesn't give you a reason to run over everyone in your path. Your ascendant represents a "specialty" training you're here to take, and the sooner you master it, the easier life will be for you.

Each of the 12 signs rises over the horizon during a 24-hour period, so in rough terms, each ascendant rises over the horizon for 2 hours (more or less, depending on how quickly a particular sign rises) every day. In addition, whichever sign the Sun is in will be the sign rising at sunrise that day.

For example, in the early spring, Aries ♈ is rising at sunrise, but at sunrise in the middle of summer, Leo ♌ is rising. This means that if you were born at sunrise, both your Sun ☉ sign and ascendant would be in the same sign—and so others would see you behaving like your Sun sign. Or to put it another way, rather than wearing a different mask, you'd behave like your Sun sign.

We'd like to add another dimension to your consideration of your ascendant, too. Think of it as "training" for the person you are becoming. In other words, your rising sign indicates the skills and traits you're learning to develop during your lifetime. If you're born with a Scorpio ♏ ascendant, for example, much of what you do might be connected with learning about control, both self-control and a need to control others.

Your ascendant might also be revealed in the clothes you wear, car you drive, or any of the other ways you "show" yourself to the world. Your ascendant is as much a part of you as your Sun sign—but it's often more obvious to others.

In Chapter 9, we'll show you a simple way to find your ascendant. Then we'll explore what the "mask" of your ascendant reveals about you.

The Sun ☉, the Moon ☽, the Planets, and the Nodes ☊☋

Because it stands for your self, your willpower, and your creativity, your Sun ☉ sign is the strongest representation of who you really are. For simplicity, the Sun ☉ and the Moon ☽ are called planets, too, because from Earth's vantage point they move across the sky just as the planets do. In astrology, the Sun and Moon are called the luminaries, because they are responsible for lighting up our world.

Planets represent different energies within ourselves and our society, and are divided into the luminaries (Sun ☉ and Moon ☽), personal planets (Mercury ☿, Venus ♀, and Mars ♂), social planets (Jupiter ♃ and Saturn ♄), and transpersonal planets (Uranus ♅, Neptune ♆, and Pluto ♇).

The following table is a quick reference guide to each planet's symbol, and that planet's energies.

The Planets

Planet	Symbol	Energies
The Luminaries		
Sun	☉	Self, essence, life spirit, creativity, willpower
Moon	☽	Emotions, instincts, unconscious, past memories
The Personal Planets		
Mercury	☿	Mental activities, communication, intelligence
Venus	♀	Love, art, beauty, social graces, harmony, money, resources, possessions
Mars	♂	Physical energy, boldness, warrior ways, action, desires, anger, courage, ego
The Social Planets		
Jupiter	♃	Luck, abundance, wisdom, higher education, philosophy or beliefs, exploration, growth
Saturn	♄	Responsibilities, self-discipline, perseverance, limitations, structure

continues

The Planets   (continued)

Planet	Symbol	Energies
The Transpersonal Planets		
Uranus	♅	Sudden or unexpected change, originality, liberation, radicalness, intuition, authenticity
Neptune	♆	Idealism, subconscious, spirituality, intuition, clairvoyance
Pluto	♀	Power, regeneration, destruction, rebirth, transformation

Every Heavenly Body Tells a Story

Planets are the "what" of astrology. They represent the various energies of a person, including things like mental and emotional nature, desires, vitality, soul, will, consciousness, and subconscious, as well as the people in a person's life.

Every planet, in other words, tells a story. And many of these stories you already know. Remember Icarus, the silly boy who flew so close to the Sun that his wax wings melted? Remember the Roman gods: Mercury, god of communication and transportation; Venus, goddess of love and beauty; Jupiter, god of the heavens, lightning, and thunder; wrathful Neptune, god of the sea; and Pluto, god of the underworld; to name a few?

The Roman gods inspired the names of the planets.

Mercury   **Venus**   **Jupiter**   **Neptune**   **Pluto**

These same figures appear in other intuitive arts as well. One example can be found in palmistry, where the fingers and mounts of the hand are named for them. If you can remember individual gods' characteristics, they can serve as a sort of shorthand for remembering the traits of each planet—and the areas of your hand in palmistry as well.

Because each planet's stories are connected to the way that planet seems to behave, in turn, they are stories about *you*. These stories are based on a number of things, such as what sign a planet is in and where it is in your birth chart, as well as which planets it associates with and how well they get along with each other.

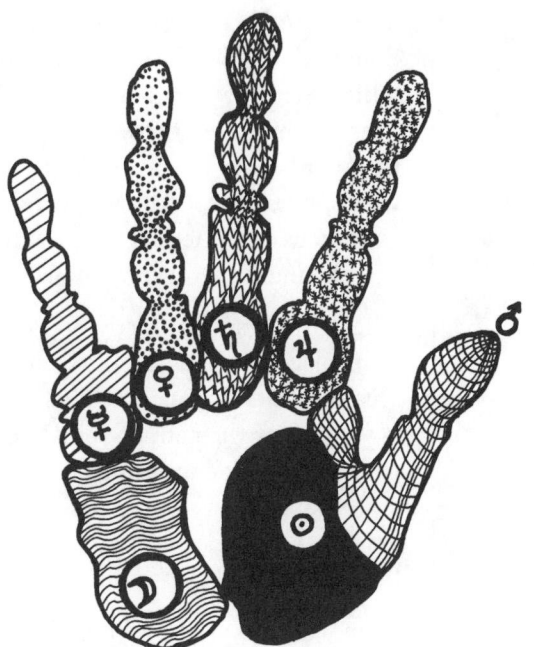

The fingers and mounts of the hand are named for the same gods who appear in astrology.

Astrology is complex, just like the planets, and so we'll be telling you some of these stories when we tell you more about each planet. Humans, after all, are storytellers for good reason. Stories help us understand who we are and why we're here. Because astrology has a similar purpose, it's natural the two should hook up in this book.

In Part 3, we'll explore the planets in more depth. We'll also show you how each planet's energy changes from sign to sign—and what this reveals about you.

> **StarFacts**
>
> Mythology is more than just stories about those Greek and Roman guys. Every culture, from Native American to African to Armenian, has its own stories, and what's interesting is how often these stories are alike. Every culture seems to have an origin myth, a flood myth, a sacrifice myth, and a trickster myth, for example—and these similarities are only the beginning.

What Are Nodes, Anyway?

Although the *Nodes* ☊☋ of the Moon are not heavenly bodies, they nonetheless add some essential information to your birth chart. Exactly opposite each other, these points are often called your past and your future. Let's look at them a little more closely.

AstroLingo

The **Nodes** physically represent moving points that relate to the Moon's orbit around Earth. Astrologically, the *South Node* ☋ represents your heredity or your past, and the *North Node* ☊ represents your possibilities for growth and where your future lies.

AstroLingo

Planetary **rulers** are in charge of certain signs; these planets and signs share certain characteristics.

The *South Node* ☋ represents your heredity or past. Some call the South Node the "point of letting go." This means that you have already learned these lessons and mastered these skills; if you continue along this path, it will be the "easy way out." In other words, because you know how to do these things extremely well, there is no growth, no challenge, and no learning gained from doing them.

The *North Node* ☊, exactly opposite the South Node in its placement, represents your possibilities, your area of greatest growth, and where your future lies. If you follow the path of your North Node, you can gain new confidence as you learn new ideas. This is the path to developing new skills, abilities, and growth. Of course, it's also the path that is less comfortable for you.

Your "comfort zone" is your South Node, but being comfortable isn't necessarily your best path.

Planetary Rulers

Every planet naturally "rules" one or more of the signs, and so, also naturally, certain planets and certain signs share certain characteristics. Planetary *rulership* means that a planet is "in charge" of a sign. For instance, no matter what sign Mars ♂ or the Sun ☉ is in, they are still in charge of Aries ♈ and Leo ♌, respectively. Leo, like the Sun, is bright and optimistic, and Aries, like Mars, is energetic and on-the-move. Following are the planets and the signs they rule.

Planetary Rulers

Planet	Sign(s) Ruled
Sun ☉	Leo ♌
Moon ☽	Cancer ♋
Mercury ☿	Gemini ♊, Virgo ♍
Venus ♀	Taurus ♉, Libra ♎
Mars ♂	Aries ♈, co-ruler of Scorpio ♏
Jupiter ♃	Sagittarius ♐, co-ruler of Pisces ♓

Planet	Sign(s) Ruled
Saturn ♄	Capricorn ♑, co-ruler of Aquarius ♒
Uranus ♅	Aquarius ♒
Neptune ♆	Pisces ♓
Pluto ♇	Scorpio ♏, co-ruler of Aries ♈

Planet Power: Where Do You Put Your Energy?

Knowing the signs your planets are in can help you see why you behave the way you do. If your Mercury ☿ is in Gemini ♊, for example, it might indicate that you're a person who's quick-thinking.

Some people have several planets in a sign other than their Sun sign. This means they'll exhibit strong characteristics of that different sign. Similarly, some people might have lots of planets in a particular *house* of their chart, and so they might spend a lot of energy in that area of their life.

In Part 3, we'll be showing you just what each planet in each sign reveals in more detail. For now, just remember that whatever signs *your* planets are in describe how you use their particular energies or functions in your life. For example, a Leo Moon ♌☾ means you will seem sunny and optimistic, but someone with an Aquarian Moon ♒☾, will seem aloof and detached.

Houses

Now, looking at the next figure, it's time to discuss what those pie slices *really* represent: They're the houses, the places where everything in your life occurs. Each of the 12 houses encompasses a specific arena of life, the stage where the drama of the planets unfolds.

Everything in your life happens in one of these houses, from where you brush your teeth to where you keep your secrets. When you look at a chart, the first house is always the pie slice just below the eastern horizon, and the other houses follow, counterclockwise, around the chart.

Heaven Knows

Are you starting to wonder how you're going to keep this all straight? It might help if you remember that planets are the "what," signs are the "how," and houses are the "where."

It might help you to think of each house as representing the horizon at the time of your birth: Half the sky was visible, and half of it was not. Below the horizon are the six houses of *personal* development—invisible, but oh-so-important. This includes areas such as your personality, personal resources, knowledge, home, creativity, health, and responsibilities.

Above the horizon are the six houses of your development in the larger world—those that are visible, in other words. These houses include areas such as your relationships, joint or shared resources, social concerns, career, goals, and the subconscious.

Each House Is an Area of Your Life

Bear in mind that the following chart shown is just the tip of the iceberg when it comes to what's in each house. We've tried to give you word associations that you'll be able to remember. Planets *in* signs appear *in* houses, or, in other words, show *how* you do *what* you do in certain *areas* of your life.

Which house and sign a planet are in is where the story of you *really* begins. This is where the particular mathematics of astrology come into play: Planets + Signs + Houses = YOU. If you've got Mars ♂ in Aries ♈ in your first house, for example, you're always going to put yourself first!

The houses are where the activities of your life unfold.

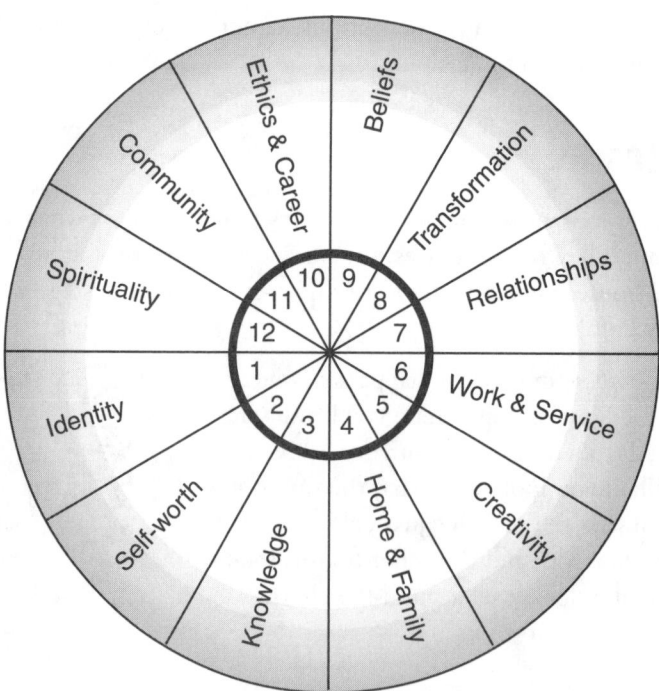

House	Area of Life
1st	Physical self, personality, early childhood
2nd	Possessions, earning abilities, self-esteem
3rd	Knowledge, siblings, environment
4th	Home and family, foundation of life
5th	Creativity, fun, romance, risk, children
6th	Personal responsibilities, health, service
7th	Primary relationships, partnerships
8th	Joint resources, sex, death, rebirth
9th	Social areas of higher education, philosophy, religion, law, and travel
10th	Reputation, career, social responsibilities
11th	Goals, groups, friends
12th	Subconscious, privacy, past karma

There's nothing arbitrary about the house divisions. Astrologers have been studying what's going on in each house for thousands of years—and these correlations are borne out again and again in the way we all behave.

So are you ready to learn what's in all these houses? In Chapters 15 through 18, you'll learn more about each house, and you'll *really* get to see behind those doors.

Knock, Knock, Who's There? Heavenly Bodies in Your Houses

In addition to being connected to each other through rulerships, signs and planets also are associated with certain houses. What we're going to show here is which planets and signs are *naturally* associated with each house. Remember, though, where *your* planets are depends on *your* chart. In addition, don't forget that if you have more than one planet in a particular house, that's going to indicate an *emphasis* in that area of your life, and just what that emphasis is depends on *which* planets are in *which* house. Whew!

Also, just as certain planets naturally rule certain signs, they also rule certain houses. And which planet rules which house is determined by which planet *naturally* rules the sign on the *cusp* of the house. (If we've lost you, don't worry; we'll be going over this more slowly in Chapters 15 through 18.)

AstroLingo

Cusps are the *beginning* of each house. The ascendant, for example, is the beginning of the first house, the house of self, and the next cusp is the beginning of the second house, and so on. The cusps also separate the houses from each other.

The following figure shows you which signs and which rulers and co-rulers appear *naturally* in each house.

Natural planets and natural signs in their houses.

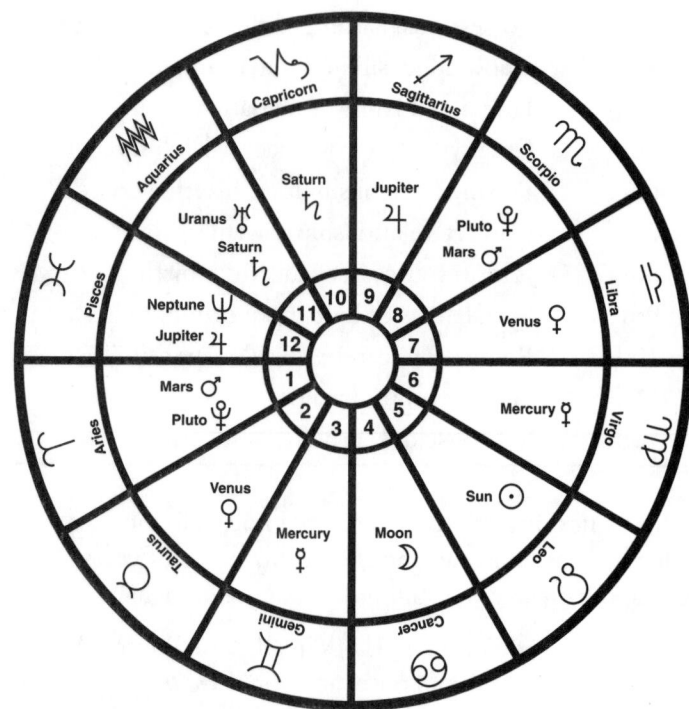

A Tour Beyond the Sun (Sign)

To illustrate the many concepts we've introduced you to in this chapter, we've provided the birth chart of *Tonight Show* host Jay Leno. Take a moment to look at Leno's chart before we begin your step-by-step tour.

What's Rising?

The ascendant, or rising sign, is the sign that is on the cusp of the first house. Leno's ascendant is Aquarius ♒. What does this say about the mask that Leno wears for the world?

For a simple beginning, let's use what you learned in Chapter 3 about energies, qualities, and elements. Aquarius ♒ has a *yang* energy, fixed quality, and Air element. This means that someone with an Aquarius ♒ ascendant will appear direct (*yang*), persistent (fixed), and intellectual and socially responsible (Air). Leno's humorous focus on current events is clearly revealed in his ascendant.

Jay Leno's birth chart.

Jay Leno
Natal Chart
Apr 28 1950
2:03 am EST +5:00
New Rochelle, NY
40°N54'41" 073°W46'58"
Geocentric
Tropical
Placidus
True Node

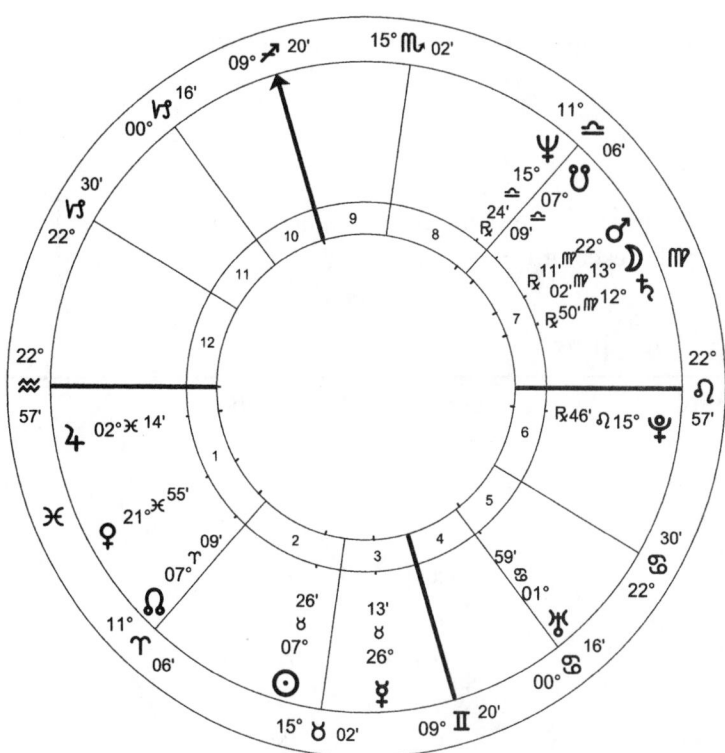

People with Aquarius ascendants have a unique ability to connect to the masses through unusual forms of communication. Leno's Aquarius rising gives him the ability to relate ideas, topical subjects, and commentary on the human condition in clever ways that are also often humorous. This ascendant indicates that his offbeat appearance is part of his demeanor; while he appears goofy on the one hand, he's direct and to-the-point on the other.

Ruled by Uranus ♅, the Aquarius ascendant loves motorbikes and cars, and enjoys being unconventional. He may appear as a fixed Air sign to us, but he's really both a liberal conservative and a conservative liberal! The older he gets, the more he'll connect with younger folks.

Leno's ascendant and all of the first house relate to his public image, so Jupiter ♃, Venus ♀, and his North Node ☊—his luck, humor, joy, attraction, and fresh approach, in other words—are integral parts of his personality and the public "mask" he wears for the world. Plus, Leno reveals his third house Mercury ☿—the communicator of the zodiac in the house of communication—with his positive, upbeat energy in both his monologues and celebrity interviews.

You'll learn more about the Aquarius ascendant as well as the other 11 rising signs in Chapter 9.

The Planets

The planets are represented by the large symbols in each house. Use the table we've provided to locate the sign for each of Leno's planets.

Jay Leno's Planets in Their Signs

Planet	Symbol	Sign	Symbol
Sun	☉	Taurus	♉
Moon	☽	Virgo	♍
Mercury	☿	Taurus	♉
Venus	♀	Pisces	♓
Mars	♂	Virgo	♍
Jupiter	♃	Pisces	♓
Saturn	♄	Virgo	♍
Uranus	♅	Cancer	♋
Neptune	♆	Libra	♎
Pluto	♇	Leo	♌

Next, locate Leno's North ☊ and South ☋ Nodes. That's right: his South Node ☋ is in Libra ♎ in his seventh house, while his North Node ☊ is in Aries ♈ in his first house. If you'd like to find out what this nodal pairing reveals about what's easy and difficult for Leno, you can sneak a peak at Chapters 13 and 15. *Hint:* It's about using relationship skills to create consensus. Sound like a talk show host you know?

Who's in Charge?

To illustrate planetary rulership, let's look at a particularly crowded house in Leno's chart. This also happens to be the seventh house, which is ruled by the planet on his descendant. In this case, the sign on the descendant is Leo ♌, which is ruled by the Sun ☉. This means that all the world's a stage to Leno, and that the planets here work at partnerships that further his sunny outlook (these are seventh house energies).

What planets do we find in Leno's seventh house? First of all, his Moon ☽. This means that seventh house matters are an emotional focal point. Of course, with so many planets clustered here, we already know this is an important area. Simply put, with a Virgo ♍ Moon ☽ in the seventh house, Leno will seek his emotional support through service and partnership.

Other planets in Leno's seventh house are Mars ♂ and Saturn ♄. Mars ♂ in Virgo ♍ in the seventh house seeks action through service to partnership, and Saturn ♄ in Virgo ♍ in the seventh house seeks to fulfill concrete goals and dreams in this same way.

Are you beginning to see how the signs, planets, and houses come together in your birth chart? The last thing we want to note about Leno's chart is that several houses appear to be empty. But no astrological house is ever "empty." When there are no planets in a house, we look at that house's cusp sign. Leno's fourth house of domestic activity, for example, has Gemini ♊ on the cusp.

The fourth house's *natural* ruling sign is Cancer ♋, which in Leno's chart is on the cusp of his fifth house, whose natural ruling sign is—*aha!*—Leo ♌. In other words, Leno's fourth house areas are tied in not only with his seventh house areas, but with his second house areas (where his Sun ☉ resides, as well).

Whew! Are you beginning to see why becoming an astrologer takes years of training? Never fear. We'll take you one step at a time. To begin, in Part 2, we'll reveal everything you ever wanted to know about the astrological signs.

The Least You Need to Know

- Your ascendant is the mask you wear for the world.
- The planets represent different parts of you, the "what" of you and your life.
- Every planet rules at least one sign.
- The Moon's Nodes represent your past and your future.
- Houses represent the areas of your life.
- Each sign and its corresponding ruler are associated with one of the houses in the natural charts.

Part  Touring the Zodiac: Sun ☉ Signs and Ascendants

"Hi. What's your sign?" Although you might know the answer to that question, it's only the beginning when it comes to astrology. Now you'll move beyond the basics to what your Sun ☉ sign and ascendant can tell you about yourself.

In the chapters that follow, we'll tour the wheel of the zodiac from Aries ♈ to Pisces ♓. You'll discover the best and most challenging characteristics of each astrological sign, as well as how they behave in love, at home, at work, and with money. Then, you'll take a closer look at each ascendant, or rising sign—which is something quite separate from your Sun sign— and get more keys to your own particular uniqueness.

Chapter 5

Spring Signs: Aries ♈, Taurus ♉, and Gemini ♊

In This Chapter

- Aries ♈, the Ram: leading the charge
- Taurus ♉, the Bull: keeping the home fires simmering
- Gemini ♊, the Twins: quick-witted, quicksilver

The first three zodiac signs, Aries ♈, Taurus ♉, and Gemini ♊, have little in common: Aries likes to get things going; Taurus likes to keep them as they are; and Gemini likes to talk about them! But they do have *one* thing in common: They're all signs of spring.

Aries ♈, the Ram: Leading the Charge

How many Aries does it take to screw in a light bulb?

One, but you better get the hell out of the way.

It's no accident that Aries is the first sign; if it hadn't been, it would have rearranged the zodiac to get there! Aries is the sign of the pioneer, the daredevil, and the person who just won't say "No." In legend, the Ram often came to the rescue, and, in fact, that's how Aries ended up as a constellation, as a reward from Jupiter for trying to save some children from the machinations of their wicked stepmother.

Nothing can stop the Ram; as the first of the cardinal signs, no one has a stronger will. Rams want to be where the action is and will do anything to make sure they get there first. Don't stand in a Ram's way. You're likely to get run down by this Butthead of the zodiac!

Rams are the only fire sign with a cardinal quality, which means they like to start things, but might not want to finish them. (As you learned in Chapter 3, qualities represent different types of activities and are related to where in a season a sign falls. Cardinal signs—Aries ♈, Cancer ♋, Libra ♎, and Capricorn ♑—start each season and are signs of beginnings.) Because Rams are also a fire sign, they're enthusiastic and impulsively go off to start something without giving it much thought beforehand. Fools rush in where angels fear to tread, true, but rushing in takes great courage, and Rams have plenty of that!

The First Zodiac Sign

Aries, the Ram ♈	March 21 to April 20
Element	Fire
Quality	Cardinal
Energy	*Yang*
Rulers	Mars ♂ and Pluto ♇
Color	Red
Gem	Diamond
Anatomy	Head and face
Keywords	Pioneering, leading, new beginnings
Archetypes	Aragorn, *Tomb Raider*'s Lara Croft, Luke Skywalker, Neo from *The Matrix*, the cowboy of the American West
Celeb Rams	Norah Jones, Martin Lawrence, Mariah Carey, Reese Witherspoon, Russell Crowe, Eddie Murphy, Marlon Brando, Tennessee Williams
Tarot suit	Wands
Tarot Major Arcana card	0 The Fool, innocence and openness

The Best and Worst of Ram

Rams are assertive, direct, and straightforward, but this also means that they can be aggressive, blunt, or impatient. Strong-willed Rams can be remarkably single-minded when they have a goal in sight, but this single-mindedness can make them tactless, blind to side issues, or just plain irritating.

The symbol for Aries ♈ could be interpreted to represent the eyebrows and the nose—the face, in other words—the part of the body that's under Ram's rulership. Or it could be interpreted as a sign of the emergence of self, of beginnings. It also represents the constellation Aries, which can be found in the sky standing erect, its head facing toward Mars.

Rams like challenges and are often wonderful leaders. Their courage can inspire others to follow their lead, and their confidence and enthusiasm get everybody where they're going.

But anyone who likes a challenge also likes a good fight, and Rams can be argumentative. At their worst, they're steamrollers, running over anything that stands in their way. But at their best, Rams are idea people who can inspire others to help those ideas see the light of day.

AstroLingo

This is the symbol for Aries, the Ram: ♈.

Rams in Love

Rams in love won't take no for an answer; they'll pursue their beloved to the ends of the world—and beyond, if necessary. Rams have the happiest love matches with other Fire signs: other Aries ♈, Leos ♌, or Sagittarians ♐; signs who, like Ram, crave excitement and passion.

If those fires don't keep burning, don't expect Rams to stick around. They like relationships that can contain the fire, and may seek lovers who are dependent on them for love but independent in other ways.

Rams can be jealous; they expect their love to give them the same fiery attention that they're giving. But Rams also enjoy sharing everything with a lover they trust, and their ambition for those they love, like their ambition for themselves, knows no bounds.

Rams and all Air signs do well together: Ram's opposite, Libra ♎, for example, can provide some air to keep the fire burning, but Ram may get tired of Libra's standards. The other Air signs, Gemini ♊ and Aquarius ♒, can also feed Ram's fire. But Ram is not a "householder" sign, and that's one reason why it doesn't do well with Cancer ♋ and Capricorn ♑. Love requires compromise and meeting the needs of others, and this is very hard for Rams to do.

From a mythic point of view, Aries is the cowboy of the American West, the Rugged Individualist, the Wild Woman, or even the goddess Diana or Artemis. None of these types are high on settling down to build a nest, especially when they're young. These are adventurers, and they don't care much about dirty dishes or clamoring kids.

The Healthy Ram

Aries rules the head and face and also represents the eyes and the brain. With this influence, it's easy to see why Rams are the quick thinkers of the zodiac, but also why they're prone to injuries—they sometimes leap before they look. At the same time, because they're quick to anger at both real and imagined slights, Rams may be susceptible to headaches and nervousness. The best health advice Rams could get would be to slow down—but don't expect them to listen.

Heaven Knows

One of the most important lessons Rams can learn is cooperation. If they learn that the help of others can only further their own creativity and desires, they can move beyond their Ram-centeredness and make enormous marks on the world.

Mars ♂, Aries' ruler, represents the blood and iron, and so Rams need to get enough iron to keep them oxygenated and keep their hemoglobin up. They also need vitamin B_{12}, which is required for the formation of red blood cells and metabolism, and potassium, which is necessary for maintaining their muscles and heart rate.

Rams at Home

There's never a dull moment with a Ram at home. Like adolescents, Rams see all the world has to offer—and want to experience it all, too. But, also like adolescents, Rams might see that world from a self-centered point of view, and that can make life with a Ram a challenge. One thing's for sure: Don't expect to find Rams snoozing next to the fire. They're the ones throwing more logs on, just to see what happens!

Rams at Work

Rams need work that holds their interest, things that totally involve them and allow them the freedom to express themselves. They don't like to take orders, and they'll always try to climb to the top themselves. Their love of competition means that they won't let setbacks stand in their way, and their eagerness for new experience means they'll jump whenever they see a new opportunity.

Rams are often found in positions that need "idea people"; they're project leaders—as long as there's someone else around to handle the details. Rams also do well in creative fields, where their fiery independence can find self-expression.

Some Aries like to work outdoors like the archetypal cowboy of the American West or in construction, and many prefer work that enables them to maintain their independence. This can include areas like outside sales, consulting, or contract work.

Rams and Their Money

Impulsive Rams sometimes spend first and think later—or don't even bother to think later! Money for a Ram is one more way of getting ahead, and getting ahead is Ram's credo. Rams can be—and often are—generous, especially when it comes to pursuing something or someone they want. With money, though, Rams might do well to turn their cash over to an Earth sign; someone who won't burn it quite so quickly (there's that fire …). They'll often be the ones to see ways to make money, but it might just as often be others who take advantage of Ram's moneymaking ideas.

Taurus ♉, the Bull: Keeping the Home Fires Simmering

How many Tauruses does it take to screw in a light bulb?

One, but she'll do it when she's good and ready.

No one is more down to earth than the passive, fixed, Earth sign, Taurus ♉. All of Bull's feet are planted firmly on the ground, and Bull's calm and dependability make a Bull a friend you can count on. Hand in hand with that dependability, Bulls can be conservative and cautious, so they're usually perfectly happy with the way things are.

Bulls' connection with the earth means they're often materially wealthy, but Bulls' wealth can also be found in the cozy homes they create: Bulls like to sit calmly in their favorite chair, maybe smoking their favorite pipe or reading their favorite paper, perfectly content if nothing ever changes.

AstroLingo

This is the symbol for Taurus, the Bull: ♉.

But this desire for harmony goes beyond the self: Bulls also seek a harmony with everything on earth. You're likely to find Bulls living in the country, but even if they live in the city, you'll find them surrounded by plants or working in their garden. Bulls crave silence, too, the silence that comes with inner serenity, and they are often people of few words. Bulls are the most physical of the signs—everything they know, they know through the body. This is because they're ruled by Venus ♀, the ruler of the senses.

The Second Zodiac Sign

Taurus, the Bull ♉	April 20 to May 21
Element	Earth
Quality	Fixed
Energy	*Yin*
Ruler	Venus ♀
Color	Green
Gem	Emerald
Anatomy	Neck and throat
Keywords	Ownership, dependability, sensuality
Archetypes	Marmie from *Little Women*, Dustin Hoffman's character in *Kramer vs. Kramer*, Aphrodite, Osiris
Celeb Bulls	Jay Leno, Jack Nicholson, Michelle Pfeiffer, George Clooney, Cher, Andie MacDowell, George Lucas
Tarot suit	Pentacles
Tarot Major Arcana card	5 The Hierophant, steadfast conformity

The Best and Worst of Bull

At their best, Bulls create a calm in the midst of storms all around them. They're connected solidly to their bodies and to their homes, have good jobs, good friends, good marriages, and good children. They're the people everyone else turns to: They're who you call if you have a flat tire at 2 A.M., and, though they may be reluctant to get out of bed, they'll be the ones you know you can rely on.

AstroLingo

Opposite signs, or a **polarity,** are signs that appear directly across from each other in the zodiac. Taurus ♉ and Scorpio ♏ are opposites.

But in their complacency, Bulls may be resistant to change, and can become dogmatic or even preachy. Bulls can't understand what all the excitement's about, and they may be the first to tell you all this New Age stuff is a lot of bunk. Bulls can be lazy as well—too comfortable to get out of that chair, or they can get so caught up in their earthly possessions that life itself passes them by.

Bulls in Love

Security and stability … a Bull in love stays in love. Romance and love are one and the same to sensuous, earthbound Bulls, and they're nothing if not patient when it comes to making sure that the love they find is the right one. A Bull will always be there for you—and expects the same in return.

StarFacts
In ancient Egypt, Osiris, the God of the Dead and the Underworld, was represented as a man with a bull's head. Living manifestations of Osiris were selected by the priests and revered. Osiris remains with us today. Look on the back of a $1 bill: There's an eye (the symbol of Osiris) above a pyramid!
Aphrodite also represented Taurus. After all, Taurus is ruled by Venus. She represented the qualities of deep intimacy, as well as beauty. Aphrodite was beautiful not to attract men, but to celebrate herself and her high standards. She was intimate only with those men who met her high standards for honor and love!

Bulls don't like change, so they might show some jealousy if the stability they create seems threatened in some way. A Taurean partner is one you can always depend on, though, and, although it may seem dull at times, you can rest assured they're with you for the long haul.

Bulls are attracted to Water signs, especially Cancer ♋ and Pisces ♓. But many Bulls or Rising Bulls find their mate in a Scorpio ♏, Bull's opposite. Bulls get along well with householder Cancers, as Bulls like their comfort. Remember: Earth and water go well together, creating beautiful lakes.

Taureans are often attracted to the more lively signs like Aries ♈, Gemini ♊, or Sagittarius ♐, but quickly become annoyed when all these signs want to do is go out and play. They're most comfortable with other Earth signs, whose reliability and need for established routine match their own. Don't expect many fireworks here, though, just everything in its place, as it should be.

The Healthy Bull

The Bull rules the neck and throat and so the entire metabolic system. The thyroid gland in particular can be a problem for Bulls: They might not properly convert what they eat into energy and so can be prone to gain weight. Their love of inaction feeds this tendency as well. But the throat is also where singing comes from, and many Bulls are well-known singers: Barbra Streisand, Bing Crosby, and Ella Fitzgerald, to name just a few.

Iodine is necessary for the development and functioning of the thyroid gland, which is ruled by Taurus. Other vitamins and minerals that are important to Taurus are selenium, bioflavenoids, and vitamin E, which work together to maintain beauty and promote normal body growth, fertility, and metabolic action. With Venus being Bulls' ruler, getting enough of these nutrients is even more important than usual.

Bulls at Home

Home is where Bulls thrive: They collect, they arrange, they make it into a womb where they and those they love can comfortably relax. Bulls may be collectors, too: With their Venus ruler, they have an appreciation for beauty. Their homes might be filled with music and books as well as paintings and sculpture. They're also likely to know a great deal about some special area of expertise, such as the breeding habits of iguanas or the batting averages of White Sox pitchers.

Bulls crave comfort, security, and calm, and their homes reflect that desire. A Bull's home is always a good place to show up at dinnertime. Not only will there be something wonderful cooking, but you're sure to be invited to stay!

Bulls at Work

No one knows a good opportunity like a Bull, especially an opportunity that promises long-term stability. Even Merrill Lynch knows this: They're "bullish on America," remember? Connected to the earth, Bulls can do well with real estate or land deals. But Bulls don't want to build the homes and buildings (Aries ♈ does that); they want to *own* the land, home, or building as an investment.

Star-Crossed

There's nothing wrong with a little security, but Bulls need to beware of taking it to extremes. If Bulls' love of possessions crosses the line from comfort to acquisition, they may lose sight of enjoying things in the here and now. Great planners for the future that they are, Bulls need to beware of becoming so prepared that there's nothing to enjoy now.

Bulls' connection to the earth makes them practical in nature. They aren't going to set off on an impulsive whim. They might be interested in finance, for example, or banking, or the things they can build with money and resources.

Bulls make wonderful employees, too: They're the ones who show up even on snow days, the ones who get the proposal in on time. Because Venus is their ruler, many Bulls are talented folks who sing, write, or perform music, sculpt, or enjoy other creative endeavors. Many Bulls use their voices for voice-overs or are radio announcers or disc jockeys.

Bulls and Their Money

Bulls are wonderful providers and may acquire a great deal of money and a wealth of possessions. But they also need to be careful not to cross the line into materialism, wealth for its own sake, or extravagance. There's a danger of stinginess, and Bulls might hoard their money or hide it away where it will be "safe." But as the ultimate Taurean desire is for earthly harmony, they are far more likely to use their wealth to share their desire for comfort with those they love.

Gemini ♊, the Twins: Quick-Witted, Quicksilver

How many Geminis does it take to screw in a light bulb?

Two.

Twins never miss a thing; their goal is to see everything. Gemini ♊ is a mutable sign, which signifies change; a *yang* sign, which signifies motion; and an Air sign, which signifies the mind. In their quest for knowledge, Twins are always in motion, always alert, always trying to live not just two, but as many lives as they can, all at one time. Often called a dualistic sign, Twins are really deceptively simple: It's all based on avid curiosity, on finding things out and then quickly moving on to something else.

Twins have been called the Great Communicators, too, and with Mercury as their ruler, it's easy to see why. But sometimes words can mask meaning, and that's another paradox of Twins: Meaning is not really what they're after; it's the ideas themselves.

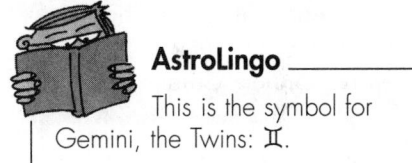

AstroLingo

This is the symbol for Gemini, the Twins: ♊.

The Third Zodiac Sign

Gemini, the Twins ♊	May 21 to June 22
Element	Air
Quality	Mutable
Energy	*Yang*
Ruler	Mercury ☿
Color	Yellow
Gem	Agate
Anatomy	Hands, arms, shoulders, lungs
Keywords	Mentality, communication, versatility

continues

The Third Zodiac Sign (continued)

Gemini, the Twins ♊	May 21 to June 22
Archetypes	Hermione of *Harry Potter*, Castor and Pollux, Coyote the Trickster
Celeb Twins	George H. W. Bush, Marilyn Monroe, Clint Eastwood, Elizabeth Hurley, Rupert Everett, Mike Myers, Joseph Fiennes
Tarot suit	Swords
Tarot Major Arcana card	6 The Lovers, options and choices

The Best and Worst of Twins

Twins can be amusing, witty, quick, and flexible—and they can be glib, sarcastic, fickle, and devious. Two sides of the same coin, and it's all too easy for a Twin to flip back and forth between them. At their best, Twins are masters of invention, clever and adaptable, never afraid to try something new. But this same eagerness to try everything can lead them to be scatterbrained or restless, even unreliable or ungrateful.

At their weakest, Twins can run themselves to emotional exhaustion, or feel that nothing matters. At their strongest, their wide variety of interests brings them many friends and experiences, and their quick mind enables them to take it all in. You can always count on a Twin to be the life of the party!

> **StarFacts**
>
> The symbol for Gemini ♊ may be merely the Roman numeral II, but it also represents the parts of the body ruled by this third sign: the hands, arms, shoulders, and lungs. Taking it still one step further, this symbol suggests the dual sides of human nature: mind and soul. On the other hand, maybe it just a pair of twins!

Twins' flexibility and adaptability arise because this is a mutable sign, and mutability means changeability. Mutable signs, such as Gemini ♊, occur as the season is changing and so are associated with transitions. Other mutable signs are Virgo ♍, Sagittarius ♐, and Pisces ♓.

Geminis are also very resourceful because they've seen so much, and that's part of their mutability, too: The more you're willing to change, after all, the more you're going to see.

Twins in Love

The Twins of the Gemini myth, Castor and Pollux, chose to be united forever in the sky rather than separated for even a moment, and so Gemini is obviously a sign of relationships. Translated to love, though, Twins have so many relationships that they can all seem a little too casual. This is because Gemini's a mutable sign. It's not that a Twin won't give you all the attention you want, it's that a Twin can't. There's too much else going on!

Here's where Twins' fickleness can come into play: Someone who seemed fascinating last week is a known quantity this week and so is no longer interesting. But Twins also can be the ideal partners: They're charming, witty, generous, and genuinely interested in you—it's keeping that interest that's the hard part. Meet them on their own ground—wit and imagination—and let them know they can trust you by trusting them.

Other Air signs—other Geminis ♊, Librans ♎, and Aquarians ♒—are always a good bet for Twins; Air signs are lighthearted and understand each other's need for mental stimulation. At the same time, though, two Air signs might never come down from the clouds. If they do, they might find there's no place to land.

Because air feeds fire, Twins can do well with Aries ♈, Leo ♌, and Sagittarius ♐, the Fire signs. Down-to-earth Virgo ♍ is a good match, too: With the same quality (mutable) and ruler (Venus) as Gemini, Twins and Virgos can both challenge and learn a lot from each other.

Healthy Twins

No other sign can benefit quite so much from learning to breathe, learning to relax, and taking deep breaths and then letting them out. Twins are always on the move, moving their arms like wings much of the time, and all this rushing around can mean they don't stop and smell the roses like they should. Gemini rules the hands, arms, shoulders, and lungs, and this grouping reflects yet another of Twins' dualities, the need to flit about and the need to breathe deeply and relax. If Twins don't learn to relax, all that flying around can lead to emotional exhaustion.

> **CAUTION**
>
> **Star-Crossed**
>
> No sign is more prone to the dangers of running in circles than Gemini. Twins are so fond of motion that they might not notice that their motion isn't leading them anywhere. Over-stimulation can lead to jumpiness, insomnia, or, as already mentioned, emotional exhaustion. Twins need stoplights or they'll never stop!

Twins at Home

Twins at home—now, there's a phrase that's hard to interpret: Twins don't often stay put long enough to let them see where home is. But maybe that's exactly it: Twins are at home wherever they happen to be. Twins are seldom content to sit still and watch the world go by; they'd rather be on that world and going by with it!

Don't forget that Twins are great communicators, so if they *are* at home, you're likely to find them on the phone or gathering new information from reading or watching TV.

Twins at Work

Twins need mental challenges to keep them stimulated on the job, and it can't be the same challenge over and over again. Careers like advertising, writing, broadcasting, and public relations appeal to Twins because they're always presenting new challenges to Twins' inquiring minds. Don't rule out technical fields, though; the right opportunity might offer Twins just the mental somersaults they need.

Twins are often found in sales positions or in other jobs where there is a lot of contact with other people. They can be "silver-tongued" with their wit and communication abilities, so they're excellent at persuading or influencing others. This literally translates to selling products or services, or selling ideas to others.

Twins and Their Money

Twins like to spend their money on information, computers, travel, and cars, things that will feed their need for new ideas, communication, movement, and action. Twins don't worry much about spending, either, and are apt to max out their credit cards and then sign up for another. It's not money that concerns Twins, it's information; and any way they can get it, they will, including buying it.

In the next chapter, we'll look at Cancer ♋, Leo ♌, and Virgo ♍, the summer signs.

The Least You Need to Know

◆ The signs of spring are Aries ♈, Taurus ♉, and Gemini ♊.

◆ Cardinal Aries ♈ likes to lead and pioneer.

◆ Fixed Taurus ♉ is dependable and sensual.

◆ Mutable Gemini ♊ is a versatile quick thinker.

Chapter 6

Summer Signs: Cancer ♋, Leo ♌, and Virgo ♍

In This Chapter

◆ Cancer ♋, the Crab: home is where the heart is

◆ Leo ♌, the Lion: king of the jungle

◆ Virgo ♍, the Virgin: practical perfection

The signs of summer, Cancer ♋, Leo ♌, and Virgo ♍, might share a season, but each is otherwise unique. Emotional Cancer is a nurturer; bright, sunny Leo seeks the spotlight; and meticulous Virgo improves herself by helping others learn about sacred patterns.

Cancer ♋, the Crab: Wear Your Heart on Your Sleeve

How many Cancers does it take to screw in a light bulb?

One, but his therapist has to talk him into it.

Touchy, touchy, touchy: No one else feels like a Crab. And no one retreats like a Crab, either: Quick to hurt, they're also quick to crawl into their shells. But remember, crabs' shells are also their houses. Crabs are nurturers, too: The Mamas and Papas of the zodiac.

Star-Crossed

Wound Crabs, and they'll never forget it; Crabs will carry grudges for life. Befriend Crabs, and they'll never forget either; Crabs are famous for keeping in touch with old friends, old loves, and old times. And what a memory! Need to know who was wearing what at that party back in 1965? Ask any Crab—chances are they'll remember the menu as well!

Others look to Crabs for warmth and understanding, and Crabs always lend a sympathetic ear, lap, or shoulder. But these Moon-ruled ☽ children won't look to get the same from you. They might be the most sensitive sign of the zodiac, but they're also the least likely to let you know what they're feeling. Crabs hide their emotions behind what they believe is an impenetrable shell.

For Crabs, it's all about security; in fact, that's the major point of Cancer. Crabs are learning about emotional and physical security, as well as responsible nurturing. After the primal instincts of Ram, the building of Bull, and the thinking and mental development of Twins, there's the emotional foundation of Crabs, which can take many forms, like a house—or a shell.

The Fourth Zodiac Sign

Cancer, the Crab ♋	June 22 to July 23
Element	Water
Quality	Cardinal
Energy	*Yin*
Ruler	Moon ☽
Color	Silver
Gem	Pearl
Anatomy	Stomach and breasts
Keywords	Feeling, sensitivity, nurturing
Archetypes	Meryl Streep's Clarissa in the film *The Hours*, Barbara Bush, Aunt Em
Celeb Crabs	Tom Cruise, Princess Di, Harrison Ford, Meryl Streep, Liv Tyler, Tom Hanks, the Dalai Lama, Ernest Hemingway
Tarot suit	Cups
Tarot Major Arcana cards	14 Temperance, patience and adaptation; 18 The Moon, imagination and feeling

The Best and Worst of Crabs

At their best, Crabs are dependable, loving, adaptable, and self-sacrificing, which means at their worst, they're clinging, oversensitive, moody, and smothering. Want a money manager? Let a Crab handle it. Need an advance? Better have those numbers ready! Late for dinner? Tell Crab your sob story. Didn't show up at all? Better move to another town!

Because one of us is a Crab, we know how easily Crabs are distracted, and how anything can set Crabs' imaginations running—in another direction. Crabs are always off on tangents. Picture a crab on the beach, always moving sideways rather than forward. They *do* get where they're going, often without the rest of us realizing they've done it. Sneaky? Yes, Crabs can be sneaky. Clever? Yes, they're that, too. Don't ever take a Crab for granted, that's for sure. They'll leave you standing in the sand, wondering which way they've gone!

AstroLingo

This is the symbol for Cancer, the Crab: ♋.

StarFacts

Many of Cancer's myths involve turtles or tortoises. In ancient Egypt, the constellation was called Stars of the Water, and its symbol was two turtles. In Roman mythology, the Crab assisted Jupiter's wife, Juno, in trying to slow down one of the many labors of Heracles (Hercules in Greek mythology). The unfortunate Crab got caught underfoot, though, so all Juno could do to reward it was place it in the heavens.

Crabs in Love

No one sends more confusing messages than a Crab; just when you think they might be interested, off they go into their shells. Crabs are so afraid of being hurt that they may *never* let you know they're interested, but on the other hand, if they decide they've got a chance with you, look out: Crabs can hang on very tightly.

Crabs who didn't feel coddled as children might seem cold and distant as adults. But in their indirect Crab way, they're really dying for attention. Crabs have a natural fear of revealing themselves—those soft insides are very vulnerable—so they're never going to approach you directly. You know those conversations that go "What's the matter?" "Nothing"? Chances are they're with a Crab.

Water signs—other Cancers ♋, Scorpios ♏, or Pisces ♓—understand things the same way Crabs do, and Pisces in particular may inspire Crabs to use their intuition.

Still, there can be too much emotion and too little thinking with these pairings. Crabs are good with Earth signs—Taurus ♉, Virgo ♍, and even their opposite, Capricorn ♑—keeping them watered and fertile. Gemini ♊ can be fun, but might feel smothered, and Leo ♌ might love the attention, but not return it.

As a Water sign, Crabs require trust in a relationship and are very cautious about giving their hearts away. The things they need most are love and security, and even if you and a Crab later part, the Crab will stay in touch and remember your birthday. Deep down, Crabs really do believe love makes the world go 'round, and if you love a Crab, you can go along for the ride.

The Healthy Crab

Nurturing Crabs rule the stomach and the breasts, sources of food and nourishment. So naturally, sensitive Crabs are prone to stomach troubles and, with their love of creating comfort through food, can also be prone to being overweight.

No sign is as sensitive to touch, and Crabs are always reaching out and touching. But they're sensitive to hot and cold, too: You'll see Crabs wearing socks in July, or, if it's very hot, scuttling into the shade or the water to cool off. Remember that Crabs' ruler is the Moon ☽, and the Moon has no light source of its own. Crabs reflect everything around them, and their emotions swing with the tides.

Vitamin A and beta-carotene are especially helpful for growth and maintenance of all mucous membranes, including the stomach and digestive tract, which is very important to a Crab. They also help build strong bones and teeth (ruled by Capricorn ♑, the opposite sign). Crabs also may have allergies, which are often aggravated by dairy products, so if digestion becomes a problem, it's best for Crabs to monitor what they eat in relation to how they feel.

Crabs at Home

Crabs' homes are their safe havens, even if they do carry their houses on their backs. It might be the pillows tossed about for comfort, or it could be those good smells coming from the kitchen, but you'll always feel like a Crab's home is a place where you can relax and unwind.

Within that cozy home, though, there's a place that's Crab's alone. It might just be a corner on a couch, but in that corner will be Crab's favorite book or blanket, and maybe a picture or two. Chances are Crab's dog or cat will snuggle up there, too, whether or not Crab's there at the moment. But rest assured there *will* be a dog or cat, or maybe more than one. Crabs nurture any creature that comes their way.

StarFacts
According to Greek (and Roman) mythology, Demeter (Ceres), goddess of the earth, was responsible for agriculture and growth. When Demeter found out that Pluto (Hades) had stolen her daughter, Persephone, and taken her to the Underworld, Demeter grieved and forbade anything on Earth to grow. Zeus (Jupiter) had Hermes (Mercury) go to the Underworld to strike a deal with Pluto. Because Persephone had eaten seven pomegranate seeds and had toured the Underworld, however, Pluto insisted that she be returned to him each year for three months (our winter months). Because of her motherly devotion, Demeter is associated with Cancer ♋, the sign of motherhood and responsible nurturing.

Crabs at Work

Although it might seem that Crabs can be too dreamy or unfocused to do well in business, it often happens that the opposite turns out to be true. Intuitive and sensitive to change, Crabs can often sense future trends and be on the cutting edge. Cancer's mothering quality might come out at work by birthing new products, projects, or companies, taking care of others by feeding them or nurturing their emotional selves via teaching.

Crabs are often found in creative areas like writing, too, because writing involves the part of motherhood that requires gestation, creating something new and unknown, and then birthing it. In addition, Crabs' empathy for others, as well as their prodigious memories, comes into play with the creative arts, helping them generate works that connect with everyone.

Crabs and Their Money

Tenacious Crabs hoard their money just like they do everything; in fact, no matter how much they accumulate, they may never feel entirely secure. Crabs don't differentiate between things and security, and because of their nature (hard on the outside, soft on the inside), they hold onto everything with a tenacious grip.

Sometimes this hoarding tendency can move into selfishness, not because Crabs don't want to help, but because they're so afraid of being hurt from the outside that they'll do anything they can to protect themselves—including keeping all their assets to themselves.

You won't often find Crabs broke; they're far too concerned with security. And, because they want this security for those they love as well, they'll make sure to create a safe haven for them, too.

Leo ♌, the Lion: King of the Jungle

How many Leos does it take to screw in a light bulb?

One, and a hallelujah chorus while she does it.

Talk about self-confidence, Lions invented it. Ruled by the Sun ☉, Lions bask in the spotlight. They're dramatic, they're bold, they're creative, and they're strong; no other sign can grab and hold the spotlight the way a Lion can.

AstroLingo

This is the symbol for Leo, the Lion: ♌.

Lions are great fun to be around, too. Their exuberance is contagious, and when they get to the party, everyone knows it's really begun. Not only *can* Leos lead, they *will* lead: Lions expect to be at the head of the line—and of the pride.

Lions don't give up, as anyone who has watched a lion chase and catch its prey can attest to. The point of being Lions is to be at one with the creative principle, and to learn how their willpower affects what they create in their lives. Self-expression and creativity are everything to Lions. Eventually they learn to follow more than just their own will, aligning themselves with the higher Self and the creative principles of the Universe.

The Fifth Zodiac Sign

Leo, the Lion ♌	July 23 to August 22
Element	Fire
Quality	Fixed
Energy	*Yang*
Ruler	Sun ☉
Color	Gold
Gem	Ruby
Anatomy	Back, spine, and heart
Keywords	Willpower, creativity, expressing the heart
Archetypes	King Arthur, The Lion King, Hercules, Hindu goddess Sarasvati, Celie in *The Color Purple*
Celeb Lions	Ben Affleck, Sandra Bullock, Lisa Kudrow, Lucille Ball, Robert DeNiro, Mick Jagger, Madonna, Woody Harrelson, Bill Clinton
Tarot suit	Wands
Tarot Major Arcana cards	8 Strength, fortitude and compassion; 19 The Sun, self-confidence

The Best and Worst of Lions

Because Leo is a fixed sign, Lions can be determined, stubborn, or even habit-bound, but confident Lions are born to lead, and they're proud, courageous, and self-assured to a fault. Lions can be generous, commanding, ambitious, and proud, and this means they can also be intolerant, demanding, self-righteous, and vain. Lions can lead others to tremendous victories, but they can be ruthless with their enemies. Because their memories are short, however, they are quick to forgive.

Because Lions are always leading, they are often surrounded by yes-men and sycophants. This, in turn, can lead to gullibility, because Lions are easily flattered and can forget that not all might love them. And, as much fun as they can be, they also can become overbearing or self-centered if things aren't going their way.

Lions are exceptionally loyal, and expect loyalty in return as well. They are very up-front about their needs and expectations, and this lack of guile can also be their undoing; Lions might do well to trust a little less, but they expect adulation, and others can't help but give it to them.

> **StarFacts**
>
> Why do so many Leos go by one name? Because they can! With the Sun ☉ as their planet, Lions live in and for the spotlight, and with that kind of lighting, they can go by any name they choose. Jackie, Lucy, Mick, Madonna, and Napoleon are just a few Leos we recognize from singular names. Others include Fidel, Tipper, and Lawrence (of Arabia).

It takes creativity to generate excitement, but Lions are among the most creative signs of the zodiac. The Sun ☉, after all, provides illumination, and it is through that light that Lions truly shine.

Lions in Love

Generous Lions expect generosity in return: They love being in love and the drama being in love provides. Lions are loyal, too, which can actually make it difficult to end a relationship with them.

Lions expect adoration, but they'll give it as well. Like kings, they'll graciously give their loyal subjects all they can. A Fire sign, they'll usually do best with other Fire signs—other Leos ♌, Sagittarians ♐, or Arians ♈—but Lions also can be caught up in the intensity of Scorpios ♏ or the refinement of Libras ♎.

Airy Geminis ♊ and Aquarians ♒ (Lions' opposite) are also good matches; remember that opposites attract. Lions learn a lot in particular from the detached Aquarian, who can provide them with perspective and give them balance.

The Healthy Lion

No one is healthier than Lions; the ailments that touch the rest of us seem to pass them by. This strength is due in no small part to Leo's rulership of the back, spine, and heart: Even the words suggest Lions' strength.

StarFacts
The only way Hercules could slay the Lion of myth was in hand-to-paw combat, and even then, the Lion managed to bite off one of Hercules's fingers! So awed was he by his opponent's strength, Hercules used Lion's pelt for a breastplate and his jaw for a helmet, both of which helped him in his further labors.

Heaven Knows

A lion features prominently in the Strength card of the Tarot. Just as Leo ♌ is a sign of both strength and generosity, childishness and ferocity, this Major Arcana card suggests the fearless and fearful child in us all.

But Lions can be less strong emotionally. When they fail to get the adoration and respect they deserve, they can actually become physically ill. And Lions, like all cats, can be lazy, too; the only evidence of life in them may be the continual twitching of their long tails.

Because Leo rules the spine and heart, these areas also can cause them trouble when things don't go well. They might need a trip to the chiropractor or a cardiologist to get them back on track, but it's also important for them to deal with the underlying emotions that set off such problems to begin with.

Lions need plenty of magnesium and calcium on a 1:1 ratio to protect their hearts (a muscle) and circulatory systems. And Lions need to pay more attention to their potassium and salt balance than other people, because that balance is very important for their hearts. Coenzyme Q_{10}, an enzyme that strengthens the heart, might also provide them with additional energy when they get older.

Lions at Home

Lions call their homes their "castles," and they love to show them off almost as much as they love to show off themselves. Lions give great parties and won't hesitate to keep the food and wine coming.

Home is another place where Lions' generosity is evidenced: There's always a place for everyone to sleep, and friends are welcome to stay as long as they please.

If they're not entertaining, you might find Lions roaring when they're upset, but you might also hear them purring like kittens when everything is in order and they get the attention they need.

Lions at Work

No one leads like a Leo, and Lions will naturally gravitate toward careers that allow them to shine. They might be generals or presidents, but Lions might be teachers as well, firing up their students' enthusiasm with their own.

Lions can often be found in the performing arts, shining with the brightness of the Sun. In the public eye, a Lion is charismatic and magnetic, but a Lion shines even in less visible fields.

Above all, Lions need an audience (what good is it to be king without subjects?) and often choose jobs where they can get one. These fields include sales, teaching, consulting, tour guiding, management, and, of course, performing.

StarFacts
Lions are kings, and kings are Lions. The Lion of Judah and Richard the Lionhearted are just two examples, but don't forget the Queen of Sheba, daughter of the Sun ☉ (ruler of Leo ♌) who married Solomon. According to legend, all their children, the Ethiopians, were destined to be kings. There's just something regal about the noble Lions, and it's got a lot to do with the way they carry themselves: These people look and act like royalty, even when they're not. Some American Lions? Jacqueline Kennedy Onassis, Norman Schwarzkopf, and Bill Clinton. See what we mean?

Lions and Their Money

Image matters a lot to Lions, so if the checking account balance and Lions' needs are saying different things, it's the needs that are going to win out. Big night out with the gang? Count on Leo, broke or not, to pick up the tab.

Nothing's too good for a Lion, so they're not likely to notice what something costs. Lions seldom think to bargain; when they see something they want, they get it. Living the good life, according to Lions, has nothing to do with what things cost, and this makes them most generous—nearly royal in their magnanimity.

Virgo ♍, the Virgin: Practical Perfection

How many Virgos does it take to screw in a light bulb?

At least four. One to take out the light bulb, one to check the wiring, one to put in the new light bulb, and one to clean up the mess.

Purity. Perfection. Practicality. These are the Virgin values. But what does this translate to? Virgins, more than any other sign, are identified with analyzing—with examining everything in great detail, so as to improve not just themselves, but the world. And improving the world means serving more than one's self: It means serving the greater good. Virgins are very responsible people.

Virgins are about connection: They see things very clearly, and they see each part of a whole in a way that few other signs can. One of us is a Virgo, and she is forever finding the little errors her co-author didn't bother to reread for—and then, the next time through, she finds still more! This pleases her messy co-author to no end, but it pleases Virgo as well: Virgins really *like* to clean these messes up. Constant refinement means no discord, and Virgo does whatever's necessary to achieve perfection.

There's a lot of misinformation about the use of the word "virgin." A virgin is a woman whole unto herself, not just someone who has never had sex. Virgins are about finding the patterns, especially sacred patterns; and in past eras, these were the sacred priests and priestesses. They also worked in agriculture, taking care to read the natural cycles and patterns correctly so there would be enough food to feed everyone.

AstroLingo

This is the symbol for Virgo, the Virgin: ♍.

In Native American tribes, Virgin is represented by the spider, which weaves the sacred patterns in its web. This explains why many Virgins aren't very comfortable in our present society, where these sacred patterns have largely been lost or forgotten.

The Sixth Zodiac Sign

Virgo, the Virgin ♍	August 22 to September 22
Element	Earth
Quality	Mutable
Energy	*Yin*
Ruler	Mercury ☿
Color	Blue
Gem	Sapphire
Anatomy	Intestines and colon
Keywords	Service, self-improvement, sacred patterns
Archetypes	Mexico's Virgin of Juquila, Astraea, Renaissance monks who created illuminated manuscripts

Virgo, the Virgin ♍	August 22 to September 22
Celeb Virgins	Salma Hayek, Cameron Diaz, Keanu Reeves, Sean Connery, Greta Garbo, Stephen King, Sophia Loren, River Phoenix
Tarot suit	Pentacles
Tarot Major Arcana card	9 The Hermit, truth and inner guidance

The Best and Worst of Virgins

Calm-on-the-outside Virgins will fool you like no other sign. On the inside they're all restless energy, constantly seeking, constantly improving, and constantly *fixing* whatever needs to be fixed. Here is one of the zodiac's liveliest minds, a consummate problem-solver, a model of methodical efficiency, bent on beauty and perfection.

Because Virgo ♍ is an Earth sign, Virgins are very practical, and because their quality is mutable, they're resourceful as well. That same mutability also can translate into flexibility, and so Virgins can be chameleonlike, too. They might agree with you when they sense you're not going to change your mind (practical and flexible), but privately they won't change their minds either, unless it suits their purposes.

Virgins can think too much. They can find fault wherever they look—even where there's none to be found. They can be inflexible, and they can worry too much along with all that thinking. Because Virgins measure their self-esteem by weighing what they accomplish in a given day, however, they can increase their self-esteem by giving up this narrow view of what they're good for. Then they'll see themselves as whole people, with love, feelings, and other important things to offer others.

No one is more organized than a Virgin. While the rest of the world is collapsing around them, Virgins are calmly making lists of what's left. No one's more committed, either, or more willing to make sure it goes smoothly for everybody. If there's someone in the kitchen cleaning up after dinner while everyone else has gone on to another party, it's most likely a Virgin, who's probably perfectly happy to be there. Virgins *like* to work, and they do it very well.

StarFacts
Virgins have long been known as healers and those who serve, and the mythological archetypes here are no exception. Chiron was the wounded healer who couldn't heal himself but nonetheless healed others, and Astraea was a healer as well. Oaxaca, Mexico's tiny Virgin of Juquila, used Earth energy to survive the ravages of fire. Many faithful make the pilgrimage to her shrine each year to ask for special favors.

Virgins in Love

There's no denying that Virgins seek the perfect mate, but they also enjoy the pleasures of intimacy, especially when those pleasures can lead to personal growth. In her constellation in the sky, Virgo appears to be dancing, and one of her greatest joys is the fruit of consummated love.

Because Virgins like to serve, they will do whatever they can to take care of those they care about. Sometimes they can go too far, leaving the beloved with nothing to do, but often they anticipate the needs of others with prescient clarity.

As seekers of order, it's natural that Virgins seek out other Earth signs—Virgos ♍, Taureans ♉, and Capricorns ♑—but it might be the fixed intensity of Scorpio or the mutable water of Pisces ♓ that really plants the seeds of contentment for this mutable sign. Watery Cancer ♋, too, can make for strong emotional connections. But Virgins shouldn't necessarily settle for complacency just because it's tidy; they may find far more compatibility with the excitement of Gemini ♊ or Sagittarius ♐.

The Healthy Virgin

Virgins are often more concerned with health and its applications than other signs. In an Earth sign like Virgo ♍, their ruler, Mercury ☿, is very practical and interested in practical applications of knowledge. Virgins will often know about vitamins or aromatherapy; they'll know which herbs cure which ills and why your antibiotic isn't working on your pesky cold. Virgins' interest in health is largely because they're interested in practical knowledge and in sacred patterns (and what's more sacred than healing?), as well as in keeping themselves healthy.

Virgo rules the intestines and colon, and it is in these areas that problems often arise for these people. Busy Virgins need to stop what they're doing periodically to eat, and they need to relax while they eat, not rush through—or worse, work through—their meals. Virgins need to remember to serve themselves as well as they serve everyone else.

Virgins are most likely to get sick when they have problems at work (especially if they *dislike* going to work) largely because of their dedication to any given project. Workaholic Virgins need to balance work with relaxation and pleasure.

Virgins need a lot of B-complex vitamins to help control their anxiety. In addition, they need PABA (Para-aminobenzoic acid), which is important for maintaining the health of the intestines and breaking down and using proteins.

Virgins at Home

Here again, Virgins' love of service shows itself clearly. The Virgo home is tidy, efficient, and organized, but that just makes it easier to take care of all those who enter. You won't find Virgins sitting down to eat until everyone else has enough on their plates, and even then, Virgins may hover rather than sit down and join in.

Virgins are great lovers of beauty, and coupled with their understanding of botany, this can mean homes surrounded by lovely gardens and filled with thriving plants and herbs. Virgins are likely to have aloe vera growing somewhere, and are even more likely to snap off a leaf to rub on your wound.

Virgins at Work

Count yourself fortunate to have Virgins on your work team: With their love of challenge and constant need for self-improvement, they'll bring a strong dose of clarity to any project.

Virgins can be good planners, good organizers, and good finishers, but the same knack for details can also make them very strong in any field where they use their hands. Best of all, no matter what they do, Virgins are always reliable, whether they're the boss or an employee. With their desire to serve, they'll see the job gets done in a fine way.

The two largest job categories for Virgo are in the health field and any jobs that require analysis, including marketing, systems analysis, and computers. Virgins love details and excel at jobs that require detail-oriented work. Of course, as Madeline can tell you, Virgins' attention to detail makes them fine astrologers, too.

Virgins and Their Money

Detail-oriented, organized Virgins always have their checkbooks balanced and often know exactly how much money they've got in their pocket as well. Here's an area where Virgins, with their eye for every detail, can tend to be highly critical of their own abilities, but they are in reality not only able money managers, but also clever ones, staying within their budgets, never frivolous. In fact, you might often find that the folks we call "bean counters" are Virgins.

In the next chapter, we'll be looking at Libra ♎, Scorpio ♏, and Sagittarius ♐, the signs of fall.

The Least You Need to Know

◆ The signs of summer are Cancer ♋, Leo ♌, and Virgo ♍.

◆ Cardinal Cancer ♋ is a sensitive nurturer.

◆ Fixed Leo ♌ is creative and big-hearted.

◆ Mutable Virgo ♍ is concerned with service and self-improvement.

Chapter 7

Fall Signs: Libra ♎, Scorpio ♏, and Sagittarius ♐

In This Chapter

- Libra ♎, the Scales: a fine balance
- Scorpio ♏, the Scorpion: intense power
- Sagittarius ♐, the Archer: flying high

The signs of spring and summer represent personal development, and with the start of fall, we move into the signs of external development—Libra ♎, the seeker of harmony; Scorpio ♏, the transformer; and Sagittarius ♐, the explorer.

Libra ♎, the Scales: A Fine Balance

How many Libras does it take to screw in a light bulb?

Maybe one to do it and one not to do it.

Harmony. Balance. No one wants to even things out like a Libra ♎. Libra begins at the autumnal equinox, a time when the length of the day equals the length of the night, and Scales strive for such balance in all they do.

Libras are charming, and their charm is primarily due to the rulership of Venus ♀. Scales see *everything* from both sides and have a great appreciation for art and beauty. As a *yang*, cardinal sign, they generate a great deal of activity as well, especially in starting things, from diplomatic talks to friendships.

But Libra is an Air sign as well and, like all Air signs, has an active mind. In Scales' case, this takes the form of looking at one side and then the other, weighing everything over and over again. Like other cardinal signs, Libra seems constantly in motion, moving around and enjoying life.

The Seventh Zodiac Sign

Libra, the Scales ♎	September 22 to October 23
Element	Air
Quality	Cardinal
Energy	*Yang*
Ruler	Venus ♀
Color	Blue
Gem	Opal
Anatomy	Kidneys, lower back, adrenal glands
Keywords	Balance, harmony, justice
Archetypes	King Solomon, Supreme Court Justice Ruth Bader Ginsburg, parents who encourage kids to share
Celeb Scales	Nicole Kidman, Matt Damon, Gwyneth Paltrow, Will Smith, Angelina Jolie, John Lennon, Eleanor Roosevelt, Barbara Walters
Tarot suit	Swords
Tarot Major Arcana card	11 Justice, fairness and honor

The Best and Worst of Scales

Scales are social creatures, ready to share their experience with others, and quick to form partnerships. Friendly, popular, and attractive, they often are idealistic as well, eager to talk about their high principles and lofty ideas with any who will listen.

But Scales can seem affected or insincere, too eager to compromise, or worse, indecisive. Scales are often so busy weighing each side of an issue that they can never come to a conclusion or decision. Also, in their need to please others, they might forget to please themselves. Scales need to be aware of their own needs and meet them, too, not just those of other people.

At their best, Scales understand that their strength lies in creating and maintaining relationships. Scales seek to find their perfect complement, their other half, to complete the balance. They also want to find balance in other things, not just relationships.

Libra is the sign of justice and so is represented by a blindfolded Venus ♀, who holds the scales of Libra ♎ in one hand and the sword of Mars ♂/Aries ♈ (its opposite) in the other. The goal for Libra is the attainment of inner harmony and a reconciliation of opposites. Not an easy task, but if anyone can do it, Libra can.

AstroLingo

This is the symbol for Libra, the Scales: ♎.

Scales in Love

Scales love to be loved and admired, and they give much in return as well. Constantly testing their powers of attraction, they may seem flirtatious and flighty, but all the while Scales are seeking their other half. Scales are romantics, too, and they love to "set the mood" for romance by creating an atmosphere of beauty to match their feelings.

Air signs—Geminis ♊, Aquarians ♒, other Librans ♎—with their easy talk and quick minds, are an obvious match for Scales, but there are interesting possibilities with Scales' opposite, Aries ♈, as well, though each sign might believe the other too selfish. Scales can thrive with Leo's ♌ generosity, or they might find the balance they seek through an adventure with Sagittarius ♐.

Heaven Knows

The prime purpose of Scales is to create relationships with others. Libra ♎ is the opposite of Aries ♈, where people are concerned with themselves. Here we see the concern for others and the incorporation of both perspectives, "mine" and "theirs."

Scales are at their strongest with other people, and yet their focus in a relationship is on themselves. Scales' self-concept is a reflective one, seen through others' eyes rather than their own. At the same time, Scales might hide their own feelings in order to give an appearance of balance. Scales would do well to remember that making a decision is not always a tipping of the scales!

Healthy Scales

Graceful Scales should pay attention to inner fitness as well as outer fitness; their tendency toward lower back or kidney problems is a direct result of keeping things inside to avoid creating discord. As in love, healthy Scales need to bring their ideals down to an earthly scale.

Scales also can benefit from holistic aids like aromatherapy, and the lovely scents and properties of rose oil or jasmine can help create the inner harmony Scales seek. As a sign ruled by Venus, after all, Scales are very sensitive to smells all around them.

For Scales, extra potassium might be needed to balance the water level in the body and stimulate the kidneys to eliminate wastes. Vitamin E, selenium, and vitamin P (or bioflavenoids) are very helpful for preserving the beauty of Libra.

Scales at Home

Scales' homes are lovely places filled with *objets d'art*, reflections of the beauty of Librans themselves. True to their need for others, Scales are among the great hosts of the zodiac, filling their homes with other people as well as those people's conversations, ideas, and, often, their music.

Scales also enjoy the comforts of life and will not hesitate to make certain that their home reflects them. Because Scales seek harmony and balance above all, this is what you will find in their homes.

Still, all that waffling we've mentioned can make life with Scales rough going at times. Their constant weighing of things can make decision time difficult, and their ideals can mean they seek a harmony impossible to find here on Earth. Still, this results in a home that is singularly lovely, as befits the home of a Venus-ruled sign!

⚠ CAUTION

Star-Crossed _____

Signs ruled by Venus ♀ are the most romantic of the zodiac, and Libra is no exception. But this same romanticism can translate to a search for an ideal mate as well, and Librans should beware of the disappointment that can occur when such high expectations are brought down to Earth. Another danger is that Scales may refuse to acknowledge the beloved's true self and instead keep their ideal of their partner up on a pedestal.

Scales at Work

Social Libras shine at work. They are often leaders, showing others the way, but with their need for balance and harmony, they are often partners, too, using their knack for balance and harmony with others to achieve great things.

Scales' charm comes into play at work, too, and they may have a knack for public relations or sales. Or Scales' love of beauty might translate into a career in the arts, or in fashion or interior design.

You might expect Scales to be judges and lawyers, but though they often are found in these fields, their tendency to vacillate rather than come to a final decision can sometimes hamper them.

On the other hand (a favorite Libra phrase), these same qualities can make Scales fine counselors, where their ability to hear two sides of an issue rather than take sides is a decided asset. And for the same reason, they can be remarkable teachers, translating a broad array of ideas into a range of possibilities.

Scales and Their Money

Money for Scales is a means to an end, and that end is beauty and harmony. Scales need to be aware, however, that things and their appearance cannot give or replace inner security and harmony, and they might find that hanging on to a little "mad money" could bring them much closer to such balance than they would have thought possible.

Scales are more likely to invest in things and people than in long-term securities, because they like to see an immediate return on their investment—in the form of beauty and harmony. The inward reflects the outward here as in no other sign: To Scales, appearances really *do* matter.

Scorpio ♏, the Scorpion: Intense Power

How many Scorpios does it take to screw in a light bulb?

None. They like the dark.

Scorps are intense. They're dealing, after all, with life and death, and, by extension, with birth and sex. Scorpions are all about mystery, about how that poison stinger can so quickly change life into death, and Scorps can be both penetrating and incisive. Scorpio ♏ is one of the signs that has two rulers, Pluto ♀ and Mars ♂. That's why this sign can be quite a warrior, and very powerful. Combined with their fixed nature, these people never give up.

Like all Water signs, Scorps are more concerned with feelings than appearances, and as a fixed sign, they're often resistant to change. Scorps' ability to see through others' facades can serve them well, and they can wait forever for the right moment to get even or make their move.

StarFacts

According to Navajo myth, Grandmother Spider is the Grandmother of all the people (the Diné, as the Navajo call themselves). Whenever the people seem lost or confused, it is Grandmother Spider who will speak to them from her ever-evolving web, to remind them that they already know the way—and that they must simply look inside themselves!

Scorps are constantly probing beneath the obvious face of things, seeking what lies beneath. One of their rulers is Pluto ♀, the invisible planet that rules beginnings and ends, both of which, like Pluto itself, occur out of natural sight.

Scorpions' intensity and probing might make them sound humorless and frightening, but these same characteristics create both passion and excitement as well. You might feel as if a Scorpion is looking right through you, but the feeling might be an invigorating one.

The Eighth Zodiac Sign

Scorpio, the Scorpio ♏	October 23 to November 22
Element	Water
Quality	Fixed
Energy	*Yin*
Rulers	Pluto ♀ and Mars ♂
Colors	Burgundy, Black
Gem	Topaz
Anatomy	Genitals, urinary and reproductive systems
Keywords	Desire, transformation, power
Archetypes	The Phoenix, The Scorpion King, Grandmother Spider
Celeb Scorps	Calista Flockhart, Jodie Foster, Leonardo DiCaprio, Bill Gates, Georgia O'Keeffe, Dan Rather, Winona Ryder, Hilary Clinton
Tarot suit	Cups
Tarot Major Arcana card	13 Death, transformation and regeneration

The Best and Worst of Scorpions

Scorps use what many astrologers call Scorpionic power to achieve their ends. But maybe we should just look at that power itself, because Scorpio is the zodiac's most powerful sign.

Scorpio ♏ appears in the zodiac at a time when the earth seems to be dying: Leaves fall from the trees; hibernating animals retreat to their caves; even humans go inside their houses and sit by their fires. But this retreat is in reality a regeneration, a rebirth, and this is the true source of Scorpio's power. In Scorpio's case, still waters really *do* run deep!

In pop astrology, you'll often find this power called sex, and yes, Scorpios *do* have a strongly developed sexuality. Sometimes, though, they might disguise this even from themselves, in which case they may constantly be seeking something they can't quite name.

Sometimes Scorps sublimate this energy into other projects, and they might be very aware of doing it. At their worst, they may choose to use their magnetism to coerce others in fanatical ways, like Scorpio Charles Manson.

Scorpio is also associated with death, but in its astrological sense, death refers to transformation and rebirth rather than oblivion. The Death card of the Tarot represents the potential for transformation that is the essence of Scorpionic power as well.

At their best, Scorpios are magnetic leaders, like Billy Graham: shrewd, faith-inspiring, compassionate, and brave. At their worst, they're manipulative, vengeful, or even cruel. Like the nuclear energy that shares Pluto's ♀ rule, they can use their power for good or evil, and Scorps would do well to use their tremendous energy and power in positive ways, such as healing and learning control.

AstroLingo

This is the symbol for Scorpio, the Scorpion: ♏.

StarFacts

Scorpio's symbol ♏ is a pictorial representation of a scorpion's stinger connected to the human reproduction organs. In ancient times, it also represented the mythical phoenix, a bird that continually regenerated from its own ashes. Scorpio was believed to represent the serpent in Adam and Eve, and an eagle. One thing's clear: No other sign of the zodiac is so concerned with the cycles of life.

Scorps in Love

Although Scorps might know everyone else's heart of hearts, they'll seldom reveal their own. When they do, though, they share a depth of passion no other sign can. Like their relatives the spiders, Scorps will weave a web of romance, attracting partners with their intricacy and magnetism. But they're also quick to retreat if they feel threatened—and after Scorps have hidden, it might be hard to get them to reveal themselves again. You'd also do well not to injure a Scorp in love; their vengeance has a long memory and a fierce sting.

Don't forget that Scorpio ♏ is a Water sign, sometimes emotional, sometimes moody, always slow to commit but very loyal when they do. Other Water signs might be the most comfortable match for Scorp romance: Scorp may see other signs' approaches to love with too much clarity for romance. Earth signs, like Taurus ♉, Virgo ♍, and Capricorn ♑—fed by Water—can do very well with Scorps. And Taurus ♉ is Scorps' opposite, as well, very sensuous and pleasure-loving, an interesting match for Scorpio's intensity.

The Healthy Scorp

So reluctant are they to let anything out in the open, retentive Scorps may be prone to urinary tract infections or constipation. But they also have the potential to be great healers, not just of themselves but of others, because of their strong regenerative and transforming powers.

Healthy Scorps pay attention to their dreams, for both their informative and their imaginative power, and they should pay attention to what they eat and drink as well: Scorps' intake can truly make a big difference in how they feel. Any relaxation techniques that help Scorps get rid of old resentments and anger could also help them feel their best. But Scorps' most important health lesson is to let go—of repressed jealousy, anger, and resentment.

Scorps need to get adequate amounts of zinc or zinc supplements in their diets. This is essential for the growth, development, and functioning of the reproductive organs and prostate gland, as well as the general healing process, both of which are important for Scorps.

Scorps at Home

Because Scorps require power and control, life at home can be full of struggles— power struggles! Or it can be a place where Scorps keep "everyone in line" until they get married and have children. But no matter what the kids or spouse do, Scorps are ready to defend them with their lives and stingers if necessary. Loyalty is very important to them.

When Scorps are unhappy, though, they head off to be alone—and heaven help you if you disturb them! Scorps usually need and want time alone regularly, to process their intense feelings. Without time alone, it can become very hard for Scorps to maintain their sense of control. For this reason, Scorps need their own hiding place at home, where no one else will bother them. This isn't just a corner in a room, either, but an entire room that they can call their own.

When Scorps *are* able to control themselves instead of others, they are very loving and loyal, and can give a great deal of themselves to their families and mates.

Heaven Knows _____

Scorps are focused on regeneration and rebirth: You can't have new life without those things. Thousands of years ago, this sign was associated with sorcery and the study of mysteries that increased personal energy, like tantric energy. This sign isn't always entirely comfortable in our present society, where "getting in touch with one's feelings" translates to not letting them be in charge.

Scorps at Work

Scorps thrive on change, and a career that requires any renovation or strategy works very well for them. They might find creative outlets for those transforming energies, or they might be in the healing arts as doctors or counselors. Scorps also can do very well in fields like research or science—anything requiring that penetrating, probing eye will benefit from a Scorp touch.

Scorps also are often involved in reviving the environment or cleaning up waste in some way. Scorpio is involved in eliminating toxins and regeneration, and that's why they excel at these jobs.

As the most powerful zodiac sign, Scorps also do well in any position where they can wield that power, be it management, finance, or directing. But that power also means that any field Scorps choose will benefit from their influence: Even the seemingly meaningless is transformed when a Scorp is in charge.

Scorps and Their Money

Here again Scorps' retentive ways come to the forefront, and a Scorp and his money are not soon parted. Scorps understand the dynamics of power and money, and their conservative approach pays off here as well.

Scorps will amass cash quietly in the background and then use it to achieve their ends. Outward appearances mean little to Scorps; to them, it's all about control and transformation, and they'll apply their money only where they feel it's necessary.

Sagittarius ♐, the Archer: Flying High

How many Sagittarians does it take to screw in a light bulb?

One, and eleven other signs to revolve around him.

The Archer's arrow searches for meaning, and Sagittarius ♐ can be thought of as the gypsy, the student, and the philosopher, all rolled into one. No other sign is so focused on finding life's basic truth. Archers burn with this need to understand, and, as a mutable sign, they thrive on the changes this search can provide.

Because this is a *yang* sign, Archers are always moving toward more and more experience. It's also a party sign, and the party is marked by the Fire sign's enthusiasm, high spirits, and a whole lot of fun. Archers' optimism is contagious, and their honesty and directness can be a breath of fresh air.

The Ninth Zodiac Sign

Sagittarius, the Archer ♐	November 22 to December 22
Element	Fire
Quality	Mutable
Energy	*Yang*
Ruler	Jupiter ♃
Color	Purple
Gem	Turquoise
Anatomy	Liver, hips, and thighs
Keywords	Understanding, enthusiasm, exploration
Archetypes	Diana the Huntress, Indiana Jones, the Centaur

Sagittarius, the Archer ♐	November 22 to December 22
Celeb Archers	Brad Pitt, Ben Stiller, Lucy Liu, Britney Spears, Woody Allen, Kim Basinger, Walt Disney
Tarot suit	Wands
Tarot Major Arcana card	7 The Chariot, winged victory

The Best and Worst of Archers

Archers thrive on independence and freedom, and they never tire of a change of scenery. Sure, they might forget your date or miss that important deadline, but you can also count on them to get even the dullest of parties moving. Archers are ruled by Jupiter ♃, the king of the Roman gods, and the planet of good fortune, optimism, expansion, and abundance. (The word *jovial* is a derivative of the Latin form of Jupiter.) Jupiter is a fortunate ruler, and Archers tend to be freedom-loving, energetic people.

Archers' enthusiasm is bound to be contagious, but their lack of commitment can annoy other more responsible signs. Their generosity might spill into excessiveness, their optimism might make them blind to details, and their honesty can make their remarks sound blunt or inconsiderate. But the carefree adventurousness of Sagittarius can be a welcome change.

StarFacts

In Greek mythology, the best and bravest hunter was a woman, Diana (also called Artemis). Protector of the wild animals, Diana was the guardian of all women as well, and whenever a woman died quickly and painlessly, she was said to have been slain by one of Diana's arrows. Another Archer myth is that of the Centaur, half human, half beast. You may remember them in living color, prancing and galloping around during Beethoven's *Sixth Symphony* in *Fantasia* (and that's a pretty good picture of Centaur life: one big party!). But remember that half of the Centaur is human, and hence thinking and searching for meaning and truth, like an Archer.

Most dangerous to Archers can be their tendency toward dogma. Because they're seeking a universal truth rather than an individual one, they might mistake a trend for that truth and then become rather preachy about its powers. But Archers truly do wish to unite all people under one idea, and if they believe they've found it, they're eager to share it with all.

AstroLingo

This is the symbol for Sagittarius, the Archer: ♐.

In the long run, for Archers, it's the getting there that's more than half the fun: Archers love travel, new places, and seeking. Go along for the ride if you dare. Of course, if you're an Archer yourself, you won't think twice.

Archers in Love

Commitment? Sure. Just don't expect it to go on too long. Mutable Archers are always on the move, and if they do find their true love, they might have left a bevy of admirers behind, trying in vain to find their tracks.

Love is fun! Romance is a gas! Passion is excitement! See how Sagittarius breeds exclamation points? Those who require loyalty and longevity in love might do well to look elsewhere, but if you're looking for a good time, call 1-800-ARCHER.

Archers aren't just looking for a good time, although that's part of it: They want a trail-mate for their journey. They're here to seek, and householders aren't particularly interested in living a life on the trail. It takes a special person to want to adventure off with a Sag; the future is so open to possibilities, but also so unsettled. This isn't the person you want if you're after a mate to "settle down" with. But for another adventurer, a Sag is a great journeyer.

Archers aren't concerned with details, which means they can drive more detail-oriented signs like Virgo ♍ to distraction. And Archers expect that everyone will want to have as much fun as they do, which tends to leave Scorpio ♏ and Taurus ♉ back in the dust, too. Archers will do best with other Fire signs, where the romance can be both fiery and adventurous. Just don't forget that air feeds fire, too: Gemini ♊, Libra ♎, and Aquarius ♒ might have just the kind of surprises that Archers love.

The Healthy Archer

Energetic Archers can sometimes forget to slow down. And while they're galloping along, they might be gathering more and more new projects before they've finished any they've already started. All this running can make them prone to nervous exhaustion or just plain confusion. Sometimes it's necessary for racing-ahead Archers to S-T-O-P.

Sagittarius ♐ rules the hips, thighs, and liver, all of which can be severely harmed by overindulgence. Archers would do well to work on exercises that help them stay centered physically, and this, in turn, will help them not to lose sight of the big picture they envision.

Archers need to be aware of the problems of excess sugar, fat, or even alcohol; all can harm their livers. Too much overindulgence in these foods can really slow them down and make them sick. Archers need adequate amounts of vitamin K, inositol, manganese, and molybdenum to maintain normal liver function and metabolize fats. Detoxifying their liver around mid-life also can prevent major health problems later.

Archers at Home

Archers are great entertainers, and everyone loves a party at Archer's house. Yes, they might forget to serve—or even to make—a main course, but all will be having too much fun to care.

You won't often find children at Archer's house, though. This adventurous sign doesn't want to be tied down. Archers like to feel free to set out for the next adventure, and home can just as easily be a tent in the Serengeti or on Mt. Denali as a bachelor/ette pad in the French Quarter or on Beale Street.

But wherever Archer's tent is pitched, you can be sure that's where you'll find the action.

Archers at Work

Because Archers tend to lose interest before a project is completed, it's best to have them on your idea team. Archers do well, though, in all areas of communications, or anywhere a sense of humor and excitement are needed, and they may be clowns, tricksters, or even court jesters. They'll also do well as *National Geographic* photographers—or any kind of photographer.

Archers also can be found in positions that require risk, from the stock market to test piloting. They may be gamblers: Archers believe in their luck, and that optimism really does make them lucky.

Archers are often found in education, medicine, the legal system, foreign relations, the travel industry, or traveling for business, such as importers/exporters, or in sales. Archers tend to be highly educated and very well read; Sagittarius often produces philosophers, preachers, or anyone associated with inspiring others.

Archers and Their Money

Overconfident Archers tend to overextend themselves (and by extension, their resources) for the sake of a good time. But here again, their luck comes into play: Archers will put their last $100 on that 50-to-1 shot—and it has a good chance of coming in. You can bet that Archers, if they can hang in the game long enough, will go for the high stakes like John Corbett's character in the TV series *Lucky* who wins a million in the World Championship of Poker (only to lose it all a year later), whether or not they've got a lifeline or two or three intact—which is a good time to count on that Archer luck!

StarFacts

One of the best-known Archers at work was Gene Roddenberry, the creator of *Star Trek*. Deep in the heart of the 1960s, Roddenberry created a crew that included an African American woman, a Russian, an Asian, and an alien! Old *Star Trek* shows may look dated now, but back then, Roddenberry's vision was truly revolutionary—and *very* Archerlike.

Because they're more interested in the big picture than the little details, Archers may forget that they borrowed that $20 from you as soon as they've got it in their hand. Their irresponsibility with money may irk their more dependable friends to no end. But those same dependable friends will always come through for Archers, and because Archers know it, they don't sweat it.

As a mutable sign, Archers can be very resourceful, so they're able to scrape something together, even if they're broke. Of course, that could lead back to borrowing from others. Very resourceful of them!

In the next chapter, we'll be looking at Capricorn ♑, Aquarius ♒, and Pisces ♓, the signs of winter.

The Least You Need to Know

♦ The signs of fall are Libra ♎, Scorpio ♏, and Sagittarius ♐.

♦ Cardinal Libra ♎ seeks balance and harmony.

♦ Fixed Scorpio ♏ desires transformation and power.

♦ Mutable Sagittarius ♐ is an enthusiastic explorer.

Winter Signs: Capricorn ♑, Aquarius ♒, and Pisces ♓

In This Chapter

- ◆ Capricorn ♑, the Goat: ain't no mountain high enough
- ◆ Aquarius ♒, the Water Bearer: the quiet revolutionaries
- ◆ Pisces ♓, the Fishes: how deep is the ocean?

Perhaps no three signs are more different than the signs of winter: Capricorn ♑, Aquarius ♒, and Pisces ♓. Capricorn is the organized, goal-setting achiever; Aquarius is the inventive, humanitarian revolutionary; and Pisces is the compassionate, all-understanding healer.

Capricorn ♑, the Goat: Ain't No Mountain High Enough

How many Capricorns does it take to screw in a light bulb?

One, but it has to be her idea.

No sign's public persona is closer to its values than a Goat's, and no sign is more directed toward its goals. Intense and practical, Goats will bide their time, waiting for the right moment to climb that peak, because after they do, they intend to stay there.

Self-control, of both will and emotion, helps Goats achieve their aims. As the cardinal Earth sign, Goat is decidedly down to earth in its efforts, and, with its *yin* energy, a Goat uses the mind rather than physical force to reach its goals.

But Capricorn ♑ isn't just any goat; it's a sea-goat, and, as a creature that's half fish, it also can use water's deeper powers to its advantage. Ultimately, though, Goats' goals are always down-to-earth, so, no matter what their means to get there, their ends are always practical and constructive.

Capricorn is society's "elder." Goats are here to accept responsibility for helping others and building a society that meets the needs of the people. They also want to build something stable and enduring; after all, this sign is ruled by Saturn ♄, also known as Father Time.

AstroLingo

This is the symbol for Capricorn, the Goat: ♑.

Goats are meant to create a balance between conscientious nurturing and meeting the responsibilities of being the elders. People don't become elders when they're young, though, so Goats understand the patience required to learn what's important.

The Tenth Zodiac Sign

Capricorn, the Goat ♑	December 22 to January 21
Element	Earth
Quality	Cardinal
Energy	*Yin*
Ruler	Saturn ♄
Color	Brown
Gem	Garnet
Anatomy	Bones, joints, and knees
Keywords	Achievement, structure, organization
Archetypes	Father Time, Cronus, Howard Roark, the gifted architect in Ayn Rand's novel, *The Fountainhead*, Joan of Arc
Celeb Goats	Cuba Gooding Jr., Ricky Martin, Tracey Ullman, Kate Moss, Mel Gibson, Muhammad Ali, Martin Luther King Jr.

Capricorn, the Goat ♑	December 22 to January 21
Tarot suit	Pentacles
Tarot Major Arcana cards	15 The Devil, materialism, obsession; 21 The World, attainment

The Best and Worst of Goats

It can be lonely at the top, but if Goats want to be there, they'll learn to live with solitude. At their best, Goats are ambitious, organized, efficient, and responsible, but they also can be cold, calculating, suspicious, and rigid. And Goats are often hardest on themselves.

In their effort to achieve security, Goats might step on anything, or anyone, that stands in their way. But they can be surprisingly kind, too, especially to those who have done them favors or kindnesses. Goats are motivated by pride; they don't like to be beholden, and they'll repay favors generously.

Goats' practicality can be a welcome asset in the cold of winter: The logs will be stacked and ready next to the door, and the cupboard will be filled with all that's needed to get through the cold months. And Goats will surprise you, too, with their quiet, dry wit helping to pass the winter nights.

Goats in Love

Goats seek their approval from the world-at-large, which might make personal relationships seem secondary to them, but after you discover Goats' dry sense of humor, you'll find a way to their hearts as well.

Heaven Knows

It's cold at the start of winter, and Capricorn's a cold sign, cold and calculating. Unlike another climber, the Ram, the Goat's steps are slow and sure: Goats want to make sure they get where they're going, so they're careful to take their time. With their energy turned inward, toward self-control, Goats quietly and steadily work toward their goals. And ruled by practical Saturn ♄, they're bound to get there, too.

When you penetrate a Goat's icy reserve, you'll find the possibilities for deep love and strong loyalty. With their deepest feelings buried beneath the surface, Goats protect those they care for, and they'll stick around when the going gets tough.

Stability matters more to Goats than to any other sign, so when it comes to romance, they'll seek comfort over pleasure, and longevity over romance. Goats do well with other Earth signs, but it is with Water signs that the best connections may occur: A nurturing Cancer ♋, passionate Scorpio ♏, or sympathetic Pisces ♓ might help a Goat grow in new ways.

The Healthy Goat

Goats can be pessimistic, and they need to beware of the melancholy that pessimism can bring. But cautious Goats often live long, long lives: Helena Rubinstein, Albert Schweitzer, and Carl Sandburg lived well into their 90s, for example. What seems to shorten Goats' lives most often is their potential power: Both Joan of Arc and Martin Luther King Jr. were Goats, after all.

Many Goat afflictions are due to too much rigidity in their thinking or behavior: The difficulty of representing tradition is getting too rigid about it. Eventually this can translate into arthritis or rheumatism.

As for vitamins, what else? Goats need calcium to build those bones and teeth, as well as to keep their nerves under control. Goats also need plenty of vitamin C, which is necessary for healthy skin, ligaments, bones, teeth, and gums. And they need to get enough vitamin D and magnesium for utilizing the calcium to build their bones.

Capricorn rules the skeleton, bones, and teeth, all the structural aspects of the body that Goats are associated with. For this reason, alternative therapies that deal with the structure of the body, such as chiropractic therapy or Feldenkrais, a form of structural and physical therapy, are very appropriate for Goats.

Heaven Knows

More Presidents of the United States have been born with their Sun ☉ or Moon ☽ in Capricorn ♑ than any other sign. Why? Because Goats' ambitions, shrewdness, and slow, steady movement toward their goals are just what are required for executive positions. Goats aspire to the top spot, and they get there, too!

Goats at Home

Our favorite Goats seem to understand the importance of a place of their own, a quiet, private retreat from all the trappings that can come with power. Here they'll have their favorite music playing, their favorite pictures on the walls, and their favorite books stacked up next to their favorite chair.

Like all Earth signs, Goats appreciate the comforts of home, but they're more likely to use it as a getaway than a base of operations. Goats know the importance of strong foundations, and their home will be warm and secure, a haven from those cold winter storms.

Goats at Work

Goats like to be in charge, and if they don't start there, it's usually where they'll end up. Rags-to-riches Goats abound, such as Howard Hughes and Aristotle Onassis, as well as powerful Goats, such as Mao Tse-tung and Joseph Stalin.

The older Goats get, the more rewarding their lives are likely to become. Once they've achieved the power they've sought, they can relax with the wisdom they've gained and the lessons they can share with others. Many Goats live long lives as writers or artists, including J. R. R. Tolkien, Alfred Stieglitz, and Anton Chekhov. And Goats are found in business, where there are a lot of mountains to climb. As Goats are very achievement-oriented, you'll find them at the tops of many fields—and mountains.

StarFacts

Have you heard the one about Cronus (another name for Saturn ♄, Capricorn's ♑ ruler), who ate his children, because he was certain one of them was going to overthrow him? Talk about being rigid and sticking to tradition! Fortunately, his wife substituted a rock for one of the kids, who just happened to be Zeus, also known as Jupiter. Jupiter later went on to lead his brothers and sisters, who were freed (alive) from their father's stomach, in what seems to be a justified revolt against their father.

Goats and Their Money

Goats understand the power that can come with money, and, as a cardinal sign, they're likely to do things with it in order to turn it into even more money: buying, selling, and making deals. Goats use their money to attain and maintain power. Money means control to a Goat, and control and power are Goats' driving forces. They also are generous with their money once they have it, but the generosity is tied to their power and prestige: Goats truly understand the phrase "Money talks."

Aquarius ♒, the Water Bearer: The Quiet Revolutionaries

How many Aquarians does it take to screw in a light bulb?

One, and he has to use the latest technology to do it.

Aquarius ♒ is where you'll find the zodiac's eccentric individualists and crazy inventors. Anything out of the ordinary interests this independent sign, and Water Bearers are often trendspotters and trendsetters.

Water Bearers' fixed Air represents persistent development of the intellect through communication, and their planetary influence, Uranus ♅, means they'll be committed to innovation and change. Aquarians will often be progressive and open-minded, but that fixed quality means they'll often be fixed in their opinions as well.

Most W-Bs find Earth to be a very dense place. Most of them are 50 years or more ahead of their time, and talking to the rest of us can seem like a difficult and laborious process. Aquarians often feel like they're visiting from another planet, because their ideas are so advanced. Trouble is, sometimes they forget their missions after they get here and find out how dense this place really is.

So why is it that Aquarius, the Water Bearer, is an Air sign, not a Water sign? Good question. But look at this sign's symbol, ≈, to find your answer. This water is in the form of waves, which are caused by wind: the motion of air on water. These wavy lines also represent the serpents of knowledge; the parts of the body ruled by Aquarius, the ankles and the circulatory system; and lightning that cleans air and leaves that "ozone buzz." Remember that this name doesn't refer to the water itself but to its carrier: Aquarius is the "water bearer," the most human of the signs.

AstroLingo

This is the symbol for Aquarius, the Water Bearer: ≈.

Water Bearers will do anything to avoid boredom, and they care little for what others think, especially after they've determined their own particular cause. Their ambition is for humankind rather than just themselves, and you'll find some of the great progressive thinkers here: Charles Darwin, Abraham Lincoln, Thomas Edison, and Franklin Delano Roosevelt, for example.

The Eleventh Zodiac Sign

Aquarius, the Water Bearer ≈	January 21 to February 19
Element	Air
Quality	Fixed
Energy	*Yang*
Rulers	Uranus ♅ and Saturn ♄
Color	Violet
Gem	Amethyst
Anatomy	Ankles and circulation
Keywords	Humanitarian, unique, revolutionary
Archetypes	Noah's Ark, *Star Trek*'s Spock, Glinda from *The Wizard of Oz*

Aquarius, the Water Bearer ≈	January 21 to February 19
Celeb W-Bs	Christina Ricci, Heather Graham, Edward Burns, Oprah Winfrey, Chris Rock, Wolfgang Amadeus Mozart, Virginia Woolf, Paul Newman
Tarot suit	Swords
Tarot Major Arcana card	17 The Star, hope and faith

The Best and Worst of W-Bs

Idealistic, inventive, and original, W-Bs can all-too-easily seem aloof, detached, or just plain cranky. W-Bs' tendency to go against the grain can separate them from other people, even the more abstract "humanity" they are trying to help.

More than any other sign, W-Bs have a human connection, and they seek to bring all humans together without regard for any of the imaginary divisions humans themselves have created. This same disregard for human difference, though, might leave W-Bs without any close relationships of their own. Have you ever heard the line, "I love humankind. It's people I can't stand?" It's likely this was first spoken by an Aquarian.

W-Bs' strongest trait is their intellectual independence, their refusal to be pigeonholed. W-Bs really do hear a "different drummer," and it may even be they who are playing those drums. W-Bs can be radicals, renegades, or bohemians, too, but depending on other factors in the chart, this might not be obvious. They can look perfectly normal yet have very different ideas. So even though they might pass for one of us, they don't *feel* like us.

It's almost as though they're aliens from another star system, living in human bodies. W-Bs often experiment with or observe friends, mates, or partners, just to see what they will do under a particular set of circumstances, and they can be very detached about this process—although the results might be enough to keep them interested in a person!

W-Bs in Love

Independent W-Bs need partners who understand that independence and who won't feel threatened by it, and in return they'll offer their partners the same kind of freedom. With the right partner, W-Bs will be constant and true: Remember, this is a fixed sign, reluctant to change after it's established what it considers the right path.

Some W-Bs may sacrifice personal relationships to pursue a greater good, and some may seem aloof even in the best of relationships. Sometimes W-Bs' relationships themselves will become laboratories for their creativity, as they did in the cases of James Joyce, Federico Fellini, Gertrude Stein, and W. Somerset Maugham. W-Bs are always seeking what's best for humankind, and they can sometimes lose sight of individual humans in the process.

Air signs—Gemini ♊, Libra ♎, other Aquarians ♒—will naturally combine well with Aquarius, but pay attention to the fire-feeding capabilities of air, too: The innovation of a W-B might be just what Aries ♈, Leo ♌, or Sagittarius ♐ needs for some mutual excitement.

StarFacts

There's a lot of disagreement about just when the Age of Aquarius will or did begin. But what *is* agreed on is just what the Age of Aquarius means, and you'll see a lot of those same traits in an Aquarian person: tolerance, independence, progressiveness, and altruism. The Aquarian Age heralds important leaps in science and technology, logical progressions, and greater global connections. Does this sound familiar? It should: Many believe the Age of Aquarius has already begun.

The Healthy W-B

The ankles and the circulatory system are ruled by Aquarius ♒: The ankles support our ability to stand, and circulation is the movement of our very lifeblood through our bodies. W-Bs are the very essence of human existence, and it's important that in their tendency to think and see globally, they don't lose sight of these areas closer to home.

Vitamins and, of course, eating right can keep W-Bs at their fittest. W-Bs need magnesium—and plenty of it—in their diets to keep their circulation and heart (Leo is their opposite) in good shape. Magnesium also is needed for the electrical charges that move nutrients in and out of cells, as well as for absorbing and using vitamins and minerals.

W-Bs might heal well with acupuncture or chiropractic, because Saturn ♄ is their co-ruler and these healing techniques deal with the nervous system and their energy. Exercise also plays an important role; with their heads in the clouds, W-Bs might forget that they have a body to take care of as well!

W-Bs hold the mind and spirit in high esteem, but they need to pay attention to what connects them to the rest of humanity, too, and to keep their lifeblood circulating freely.

W-Bs at Home

W-Bs' home is the world, and they populate that world with a variety of people, especially the unusual, the eccentric, and those who are just plain different. "Live and let live" is a W-B motto, and they'll open their doors to anyone who needs their shelter. W-Bs believe that they can change people's lives just by being a part of them, and if their homes sometimes resemble Noah's Arks of humanity, it's no coincidence.

Even though they may seem aloof, W-B's individual goals are always based on a greater good. This holds true at home, too: Altruistic and giving, W-Bs share their homes with all.

W-Bs at Work

Clever, original W-Bs can excel in any profession in which creativity is a plus. This isn't limited just to the arts, either, but can extend to scientific innovation and invention, to public service or civil rights reform, even to owning a business of their own or marketing someone else's unique ideas. Many also work in broadcast media.

StarFacts

Among the myths associated with the sign of Aquarius ♒ are the great deluge myths: Noah's Ark in the Judeo-Christian tradition and Deucalion and Pyrrha in the Greek tradition. According to this myth, after surviving the Greek deluge by building a wooden box to float in, Deucalion and Pyrrha created a new race of people by throwing rocks over their shoulders: The rocks that Deucalion threw became men, and the rocks that Pyrrha threw became women. Talk about innovation!

W-Bs understand that the future is where innovation lies, and their careers may often lead others toward that future. Charles Lindbergh was a W-B, for example, and Ronald Reagan. W-Bs may also be geniuses within their chosen field, like golfer Jack Nicklaus or dancer Mikhail Baryshnikov.

W-Bs can be revolutionaries, sometimes associated with actual government revolutions, like Boris Yeltsin and Angela Davis, and they're often associated with ideas, causes, or inventions that eventually revolutionize the world.

But no matter where they work, you can count on W-Bs to be the ones at the cutting edge, the ones with ideas, the ones with creative solutions to the problems everyone else thought insoluble.

W-Bs and Their Money

W-Bs are givers rather than keepers, and with their vision focused on the future, they're not likely to concern themselves with the here and now. This can translate into a disregard for money, including a tendency to go beyond their budgets or overextend themselves in other ways.

With their vision for the future, though, W-Bs can potentially do well in speculative ventures, especially in areas that will use new technology. Well-selected investments in these areas now can protect W-Bs moving into their more uncertain futures.

Pisces ♓, the Fishes: How Deep Is the Ocean?

How many Pisceans does it take to screw in a light bulb?

The light went out?

Mutable water: from solid (ice) to liquid to gas (vapor). This is the character of Pisces ♓, changing according to outside conditions. And yet Fishes live largely in the world of the imagination, the realm of dreams, where objects and events seem to have no connection to outer reality. What's going on here?

This last sign creates the possibility to move beyond self into transcendence, represented to humans as the world of dreams and faith. But this also can be a world of sheer escapism, where dreaming is done for its own sake. Fishes, we could say, can either sink or swim.

Put another way, Fishes know which way the river is running and might swim with it or against it. Swimming against it can mean they might find a way to another stream ("hooked" Fishes can channel their addictions, for example), while swimming with it might mean, quite literally, "going with the flow," and living intuitively.

Fishes are highly intuitive, and Pisces is the sign that merges with others so easily that these people don't always know what's theirs and what belongs to someone else. Fishes are frequently so sensitive to the vibrations of others that they can go into work and instantly feel how others are doing. Unfortunately, they also might unconsciously take responsibility for how others are doing, or wonder why they feel so bad—especially when they woke up feeling so good!

For this reason, Fishes can have a hard time maintaining their boundaries and knowing what *they're* feeling, as opposed to what others are feeling. The reason for this boundary stuff goes back to the main point of Pisces, which is to merge with others, and, eventually, the Source or God. Fishes are in a highly spiritual sign, living in a very nonspiritual world. For this reason it's easy for them to get off-track by merging with the wrong people and to get away from their true spiritual focus.

Above all, Fishes are here to give, not just to those like themselves, but to anyone who needs their help, love, attention, or whatever. Mulder of *The X-Files* is probably a Pisces, or else he has a strong Neptune! After all, his poster read: "I want to believe." Scully: "Time can't just disappear … it's a universal invariant!" Mulder: "Not in this zip code."

StarFacts

True to the Piscean paradox, here's a symbol ♓ with multiple meanings. It represents two fishes tied together; a picture of the human feet, which Pisces rules; or two crescent moons, connected by a straight line—emotion and higher consciousness tied down to the material world. No wonder Fishes so often feel misunderstood and yet have so many possibilities. Even their symbol is all-encompassing! Pisces is associated with baptism, spiritual cleansing, and renewal, and Venus ♀ is "exalted" here, which means that the love and beauty she rules are of a universal rather than a personal nature. Fishes are a symbol of divine purity; the birth of Christ is associated with the beginning of the Age of Pisces.

The Twelfth Zodiac Sign

Pisces, the Fishes ♓	February 19 to March 21
Element	Water
Quality	Mutable
Energy	*Yin*
Rulers	Neptune ♆ and Jupiter ♃
Color	Sea-green
Gem	Aquamarine
Anatomy	Feet, immune system, hormonal system
Keywords	Compassion, universality, inclusiveness
Archetypes	The Empath, Mulder from *The X-Files*, Buddhist goddess Kwan Yin
Celeb Fishes	Queen Latifah, Bruce Willis, Drew Barrymore, Thora Birch, Billy Crystal, Mikhail Gorbachev, Liza Minnelli, Ralph Nader, Elizabeth Taylor
Tarot suit	Cups
Tarot Major Arcana card	18 The Moon

The Best and Worst of Fishes

Compassionate Fishes can see deep into the human psyche, probe the depths of emotions, lend a sympathetic ear, or play an intuitive hunch. But they can also be oh-so-sad, shy, timid, or just plain impractical. Fishes can seem both lazy and over-talkative, the talk seeming to go on and on about any number of unlikely possibilities.

But Fishes can change, too, and change can be good: It can mean adaptability. Because of their extraordinary sensitivity, Fishes are often creative artistically, and their understanding of people sometimes seems limitless (though the understanding doesn't always extend to themselves).

Pisces ♓ is the sign that represents spirituality (not religion, like Sagittarius ♐), a true need to have a relationship with a higher power. When these spiritual needs aren't fulfilled, Fishes can become involved in the negative side of this energy, which is escapism. That's where the drugs, alcohol, or sugar addictions come in, as well as the wrong kinds of people.

AstroLingo

This is the symbol for Pisces, the Fishes: ♓.

Fishes need to learn to live by faith and intuition: Once they do this, they're on the right track. Physicist Albert Einstein was a Pisces, and his theories were "impractical," but correct. Does the universe need dreamers and people who can transcend the boundaries of normal reality? And does that make them impractical? Or just different from the rest of us?

Fishes in Love

Kind, perceptive, sensitive Fishes look at the inner soul of others, at the essence rather than the surface. Fishes are truly seeking their soul mates, the most profound love possible and so might be disappointed when real people fail to live up to their idealistic expectations.

Fishes in love can create an enchanting place where love happens, a space separate from the rest of the world for Fishes and their loved ones alone. Fishes feel, and they can translate that feeling, too: You'll always know when you're the object of Fishes' affection.

Water, water, water: Of course Fishes will do well with Cancers ♋, Scorpios ♏, and other Pisces ♓. But here's a sign where empathy can go far—if Fishes are careful. More flighty signs like Gemini ♊, Libra ♎, and Aquarius ♒ may leave Fishes swimming in their wake—or raise them to new heights of awareness.

Fishes can do especially well with nurturing Earth signs, and Earth signs' practicality can also keep Fishes' tendency toward flights of fancy a little more rooted. As in all areas, though, Fishes need to beware of those who would take advantage of them: They're quick to trust, and all too easily hurt. Impressionable Fishes can fall for just about any hard-luck story; dreamers themselves, they can easily get caught up in the dreams of others as well. Fishes can tend toward addiction, too, whether in food, alcohol, drugs, or simply the wrong kinds of people. Sometimes, their lives can seem filled with trouble.

Healthy Fishes

Fishes can tend to overindulge, and need to be careful to limit their intake of everything from bread to wine. Fishes may be overweight or have a tendency to retain water. Pisces rules the feet, and Fishes should take particular care to avoid sprains, or even breaks, to that sensitive area.

Fishes don't always take care of themselves as well as they do others, but one way to start would be through a holistic fitness regimen that takes into account both body and soul. One vitamin that can help Fishes feel their best is pantothenic acid, which helps stimulate their adrenal glands and increase their immune systems. Because Pisces appears to rule the immune system, all aids to this system—such as Astragalus or Echinacea herbs—are helpful for Fishes.

Pisces also seems to be in charge of hormones, so keeping them in balance is very important. Fishes are very sensitive to foods and poisons in their environment, and might need to be detoxified more frequently than any other sign. Alcohol and drugs are very difficult for them to process. Even prescription drugs can wreak havoc on their systems, so it's very important for Fishes to watch their intake and notice the changes in their bodies.

StarFacts
Fishes often channel their imagination and creativity into the arts: The great Italian Renaissance artist Michelangelo Buonarroti was a Pisces, and so were French Impressionist painter Auguste Renoir and Polish Romantic composer Frederic Chopin. Fishes do best when they believe in themselves and their dreams the same way they believe in others' dreams—but this isn't always an easy task.

Fishes at Home

Fishes use their homes as places for spiritual renewal—or spiritual abuse. Just as they might swim with or against the current, they might use their homes as refuges or dens of iniquity, and the choices they make will spill over into other areas of their life as well.

If Fishes find true love, they're more likely to create a home as refuge, and Fishes would do well to create their own hidden cave, a place to renew themselves, to meditate, and to be introspective. Retreat can bring healthy renewal.

Fishes at Work

Because Fishes love to combine their real life with their imaginary one, they can often be found in the world of theater or film, or in any of the arts. But they also can do quite well in business or even politics, where their sensitivity can give them powerful insights less intuitive signs might miss.

Fishes like to work behind the scenes or alone: Fame and recognition aren't what drive them. Because of this, Fishes can be great manipulators or builders. Or they may be photographers, beautifully capturing others' spirits on film.

Fishes are often found, too, in areas where their capabilities for the spiritual can be used: They may be astrologers or monks, religious leaders or healers. Fishes are known for their ability to sacrifice themselves for others.

Pisces also deals with images, so these people are gifted at leading others through visualization experiences and meditations and bringing people to a higher level of awareness and consciousness. Above all, Fishes are here to help the rest of us transcend our normal ruts, beliefs, and boundaries, and see the illusions we live under.

Fishes and Their Money

Here again, Fishes need to be wary of others' stories: They're all too easily convinced to hand over their life savings to help a friend (or anyone) they think is in need. Money can swim in and out of Fishes' lives as mysteriously as everything and everyone else does, and impractical Fishes don't always understand why.

Because they're not really prone to moneymaking enterprises themselves, Fishes' money might come from outside sources, and it might go back outside, too. Many Fishes work in the service sector, so they may not get the kind of money that business enterprises pay. But what Fishes *are* good at are the dreams where all good ideas—including potential moneymaking ones—begin. Here's a sign whose intuitive hunches are always worth pursuing.

The Least You Need to Know

◆ The signs of winter are Capricorn ♑, Aquarius ♒, and Pisces ♓.

◆ Cardinal Capricorns ♑ seek structure and achievement.

◆ Fixed Aquarians ♒ are innovative and humanitarian.

◆ Mutable Pisces ♓ are compassionate to all.

Chapter **9**

Ascendants: The Mask You Wear for the World

In This Chapter

- ◆ The costume you selected at your birth
- ◆ Finding your ascendant
- ◆ What your ascendant reveals about you
- ◆ Ascendants, sign by sign

Remember choosing who you wanted to "be" for Halloween? Your parents may have laughed at your insistence that you "had to" be Spiderman, or the Little Mermaid, or Luke Skywalker, or Hopalong Cassidy (we're probably dating ourselves here …).

Your ascendant is the daily costume you selected at the moment you were born: It's the mask you wear every day, the "you" everybody else sees. And it might be connected to the character you wanted to be for Halloween, too.

What's Rising?

Let's start by finding your ascendant. The most idiot-proof way is to have a computer with the appropriate software find it for you, but there are some simplified methods that you can use. All you need to know is the time and date of your birth. This method isn't foolproof, but it works much of the time. Got those numbers? Now, just follow these step-by-step instructions:

1. Write your birth date and time in the appropriate "slice" for the time of day you were born. We're using brilliant actor Denzel Washington's birth date and time—0:09 A.M. on December 28, 1954—in our example. Washington's birth chart appears in the following figure.

Birth chart for Denzel Washington.

Denzel Washington
Natal Chart
Dec 28 1954
0:09 am EST +5:00
Mount Vernon, NY
40°N54' 073°W50'
Geocentric
Tropical
Placidus
True Node

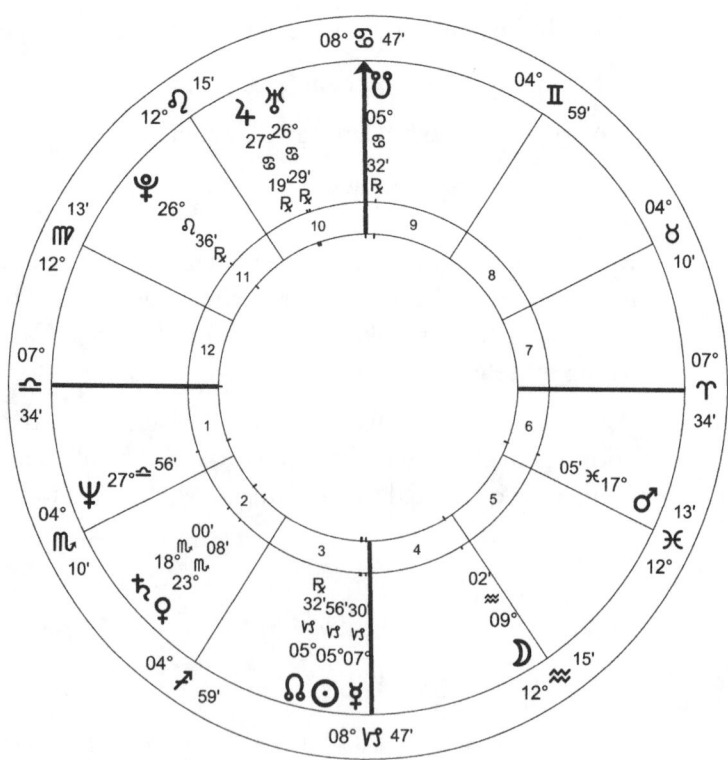

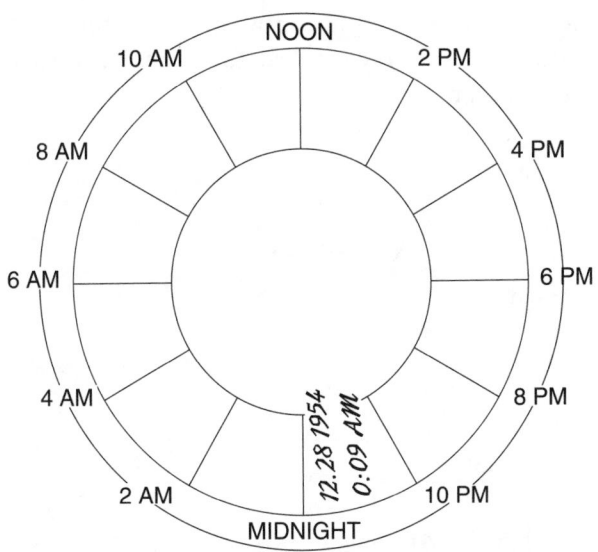

Write your birth date and time in the appropriate slice. We've filled in Denzel Washington's stats in this example.

2. Using the zodiac on the tear-out reference card at the beginning of this book, find your Sun ☉ sign.

3. Draw your Sun sign in the same "slice" in which you wrote your birth date.

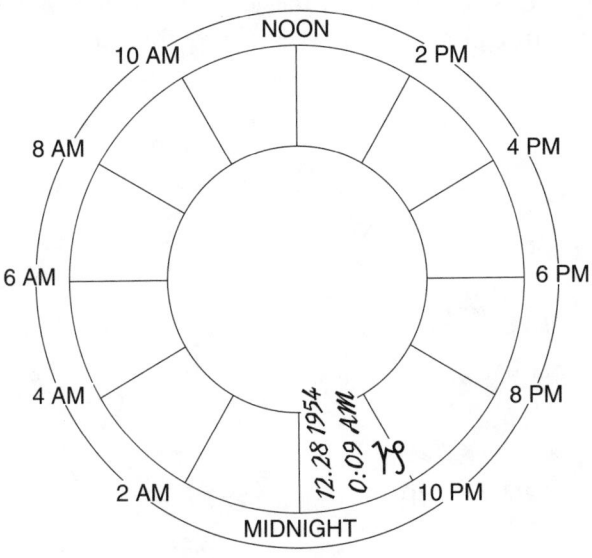

Draw your Sun sign in the appropriate slice. We filled in Denzel's Sun sign: Capricorn ♑.

4. Now, going in a *counterclockwise* direction, draw the rest of the signs, in order, in each "slice." If you drew Aries ♈ in your slice, for example, you should follow with Taurus ♉, Gemini ♊, and so on.

Draw the signs counterclockwise on the chart. We've done this on Denzel's behalf.

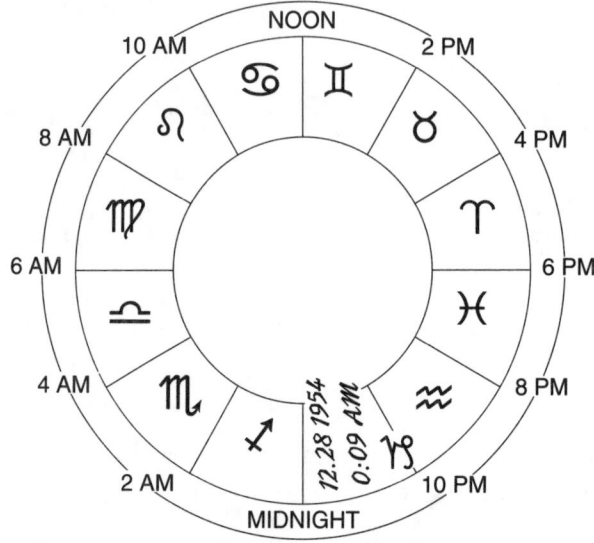

5. Now look to see which sign is shown at the "eastern horizon" of your chart. Remember, on an astrological chart, the "east" is on the left. "X" marks the spot.

"X" marks the spot. Note that the symbol for Libra ♎ in the house just below the eastern horizon is circled— this sign is the ascendant for Denzel Washington.

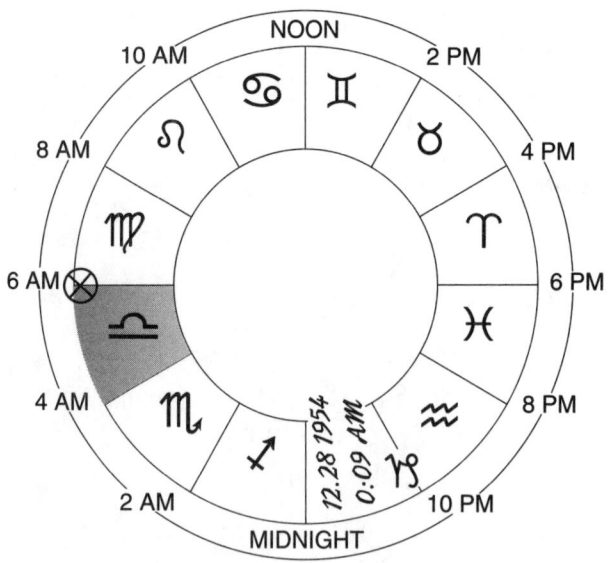

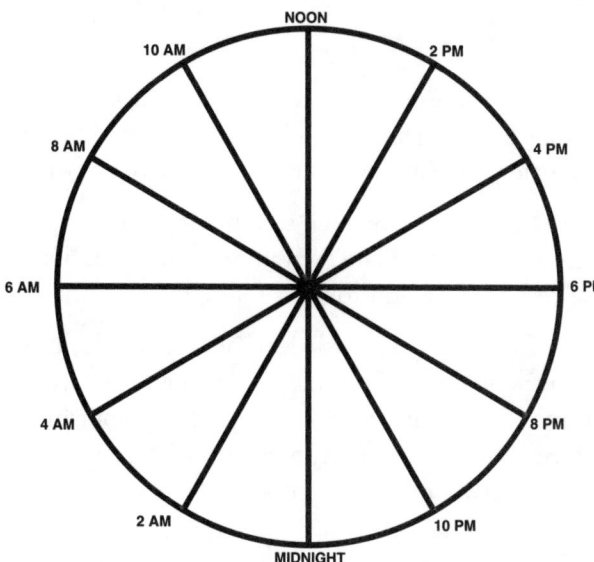

Use this blank chart with ascendant times to figure out what your ascendant is. Follow the same procedures we just used to figure out Denzel Washington's ascendant.

It's important that you know your exact birth time for this method to work. We tried it first for singer Norah Jones, but her exact birth time isn't known. Even when you *do* know the exact birth time, this method isn't idiot-proof, as we discovered when we tried it for *Tonight Show* host Jay Leno. That's because while this shortcut method of finding your ascendant often works, it doesn't utilize the calculations required to be certain. In some cases, we'll get a "false positive"—as we knew for Jay Leno because we had his birth chart to guide us. (You first saw Jay's birth chart in Chapter 4.) Denzel Washington himself is a tricky example for figuring an ascendant through this method, as his birth time is so close to midnight. The best method for clearly determining your ascendant is to consult an accurate astrological birth chart.

Got your ascendant, or rising sign, figured out? Read on to find out what your rising sign reveals about you.

Star-Crossed

Sometimes the information for the ascendant you found using our quick method might seem all "wrong." If this is so, read the information for the ascendants immediately before and after it as well. The quick method is approximate, not exact, so it is possible that you might get a "wrong" reading from it—but it will be close.

Rising Signs

As you recall from Chapter 4, your ascendant reveals a great deal about the way you express yourself. Unless your Sun sign and ascendant are the same (which means you were born at sunrise), the true you is hiding behind the mask of your rising sign.

As you discovered in the last four chapters, each sign has its own unique characteristics. These characteristics are your ascendant, or outward manifestation, so you put on that sign's face for the rest of the world to see.

We'd like to add another dimension to your consideration of your ascendant, too: Think of it as "training" for the person you are becoming. In other words, your rising sign indicates the skills and traits you're learning to develop during your lifetime. If you're born with a Scorpio ♏ ascendant, for example, much of what you do might be connected with learning about control, both self-control and a need to control others.

Rising Signs of Spring

As you'll recall from the Sun sign chapters, the signs of spring have little in common other than their season. The same holds true for these signs when they're rising: An Aries ♈ ascendant is learning about independence; a Taurus ♉ ascendant is learning to appreciate the finer things in life; and a Gemini ♊ ascendant is learning, well, about learning.

Ram Rising: The Aries ♈ Ascendant

- ◆ Keynote: striving forward
- ◆ Training for independence

Ram Rising is like taking the "Aries training." This is someone who's learning to develop a strong, individuated self, learning how to play, and to become independent, spontaneous, and free of restrictions in the process. It's also important for Rising Rams to learn qualities of courage, trust (especially in themselves), and even innocence.

Ram ascendants really *are* ascending, always pushing themselves forward, always striving for the next peak. Those with a Ram ascendant are often the ones making the decisions, and they've got strong likes and dislikes to back up those decisions. But Ram ascendants might mistake impulsiveness for a need for action and might not stop long enough to see what they really want. Rising Rams may appear pushy or rude; but remember, an ascendant is a mask, and what appears to be arrogance may be covering up something else entirely.

Bull Rising: The Taurus ♉ Ascendant

- ◆ Keynote: seeking identity through substance

- ◆ Training for aesthetic appreciation

Rising Bulls seem placid and easygoing, have charming manners, and never impose their opinions on others. They don't want to upset the apple cart. They like it the way it is, full of apples.

You could think of Bull Rising as someone who is "training" to learn about beauty. Rising Bulls' lesson is to understand the nature of physical experience, aesthetics, and the nature of intimacy. As shamanic astrologer Daniel Giamarro says, the enlightened path for one with this training "is the Garden of Eden, to bring spirit into matter all the way, so one can totally enjoy it." This training helps Bulls learn to be fully present in life and increase their life force energy.

Bull ascendants seek their identity through substance, whether it be possessions, connections, or creation. Rising Bulls always seek to "keep a handle" on things, but their love of food, drink, and yes, sex, can make them momentarily forget that stability is their main goal.

> **Star-Crossed**
>
> Like those with a Taurean ♉ Sun sign, Rising Bulls need to remember to love things for their own sake rather than for what they might represent. For Rising Bulls, possessions are merely a mask.

Twins Rising: The Gemini ♊ Ascendant

- ◆ Keynote: emotion in motion

- ◆ Training for truthful communication

Motion. That's what you're going to see in a Rising Twin. Restlessness is the hallmark of this ascendant, and Rising Twins find their identity by making as many contacts as possible. Rising Twins are often the life of the party and, in fact, are often *giving* the party.

At the same time, Rising Twins are learning to be the eternal youth, free spirit, entertainer, artist, or comedian. They can also be the troubadour minstrel, court jester, trickster, or clown, or the coyote that leaves a surprise. Remember that the court jester was the only one who could tell the King the truth and not be killed for it (another form of messenger). Rising Twins are learning these abilities, as well as how to communicate truthfully without getting creamed for it.

Heaven Knows _____

Remember that Gemini ♊ is the first of the Air signs. Air is the element of mental activity, so Rising Twins are always thinking about what's next.

A Gemini ♊ ascendant will appear excitable and quick—and also prone to upset. At the same time, there's an aloofness here: Twins' connections are made on a mental field, which can often leave emotions out in the cold.

Rising Twins' motion might mask many things, but remember, an ascendant is just that—a mask. And if anyone knows how to wear a mask, it's a Rising Twin.

The Rising Signs of Summer

They might all be signs of summer, but that's where the resemblance between these three rising signs ends. A Cancer ♋ ascendant is learning about emotion; a Leo ♌ ascendant is learning to trust him or herself; and a Virgo ♍ ascendant is learning his or her own particular sacred work.

Crabs Rising: The Cancer ♋ Ascendant

◆ Keynote: learning responsible love and nurturing

◆ Training for family foundations

Rising Crabs are talkative, especially about feelings, but they're also moody and changeable, because their ruler, the Moon ☽, changes signs every few days. At the same time, Rising Crabs are compassionate and receptive. They know what's happening with everyone around them, because they're sensitive to others. Family and traditions are important to them. But they can be crabby and irritable at times, too.

Heaven Knows _____

It can seem deceptively easy to get to know a Rising Crab: They seem so soft and personal. But like those with Crab Sun signs, Rising Crabs wear a hard, tough shell that can sometimes get in the way.

Rising Crabs are learning about the nature of family, home, and roots, as well as how to love and nurture so that their children will have a safe foundation and a concern for the welfare of generations to come. They also are learning how to responsibly nurture, love, and support their offspring or creative projects until they reach maturity. This "training" teaches them how to redefine "family," while providing support and nurturing in an appropriate way.

Rising Crabs may be indirect in their approach to things and quick to take things personally. Above all, they seem to react to all things emotionally, feeling rather than thinking their way through conflict. That's because, in the case of Crab Rising, there are two shells: the ascendant mask and the Crab shell itself.

Lion Rising: The Leo ♌ Ascendant

♦ Keynote: developing self-confidence

♦ Training for self-approval before the approval of others

Rising Lions present the world with a bright, sunny, confident exterior, coupled with a flair for the dramatic. How much has this got to do with the inner being beneath the show? That depends on the individual.

One of the primary lessons of being a Rising Lion is to learn to give up needing other people's approval, respect, and admiration. This usually doesn't happen until the person is able to choose self-approval and self-respect over that of other people. When it does happen, though, Rising Lions suddenly gain more respect and admiration from others than they had when they were trying to please others. Self-approval is the key to a Rising Lion.

An ascendant Lion might help to develop self-confidence, because the outer person will be projecting self-confidence as a matter of course. After a while, this can become second nature, helping those who are less confident overcome a lack of faith in themselves.

No other sign can mask quite so well as Leo ♌, and no other mask can fit so well that you forget it's a mask. But beneath all the roar the Lion can be a real pussycat.

Virgin Rising: The Virgo ♍ Ascendant

♦ Keynote: a process of self-improvement and refinement

♦ Training for finding the sacred patterns of the universe

When you meet Rising Virgins, the first thing you may notice is that they're refined and soft-spoken. A man with Virgin Rising might look like a quintessential British gentleman, for example. Rising Virgins might not say much until they've adequately sized you and the situation up. Because these people are analytical, they'll probably ask you several questions, rather than assume anything. Rising Virgins also can be very witty people, because they're Mercury-ruled.

Rising Virgins are learning to develop a new understanding of how they can contribute to our present culture and the nature of sacred work in today's world. Once they understand what their sacred work is, they can learn to co-create with the patterns of the Universe.

Rising Virgins may be learning to put things in perspective, or they may have a tendency to let small details take on meanings far beyond their actual importance. Work will matter a great deal to Rising Virgos and might well be their most effective mask.

The Rising Signs of Fall

They may all be signs of Fall, but that's where the resemblance between these three rising signs ends. With a Libra ♎ ascendant, you're learning to find equilibrium in all things; with a Scorpio ♏ ascendant, you're learning about your own personal power; and with a Sagittarius ♐ ascendant, you're learning to seek out new adventures.

Scales Rising: The Libra ♎ Ascendant

- ◆ Keynote: creating conscious, equal relationships and partnerships
- ◆ Training for balance and justice

Rising Scales often have refined and delicate features, a certain beauty and charm, and a manner of dressing that is always clean, neat, and in good taste, with a strong sense of style and color. They might also have a well-developed sense of diplomacy and refined social graces. Rising Scales are very personable and charming as well.

Rising Libras are learning about consciousness, equal relationships, and partnerships. This is not about defining who you are by whom you're with, but actually learning—through constant interaction—about relationships as a spiritual path. This "training" is about refining one's awareness.

Rising Scales' need for companionship or partnership is balanced by their desire for fair play, peace, balance, and harmony, and after their need for love is satisfied, their desire for social justice will kick in.

Scorp Rising: The Scorpio ♏ Ascendant

- ◆ Keynote: the life force as a path to the God of your understanding, the Universe, or the Source

- ◆ Training for personal magnetism

There's nothing halfway about a Rising Scorp; they put the whole force of their personality behind everything they do. Rising Scorps are often very magnetic and attract others very easily: Their magnetism is one of the reasons it's so easy for these people to gain power: Others give it to them.

Another aspect of Rising Scorps' personalities is their intensity. Someone once described this personality as similar to Oya, the Nigerian goddess of rainstorms and sudden change stirring up a calm, motionless lake. Watery Rising Scorps aren't really interested in surface chitchat, and their intensity might initially intimidate others.

Rising Scorps are learning about the life force as a path to the God of their understanding, the Universe, or the Source. As part of this "training," Rising Scorps might experience powerful and intense feelings, which they will then learn to master to fully understand their experiences.

Scorp Rising is a strong indicator of people born with a need to control, because that's when things feel safest to them. There may have been major difficulties in the early environment and home life that encouraged them to take control so they would feel safe. After all, people don't worry about feeling safe unless they feel very vulnerable. Rising Scorps' greatest challenge is to learn how to control themselves and stop controlling others.

The mask of Scorpio is secrecy; Scorpio Rising can act as a double disguise. Rising Scorps might use manipulation or deception to rise to power, and they might move quietly in the wings until their rise has been completed.

> **Heaven Knows**
>
> Many of the twentieth century's most influential leaders have had Rising Scorps: Gandhi, Mussolini, and Stalin, to name three. Although it's clear that Rising Scorps' quest for power is separate from questions of good and evil, it's equally clear that it is a given.

Archer Rising: The Sagittarius ♐ Ascendant

- ◆ Keynote: seeking adventure, new horizons, and spiritual growth

- ◆ Training "to boldly go where no one has gone before"

The world of Rising Archers is filled with possibilities, and these people are unusually optimistic. Rising Archers are explorers. They need to see new territory, so goals and challenges are very important to them.

Rising Archers often have long thin faces, with high foreheads, rather like horses, and they might shake their heads, just as horses toss their manes. Rising Archers tend to hide their problems and troubles behind humor, and they don't want others to be worried about them. Part of this is because they can't stand to worry about themselves, so they don't want others to do so either.

With Jupiter ♃ as the ruler of their ascendant, Rising Archers are often jovial, happy-go-lucky, enthusiastic, and optimistic, always seeking to find the truth, and they will approach the world as if it's their own oyster, filled with possibilities.

Rising Archers are like trainees on a Star Fleet spaceship, learning "to boldly go where no one has gone before." They are learning about the meaning of life and expanding their inner selves to the furthest horizons possible. Adventure and spiritual growth go hand in hand with Archer Rising.

> **StarFacts**
>
> With their strong philosophical outlook and/or strong religious nature, Rising Archers believe that something better is just around the corner, even when things go wrong. Rising Archers always seem to be shooting their arrows in order to have new challenges and goals. Having to do the same things over and over again drives them crazy.

The Rising Signs of Winter

They may all be signs of winter, but these three rising signs have little in common beyond that: A Capricorn ♑ ascendant is learning about responsibility; an Aquarius ♒ ascendant is learning about the bigger picture; and a Pisces ♓ ascendant is learning about empathy and giving.

Goat Rising: The Capricorn ♑ Ascendant

- ◆ Keynote: being responsible for yourself and others
- ◆ Training to take care of business—and everything else, too

Rising Goats are learning about what it means to be responsible for not just themselves, but others, too. Part of this "training" is learning the rules, and part is being available to help others, but the tough side is that Rising Goats might begin to believe that they are responsible for *all* the problems around them (rather like a scapegoat!) and that they must carry the burden for others. Rising Goats would better help themselves by learning how to oversee their territory, as well as learning new ways to create family and community.

Rising Goats can be worriers. They'll worry about what's going wrong in their youth, what can go wrong in their middle age, and about death in their old age. And they can tend to be quiet and reserved, though this often masks an active mind and tremendous willpower.

It's often hard for Rising Goats to show their feelings; their mask of reserve might be doubly thick because Capricorn ♑ is a naturally quiet sign. What you'll find on the surface with a Rising Goat is a need for order, a constant checking of the details to make sure everything is going smoothly—and a sometimes obsessive certainty that it's not. It's all part of learning about responsibility.

Rising Goats may remind other less practical signs that they need to attend to what matters, and so they sometimes seem to be "wet blankets." But underneath all this careful planning, you may find someone who's a whole lot of fun.

W-B Rising: The Aquarius ♒ Ascendant

- ◆ Keynote: progressive forward-thinkers
- ◆ Training for cosmic consciousness

Rising W-Bs appear to be forward-thinking and progressive, friendly, and open to new ideas, but they also may be intolerant of others' shortcomings and quite sarcastic.

Rising W-Bs are full of contradictions: They love to travel, and they love to stay at home; they're friendly and outgoing, and they're moody and aloof. Mind-wise, they can be both scientific and artistic, and they might be involved in two very separate areas of work.

Rising W-Bs are magnetic—this sign is associated with electricity—so people with this rising sign appear unusual in some way and attract many people to them. This is often the ascendant of celebrities or people who work in broadcasting. Jay Leno, for example, has Aquarius Rising. Rising W-Bs are taking the "training" of achieving cosmic consciousness. They're here to learn how to detach from the physical and emotional planes so they can focus on spirit and the higher planes.

No matter what the challenge, W-B Rising always goes forth with a spirit of adventure. They might forsake human connections for ideas, but they are always on the cutting edge. Take Carl Jung, for example. He had an Aquarius rising.

Fishes Rising: The Pisces ♓ Ascendant

- ◆ Keynote: learning how to give in a healthy way
- ◆ Training for giving, without giving all

Rising Fishes want the world to appear ideal, and if it doesn't, they'll ignore anything that doesn't color the picture the way they want. They'll show endless goodwill toward others, often to the detriment of themselves, and will often get caught up in pipe dreams and get-rich-quick schemes, both their own and others'.

Rising Fishes need to learn about giving in a healthy way, including giving unconditional love to everyone—not just family, clan, tribe, or race—as other signs do. This "training" teaches them to be there for others and to merge themselves and their energy with others to help anyone who needs it.

Rising Fishes also are learning how to be in the flow of life, instead of trying to control things. This is a "giver training," but Rising Fishes also learn to offer help to anyone, not just those who look, think, and act like them.

Quick to be sentimental, Rising Fishes will cry over anyone's spilled milk. Their bodies are basically one big antenna, catching all the pain and pleasure the world has to offer, and their moods will change as often as the tides—or even more often. Rising Fishes' eyes might be watery-looking, and have an ethereal look to them.

The mask here is feeling, a curious mask, because feeling would seem to be an internal sense. But the Rising Fishes' seemingly quick emotions may be covering something else entirely—or they could just be the tip of the watery iceberg.

The Least You Need to Know

- ◆ Your ascendant is the mask you wear for the world.
- ◆ You can usually find your ascendant using the pie charts we provide in this chapter.
- ◆ Your ascendant reveals your mode of self-expression.
- ◆ You can think of your rising sign as a kind of lifelong "training" for the lesson you most need to learn.

Part 3

Heavenly Bodies and Your Astrological Birth Chart

It's time to move beyond the Sun ☉ signs to planets in the astrological signs. Here is where it will be a good idea to have your birth chart in hand before you begin, but even if you don't, you might be able to figure out which planets you have in which signs by the descriptions we provide. Think of the astrological signs as the *way* you do things, and the planets as the *energy* with which you do them.

You'll also learn about planetary retrogrades, where the motion of a given planet appears, for a time, to be moving backward from Earth's perspective. You'll learn the difference between personal retrogrades and transiting retrogrades, and discover why knowing when planets are retrograde can help you chart your own course.

When the Moon Is in the Seventh House

In This Chapter

- ◆ Lessons in housekeeping
- ◆ A house is more than a home
- ◆ The planets as landlords
- ◆ Retrograde planets
- ◆ Why Neptune and Pluto are special

Houses are the stages where the drama of your planets in their signs unfolds, the places where *who you are* is made visible by *what you do*. Think of the houses as the various places where you live your external life, just as your home, your office, and your car are some of the locations for your life. Some may be places you'd rather avoid, and some may be places you'd love to never leave, but each of them is very much a part of you.

Lessons in Housekeeping

You will recall that each of the 12 houses encompasses a specific arena of life. The first house is the pie slice just below your eastern horizon, and the other houses follow, counterclockwise, around your astrological birth chart. The dividing lines between the houses are called *cusps*. Each cusp begins a new house; think of them as doors into the houses.

Remember, too, to think of each house as representing the space above and below the horizon of your birth chart: Half the sky is visible, and half of it isn't. Below the horizon are the six houses of *personal* development that aren't generally visible to others. These include areas such as your personality, knowledge, possessions, home, creativity, responsibilities, health, and the way you help serve others.

Above the horizon are the six houses of your development in the larger world that others can more readily see. These include areas such as your relationships, shared resources, social concerns, career, goals, and your unconscious.

> **AstroLingo**
>
> **Cusps** are the dividing lines between the houses and are the beginning of each house as well. The cusps of the houses determine which house a planet is in.

> **Heaven Knows**
>
> Among the 12 houses are all the areas of experience any human will encounter, and so *everything* in your life shows up in one of your houses—everything from early childhood to sex, death, and taxes!

A House Is More Than a Home

Houses reveal *where* in our lives we have lessons to learn. If, for example, you seem to have a pattern of picking the wrong type of friend or lover, you probably have a lesson related to your seventh house that you haven't quite mastered yet. Or if every time it seems you've finally settled down "for good," you suddenly up and move again, maybe you haven't quite resolved a home issue that would make your fourth house feel comfortable or stable.

Your first house is also called your *ascendant* house, so it is where we find the you that the world sees: your personality and your physical self. Each house, just like each sign, also has a *quality*.

The first house, for example, is also one of four *angular* houses (which correlate to the *cardinal* signs). The angular houses represent your *strongest personal influences*: The first house is your "identity project"; the fourth house, your "foundation or home project"; the seventh house, your "relationship project"; and the tenth house your "social role or career project."

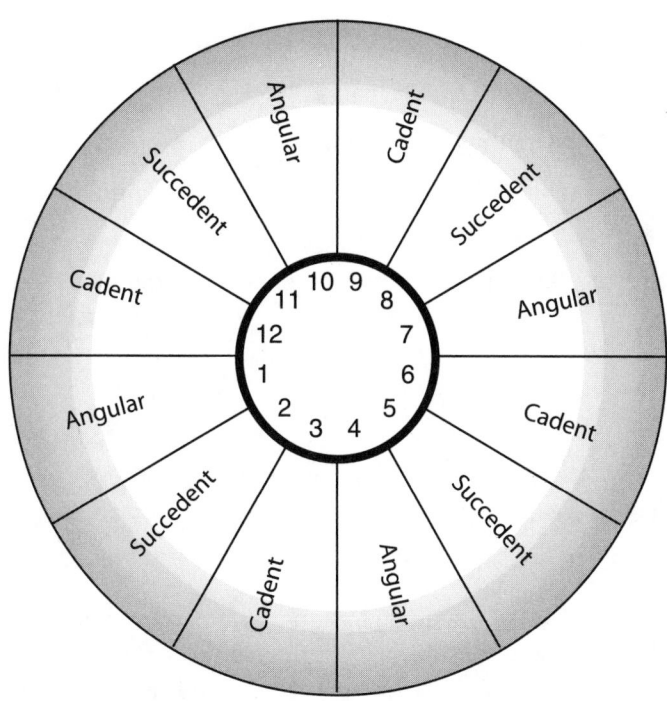

The cardinal houses represent personal influences, the succedent houses represent areas of personal stability, and the cadent houses represent social areas and higher purposes.

The Cardinal, or Angular, Houses

The First House	Physical self and personality
The Fourth House	Home and the foundation of your life
The Seventh House	Primary relationships
The Tenth House	Reputation and career

AstroLingo _____

The **angular** houses are houses with potential for dynamic action. The first, fourth, seventh, and tenth houses are angular. They correspond to the natural cardinal signs, which are Aries ♈, Cancer ♋, Libra ♎, and Capricorn ♑.

The second set of houses, called the *succedent* houses, corresponds to the natural fixed signs and represents *the areas of your life concerned with resources:* what you own, how you earn money, your creative capabilities, your shared resources, and the friends and groups that help you achieve your goals.

The Succedent Houses

The Second House	Possessions, self-esteem, and earning abilities
The Fifth House	Creativity, children, risk-taking, romance
The Eighth House	Shared resources, taxes, insurance, intimate relationships, transformation
The Eleventh House	Groups you work with to achieve your goals and desires

AstroLingo

The **succedent** houses, which correspond to the natural fixed signs, are houses that give us stability and purpose. They're the second, fifth, eighth, and eleventh houses. They correspond to the natural fixed signs: Taurus ♉, Leo ♌, Scorpio ♏, and Aquarius ♒.

The last set of houses corresponds to the mutable signs. These *cadent* houses are concerned with your *human relationships and transitions;* notice how each of these houses encompasses a much *wider* scope of activities than the angular and succedent houses do.

The Cadent Houses

The Third House	Knowledge, short trips, siblings, local environment, and neighbors
The Sixth House	Daily responsibilities, health, service to others, and co-workers
The Ninth House	Social areas: higher education, philosophy, religion, law, travel, and foreign concerns
The Twelfth House	Subconscious, the unknown

AstroLingo

The **cadent** houses, which correspond to the mutable signs, are the most adaptable group. The third, sixth, ninth, and twelfth houses are cadent and are primarily concerned with relationships and transitional states. They correspond to the natural mutable signs, Gemini ♊, Virgo ♍, Sagittarius ♐, and Pisces ♓.

What's Behind Those Doors?

In addition to being divided by quality, houses are also divided by *element*. The following chart shows these divisions and their meanings.

Houses by Element

Fire: Houses of Personal Life

First House: body
Fifth House: soul
Ninth House: spirit, mind

Earth: Houses of Substance

Second House: possessions and earning abilities
Sixth House: occupation and daily work
Tenth House: reputation and social role

Air: Houses of Relationships

Third House: relationships we don't choose (siblings, neighbors)
Seventh House: relationships we do choose (lovers, partners, friends)
Eleventh House: relationships of shared interests

Water: Houses of Endings

Fourth House: the end of the physical body
Eighth House: liberation of the soul, death
Twelfth House: the results of the life we choose

Remembering these divisions also will help you to learn which area each house represents. Yes, we know: There's a *lot* to learn. Think of it as home schooling!

Star Gazing: Heavenly Bodies in Your Astrological Chart

Knowing which planets appear in which signs and in which houses begins to reveal the story of you. The following keywords will help you remember what's what among the heavenly bodies.

Heavenly Keywords		
Signs	The way you do things	How
Planets	Energies; what you like to do	What
Houses	Areas of your life	Where

Here's an example: If you have Venus ♀ in Libra ♎ in your second house, what you own will be very attractive. You'll also count your ability to create harmonious relationships as one of your important talents.

Where Are the Heavenly Bodies?

Below, we've provided that terror-ific writer Stephen King's birth chart. In Chapter 4, we looked at Jay Leno's birth chart to see what signs the planets appeared in. Now, with Stephen King, we're going to add the planets as well. Here are King's planets in their signs and houses.

Birth chart for Stephen King.

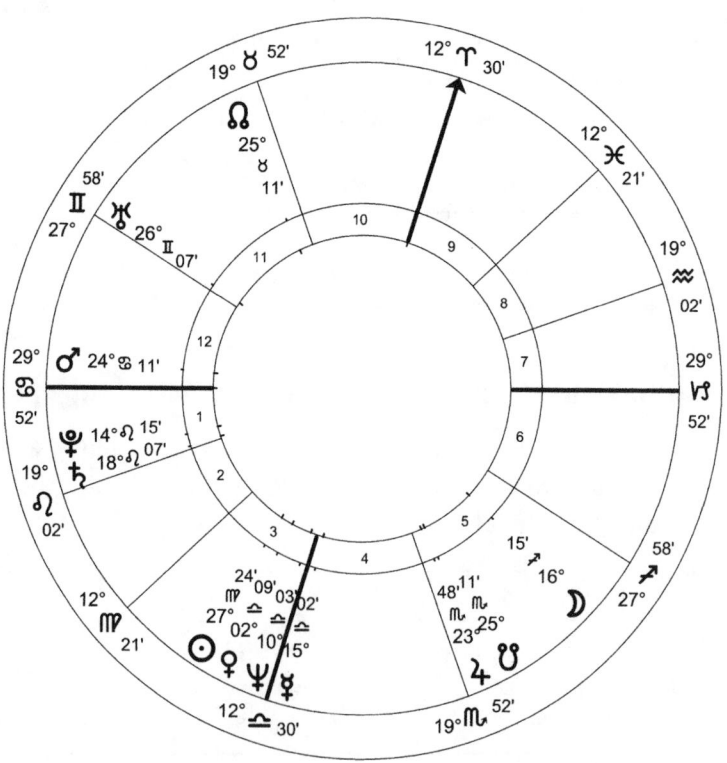

Stephen King
Natal Chart
Sep 21 1947
1:30 am EDT +4:00
Portland, ME
43°N39'41" 070°W15'21"
Geocentric
Tropical
Placidus
True Node

Stephen King's Planets in Their Signs and Houses

Planet	Symbol	Sign	Symbol	House
Sun	☉	Virgo	♍	Third
Moon	☽	Sagittarius	♐	Fifth
Mercury	☿	Libra	♎	Fourth
Venus	♀	Libra	♎	Third
Mars	♂	Cancer	♋	Twelfth
Jupiter	♃	Scorpio	♏	Fifth
Saturn	♄	Leo	♌	First
Uranus	♅	Gemini	♊	Eleventh
Neptune	♆	Libra	♎	Third
Pluto	♇	Leo	♌	First
South Node	☋	Scorpio	♏	Fifth
North Node	☊	Taurus	♉	Eleventh

The Planets as Landlords

In Chapter 4 you read about rulerships. When a planet is the *ruler* of a particular sign, we think of it as the "landlord." It might help to actually think of these planets as the ones that are collecting the rent, making sure the toilets flush and the lawn gets mowed.

Landlord planets "own" the houses they're in charge of, so they have the final say about what's happening in that area of your life. In other words, no matter which planets are "renting," or "in" a house, the landlord's the one calling the shots.

Here's where we need to review the rulership of signs in order to determine the ruler of each house in your chart. Once again, we'll use Stephen King's chart to show you what we mean. And we've also provided you with a list of planetary rulers.

AstroLingo

The planetary **ruler** of a sign is the "landlord" of the house with that sign on its door (or cusp). This means that planet is "in charge" of what occurs in that area of life.

Natural Planetary Rulers

Planet	Sign(s) Ruled
Sun ☉	Leo ♌
Moon ☽	Cancer ♋
Mercury ☿	Gemini ♊, Virgo ♍
Venus ♀	Taurus ♉, Libra ♎
Mars ♂	Aries ♈, co-ruler of Scorpio ♏
Jupiter ♃	Sagittarius ♐, co-ruler of Pisces ♓
Saturn ♄	Capricorn ♑, co-ruler of Aquarius ♒
Uranus ♅	Aquarius ♒
Neptune ♆	Pisces ♓
Pluto ♇	Scorpio ♏, co-ruler of Aries ♈

King's Landlords

House	Sign on Cusp	Landlord(s) or Ruler(s)
First	Cancer ♋	Moon ☽
Second	Leo ♌	Sun ☉
Third	Virgo ♍	Mercury ☿
Fourth	Libra ♎	Venus ♀
Fifth	Scorpio ♏	Pluto ♇, Mars ♂
Sixth	Sagittarius ♐	Jupiter ♃
Seventh	Capricorn ♑	Saturn ♄
Eighth	Aquarius ♒	Uranus ♅, Saturn ♄
Ninth	Pisces ♓	Neptune ♆, Jupiter ♃
Tenth	Aries ♈	Mars ♂
Eleventh	Taurus ♉	Venus ♀
Twelfth	Gemini ♊	Mercury ☿

Remember, even if a house appears "empty" on a birth chart, it nonetheless has a landlord. The planets in any house are sort of "renting" the area, but the landlord has the final say about what goes on in that area of life. The exception to this is when a landlord actually occupies the house it rules; in that case, it's not a renter, but an in-residence landlord. This means that it's going to be keeping a particularly close eye on what goes on in that house.

No matter where the landlord "lives," though, if it's not in the house it rules, whatever is happening to it affects the house it *owns* as well. We could say that the house is "owned" by an absentee landlord.

Let's use King's Capricorn ♑ on the seventh house cusp as an example. Saturn ♄ would be the landlord here. Now, whatever sign the landlord is actually in will change the way it acts—the sign affects its style, in other words.

On King's chart, his Saturn ♄ is in Leo ♌ in the first house, indicating that, although he's supremely self-assured, he also has a need for recognition that he can fulfill through self-discipline, organization, and persistence. Additionally, Saturn ♄ is next to his Pluto ♇, which is also in Leo ♌, providing plenty of independence to fulfill his special destiny. This brief example begins to show you just how interconnected all the areas of your life are. Although you might have already "known" these things on some level, astrology maps them out for you in a way that's easy to understand. That's why we call it a map of you.

When Planets Seem Backward: Retrogrades ℞

When planets are *retrograde*, they appear from our vantage here on Earth to be moving backward. Think of it as that moment when you pass a car going in the same direction you are when that car appears to be going backward. When this same thing happens to our Earthly view of other planets—because each planet travels its orbit around the Sun at a different speed—we call it *retrograde* motion. The symbol to denote a retrograde planet on an astrological birth chart is ℞.

When you have retrograde planets in your birth chart, you need to pay special attention to those planets' energies. Chapter 14 is devoted entirely to this concept.

> **AstroLingo**
>
> When planets are **retrograde,** their motion, seen from an Earthly perspective, appears to be in reverse (but this is not actually so; planets can only move in one direction along their orbits).

Why Neptune ♆ and Pluto ♇ Are Special

Poky Neptune ♆ and Pluto ♇ are such "slow" planets from our Earthly vantage point that they're called "generational" planets. A whole generation usually has these planets in the same sign.

Right now Pluto is on the "fast" part of its cycle: It's "only" taking about 11 years to get through a sign! At its slowest, Pluto takes about *30* years (speed is relative, after all), which might help explain why time seems speeded up these days. Neptune also takes a while to go through one sign—about 14 years—so it's called a generational planet, too.

Both of these planets are "late" discoveries. Three planets were discovered relatively recently: Uranus ♅ was first noted in 1781, Neptune ♆ in 1846, and Pluto ♇ in 1930. Naturally, modern astrologers have had to study these new discoveries to find how they fit into the larger scheme and how they correspond to other developments in our evolution. In so doing, they've learned that Uranus is associated with scientific invention and innovative ideas, as well as revolutions; Neptune is connected to film, psychic abilities, and psychology; and Pluto is aligned with both atomic energy and the collective unconscious.

> **Star-Crossed**
>
> You may remember the recent heated discussion among astronomers as to whether Pluto ♇ was really a planet. Considering Pluto's area of "expertise," this potential for transformation probably wasn't a surprise!

Because Neptune and Pluto move so slowly, we're only going to look at each of them in the signs for people who are (or soon will be) alive now, approximately a 100-year span. If you don't fit into this time span, call us right away. You belong in the *Guinness Book of World Records!*

StarFacts

Interestingly, there's a correlation between a planet's discovery and concurrent scientific discoveries connected with that planet's energies. For example, there was no psychology at all until Neptune was discovered in 1846—and *then* Freud unlocked the subconscious. And we had to wait for Pluto's "discovery" in 1930 to unlock the secrets of nuclear power. Who knows what's next …

The Least You Need to Know

- The 12 houses are the areas of human experience.

- Houses are described by quality and in a way that's similar to the elements.

- All houses have a "landlord," which is the planet that's in charge of the sign on its cusp. The landlord planet has final say about what's happening in that area of life.

- Every planet rules at least one sign.

- Retrograde planets seem to reverse their energies.

- Neptune ♆ and Pluto ♇ are "generational" planets, so a whole generation might have these planets in the same sign, and they apply to the collective.

Chapter 11

The Inner Planets: Who Are You?

In This Chapter

- ◆ The Sun ☉: Mr. BIG
- ◆ The Moon ☽: bewitched, bothered, and bewildered
- ◆ Mercury ☿: instant messaging
- ◆ Venus ♀: beauty and the beast
- ◆ Mars ♂: war and peace

Originally, we had planned to put abbreviated planet tables in the appendix for you, but it turned out that even abbreviated tables would have run over 100 pages! So instead, we recommend that you get your chart done at one of the online sites that provides the service (see Appendix A) or at a nearby metaphysical bookstore.

For the mathematically inclined, you can learn how a birth chart is calculated in Chapters 19 and 20. There are few astrologers who calculate birth charts "the old-fashioned way" now that simple computer programs do all the hard stuff. We've used the popular Solar Fire software program from Astrolabe (www.alabe.com) to generate the charts you see in this book. But it's nonetheless instructive to find out what goes into chart calculations.

AstroLingo

The **luminaries,** the Sun ☉ and the Moon ☾, are so named because they are the planets that provide light to us here on Earth.

No matter which option you choose, you'll need to have your birth chart in hand so you'll know exactly where your planets are located before you read these next chapters.

In this chapter, we'll look at the *luminaries* and the *personal* planets, which reveal the behavior and characteristics that make you unique.

The Sun ☉: Mr. BIG

As the central, life-giving force of our solar system, the Sun naturally plays an important role in what you are like, describing the nature of your individual approach to life itself.

StarFacts

According to Cheyenne myth, it was Grandmother Spider who brought the light of the Sun to the people, carrying just enough in a bowl she made of clay to light the sky slowly from east to west. Even today, the spider's web looks just like the Sun and its rays, and the spider rises to spin her web early in the morning, before the Sun is fully up.

When you ask someone what their sign is, the answer will be their Sun sign. But as you probably can see by now, your Sun sign is only the beginning. It characterizes your sense of purpose, creativity, willpower, and how you develop consciousness, as well as begins to answer the question, "Who am I?" But there's a whole lot more to you than your senses of self and purpose, right?

For more information about the specific possibilities of the Sun in each sign, you should refer back to the detailed Sun sign profiles in Chapters 5 through 8. But for information on other dimensions of yourself and that "whole lot more," keep reading.

The Moon ☾: Bewitched, Bothered, and Bewildered

The Moon is the third part of what could be called the most important triangle of astrology: the combination of Sun ☉ sign, ascendant, and Moon ☾ sign. Mother Moon, the body closest to Earth in the sky, represents what could be called your feminine side, and in fact, the Moon has four primary phases, each one representing a different aspect of the feminine nature. The Moon's phases consist of the New Moon, Waxing Moon (First Quarter), Full Moon, and Waning Moon (Third Quarter). But there are also Dark Moons and Blue Moons to consider!

New Moon   **Waxing Moon**   **Full Moon**   **Waning Moon**   *The phases of the Moon* ☽.

StarFacts

In ancient times the Moon was regarded as the Mansion of the Fathers, where the souls of the dead were waiting to return for rebirth. In Greek tradition, the Moon, who was called Selene, fell so in love with a beautiful young man named Endymion that she chose him to lie beside her for eternity. The legend goes that Endymion sleeps, forever unconscious, the stuff of dreams and the natural territory of the Moon.

◆ The early crescent or New Moon is the young maiden—also represented by Taurus ♉—and its corresponding myth is Diana the Hunter with her bow. This Moon enjoys all the possibilities before her.

◆ The Waxing, First Quarter Moon represents a young woman just ready to flower, including the mythical Persephone, who's spirited away by Hades at the height of her beauty because he can't resist it. This Moon is associated with Aries ♈, the first sign of the zodiac.

◆ Then there's the Full Moon, the mother pregnant and full with her baby, who gives birth. This Moon is associated with Cancer ♋ and the fertility goddesses. Many believe that all sorts of odd human behaviors are due to the Full Moon, and many legends (think of werewolves, for example) have grown from that belief. Hospitals have long noted an increase in emergency room visits during Full Moons, and civil unrest is more likely to occur during these periods as well.

◆ Next, there's the Waning or Third Quarter Moon, associated with Virgo ♍, the earth Goddess, who is responsible for the harvest. This Moon represents the mature woman who must release her child (like Demeter and her daughter, Persephone, or Mary and Christ) so the child can fulfill his destiny.

StarFacts

What's a Blue Moon? And why do things only happen "once in a Blue Moon"? Well, there are usually 13 Full Moons each year, and, although the lunar cycle is about 29½ days, months are anywhere from 28 to 31 days. Once in a Blue Moon, there are two Full Moons during one month, and that second Full Moon is called the "Blue Moon."

◆ The Dark Moon is associated with the old crone, the wise woman. This is also Scorpio ♏, or Hecate, who has knowledge of healing and other ancient wisdom and who mourns for the loss of her child.

As you can see, the Moon is the main model for all the feminine energies and roles. Now in a man's chart, the Moon represents his feminine side, which he might choose to project through the women in his life—his mother, lover, or wife, for example—if he doesn't express it directly, as well as his intuition.

But there's still more to the Moon. It also represents your mother, or the nurturing person who raised you, and this is true regardless of gender. Although women tend to express their Moon more directly, men often project their Moon through the women in their life. These days, men are learning to show more of their feminine energy and express their feelings.

> **StarFacts**
>
> In the past, people knew their Moon ☽ sign instead of their Sun ☉ sign, because it was considered more important. Because our western society prefers to emphasize the more "masculine" characteristics of individuality, achievement, and goals, the Sun sign is now considered more important.

Because we've called your Sun ☉ your sense of purpose and self, let's call your Moon ☽ your emotions. On your birth chart, the sign where your Moon ☽ is reveals your emotional nature, memories, habits, and patterns, especially your unconscious patterns.

The Moon's light is not its own, but is reflected from the Sun, and the emotions the Moon rules can change as quickly as that light. Your Moon, in other words, shows how you feel.

Moonshine: The Moon ☽ in Each Zodiac Sign

Because the Moon moves very fast (about 12 degrees per day), on the days when the Moon changes signs, your Moon could either be in the sign the Moon was in on the previous day or in the new sign.

Your birth chart should show the correct placement, but if your birth time is off even a little, your Moon's placement may be incorrect. For this reason, if the description of the Moon sign that appears below doesn't seem quite right to you, read the descriptions before and after it to see if your Moon is actually in a different sign.

Moon in Aries ☽ ♈

An Aries Moon indicates directness and spontaneity, an emotional nature that is energetic and sometimes excitable, a person who is both daring and independent. People with Aries Moons won't be long on patience as a rule, but they will have a knack for getting others to do what they want. Self-confident in love, they'll have little use for shrinking violets or those who seem to hesitate. Life for a person with an Aries Moon might hide a sense of insecurity, but it's also one that is always moving forward. More than any other sign, Aries feels with its *head*.

Moon in Taurus ☽ ♉

In the stable sign of Taurus, the Moon is at its best: Its emotional nature is trustworthy, warm, and affectionate. It may take a Taurus Moon a while to make up its mind, but once it does, nothing will make it change, and people with Taurus Moons marry for life. Taurus's Venus ♀ ruler is manifested here as a love of beauty, and people with Taurus Moons are artistic, romantic, and have a great love of creature comforts. The downside is that a Taurus Moon can be rigid or obstinate (remember, Taurus is a bull), because above all it needs to feel stable, safe, and secure. But Taurus feels with its *senses*, making this overall a steady and reliable Moon sign.

Moon in Gemini ☽ ♊

Mutable Gemini makes for a restless and erratic Moon, but this Moon sign also is marked by a lively, inquisitive emotional nature, quick to laugh and make others laugh, and just as quick to flip-flop to a darker mood. A Gemini Moon is curious, too, needing constant stimulation, and talkative Gemini makes this Moon quick to let others know its feelings as well. Gemini Moons also spend a lot of time trying to analyze their feelings themselves, because Gemini is a thinking sign. A Moon in Gemini feels with its *mind*, a most unusual combination.

> **StarFacts**
>
> Want an example of a Moon in Gemini, feeling with his mind, and then analyzing his feelings? How about Sigmund Freud? We rest our case.

Moon in Cancer ☽ ♋

The Moon is at home in Cancer, the sign that it naturally rules. Cancer Moons have an emotional nature that is both receptive and retentive—storing away impressions, reactions, information, and yes, feelings, until they need them, and this often makes them writers or actors (or both). With a Moon in Cancer, a person is likely to be both imaginative and creative, while underneath feeling vulnerable, touchy, moody, and easily hurt. All of this, though, is hidden under Cancer's hard shell. But because a Moon in Cancer feels with its *feelings*, it is also a warmhearted and romantic combination.

Moon in Leo ☽ ♌

Exuberant Moon in Leo has strong emotions and refuses to be limited by what it feels are narrow-minded or limiting ideas: It likes its heart to be in whatever it's doing. Leo Moons have an emotional nature that is usually both affectionate and outgoing, and often charismatic as well, but they can easily be hurt if they feel they're not being appreciated, which can be any time the spotlight's not shining on them. A natural performer and a hearty lover, Moon in Leo feels with its *heart*—strongly, openly, and joyfully.

Moon in Virgo ☽ ♍

Virgo Moons like to see things—and figure them out—for themselves. Intelligent and practical, they spend whatever time is needed to get to the bottom of what they're feeling, to not just take it apart, but to put it together again so that it makes perfect sense, a prospect that delights Virgo to no end. Step by step, Moons in Virgo approach everything they do with logic and efficiency, so they can be frustrated by less methodical minds. Conversely, their precision can sometimes seem too rigid to others, but a Moon in Virgo feels with its *logic*, using its discriminating emotional nature to create a well-ordered emotional life for itself.

Moon in Libra ☽ ♎

Moons in Libra are partnership Moons. They love the way things and people fit together to create harmony, and they seek to create an atmosphere where everything seems to fall naturally into place. The most social of Moons, Moon in Libra can seem superficial or shallow, but in reality its emotional nature cannot help but express its feelings through the way things look and feel. Naturally gracious and the most hospitable of hosts, Moon in Libra feels good when everyone else feels good. To Moon in Libra, the outward appearance reflects the inward; Moon in Libra feels through *others*.

Moon in Scorpio ☽ ♏

A Moon in Scorpio is so intense, it spends a great deal of energy protecting itself from its own emotions. Well aware of how powerful emotions can be (and never satisfied with superficial answers) Scorpio Moons can be suspicious of others, quick to judge, and hold grudges for a very, very long time. At the same time, they have a desire to understand deep mysteries and get to the bottom of things, which makes Scorpio Moons' emotional nature both intuitive and potent, capable of stronger feeling than any other Moon sign. Scorpio Moons often seek their soul mates. Above all, Scorpio Moons feel with their *intense emotions*.

Moon in Sagittarius ☽ ♐

Adaptable Moon in Sagittarius is always out there, with an emotional nature made for making friends and experiencing the new and unexpected. Sagittarius Moons love adventure, excitement, discovery, and a plain old good time. You won't find shrinking violets here, nor will you find moody brooders. You might not find anyone here: Sagittarius Moons love to be free, and they may be off on yet another adventure. Moon in Sagittarius is eager for the truth and in seeking that truth will feel through its *experiences*.

Moon in Capricorn ☽ ♑

Cold Moon in Capricorn might seem reserved and remote, but what it's really doing is planning its own success. Capricorn Moons thrive on challenges and the successes completing challenges can bring them, and they're not very big on what they view as excessive emotion. With a self-controlled and cautious emotional nature, those with a Capricorn Moon's discipline and determination can achieve tremendous successes in their lives, but there also can be an emotional cost. Capricorn Moons need to be needed, but because they feel through *control*, they may not allow others to get too close.

> **Star-Crossed**
>
> Capricorn Moons often become world leaders, but this might be because they mistake control (external approval) for love (internal approval). Napoleon had a Capricorn Moon, for example, and so did Abraham Lincoln and Indira Gandhi. Capricorn Moons' determination can help them achieve the power they seek, but they also might find that it's lonely at the top.

Moon in Aquarius ☽ ♒

You might find it hard to get close to an independent Moon in Aquarius. Being different is as necessary to this Moon as breathing, and anything that furthers Aquarian Moons' uniqueness holds their attention. Intuitively strong, Moons in Aquarius often make new discoveries, but they also might discover that new territories are lonely places. Others adore Moons in Aquarius, but they'll find what really attracts these independent Moons is unattainability. Progressive Aquarian Moons feel through their *individuality*, with an emotional nature that is cool, impartial, and ultimately on its own.

Moon in Pisces ☽ ♓

Dreamy Moons in Pisces always believe the best about everyone and everything, and so they're constantly setting themselves up for disappointment. With their sensitive and compassionate emotional nature, Pisces Moons forgive just about anything, too, but they're also easily hurt and may sometimes feel sorry for themselves. Moons in

Pisces can confuse dream with reality, which makes this a most creative Moon, although when they find they really live in reality, not in a dream, it can be a jarring jolt. Idealistic and romantic Pisces Moons feel through their *imaginations*.

Mercury ☿: Instant Messaging

Mercury is in charge of thinking and communications—what we know and how we know it. As the planet closest to the Sun, Mercury is fast, it's hot, and it's small—small but mighty, that is. Here is where you'll find all the faculties of the mind: logic and reason, intelligence and education. Mercury's tool is language, and its method is transmittal.

StarFacts
Who was that winged man? In Greek mythology, Mercury was called Hermes and was the messenger for the gods—the UPS guy with wings on his feet, passing notes, with hot-off-the-Mount gossip and godly orders in a pre-PC version of e-mail. Naturally, modern Mercury loves e-mail, as well as cell phones, FedEx, and caller ID. It's no coincidence that Mercury's corresponding sign is Gemini ♊. The two are probably passing notes right this minute!

How You Think: Mercury ☿ in Each Zodiac Sign

Are you the one strangers on airplanes tell their stories to, or are you reading the paper by the fire—or rewriting the headlines in the newsroom? Reading and writing, talking and listening, watching and thinking: This is your brain on Mercury. Any questions? The sign your Mercury is in describes your mental nature, how you think and communicate.

Mercury in Aries ☿ ♈

Quick, imaginative, and always trying to be first in everything: That's Mercury in Aries. Of course, this can also indicate an impetuous, premature, and headstrong nature, but no matter which way Mercury goes, in Aries it's always spontaneous and immediate. Running ahead before it gets all the facts, Mercury in Aries might jump to conclusions, but it is always an *active* mind.

Mercury in Taurus ☿ ♉

If Mercury is in Taurus, it's always prepared. And it's always sure, too, that its ideas, opinions, and beliefs are the right ones. This can mean that Taurus Mercuries won't always listen. But why should they, when they already know the answer? Mercury in Taurus isn't one to jump to conclusions, though; this is Mercury in its easy chair, a *comfortable* mind.

Mercury in Gemini ☿ ♊

Mercury in Gemini is full of unprocessed data and ideas, and it has the words to let others know what it means. Mercury is at home in Gemini, a quick, agile mind that's witty and charming. Although sometimes this can slip over the line into gossip, Mercury in Gemini wants to get the message across, you know? Mercury in Gemini is a *communicating* mind, the inquiring mind that wants to know.

Mercury in Cancer ☿ ♋

Mercury in Cancer might be picking up everyone else's signals; Mercury is as much a receiver as a transmitter in this sign. If there's such a thing as an earthly empath Mercury in Cancer might be it: These people always seem to intuit what others are thinking without a word being said, and, Mercury in Cancer is an *intuitive* mind. There's also a good chance that, with their good memory and strong poetic powers, they'll write it all down, too!

Mercury in Leo ☿ ♌

Here's a Mercury with heart, thinking with its heart. Outspoken and optimistic, Leo Mercuries also are strong in purpose, dramatic, and idealistic, although they aren't likely to sweat the little stuff. This is a Mercury with the charisma to lead and to convince others to follow its lead. Mercury in Leo is a *creative* mind, one that others will willingly follow.

Mercury in Virgo ☿ ♍

Impartial Mercury in Virgo sorts all those details into their proper files, where its logic and precision can find the heart of the matter. That's where Mercury in Virgo works its magic, with its fine intelligence systematically clarifying and refining the information, and understanding the patterns. Mercury in Virgo is a *logical* mind, analytical, practical, and a quick learner.

Mercury in Libra ☿ ♎

Rational Mercury in the sign of balance will endlessly weigh both sides of any issue and make comparisons, seeking to find the perfect choice. Of course, there is no perfect choice, but that doesn't mean Mercury in Libra won't keep looking. Diplomatic and charming, this Mercury might do best if someone else can make the final decisions, but he or she will make sure to provide information that covers every angle. Mercury in Libra is a *balancing* mind.

> **StarFacts**
>
> Probing Mercuries in Scorpio include Indian leader Mohandas Ghandi, scientist Marie Curie, and former English Prime Minister Winston Churchill.

Mercury in Scorpio ☿ ♏

Mercury in Scorpio sees right through semantic disguises to the real meaning behind the words. Mercury here can be critical and quick to judge, and it's not going to waste time with frivolity, either. Mercury in Scorpio is a *probing* mind, one that gets to the heart of the matter.

Mercury in Sagittarius ☿ ♐

Frank and open-minded, Mercury in Sagittarius may speak before it thinks. Sagittarian Mercuries love to learn and are quick to explore new ideas, but they also might not stick to any one idea for very long. For this reason, lengthy projects are not always Mercury in Sagittarius's forte. But Mercury in Sag is a *seeking* mind, almost childlike in its discovery of whatever it finds.

Mercury in Capricorn ☿ ♑

In Capricorn, Mercury is a hard worker, storing up those facts and figures for future practical use. Cautious and methodical, Mercury in Capricorn knows what it wants and how it plans to get it. Because what matters here is how the mind is used and what it is used for, Mercury in Capricorn is an *organized* mind.

Mercury in Aquarius ☿ ♒

Mercury in Aquarius seldom misses a thing and in addition has a knack for grasping abstract ideas. As an observer of people and their motivations, Mercury in Aquarius loves to predict human reactions, too. With its open mind and scientific approach, Mercury in Aquarius might be on the forefront of new discoveries. Always original and unorthodox, Mercury in Aquarius is an *inventive* mind.

Mercury in Pisces ☿ ♓

Mercury in Pisces moves to the intuitive side of the mind, which means its conclusions might not be based on logic. It's imagination that is the most finely tuned here, and Mercury in Pisces is often sensitive and receptive. Well tuned, Mercury in Pisces may seem psychic, though at its worst, it can seem pessimistic and confused. No matter which, though, Mercury in Pisces is a *reflective* mind.

Venus ♀: Beauty and the Beast

It's not just that old Bobby Darin song that makes us think of Venus as the goddess of beauty; the association is so deeply entrenched that it can make us forget the other areas that the planet closest to us rules. Venus is the goddess of balance and harmony, in charge of how we feel not only about our relationships and social connections, but also about what we possess.

StarFacts
As an archetype, Venus is characterized by the beautiful woman. Some Venus myths you may never have thought associated with her are those of Rapunzel, Snow White, and Cinderella. In each of these tales, there are plots afoot to separate Venus from her true love (and so, her fate). True love, of course, always triumphs, because, as we already know, you can't keep someone from her fate—especially a goddess archetype.

Venus's Earth nature is represented in her rulership of Taurus ♉, where she manifests herself as a connection to one's resources and inherent gifts. In Taurus, Venus is sensuous and devoted to comfort and pleasure. Your possessions and your self-esteem are closely connected; without good self-esteem, you might not have many resources. And both of these are tied together through Venus.

Venus's Air nature can be found in her rulership of Libra ♎, which concerns itself with the social graces and with marriage. This is where you'll find the Venus of romance and partnerships.

> **Heaven Knows**
>
> Many believe that if you are male, your Venus will represent the type of woman to whom you will be attracted, and if you are female, your Venus is your ideal feminine self. But Venus also is strongly associated with your creativity and self-esteem, and those are certainly not divided along male/female lines!

How You Love: Venus ♀ in Each Zodiac Sign

A prominent Venus in your birth chart means that how you love and connect to your surroundings is very important to you. Venus in the signs describes your love nature, your ability to attract money and worldly goods, and how you deal with relationships in general. So let's walk Venus through each of the signs and see what they indicate.

Venus in Aries ♀ ♈

In impulsive Aries, Venus can fall head-over-heels in love and then might later realize that she was falling in love with someone other than the person she thought! Physical appearance will be what grabs Aries Venuses first, and they don't much go for slobs or messes. Demonstrative and enthusiastic, Venus in Aries loves to give gifts but also can be demanding and selfish. But these people are also quick thinkers, creative and artistic. Most of all, Venus in Aries is an *enthusiastic* love.

Venus in Taurus ♀ ♉

Venus in Taurus is never impulsive. They take their time in love, as they do in everything. And because love can be everything to Taurus Venuses, they can become very possessive about those they do love. Venus is in its Earth rulership sign here, and so in addition to its stability, it also has a strong aesthetic sense, which often manifests itself in beautiful surroundings. Charming, sensual, and artistic, you could call Venus in Taurus a *steadfast* love.

Venus in Gemini ♀ ♊

Venus in Gemini is both lighthearted and emotionally objective. Venus here likes intellectual stimulation as much as romance. There's a tendency toward lack of commitment: They're far too lighthearted to stay in one place for long and can be quite the flirts. With Venus here, you may find literary talent or, at the very least, a love of language, and sociability is very important as well. Not surprisingly, Venus in Gemini is a *communicating* love.

Venus in Cancer ♀ ♋

In watery Cancer, Venus is both romantic and sensitive. Venus here can become a little too attached to people and possessions. But security is important to people with Venus in Cancer, too, so they're not likely to rush into anything. Once they do feel secure, though, they are sensitive and loyal and make everyone feel at home. If they don't have a home to take care of, they'll care for the world. For these reasons and more, Venus in Cancer is a *nurturing* love.

Venus in Leo ♀ ♌

Venus in Leo can translate into a love of self-expression and a flair for the dramatic, but this also is a generous and selfless association. Leo Venuses seem to attract the love of others without even trying because they're just plain likable. They also love fine things, and when they're in love, they love to share those things, too. Ardent and romantic, above all, Venus in Leo is a *passionate* love.

Venus in Virgo ♀ ♍

Precisely tuned to social, emotional, and artistic values, Venus in Virgo knows what it likes—and what it doesn't. Venus here can be more sincerely affectionate than any other sign, and also can manifest itself as someone with a strong business sense, or who loves to serve others in some way. Sometimes shy or soft-spoken, more than anything, Venus in Virgo is a *discerning* love.

Venus in Libra ♀ ♎

"Falling in Love with Love" could be Venus in Libra's theme song: Romantic ideals seem to have been invented here. Because Venus is in its natural Air sign in Libra, its ideals might be manifested in strong partnerships or a creative ability to create harmony and beauty in one's environment. Venus in Libra can care so much about the social graces that it might sometimes be seen as superficial or snobbish, but that's not really what's going on. Gracious and appreciative, Venus in Libra is a *romantic* love.

Venus in Scorpio ♀ ♏

In Scorpio, Venus can be an all-consuming passion: This sign is both sensuous and intense, after all. Love has power in Venus in Scorpio, and consequently there's a deep need to find true love and all the passion that true love can bring. Venus in Scorpio cares about security, too, which can translate into partnerships that lead to that security—or a deep-seeded resentment if Scorpio has been hurt. Passionate and intense, Venus in Scorpio is a *powerful* love.

Venus in Sagittarius ♀ ♐

Lighthearted and idealistic, Venus in Sagittarius is all about the adventure and excitement love can bring, so it's not always a love that lasts. Friendships do last here, though, and Venus in Sagittarius always has lots of friends. Venus's aesthetic sense usually manifests itself in a creative lifestyle in Sagittarius, because Venus loves its freedom here. Outgoing and perhaps even flirtatious, Venus in Sagittarius is an *expansive* love.

Venus in Capricorn ♀ ♑

Careful, cautious Venus in Capricorn makes for a steadfast and loyal companion, one who will stand the test of time. Venus here takes personal attachments very seriously and is often attached to its possessions as much as to people. Once love has been proven to Venus in Capricorn, you'll find commitment, honesty, and a lover who is constant and resourceful. Responsible and loyal, Venus in Capricorn is a *dedicated* love.

Venus in Aquarius ♀ ♒

Venus in Aquarius can seem emotionally detached, but there also can be a great originality to the way Venus approaches love here. Helpful, charitable, and giving, Venus in Aquarius not only has many friends, but also often has a variety of friends. Of course, Venus in Aquarius can't stand what it perceives as emotional scenes, and will just walk away from them. Because Venus in Aquarius cares a great deal about freedom and openness, it's not likely to be possessive, and might even be curious about sharing its love with others. Cool, calm, and collected, Venus in Aquarius is a *detached and magnetic* love.

> **StarFacts**
>
> Venus in Pisces celebrities include poet Elizabeth Barrett Browning, psychic Edgar Cayce, and civil rights leader Martin Luther King Jr. Remember, empathy and compassion are key here.

Venus in Pisces ♀ ♓

Compassionate and sympathetic, Venus in Pisces can actually love too much, although we're not sure there really is such a thing. Venus in Pisces is intuitive about love, and with its true empathy for others, relates to art, poetry, nature, and animals. Venus in Pisces is often highly imaginative and creative as well, putting its feelings into writing, acting, or music. Generous Venus in Pisces is often attracted to the underdog and is, above all, an *unconditional* love.

Mars ♂: War and Peace

There's a long-lived tendency to equate Mars with aggression and war, and that's no accident: This is the planet of action and warrior ways, after all. But Mars is about much more than that, of course, and here we will find how we manifest everything from physical energy and desires to our egos and how we deal with (or don't deal with!) our anger.

Mars represents courage and so is bold and courageous in certain signs—but not all of them. You could think of your Mars as your "assertiveness training": Your Mars can show you how you're going to fight your battles—and how you might have seemingly pointless conflicts.

StarFacts

Fiery Mars is the war god, but that's not all there is to him. The Hebrew word for Mars is *M'Adam*, which should look vaguely familiar: It's Adam, the first man. Just as Venus ♀ is the archetypal woman, Mars ♂ can be thought of as the archetypal man: goal-oriented, physical in his approach, and a protector of those who need protecting. Don't think of him as just a warrior, though; think of him as the one in the lead—like Adam.

How You're Driven: Mars in Each Zodiac Sign

Because this is how your independence can be found, your Mars sign can indicate how you're going to begin to separate your battles from the battles of others, and in the process find your path to personal achievement and success. Mars in the signs describes how you express your energies, assert yourself, and go about meeting your needs and desires.

Mars in Aries ♂ ♈

Independent Mars in Aries is both energetic and self-assured, a courageous go-getter who doesn't often let anything stand in its way. Because there's lots of enthusiasm here, you'll often find Mars in Aries leading, and that's fine with them, as they love to get their own way. Mars in Aries can be aggressive and even pushy, but Aries is Mars's natural home, and so is a *courageous and honest* energy.

Mars in Taurus ♂ ♉

Dogged and persistent, Mars in Taurus is not easily deterred from its steady course toward success. Mars in Taurus is a skilled artisan, often very successful in business, and passionate and sensuous as well. Sometimes Mars in Taurus's patient movement toward its goals can seem more like plodding, and its sensuous nature can become jealous and possessive. But Mars in Taurus is a *determined* energy, methodical and practical.

Mars in Gemini ♂ ♊

Versatile Mars in Gemini is a real go-getter, quick to think, quick to act—and quick to move on. Mars here often has great dexterity, and is incisive, decisive, and resourceful. At the same time, Gemini Mars can seem to jump to conclusions, to manifest in nervous energy, or to appear restless or even flighty. But Gemini Mars can be magical in its ability to communicate; this is a *lively* energy.

Mars in Cancer ♂ ♋

Mars in Cancer might keep things inside, but this can translate into enormous power of will. Mars goes subtle in Cancer, getting what it wants in often indirect ways, but because Mars is also intuitive and instinctive here, it might know exactly how to get what it wants. Mars in Cancer's protective custody can make it defensive, or even argumentative, but it also knows what it wants. Mars in Cancer is a *protective* energy.

Mars in Leo ♂ ♌

Mars's Fire element gets accentuated in Leo, and it has no problem putting its big ideas into action. Mars is generous here, too, and its enthusiasm and drama lead others to follow its often magnetic drive. There's also a tendency toward vanity and self-righteousness in Leo Mars, but those can be part of what makes this such a self-confident placement. In Leo, Mars is a *passionate* energy.

Mars in Virgo ♂ ♍

Cool, logical, and precise, Mars in Virgo works very hard to achieve its ambitions—and may even be a workaholic. Mars in Virgo is good at separating its emotions from what needs to be done, bringing both discipline and industry to everything it wants to do. Mars in Virgo is highly skilled with fine motor skills or handwork, and surgeons and craftsmen often have this placement. Mars here can be strongly passionate, especially for what it sees as the right cause. Mars in Virgo is a *systematic* energy, clever and shrewd.

Mars in Libra ♂ ♎

Charming, generous Mars in Libra has a strong sense of justice but cannot always take one side or the other. The primary need here is for active, equal relationships. Social Libra translates into someone who may be making the introductions and connections to further projects, but it also can mean an aversion to standing alone. Principled, cooperative, and idealistic, Mars in Libra is a *balanced* energy.

Mars in Scorpio ♂ ♏

In Scorpio, Mars manifests itself in self-reliance, self-discipline, and determination. With its powerful desires (which it prefers to keep to itself, because this is a very secretive energy), intense Mars in Scorpio means to get what it wants. Mars here can be courageous or set in its ways and so can also be charismatic or stubborn—or both. Forceful and thorough, Mars in Scorpio is a *highly focused* energy.

Mars in Sagittarius ♂ ♐

Far-sighted Mars in Sagittarius is often at the forefront of adventure—and might be just as quickly off on yet another adventure. Mars here is daring and bold, and also open and honest, but its energies can be scattered, and its openness a little too frank for some. Because Mars in Sagittarius has strong philosophical or religious convictions, it can manifest itself in a cause or patriotism. Above all, Mars in Sagittarius is an *exploring* energy.

> **StarFacts**
>
> Hey—listen to the music! Mars in Sagittarius folks include drummer Gene Krupa, composers John Philip Sousa and Johann Sebastian Bach, and singer Joan Baez.

Mars in Capricorn ♂ ♑

In Capricorn, Mars has everything under control: It's persistent, ordered, disciplined, and authoritative. Mars in Capricorn wants success, and it's willing to work to get there. There's no impulsiveness here; Mars in Capricorn always makes plans, and then follows through on them. Depending on what Mars in Capricorn wants, it can seem disinterested in areas that don't matter to it. Above all, Mars in Capricorn is a *controlled* energy.

Mars in Aquarius ♂ ♒

Mars in Aquarius can be the eccentric's success story: Here is where you'll find Howard Hughes's Mars, and Leonardo da Vinci's, to name but two. Mars in Aquarius isn't afraid to experiment, and it has high principles and technical expertise to go along with its originality. Mars in Aquarius can be impatient with those who don't share its ideals, and it can seem decidedly detached from the mainstream, but Mars here is a *progressive* energy, looking toward the future as if it were already here.

Mars in Pisces ♂ ♓

Mars in Pisces has the gifts of imagination, sensitivity, and intuition, which are often manifested in the creative fields. Mars here seeks involvement, whether with a partner, an idea, or a passion, and will often shoulder others' responsibilities without complaint. In fact, Mars can be self-sacrificing here—or it can inspire others in some way. Pisces Mars can be unfocused, too, or even restless. Above all Mars in Pisces is a *subtle* energy.

The Least You Need to Know

◆ Your Moon ☽ reveals your emotional nature.

◆ Your Mercury ☿ reveals your mental nature.

◆ Your Venus ♀ reveals your love nature.

◆ Your Mars ♂ reveals how you act.

Chapter 12

The Social Planets: You and Your World

In This Chapter

♦ The social planets: rewards and limits

♦ Jupiter ♃: here comes Santa Claus

♦ Saturn ♄: just the facts, ma'am

The *luminaries* and *personal planets* that you read about in Chapter 11—the Sun ☉, Moon ☽, Mercury ☿, Venus ♀, and Mars ♂—manifest their energies in the ways you reveal *yourself*. The *social planets*, Jupiter ♃ and Saturn ♄, manifest their energies in your *interactions with the world around you*.

These two planets are more socially oriented for a number of reasons. First of all, their orbits take longer than those of the personal planets, and so their connections to us are going to manifest in ways that affect far more than our own world.

Second, because those orbits take longer, people of a certain age are going to have certain things in common. Jupiter, for example, takes 12 years to complete its cycle around the Sun, so it takes one year to pass through each sign of the zodiac. That means that everyone of a certain age will share Jupiter in the same sign and have common social values.

Last, these planets are associated with our more social aspects. Jupiter represents our philosophy, higher education, and religious beliefs; Saturn represents our responsibilities, structures, communities, and organizations.

Jupiter ♃: Here Comes Santa Claus

Jupiter represents your confidence and vitality, and symbolizes growth, optimism, success, and generosity. Astrologers look at your Jupiter to find your opportunities for expansion and success, as well as to see how you might use your higher mind and education, faith, religion, or philosophy to achieve those goals.

Jupiter can be excessive: This is the planet of overindulgence and overextension. But your expansive and optimistic Jupiter will always reveal how you grow and change.

How You Grow: Jupiter ♃ in Each Zodiac Sign

Jupiter in the signs describes how you expand yourself by working with others in society. It also reveals your belief system, your interest in higher education, and how you do things on a large scale. Jupiter in the signs also shows how you might benefit materially, as well as how you might be confident—or overconfident.

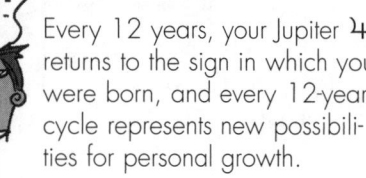

> **StarFacts**
>
> The father of all gods and men, a Jupiter archetype can be found in every type of mythology. Because it's always expansive, generous, and cheerful, it should come as no surprise that the Jupiter archetype most familiar to western cultures is Santa Claus. That's right—jolly old St. Nick!

> **Heaven Knows**
>
> Every 12 years, your Jupiter ♃ returns to the sign in which you were born, and every 12-year cycle represents new possibilities for personal growth.

Jupiter in Aries ♃ ♈

In Aries, Jupiter has a child's enthusiasm, an independent spirit, and a need to strike out on its own. This also is a very courageous Jupiter, but because of this exceptional courage, it can also be the "fool who rushes in where angels fear to tread." There will be a natural talent for leadership here, and Jupiter in Aries is often innovative as well. Although it can sometimes be rash or naive, Jupiter in Aries grows *enthusiastically*.

Jupiter in Taurus ♃ ♉

Jupiter in Taurus understands the value of life, money, and resources and likes the things that money buys: Taurus is the money sign, and Jupiter brings abundance, so it's a good match. Not only does Jupiter here have an eye for art, it often is artistic itself, and might conduct its career at home. All this stability can make it a tad smug, but Jupiter in Taurus grows *steadily*.

Jupiter in Gemini ♃ ♊

Adventurous Jupiter in Gemini has a knack for getting into advantageous situations and usually does best in intellectual areas. Jupiter here is sociable, popular, and knowledgeable about a wide variety of interests, and can actually become an intellectual snob. Jupiter here may travel a great deal, too. Jupiter in Gemini grows *mentally*.

> **StarFacts**
>
> Jupiter in Gemini celebrities include actress Ingrid Bergman, actor Steve McQueen, composer Igor Stravinsky, and boxer Muhammad Ali.

Jupiter in Cancer ♃ ♋

Generous Jupiter in Cancer is sympathetic toward others, with a good nature, a good sense of humor, and an optimistic disposition. Jupiter in Cancer is good with money, too, and everything that Jupiter in Cancer cares for prospers. These people can become overindulgent, both with themselves and with others, but Jupiter in Cancer grows *emotionally*.

✗ Jupiter in Leo ♃ ♌

Noble Jupiter in Leo is big-hearted and self-confident and radiates warmth and generosity. Jupiter in Leo thinks big and can inspire others to think big as well. With its flair for drama and its charismatic charm, Jupiter in Leo can sometimes get big-headed, but overall, Jupiter in Leo grows *magnanimously*.

Jupiter in Virgo ♃ ♍

Practical Jupiter in Virgo values work and service to others and can succeed through its smarts and perseverance. Even though many point to a conflict between Jupiter's expansiveness and Virgo's need for precision, these qualities don't need to cancel each other out; Jupiter in Virgo can actually use its methodical approach to growth to great ends. Jupiter in Virgo grows *pragmatically*.

Jupiter in Libra ♃ ♎

Artistic Jupiter in Libra is cooperative and charming and often finds its greatest area of growth through partnership. Morally conventional, Jupiter in Libra has a strong sense of justice and is always honorable in its dealings with others. Because this isn't a sign for the sole practitioner, Jupiter in Libra grows *socially*.

Jupiter in Scorpio ♃ ♏

Shrewd Jupiter in Scorpio has great faith in itself and takes itself very seriously. Jupiter in Scorpio indicates a strong need to probe for the truth behind religious doctrine or belief systems. These people are often involved in large-scale joint or corporate finances, and they can have a strong desire to gain wealth or control over others. Jupiter in Scorpio grows *powerfully*.

Jupiter in Sagittarius ♃ ♐

Farsighted Jupiter in Sagittarius can see its opportunities and act on them, and, with Jupiter in its rulership, the planet's expansiveness and generosity enjoy the spotlight. Optimistic and enthusiastic, Jupiter's enthusiasm pays off here. Jupiter in Sagittarius is heavily interested in philosophy, belief systems, foreign cultures, travel, and higher education. It has a strong tendency to choose a particular set of beliefs and then to try to convert others to it. Jupiter in Sagittarius grows *zealously*.

Jupiter in Capricorn ♃ ♑

Ambitious Jupiter in Capricorn seeks financial and material wealth and is patient and dedicated enough to achieve its goals. Hard work and willpower pay off here, as does fiscal conservatism. Jupiter in Capricorn has high integrity, especially in business ethics and its responsibilities. Although Jupiter in Capricorn is often charitable, it can become miserly. Jupiter in Capricorn grows *expediently*.

Jupiter in Aquarius ♃ ♒

Open-minded Jupiter in Aquarius might find its fortune through the people it meets because it's always open to new ideas and is both intuitive and impartial. Jupiter in Aquarius wants a world without class, race, or religious distinctions and works for a world that's impartial, democratic, and universal. With their tolerance for different values and lifestyles, people with Jupiter in Aquarius are idealistic and humanitarian. Sometimes rebellious, easily bored, Jupiter in Aquarius nonetheless grows *innovatively*.

Jupiter in Pisces ♃ ♓

In one of its home signs, Pisces, Jupiter's strength is its emotional depth, and others find Jupiter in Pisces friendly and unassuming. Jupiter in Pisces can mean you achieve your secret ideal. You're imaginative and creative, often finding great success in the arts. Altruistic and compassionate, Jupiter in Pisces also can be mysterious and reclusive. Jupiter in Pisces grows *imaginatively*.

Saturn ♄: Just the Facts, Ma'am

Jupiter represents your expansive side, but Saturn's all about responsibility, rules, and regulations. Your Saturn is concerned with self-discipline and self-respect, your lessons, duties, and limitations, and also represents the authority figures in your life. Later in life, it also represents your own authority.

Although Saturn's not going to be telling a whole lot of jokes, he *is* responsible for whatever lasting achievements you earn, especially your triumphs over obstacles. Saturn is your ambitious side and so is well aware of your strengths and weaknesses.

Saturn also is about security and safety, and as such is the teacher of the zodiac, with many lessons to impart—if we pay attention. In other words, there won't be any reward until you get your homework for your life lessons done!

Because Saturn represents the father or father figure, many refer to this planet as the policeman of the zodiac. We think that this is limiting and doesn't really show all the areas where Saturn's energy is manifested. After all, your Saturn is reflected in your perseverance, too.

> **StarFacts**
>
> Saturn reminds us that to live as social creatures, we must abide by certain laws that are both terrestrial and universal. In Blackfoot myth, Saturn is called "The Old Man." In one story, he tells the people he has created, "What is made law must be law. We will undo nothing that we have done." Not a fun guy to have at parties!

Heaven Knows

It takes Saturn 29½ years to complete its orbit and return to its placement at your birth. This return point can be thought of as a major life progress report, a point where you can assess your strengths and weaknesses and plan your future accordingly. In fact, this return is what makes people 30 and over different from those in their 20s, and why it's known as the "first hill"—or "over the hill."

Knowing Your Limits: Saturn ♄ in Each Zodiac Sign

Saturn in the signs describes the kinds of responsibilities you will be challenged by as well as the lessons you must learn. It also gives clues about the type of career you will have and how you relate to authority figures.

Saturn in Aries ♄ ♈

Impetuous Aries is forced to slow down with Saturn placed here, and this might be manifested in a powerful father or authority figure. Saturn in Aries is learning independence, self-reliance, patience, and initiative and can become singularly self-reliant—or headstrong, defiant, and defensive. Saturn in Aries needs to *learn to be independent and self-reliant,* and it also needs to learn to *cooperate* with others in order to be successful.

Saturn in Taurus ♄ ♉

Saturn's great strength, combined with its strong purpose, is mirrored in Taurus, and this placement can be determined and responsible. Saturn in Taurus sticks to its guns—and might make everyone else stick to them, too. Sometimes Saturn in Taurus can seem downright selfish, but that's because the lesson here is to *learn not to place so much emphasis on the material.*

Saturn in Gemini ♄ ♊

Saturn in Gemini can translate into a great capacity for problem-solving, and this placement indicates lifelong learning. Saturn disciplines flighty Gemini, giving Gemini's natural intelligence the patience it needs to succeed. The lesson for Saturn in Gemini is to *learn what one doesn't yet know.*

Saturn in Cancer ♄ ♋

Saturn in Cancer is a difficult placement and can indicate problems in early childhood that are not easily resolved. Saturn here seeks approval and security from others but does not always get it. The lesson for Saturn in Cancer is to *learn to self-nurture rather than depend on others.* If this lesson is learned, it will be manifested in a quiet and dignified self-assurance.

Saturn in Leo ♄ ♌

Saturn is tremendously self-assured in Leo and can be downright bombastic if there's nothing to stop it. People with this placement have a need for positions of leadership and power to fulfill their need for recognition and importance. Because the ego is strong here—and the values distorted—Saturn's lesson in Leo is to *learn appropriate values for managing others and for dealing with creativity, children, love, and romance.*

> **StarFacts**
>
> The charismatic placement of Saturn in Leo includes Adolf Hitler, Charlie Chaplin, Indira Gandhi—and Liberace!

Saturn in Virgo ♄ ♍

Responsible Saturn and practical Virgo work well together: Saturn helps Virgo achieve its goals. At the same time, Saturn in Virgo can be driven, letting nothing stand in its way, especially pleasure. This can make for a serious nature in this placement, and the lesson for Saturn in Virgo is to *learn that it's possible to enjoy living simply.*

> **StarFacts**
>
> Responsible Saturns in Virgo include former Chief Justice of the Supreme Court Earl Warren, former President Dwight D. Eisenhower, and German Field Marshall Erwin Rommel, the "Desert Fox" of World War II.

Saturn in Libra ♄ ♎

Saturn in Libra is responsible and fair and works very well with others. Saturn adds decisiveness to Libra's good judgment and often heralds great success in public life. This placement understands the need to establish long-lasting relationships with others to effectively build anything of long-term value. The lesson for Saturn in Libra is to *learn cooperation in order to develop long-term relationships.*

Saturn in Scorpio ♄ ♏

Saturn in Scorpio understands what makes people tick and uses this knowledge to further its goals. Serious, capable, resourceful, and insightful, Saturn in Scorpio is likely to do well wherever it decides to succeed. Because there's so much power at play here, the lesson for Saturn in Scorpio is to *use its power wisely and appropriately.*

Saturn in Sagittarius ♄ ♐

Saturn in Sagittarius can turn ideas into reality through its capacity for intellectual discipline, but it also can meet with drawbacks early in its life. As this placement grows older, it often learns wisdom as it goes, and as it does, it becomes more and more focused. Saturn in Sagittarius needs to *learn patience and perseverance.*

Saturn in Capricorn ♄ ♑

Saturn in Capricorn is happily ambitious and persistent and means to succeed—and it probably will, because Saturn rules Capricorn. Saturn here is unswerving in its goals, disciplined, and hardworking, but may be ruthless as well. The lesson for Saturn in Capricorn is that *there is more to life than one's position.*

Saturn in Aquarius ♄ ♒

Saturn in one of its home signs, Aquarius, wants to run the whole show. It wants both freedom and order, all in the same package. Saturn can actually manifest quite well in individualistic Aquarius, especially when it is "allowed" to keep its stance of detached observation, or it can fight every step of the way. Saturn in Aquarius needs to find what's inhibiting it and then *learn to set itself free*.

Saturn in Pisces ♄ ♓

Saturn in Pisces can be very resourceful, because it refuses to be pigeonholed. Its imagination can lead to creative success, but its sensitivity can mean great disappointments occur with this placement, too. The lesson for Saturn in Pisces is to *learn to trust itself in order to help others trust themselves*.

The Least You Need to Know

- The social planets show you your rewards and limits.
- Your Jupiter ♃ reveals how you grow.
- Your Saturn ♄ reveals your responsibilities and lessons.

Chapter 13

The Outer Planets and the Nodes: The Bigger Picture

In This Chapter

- Uranus ♅: born to be wild
- Neptune ♆: dream a little dream
- Pluto ♇: soul man
- The North Node ☊ and South Node ☋: back to the future

Uranus ♅, Neptune ♆, and Pluto ♇ are the *transpersonal* planets, concerned with energies beyond the self and universal connections. Uranus, the planet of the unexpected, rules revolution and invention; Neptune is the planet of dreams and hunches and the realms of the unconscious; and Pluto is the planet of change and transformation.

Always paired in opposite signs, the Nodes of the Moon represent the tensions of your life, the comfort of your past versus the uncertainty of your future. Through your Nodes, you can discover which lessons you've mastered and those you've yet to learn.

Uranus ♅: Born to Be Wild

Uranus is the Ice Man: invention, originality, sudden or unexpected change, and revolution, as well as breakthroughs, and radical ideas. The first of the three "late discoveries," Uranus was first found in 1781, so its connection with revolution should not come as a surprise.

StarFacts

In Cherokee myth, one dry summer a great fire burned all across the mountains. The people, concerned, sought out the Ice Man who lived very far in the North and was the only one who could put out such a large fire. "Yes," the Ice Man told them, "I can put out this fire." Then he unplaited his long hair and shook it, releasing first wind, then rain, then sleet, and finally, snow. At first, the wind merely made the fire larger, and then the rain made it steam, but the sleet and the snow finally put it out. In the spring, a lake appeared where the fire had burned a deep pit.

Uranus both questions and challenges authority, and transcends business-as-usual social and cultural ideas to arrive at new solutions. Uranus insists on our freedom, but it also understands that humans need to learn about freedom one step at a time.

Uranus is the planet of intuition and the sixth sense, the ruler of astrologers and inventors, and is also closely associated with electricity, technology, and electronics.

It takes Uranus 84 years to complete its orbit around the Sun and 7 years to move from one sign into another. In 1996, it passed out of Capricorn ♑—a tough place for Uranus—into Aquarius ♒, its natural sign. And on March 14, 2003, it moved into Pisces ♓. After a brief retrograde back into Aquarius in the fall of 2004, Uranus will remain in Pisces for the rest of most of our lives. Expect some exciting and surprising changes: Uranus is the planet of the future, of science, and innovation, and its domain is all that is unusual, different, or unorthodox.

Your Liberator: Uranus ♅ in Each Zodiac Sign

The sign Uranus is in reveals how your age group is unusual and shows how it manifests its desire for freedom, authenticity, and individuality. The house your personal Uranus is in describes your own uniqueness and where you need to "break the rules." It also heralds the kinds of historical changes that occur during its seven-year cycles.

Uranus in Aries ♅ ♈ (b. 1928–1934/1935)

Uranus in Aries is a pioneer, quick to make a break from the conventional and take off in new, unexplored directions for both social reform and new breakthroughs in science. The most recent Uranus in Aries generation has a strong desire to do what it wants to do. Bound and determined to stick to their guns, much of their lives were blown up by them, too: This generation's lives were heavily torn apart by World War II and the Korean War. As this generation ages, it tends to tell younger ones that they have no respect for "the good old days," which, during this last transit, included the heyday of everything from labor unions to bootleggers. Uranus in Aries liberates *impetuously*.

Uranus in Taurus ♅ ♉ (b. 1934/1935–1942)

Uranus in Taurus is very strong and signals both willpower and determination. Generationally, Uranus in Taurus's reform instincts regard attitudes toward money and freedom. This was the time of the worst of the Great Depression and the onset of World War II. Uranus in Taurus can be too materialistic, but that can be because early needs can fuel desire. Uranus in Taurus liberates *improvisationally*.

Uranus in Gemini ♅ ♊ (b. 1942–1949)

In Gemini, Uranus is both inventive and original, taking creative approaches to everything from literature to electronics, both of which concern communication. Communication of any sort is highlighted here, in fact, and these are the years of great leaps forward in science, technology, metaphysics, and universal education. Uranus in Gemini liberates *mentally*.

Uranus in Cancer ♅ ♋ (b. 1949–1955/1956)

Uranus in Cancer is very sensitive to others, with well-developed intuitive powers and a flair for the eccentric and unpredictable. This is the generation that rebelled against its parents during the Summer of Love and Woodstock, after all. Uranus in Cancer people have nontraditional ideas about home and family, preferring to be friends with their parents instead of relating to them only as traditional authoritarian figures, and they desire emotional freedom and excitement. Uranus in Cancer liberates *emotionally*.

Uranus in Leo ♅ ♌ (b. 1955/1956–1962)

Uranus in Leo has boundless determination and is perfectly willing to overthrow anything that doesn't go along with what it feels works best. New tools and new techniques for using those tools are found here, especially in areas of creative expression. This was the era of the Beat generation, including Kerouac, Burroughs, and Ginsberg, and John F. Kennedy's "New Frontier." Uranus in Leo liberates *creatively*.

Uranus in Virgo ♅ ♍ (b. 1962–1968/1969)

Uranus in Virgo is concerned with reforming work methods and attitudes toward health. Note that this period was when computers were first being used in the workplace. Technical advances are right up Uranus in Virgo's alley, as is the renewed interest in ecology, natural foods, and environmental concerns that began during this time. Uranus in Virgo liberates *discriminately*.

Uranus in Libra ♅ ♎ (b. 1968/1969–1974/1975)

Uranus in Libra has a strong social conscience and is interested in bringing about new ways of looking at old social traditions like marriage, partnership, and other social areas. One of the results of this has been "political correctness," a well-meaning idea gone somewhat amok, but Uranus here often finds unusual solutions—and friends and lovers. Uranus in Libra liberates *socially*.

Uranus in Scorpio ♅ ♏ (b. 1974/1975–1981)

Uranus in Scorpio is a powerful pairing, and during this time, both the Three Mile Island nuclear power plant and the volcano Mount St. Helens had unexpected explosions. Those born with Uranus in Scorpio are just now beginning to discover their power for change and also are discovering what can happen when power and sexuality are misunderstood, as in the case of AIDS. This pairing has the potential to awaken others to what is really happening and liberates *powerfully*.

Uranus in Sagittarius ♅ ♐ (b. 1981–1988)

Uranus in Sagittarius is optimistic and seeks the future, with a liberal and progressive outlook. This generation's intention is religious, legal, cultural, and academic reform, and all of these institutions underwent a period of public distrust during this era. Individuals born during this time have a strong belief in universal laws and the freedom to follow their own convictions. Uranus in Sagittarius liberates *progressively*.

Heaven Knows

The marriages and divorces of Prince Charles and Princess Diana and Prince Andrew and Fergie both occurred while Uranus was in Capricorn, wreaking havoc with anything that reeked of tradition.

Uranus in Capricorn ♅ ♑ (b. 1905–1912, 1988–1995/1996)

Uranus in Capricorn works at breaking down old, worn-out structures and organizations in order to create a better future, and in its most recent transit this meant everything from toppling the Berlin Wall and the Soviet Union to the American political scandals that seemed to top the news in the mid-1990s. Capricious Uranus is channeled into constructive directions in Capricorn and so liberates *constructively*.

Uranus in Aquarius ♅ ♒ (b. 1912–1919, 1995/1996–2003)

In its own sign, Uranus is radical, inventive, scientific, and universal, with a deep desire to change *everything* for the better. In this period, we had a sheep cloned, and the nearly literal explosion of e-mail, the World Wide Web, and global communication, as well as the dramatic rise and fall of the stock market. This is the period when everyone from heretics to eccentrics has their day. Uranus in Aquarius likes things to work demo-cratically, impartially, and universally, so anything that's not working according to those principles is subject to change. Uranus in Aquarius liberates *inventively*—and *democratically*.

Uranus in Pisces ♅ ♓ (b. 1919–1927, 2003–2011)

Uranus in Pisces has an abiding sense of mystery—and of the mysterious. During its last pairing, Uranus in Pisces saw everything from the Russian Revolution to the "anything goes" Roaring Twenties, as well as the great rise of the motion picture as mass entertainment. Uranus in Pisces people are often actors, or might be known for other creative abilities. Uranus in Pisces liberates *universally*.

During our current Uranus in Pisces transit, we look for a trend toward global govern-ment, creative solutions to previously insoluble problems, and the rise of a universal sensibility. Check back with us in seven years and see how we did!

Neptune ♆: Dream a Little Dream

A billion miles beyond Uranus, invisible to the naked eye, lies Neptune, the planet that governs the unknown. Neptune was discovered in 1846, shortly before Sigmund Freud was born. The areas a planet repre-sents don't find their Earthly manifestation, after all, until we on Earth "discover" that planet.

Neptune naturally represents all matters related to water and liquids, music and movies, glamour, dreams, and illusion. It also rules spirituality, ideals, hunches, and things we intuitively know. Neptune is the planet of the mystical, of fog and flattery and fra-grance, of allusion and addiction, of hypnosis and hypochondria.

> **StarFacts**
>
> In Greek mythology, the Universe was divided into three realms at creation: the heavens, ruled by Zeus (Jupiter); the underworld, ruled by Hades (Pluto); and the oceans, ruled by Poseidon (Nep-tune). So Neptune, the Sea God, is the ruler of the waters, the ruler of dreams—the ruler, in other words, of the unknown.

AstroLingo

Planetary **natives** have an astrological commonality, such as a planet in the same sign or house.

It takes Neptune 165 years to orbit the Sun and approximately 14 years to pass through each sign. Like all the generational planets, its influence will be felt during its times as well as by its *natives*, and its personal importance will be ascertained through its house position as well.

How You're Inspired: Neptune Ψ in Each Zodiac Sign

Neptune through the signs represents both your generation's spiritual urge and its urge to escape—its dreams and illusions. The house your personal Neptune lies in describes your own dreams, illusions, and spiritual needs. Most of all, Neptune's sign reveals how each generation is inspired.

Neptune moves very slowly and retrogrades about half of each year, so it often takes two years to transition to a new sign.

Neptune in Cancer Ψ♋ (b. 1901/2002–1914/1916)

Neptune in Cancer has a deep sentiment for nature and anything having to do with roots or family and is often psychic, spiritual, and idealistic. This placement indicates an abiding faith in "the good old days," and Neptune's last transit was a period when the world headed toward wars about patriotic nationalism and ethnic issues. Also during that time, President Teddy Roosevelt led a campaign against big business (opposite Capricorn, in other words) to protect the rights of the common people. Freud's work with the subconscious mind became recognized during this time as well. Neptune in Cancer natives are emotionally sensitive and intuitive, and are *sentimentally* inspired.

Neptune in Leo Ψ♌ (b. 1914/1916–1928/1929)

Neptune in Leo is romantic, idealistic, and artistic. Just think about the art styles like Cubism and Dadaism that appeared and how the big jazz bands broke through the restrictions on self-expression during this period. The Neptune in Leo generation had a flair for the dramatic and a sometimes unrealistic sense of what love and romance are all about. But Leo also rules speculation, and during this period there was a lot of unwise investment and market speculations, which led, as you might recall, to the big stock-market crash and the beginning of the Great Depression that occurred when Neptune moved into Virgo ♍. Either way, though, Neptune in Leo is *creatively* inspired.

Neptune in Virgo Ψ ♍ (b. 1928/1929–1942/1943)

Neptune in Virgo is the first generation to feel the pull between reason (rational science) and emotion (psychiatry), and also is the generation of both the Great Depression and World War II. Virgo rules employment, and there was a great lack of employment during this period. Remember, Neptune dissolves, and it certainly dissolved the high times of the Roaring '20s. During this period, the greed and pleasure of Leo were replaced with a concern for working people and service to society. Neptune in Virgo natives have a careful approach to life, a result of their tough early years, and are concerned with using ideals to achieve practical ends, although they might learn to rely more on their intuition. Neptune in Virgo is *practically* inspired.

Neptune in Libra Ψ ♎ (b. 1942/1943–1955/1957)

Neptune in romantic Libra emphasizes both idealism and love, and this generation is interested in new ways of looking at relationships and laws. This is the generation that confronted sexual equality, marched for peace, experimented with LSD, and cares deeply about injustice throughout the world. Sometimes this Neptune's intentions can have unfortunate results: The Neptune in Libra period saw the end of World War II—and then the beginning of the Cold War. Neptune in Libra was also when marriages were subject to uncertainty (war time made this difficult) and disillusionment. This period is when the divorce rate began increasing, too. Still, Neptune in Libra is *idealistically* inspired.

Neptune in Scorpio Ψ ♏ (b. 1955/1957–1970)

Neptune in Scorpio can be self-destructive—and potently powerful. The purpose of Neptune in Scorpio is to encourage spiritual regeneration. But because most people didn't follow this path during this most recent transit, it degenerated into exploiting sex for commercial purposes. The birth-control pill dissolved fears of getting pregnant, but this, in turn, led to a higher incidence of venereal diseases. This is also the generation of the drug culture and rock music, and advances in civil rights, which were connected to dissolving the established power bases. Neptune in Scorpio natives have an enormous capacity for renewal, especially spiritually, and there also can be an extraordinary capacity for psychic awareness or an interest in the occult. This period saw the beginnings of tremendous change in every facet of life; after all, Neptune in Scorpio is *intensely* inspired.

Neptune in Sagittarius Ψ♐ (b. 1970–1984)

Neptune in Sagittarius is open, honest, and idealistic, and astrologers put great store by the generations born in Sagittarius, the sign of higher learning, philosophy, and freedom. During its last transit here, we saw Watergate brought out in the open, and Jimmy Carter, an idealistic Washington outsider, elected President. Neptune's last transit also was a period of universal travel, as millions of people began to see the world. New and mystical religions sprang up all over, and music and art were often spiritually oriented. Personal fitness and outdoor sports also became popular. Neptune in Sagittarius natives often feel a need for greater religious and philosophical values and might revise existing laws or ways of thinking to reflect that need. Neptune in Sagittarius is *prophetically* inspired.

Neptune in Capricorn Ψ♑ (b. 1984–1998)

This period was a time that was recognized for its dissolving of worn-out governments and economic structures. The USSR dissolved, the Berlin Wall fell, and all around the world new countries were formed or reformed after years of being swallowed up by others. Communism collapsed, and here in the United States, we began facing the need for socialized medicine and other necessary reforms. Economic and political structures—society's organizations—are associated with Capricorn. Neptune in Capricorn natives have a deep sense of responsibility and self-discipline, and great courage and purpose to achieve their goals. Neptune in Capricorn is *constructively* inspired.

Neptune in Aquarius Ψ♒ (b. 1998–2012)

When Neptune was last in Aquarius, 1834 to 1847, it was a time of the transcendental literature movement, the first use of anesthetics, and the discovery of uranium. This was a period when many people pursued idealistic causes, campaigned for reforms such as the end of slavery, and strove for humanitarian and utopian ideals. Neptune in Aquarius natives have a knack for the abstract, resulting in new approaches to everything from the arts to the sciences. This period is expected to herald the beginning of the New Age, insofar as new social reforms to further the brotherhood and sisterhood of humankind are put into effect around the world. Witness how, 50 years after its founding, the function and service of the United Nations is being tested and explored by an increasingly global community as it recognizes the need for an effective multinational forum for issues of all natures—from political to environmental to humanitarian, and more. New technologies and achievements also are expected, which are predicted to set new trends for many years into the future. Neptune in Aquarius is *inventively* inspired.

Pluto ♀: Soul Journey

Planet Pluto is so far from Earth that it wasn't even discovered until 1930. And it was only after its discovery that scientists learned how to split the atom and about the atomic power that comes with it. As we noted in Chapter 10, Pluto survived an attempt to demote it from planetness—but that's no surprise from the planet of transformation.

It takes Pluto approximately 248 years to orbit the Sun, and it spends anywhere from 11 to 32 years in each sign, making it the most generational of the transpersonal planets. Learning what your Pluto is about takes time, as its energies are abstract, but they're also very deep and far-reaching.

StarFacts

We told you in an earlier chapter about the abduction of Persephone from the point of view of her mother, Demeter (Ceres). But let's look at it from Pluto's point of view: There he is, stuck in this dark underworld, with no one but the souls of the dead. Who can blame him for kidnapping a pretty girl to keep him company? That he lets her go for part of each year shows us Pluto's transformative powers and capacity for renewal, regeneration, and resurrection.

As the ruler of the underworld, Pluto is naturally associated with death, but death also is about renewal and transformation. Sometimes it takes an enormous setback or challenge to force us onto a new course; and remember, too, that the same force can be either creative or destructive, like atomic energy. It all depends on how that energy gets used.

Pluto's position in your birth chart can show how you're changing and represents both your transformative and destructive urges. Your Pluto truly is both your end and your beginning.

How You're Changing: Pluto ♀ in Each Zodiac Sign

On an individual basis, Pluto represents the soul's journey, its evolutionary intent or purpose, and what the soul has chosen to learn throughout the entire life. Although astrology leaves the question about belief in past lives up to each individual, there is generally an understanding that each person or soul is evolving during one's lifetime.

Certain branches of astrology also believe that each person is evolving over many lifetimes until he or she is ready to return to and merge with the Source, or the God of your understanding. Because it is the most generational planet, Pluto is personally revealed by its house position rather than its sign's. So to find your soul's evolutionary purpose, see your Pluto's house placement in one of the next four chapters.

Generationally, Pluto through the signs always indicates permanent changes for the world, both regenerative and destructive, in the areas associated with the sign it's in, and describes the major global and collective changes occurring at the time. Because Pluto moves so slowly, we're only going to look at it in the signs for people who are alive now (or soon will be).

Pluto in Gemini ♀♊ (b. 1882/1884–1912/1914)

During the last Pluto transit in Gemini, communications and transportation discoveries seemed to be a daily occurrence. Everything from the telephone to the airplane was invented during this period. Pluto in Gemini also opened up the avenues of exploring the human mind through psychoanalysis, a manifestation of the way Pluto's personal power interacts with the Gemini mind. Pluto in Gemini natives seek new ways to *communicate and transform their intellects.*

Pluto in Cancer ♀♋ (b. 1912/1914–1937/1939)

Pluto in Cancer means a major upheaval in family life, last witnessed during both World War I and the Great Depression, when millions of families were forced from their homes. Pluto in Cancer also is connected to a patriotic love of country and so is associated with the rise of nationalism during the 1930s in Germany, Italy, and Japan, as well as in the countries of the Allied Powers. Pluto in Cancer natives seek new ways to *achieve emotional security and maturity and often love to break with tradition.*

Pluto in Leo ♀♌ (b. 1937/1939–1956/1958)

Pluto in Leo is all about power: witness World War II, the Cold War, the Korean War, and McCarthyism. This period saw the first atomic bomb, dictatorships all over the world, and the creation of the state of Israel and the United Nations. Power can be used for either good or evil, and the Pluto in Leo generation, with its natural self-confidence and sense of authority, seeks new ways to *utilize power*—sometimes for good, and sometimes for not-so-good.

Pluto in Virgo ♀♍ (b. 1956/1958–1971/1972)

Tremendous changes in labor and industry resulted during the most recent Pluto in Virgo period: Computers arrived in the workplace; new medical discoveries made enormous strides in both preventing and combating disease; and humans set foot on the Moon, a technological feat unparalleled before or since. Pluto in Virgo natives are analytical, and often perfectionists, and they seek new ways to *solve profound problems.*

Pluto in Libra ♀ ♎ (b. 1971/1972–1983/1984)

The most recent Pluto in Libra period brought both prison reform (and prison riots) and changes in the arts and international relations. Libra's egalitarianism was manifested here in everything from the end of the war in Vietnam to Nixon's trip to China to the healing of the nation after the storm of Watergate. Pluto in Libra natives seek *harmony and cooperation*, and, as this generation reaches adulthood, we can already see the results of their Plutonian energies in their music and writing.

Pluto in Scorpio ♀ ♏ (b. 1983/1984–1995)

Pluto's most recent time in Scorpio saw a resurgence in interest in natural healing, and the rediscovery of New Age ideas. The most recent Pluto in Scorpio transit was the beginning of AIDS, and the period when all the "taboos"—rape, incest, sexual abuse, and scandals—came out in the open. The basic theme of this period is reform and transform. Pluto in Scorpio natives (remember, Pluto is Scorpio's ruler) are sensitive to their environment, emotionally intense, intrigued with the mysterious, and seek *spiritual regeneration*, sweeping away anything that stands in the way of their quest.

Pluto in Sagittarius ♀ ♐ (b. 1995–2008)

Pluto in Sagittarius signals the transformation of all the major social systems: education, health care, law, and religion. The latter includes a resurgence in fundamentalism and dogmatism as well as growth in spirituality. It's also interesting that the predictions for the "last pope" are expected to be fulfilled during this period, which could indicate a major shift in the Catholic religion. This certainly promises to be an era of new values in everything from philosophy and politics to foreign affairs. The Pluto in Sagittarius generation seeks *personal freedom*, but also has a great faith in human nature, and is both philosophical and humane.

The Nodes ☋☊: Back to the Future

You could think of the Moon's Nodes as the particular tensions in your life: the pull and comfort of the past versus the fear and uncertainty of the future. Always exactly opposite each other on your birth chart, your Nodes are the push-me/pull-you energies in your life.

Your South Node ☋ indicates lessons and talents that you have already mastered, what could be perceived as the "easy way out." Your South Node is your past, your history, and who you've been, and is generally believed to represent a composite of your past lives.

Because you've already mastered your South Node skills, talents, and lessons, there's no growth, learning, or challenge when you continue to use them. You also won't get any "kudos" or appreciation for using those skills, even though you do them very well. When you do use these aspects of yourself, you'll often find it depleting to do so. This is the Universe's way of encouraging you to follow the growth path of your North Node.

Your North Node ☊ indicates lessons you are here to learn, what could be perceived as "the hard way"— but worth the effort. Your North Node is your future and your greatest opportunities for growth; in short, your development path. This is where you will find fulfillment, increased confidence, and rewards for your efforts, the areas where you'll gain new knowledge, new ideas, and all types of growth, which in turn will lead to fruition.

Coming and Going: The Nodal Pairs ☊☋ in Each Zodiac Sign

Because the Nodes are always exactly opposite each other in your chart, their interpretations are likewise presented in pairs. Simply look for your North Node sign description, and your South Node will be included there, too.

North Node in Aries ☊♈/South Node in Libra ☋ ♎

A North Node in Aries/South Node in Libra is someone who has already learned cooperation and how to work with others, but might be dependent on others, too. These people now need to develop independence, initiative, and self-confidence, and learn how to stand on their own. It is an excellent placement for developing leadership abilities and using the relationship skills of the past to create a basis of support.

North Node in Taurus ☊♉/South Node in Scorpio ☋♏

A North Node in Taurus/South Node in Scorpio is someone who has already learned about power, the occult, and transformation, but might have had the rug pulled out from under them in the past. These people now need to learn a new set of values to live by, as well as how to stabilize their energies through the wise use of material resources. After they realize that the Universe provides all that they need, they can create beauty, harmony, and trust.

North Node in Gemini ☊♊/South Node in Sagittarius ☋♐

A North Node in Gemini/South Node in Sagittarius is someone who has already become accustomed to freedom and seeking their truth, but might still be on a quest.

Now the growth of these people comes from communicating with others and looking at both sides of all issues. This is an excellent opportunity to share their past philosophies and truth with others through the development of new communication skills.

North Node in Cancer ☊♋/South Node in Capricorn ☋♑

A North Node in Cancer/South Node in Capricorn is someone who has already learned about responsibilities, accomplishments, and ambition. Now, these people need to learn about being sensitive, sharing their emotions, and responsibly nurturing others. They're here to give of themselves and achieve their best by doing so.

North Node in Leo ☊♌/South Node in Aquarius ☋♒

A North Node in Leo/South Node in Aquarius is someone who has already learned about being the detached, ingenious inventor, or an eccentric humanitarian. Now these people need to learn how to share their love and heart with others, through generous and noble leadership. This is an excellent opportunity to share their innovations for humanity through leadership and love.

North Node in Virgo ☊♍/South Node in Pisces ☋♓

A North Node in Virgo/South Node in Pisces is someone who has already developed compassion, intuition, and strong sensitivity to others. Now these people need to develop discernment and learn how to serve others in practical ways. They will often find opportunities to share their compassion from their past while developing their abilities in medicine, healing, or nutrition.

North Node in Libra ☊♎/South Node in Aries ☋♈

A North Node in Libra/South Node in Aries is someone who has already developed independence, self-confidence, and initiative and knows how to stand on his or her own. Now these people need to learn about cooperation and harmony and how to work with others. This is an opportunity to grow from loving others, learning objectivity and diplomacy, and balancing their needs with those of others.

North Node in Scorpio ☊♏/South Node in Taurus ☋♉

A North Node in Scorpio/South Node in Taurus is someone who has already developed a sensuous nature and stability through the accumulation and use of resources. Now these people need to learn about the deeper aspects of life and might go through a rebirth process to do so. This is an opportunity to learn about true power, transformation, and commanding their feelings.

North Node in Sagittarius ☊♐/South Node in Gemini ☋♊

A North Node in Sagittarius/South Node in Gemini is someone who has already learned how to communicate with others, gather endless data, and see all sides of issues. Now these people are here in search of higher knowledge, truth, and to realize that although there are two sides to every issue, it is still the same coin. With effort, they can turn their knowledge into Divine Understanding.

North Node in Capricorn ☊♑/South Node in Cancer ☋♋

A North Node in Capricorn/South Node in Cancer is someone who has already developed sensitivity, emotions, and nurturing ways. Now these people need to learn about responsibilities, achievement, and maturity. They now have an opportunity to bring their caring nature from the past into responsible "elder" positions, where they can serve many other people.

North Node in Aquarius ☊♒/South Node in Leo ☋♌

A North Node in Aquarius/South Node in Leo is someone who has already developed a highly creative and loving nature but has generally been focused on his or her personal life. Now this person needs to learn how to develop an impersonal, humanitarian approach to life that serves mankind. This is a chance to use past leadership skills to create universal opportunities for all.

North Node in Pisces ☊♓/South Node in Virgo ☋♍

A North Node in Pisces/South Node in Virgo is someone who has already learned how to analyze, be practical, and serve others. Now these people need to develop compassion, intuition, and a desire not to judge others. They now have an opportunity to use their past abilities to serve others in new ways by developing universal consciousness, empathy, and understanding.

The Least You Need to Know

- Uranus ♅, Neptune ♆, and Pluto ♇ are transpersonal planets that affect a generation of people and global developments.

- Uranus ♅ reveals the quest for individuality and freedom of each generation.

- Neptune ♆ reveals how each generation is inspired.

- Pluto ♇ reveals how each generation is transforming itself and the world.

- Your South Node ☋ shows your past and the lessons you've already mastered.

- Your North Node ☊ shows your future development path.

Retrogrades ℞: One Step Forward and Two Steps Back

In This Chapter

◆ Retrograde planets: reversed energies

◆ Personal retrogrades: special attention

◆ Transiting retrogrades: planning ahead

◆ A tour of planetary retrogrades

Let's get one thing straight before we begin: Planets don't really move backward! It just looks that way from here on Earth, which is, after all, our astrological vantage point for all heavenly motion.

In this chapter, you'll learn just what it means when we say a planet is retrograde ℞. We'll also explain the difference between a personal retrograde and a transiting one. Then, we'll take you on a tour of the planets—in reverse.

A Brief History of Planetary Motion

When planets are retrograde, their energies seem to be reversed. If you think of planets as energies being expressed, then you can think of retrograde planets as energies being introspective. Although this is not actually occurring (planets can only move in one direction along their orbits), this is the way it appears to look from Earth. Astrologically, this means their energy will be reversed, reconsidered, or turned inward.

Mercury retrograde ☿℞, for example, rethinks things over and over to get communications or mental processes right, unlike direct Mercury's quicksilver approach. In such situations there is potential for mental burnout, so to speak. Similarly, Mars retrograde ♂℞ must learn not to act on aggressive instincts without thinking first. Retrograde Mars must use less impulsive ways to achieve its desires and learn to reconsider actions before taking them.

Understanding Retrograde ℞ Planets

Retrograde planets aren't "bad." Just as we humans need to retreat periodically to renew our energies, so do planets. And if you're born with a *personal retrograde*, you will be reconsidering the functions associated with that particular planet. This isn't "bad" at all. Once you understand what you need to do about that particular function, you usually master it and could be known for this quality.

Transiting retrogrades affect everyone, because while the retrograde planet is off on its retreat, the energy from it will feel "different," though it's not always something we can pinpoint. During transiting Mercury retrograde, for example, there might be communication breakdowns, or your car might stop running. It seems that massive e-mail glitches have become a hallmark of Mercury retrograde, so much so that we often get phone calls asking us if Mercury is retrograde when they occur. It usually is!

AstroLingo

A **personal retrograde** means that a planet was retrograde at the time of your birth and affects only you. **Transiting retrogrades** are related to what's happening overhead at a given moment and so affect everybody. They occur as the movements of the planets change, during our daily lives.

Note that the Sun ☉ and the Moon ☽ are never retrograde. The Sun, unlike the other planets, does not follow an orbit, but is rather the point around which all the other orbits revolve. And the Moon, of course, revolves around Earth and so does not follow an orbit like our own.

When a planet is retrograde ℞, it is closer to Earth than usual, and therefore its energies are more intense. For this reason, the strengths of the energies from these planets require more effort to be integrated, and until that happens, there can be difficulties with them.

Personal Retrogrades: Self-Expression

For an example of personal retrogrades, we've provided the chart of Muhammad Ali. We picked Ali because not one, not two, not three, not even four, but *six* planets (and his Nodes!) were retrograde at the moment of his birth.

Muhammad Ali
Natal Chart
Jan 17 1942
6:35 pm CST +6:00
Louisville, KY
38°N15'15" 085°W45'34"
Geocentric
Tropical
Placidus
True Node

Birth chart for Muhammad Ali.

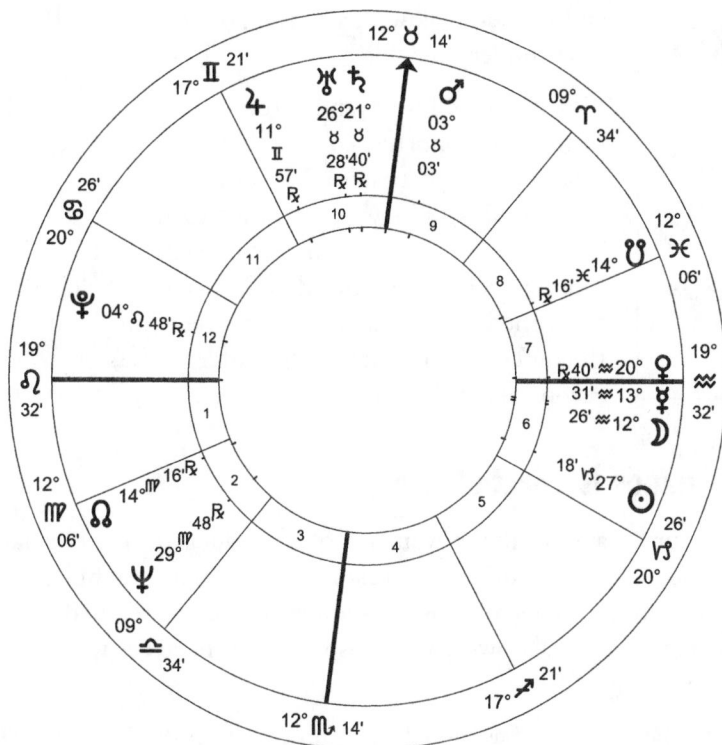

Because Ali has so many planets retrograde, we'll take them one at a time. Let's start with his retrograde Venus ♀℞, which indicates someone who will reconsider social norms. Remember that Ali was born Cassius Clay, and was among the first African American public figures to convert to Islam, and you'll see how this retrograde has manifested.

Next we have Jupiter retrograde ♃ʀ in Ali's chart. This suggests that he might find that society's religions, beliefs, philosophies, and cultural values differ from his own. When someone with personal Jupiter retrograde finds his own belief system, however, his faith will be very strong. Need we say more?

Retrograde Uranus ♅ʀ indicates a social reformer, someone who will champion what he believes is right no matter what the personal cost. Ali's championing of African American rights is recognized today as a trailblazing influence during the Civil Rights Movement.

Ali's Neptune retrograde ♆ʀ suggests a need to question and develop objectivity about matters of faith. Understanding one's spiritual path is of paramount importance to someone with Neptune retrograde. This placement reinforces Ali's retrograde Venus and Jupiter, making his conversion to Islam all the more understandable.

Finally, with Pluto ♀ and Saturn ♄ retrograde ʀ and forming a supportive conjunction (see Chapter 21 for more on conjunctions and other astrological aspects), Ali is rethinking power, authority, societal conditions and limitations. This combination actually makes him more powerful, because when he decides to do something, he is very clear about what he's doing and what the outcomes are likely to be. After all, he's probably reconsidered them more than once.

Transiting Retrogrades: Change Is a Fact of Life

Transiting retrogrades occur because of the movements of the planets during our daily lives and so affect everybody. During transiting Mercury retrograde, for example, we will notice trouble with communications, misunderstandings, missed or rescheduled appointments, and transportation breakdowns. We'll also discover mistakes we made earlier, resulting in schedule delays.

Transiting retrogrades can be thought of as global wake-up calls to rethink a particular planet's energies. Sometimes the energy is reversed, sometimes it's intensified, but no matter what, it's just not quite the same as usual.

Mercury Retrograde: Crossed Wires ☿ ℞

The purpose of Mercury retrograde is to encourage us to back up and catch up, to redo things that didn't get done the first time—or were done incorrectly—instead of constantly pushing forward. But it also can mean that expression becomes difficult, that we have trouble communicating through words, or worse, through other methods of communication like e-mail or telephones.

During Mercury retrograde, Mercury is at its closest to Earth. This is its most intense position; because this energy is "in our face," we're forced to deal with things we've glossed over, forgotten, or done wrong.

Personal Mercury Retrograde

A personal retrograde occurs when a planet is retrograde at the time of your birth. Because a retrograde planet is out of step with its function in the present culture, personal Mercury retrograde indicates people who are learning to think for themselves, especially because their thoughts and ideas will be different from those of society. This can, of course, lead to some very interesting ideas and perspectives that society needs but hasn't thought of yet. And it's Mercury retrograde people who bring these ideas back to the fold.

Star-Crossed

Astrologers chart when planetary retrogrades will occur for years in advance, to avoid costly errors. Many won't travel by air during Mercury retrograde, for example, and most wouldn't think of starting a new venture during a Mars retrograde, when we should be rethinking action rather than beginning it.

People with personal Mercury retrograde are likely to have communication problems with others, either jumping ahead or lagging behind. This often occurs when the person is caught up in processing new information and then has questions or responses to what was previously discussed—after everyone else has moved on to the next topic!

People born with Mercury retrograde are sorting through ideas, thoughts, and their own communications with greater intensity than people with Mercury direct. It takes time for them to get used to this and start understanding how to deal with it, but in the meantime, people with Mercury retrograde are sometimes likely to think too much, reprocessing the same thing over and over and then hitting mental burnout.

Retrograde Mercury is not "bad" or "good"; it's a change in Mercury's energy. Being aware of it can help you avoid costly mistakes or unnecessary misunderstandings.

Transiting Mercury Retrograde

Because it's the ruler of transportation, when Mercury is retrograde, there are more car breakdowns, traffic mess-ups, and airline delays, and travel often has some unexpected and unpleasant surprises. Rental cars might not be ready or available, or hotel reservations might not have been made or kept. Your baggage might not even show up.

> **CAUTION**
>
> **Star-Crossed**
>
> During Mercury retrograde, it's best not to buy or install new computer equipment or software because it probably won't work. During these periods, there are frequent computer overloads, which then result in breakdowns. Enormous power outages also have resulted from computer overloads during Mercury retrogrades. So do your preventive maintenance early, and back up everything.

Transiting Mercury retrograde occurs three times every year for about three weeks each time, affecting everyone. This can signal everything from software and computer problems to packages not arriving. In projects requiring communication, signals can seem "crossed," or misunderstandings can occur, and there can be missed appointments and schedule delays as well. A portion of the first edition of this book was written during a Mercury retrograde, so believe us, we know what we're talking about here.

Venus Retrograde: What's Love Got to Do with It? ♀ ℞

Venus's energies are focused on all things bright and beautiful, and that includes everything from your social life to your love life. This means that during retrograde Venus, you will reconsider and reevaluate everything from who and what you love to who loves you.

Personal Venus Retrograde

People with a personal Venus retrograde will reconsider relationships and values, especially in terms of societal norms. By comparing their lives and values to others, they realize they walk to the "beat of a different drummer" and don't fit into the mainstream. They may choose to have relationships that are different from the norm. They might, for example, follow an alternative lifestyle or even become a hermit.

Because their values are outside of the norm, these people also must learn to please and approve of themselves, instead of seeking approval from others. Once they learn this, the social pressure to conform lessens because they no longer depend on others for approval.

If you have social Venus in a personal retrograde, it can lead to feelings of social awkwardness, missed connections, and doubts about one's worth as a lover or partner. At the same time, though, this retrograde can free you to pursue new or different social values, because Venus's energies are turned inward.

Transiting Venus Retrograde

During a transiting Venus retrograde, old lovers and friends may resurface, relationship issues come to the forefront, and all types of contracts and partnerships get reconsidered, especially if they are difficult.

This is also when values get reconsidered to see if they still make sense or need adjusting. The purpose of Venus retrograde is to reconsider relationship and acquisition needs, because these change over time for everyone. So it's important to get in touch with your present values, wants, and needs, and become clear about what you want to attract.

Venus is retrograde the least amount of time of all the planets: Out of its 584-day cycle, its retrograde is not quite 6 weeks long.

Mars Retrograde: Inward Action ♂℞

Mars is the action planet, so it should come as no surprise that when it's retrograde, inward action is the name of the game. The purpose of Mars retrograde is to evaluate what motivates you and determine if you're on the correct path, doing what you should be doing.

Personal Mars Retrograde

A personal retrograde Mars means your desires, drive, ambition, and energy are turned inward, and this can result in enormous reserves of power being used to stay the course. With a personal Mars retrograde, you're here to rethink actions, desires, and such.

With a personal Mars retrograde, you will learn to operate in a different manner, take a different path, and seek to fulfill your desires in new ways. But until you learn to do this, you might overreact or be too forceful in asserting yourself. People with Mars retrograde also tend to compete with themselves instead of with others.

Transiting Mars Retrograde

During a transiting Mars retrograde, it's time to adjust your actions and aggressive instincts to ensure that they accomplish your intent, which can include going back over previous actions and redoing them. Old resentments that haven't been resolved in the past will resurface during these periods, as this is the time to develop new strategies and approaches for dealing with issues, anger, and learning assertiveness.

Mars is retrograde for about 9 to 10 weeks out of its 26-month cycle.

> **CAUTION Star-Crossed**
>
> Transiting Mars retrograde is *not* the time to make new starts, as this period is for directing your energies inward, determining where you should be headed and how you should get there. So when you try to push forward with new beginnings under this cycle, you often run into one obstacle after another.

Jupiter Retrograde: Stepping Back ♃ ℞

Because Jupiter is the planet of societal growth and expansion, when it's retrograde, you can expect that energy to turn inward. This means a personal Jupiter retrograde is someone who will be rethinking society's direction, and during a transiting Jupiter retrograde, we'll all be evaluating the direction we've been going.

Personal Jupiter Retrograde

People with a personal Jupiter retrograde find that society's religions, beliefs, philosophies, and cultural values aren't compatible with their own. They have to step back from the norms and rethink these things in order to develop their own "operating systems."

This process often results in very strong and intense faith, and, examples of people with personal Jupiter retrograde include the previously mentioned Muhammad Ali, His Holiness the Dalai Lama (see Chapter 3), Mark Twain, and Karl Marx. People with Jupiter retrograde are very intuitive, seeking answers within themselves, and they often find unusual ways to expand their lives.

People with retrograde Jupiter must grow from within before they seek growth in the outer world. What the world has to offer might not be what they need.

Transiting Jupiter Retrograde

Immediately preceding a transiting or cycling Jupiter retrograde, society, organizations, and individuals will have "gone too far" in their urges to expand and grow. Their actions in this regard will have exceeded positive limits, and Jupiter retrograde means it's time to step back.

A transiting Jupiter retrograde is the time to grow internally and prepare yourself for opportunities that will be available after Jupiter goes direct. It is particularly important to develop more understanding and awareness during these periods, to determine if what's being offered to you is what you really want.

Jupiter goes retrograde for a period of 4 months every 13 months.

Saturn Retrograde: Restructuring ♄℞

Saturn is the planet of systems and organizations, and when it's retrograde, it's time to reexamine these things and find ways to improve them. In fact, if you were born with a Saturn retrograde, you already know there are systems that need fixing, and you may well be devoting your life to doing just that.

Personal Saturn Retrograde

People born with a personal Saturn retrograde were born when systems were being reorganized and restructured to work better. Because they're aware of the deficiencies in most systems or organizations, they want to find ways to make them work.

Because Saturn represents limits, people with retrograde Saturn might not have clear or well-defined boundaries with others. This, in turn, can lead to their accepting too many responsibilities for others—or not enough for themselves. In addition, these people will be challenged to find their own definitions of success and their own social roles, because they won't relate to society's standards or norms, or their role models might not have given them the needed guidance.

> **Heaven Knows**
>
> Need an example of someone with personal Saturn retrograde? Steven Spielberg's retrograde Saturn is found in Leo in his second house of material things. No wonder his films question everything.

Transiting Saturn Retrograde

During a transiting or cyclical Saturn retrograde, it's time for all of us to restructure systems, programs, organizations, and rules in order to make them function better. Processes and policies all benefit from reexamination during this period.

On a personal level, transiting Saturn retrograde is the time to become more aware of your own authority and power and whether it fits within society's rules. It's also a time to reconsider where *you* fit within society and whether you're allowing its rules to limit you. The challenge is to objectively analyze society's patterns and expectations.

Saturn retrogrades every 12½ months for a period of 4½ months.

Uranus Retrograde: The Times, They Are A-Changing ♅℞

Uranus is the planet of the unconscious, and even when it's retrograde, this is the area where its energies will be concentrated. The difference during a retrograde is that the energy will be even more pronounced, so people born with Uranus retrograde are often in the forefront when it comes to change.

Personal Uranus Retrograde

Because Uranus is the Awakener or Liberator, it acts primarily on a person's unconscious. When Uranus is retrograde in a person's chart, the desire to reform or rebel is even stronger than when Uranus is direct. For this reason, it's very important for these people to understand the internal workings of structures and systems before they create reforms. When a person has Uranus retrograde, it's important to become as detached and objective as possible when determining what to change.

Both John F. Kennedy and Adolf Hitler had Uranus retrograde in their charts. Although both of these men were major social reformers, President Kennedy chose to use this energy to champion equal rights and humanitarian changes, while Hitler demonstrated its negative aspects by letting his ego override the welfare of others.

Transiting Uranus Retrograde

In cyclical or transiting Uranus retrogrades, it's time to ask yourself what changes are occurring in the world and how you're contributing to or working against them. It's important to see the connections between your own personal changes and those that are occurring around the world.

Uranus retrogrades for five months every year.

Neptune Retrograde: Not Just Blind Faith ♆℞

Faith and dreams: These are the areas of Neptune's energy, and when this planet is retrograde, nothing is accepted as blind faith. Whether it's the personal spiritual quest of a person with retrograde Neptune or the collective quest of society during a transiting Neptune retrograde, this planet's retrograde energy means a reexamination of hopes and beliefs.

Personal Neptune Retrograde

When Neptune is retrograde in a person's chart, there's an even stronger indication that the person needs to question and test all aspects of faith. Instead of blindly accepting faith, they're here to question it and develop objectivity regarding all the intangibles of life, such as truth, fear, hope, and inspiration. Because Neptune is closest to Earth when retrograde, its functions are intensified. For this reason, it's also commonly found in artists, musicians, poets, and those who lead spiritual lives.

Understanding their spiritual path will either be an important part of the lives of retrograde Neptune people, or they may be confused, disillusioned, or full of illusions. For these people, dreams can be an important method of accessing messages from their unconscious.

If a spiritual quest isn't pursued, retrograde Neptune people may fall into drugs, alcohol, or other escapist behaviors. Because this need to understand spirituality is so emphasized in them, they can't ignore it, and must deal with it one way or another. Ideally they question the ideas society accepts about faith, fears, truth, and understanding, and bring this information not only to themselves, but to the rest of the world as well.

Transiting Neptune Retrograde

When Neptune is retrograde cyclically or by transit, it's time for everyone to tune into the collective unconscious and notice how their own fears, illusions, confusion, or spiritual journey are connected to what's happening with humanity. You should determine if you're using your own energies in positive ways to develop faith and spirituality, or pursuing a path of escapism and disappointment.

Neptune retrogrades about five to six months every year.

Pluto Retrograde: Transformation Time ♀ ℞

When Pluto is retrograde, the one thing you can expect is the unexpected. As the planet of transformation, Pluto's energies equal change, so retrograde Pluto means a reexamination of the changes you (and society) have been making.

Personal Pluto Retrograde

When Pluto is retrograde in a person's chart, this indicates that he or she will be much more intensely focused on personal transformation and rebirth, in order to help transform the world. First these people must be reborn to new ways, though, so they can begin to impact the world positively. It's also important for them to connect their own actions, behaviors, and changes to those of humanity and see what role they're playing in it. With today's environmental concerns, these people are aware of how they impact Earth with their actions and attitudes.

Transiting Pluto Retrograde

As a cyclical or transiting period, Pluto retrograde is our signal that it's time to step back and review how each of us is either contributing to the future and evolution of mankind and Earth or working to destroy it. These are the periods when it's important to become more conscious of how we impact Earth and others.

Pluto is retrograde every year for at least five months.

The Least You Need to Know

◆ When a planet is retrograde ℞, its energies seem to be reversed.

◆ A personal retrograde means you were born with a planet retrograde. Its energies will be special to you, if this is the case.

◆ Transiting retrogrades affect us all.

◆ Each planetary retrograde presents both opportunities and challenges.

Part 4

The Twelve Astrological Houses: Unlocking the Mystery of *You*

Whether it's about you, your responsibilities, your career, your relationships, or your beliefs, the areas of your life can all be found in the astrological houses. Represented by the 12 "pie slices" of your birth chart, these areas describe every major area of your life.

In the next four chapters, we not only take an in-depth look at each house, we'll show you what it means when a planet "lives" in each house. As with Part 3, you'll likely want to keep your astrological birth chart handy as you uncover more of the story of you.

Remember: Houses are the "where" of astrology, so it's here you'll find out the areas of influence and the areas you'd prefer to avoid.

Houses in the First Quadrant: Let's Get Personal

In This Chapter

- ◆ Houses are where it is
- ◆ The first three houses: the most personal houses
- ◆ The first house: taking care of number 1
- ◆ The second house: Are you what you own?
- ◆ The third house: the street where you live

From the very beginnings of astrology, astrologers divided life into different categories. The Babylonian astrologers named these areas the houses, to represent the arenas where the drama of your life unfolds. Whereas signs are psychological processes, houses are experiential, or, as astrologer Steven Forrest puts it, "We *are* our signs, and we *do* our houses."

Because there are 12 signs and 12 houses, learning the symbolism of the signs is a big step toward learning the symbolism of the houses. Still, they aren't at all the same thing, so let's make sure you understand what the difference is.

Houses Are Where It Is

There are specific meanings to which *houses* your planets are in, which is one more step in unlocking the mystery of you. Any house in your birth chart with more than one planet in it shows an area of your life that is emphasized and strengthened. At the same time, houses without any planets are active as well. It all depends on the house's ruler, and the *aspects* it has to it. A house without planets in it could be just as strong as—or stronger than—one with planets visible. Aspects will be covered in more detail in Chapter 21.

All houses, whether empty or full, have house rulers, which describe what's happening in that area of your life. It's not like there's nothing going on just because there are no planets in a house. Remember, all houses have rulers or landlords, which are ultimately in charge of the house. On the other hand, if one of the planets "living" in a house also is its ruler, then that house has, in effect, a resident landlord. Just like a real landlord, that planet's going to have a lot of control over what happens in that particular area of life.

> **AstroLingo**
>
> The **houses** are the "where" of astrology. Each of the 12 houses encompasses a specific area of your life.

As you read in Chapter 10, the houses in your chart appear as 12 pie slices, 6 below the *horizon* and 6 above. Your horizon divides your chart into north and south, and runs from your *ascendant* to your *descendant*. On an astrological chart, south is the upper half, or houses 7 through 12, and north is the lower half, or the first 6 houses.

> **AstroLingo**
>
> When two planets are **in aspect** to each other, they're related by one of a set of geometric angles between them, some of which are beneficial or well aspected, and others that are challenging. For example, two planets that are 180° apart (±7°) are said to be opposite. There are five major aspects: conjunctions ☌ 0°, sextiles ✶ 60°, squares □ 90°, trines △ 120°, and oppositions ☍ 180°.

Like Four Points of the Compass

We introduced the concepts of your astrological ascendant, descendant, midheaven, and lower heaven in Chapter 3. Here, we'll return to the birth chart of the Dalai Lama to look at each of these points in more depth. We'll show you where to find them on His Holiness's chart, so that you in turn can find them on your own.

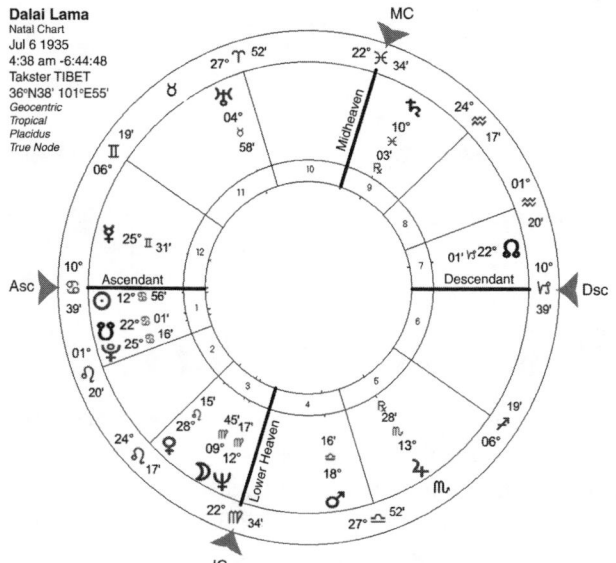

Birth chart for His Holiness the 14th Dalai Lama.

As you recall, your ascendant, or your rising sign, is the same as the sign on the cusp of your first house and represents your self-image and personality. The Dalai Lama's ascendant is Cancer ♋.

Your descendant is the sign on the cusp of your seventh house and represents how you channel your energies through partnerships and relationships. The Dalai Lama's descendant is Capricorn ♑.

In addition to the horizon line, your chart is divided by a *meridian* line, which separates your birth chart into east on the left and west on the right. The lowest point of the meridian is the lower heaven or I.C., and is the same as the cusp, or beginning, of the fourth house. This symbolizes your life's foundation, including your home and psychological roots. The Dalai Lama's lower heaven is Virgo ♍.

The highest point of the meridian is the midheaven or M.C. and is the same as the cusp, or beginning, of the tenth house. This represents your ambition, career or social role, and public image. The Dalai Lama's midheaven is Pisces ♓.

So are you ready to grab your birth chart and tour today's open houses? We promise, no pushy real estate agents! We'll start by taking you through the three houses in the first quadrant, which are all about you. See Chapter 4 if you need to review the natural associations of signs and houses.

AstroLingo

The **horizon** line on your birth chart divides your chart into north, the bottom half, and south, the upper half. It also connects your ascendant, the sign on the beginning of the first house, and your descendant, the sign on the beginning of the seventh house. The **meridian** line divides the circle of your chart into eastern and western halves. The line of your meridian connects your I.C. and your midheaven.

The First House: Taking Care of Number 1

This is the house of self, the place where your ascendant—your personality and self-image—resides. Here is where you will find your personal style, from your mannerisms to your temperament, from your disposition to your likes and dislikes, as well as a key to why you look the way you do. This house also includes your physical body and your early childhood and is closely tied to your health.

The first house: your physical self, personality, and early childhood.

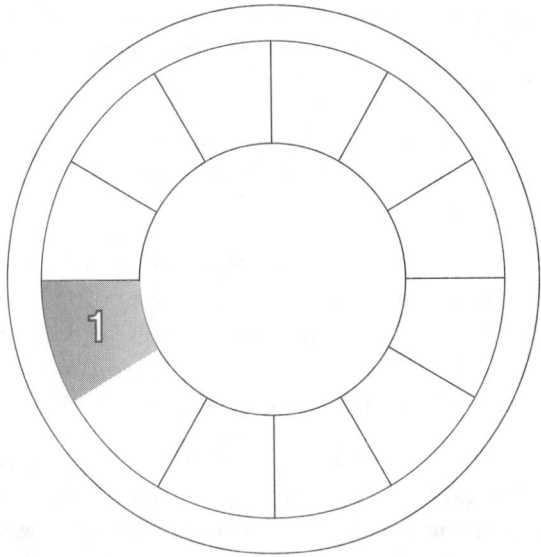

This is the house where your ascendant "lives," the place where you will find the mask that best serves your needs. Successfully navigated, the first house shows a sense of control and direction; if it is less successfully navigated, there will be a lack of self-assurance, which might manifest in a number of different ways.

Because the planet that rules the natural first house is Mars ♂ and its corresponding sign is Aries ♈, it's clear that the focus of this house is going to be your identity, or the "I Am" principle.

Heavenly Bodies and Me, Me, Me

Your *first house sign* describes your self-image and how you express your identity; its *ruler* describes where and how your identity and self-image are developed. The Aries ♈ house (*the corresponding natural sign*) shows another area of life that your identity is tied to, providing you with greater self-awareness.

The Sun ☉ in the First House

If the planet of individuality appears here, in the house of self, there's a strong sense of self and powerful leadership abilities, as well as a need for lots of attention. A first house Sun indicates a "sunny" disposition and an optimistic nature. A first house Sun *could* mean the ascendant and Sun sign are the same, but it will *always* mean that there's a strong will, tons of energy, a noble manner, and intense self-awareness.

> **StarFacts**
>
> The first house is sometimes called the house of self-interest because it not only shows what you want, but how you're going to get it. Self-interest has gotten a bad rap lately, don't you think? What's wrong with getting what you want from life, after all?

The Moon ☽ in the First House

A first house Moon indicates imaginative self-expression and a desire to be admired and appreciated. To first house Moons, everything can depend on how they feel. Their expression is changeable and moody, and they're highly impressionable—which might also indicate psychic abilities. Their personal identity is often strongly influenced by their early childhood, family, and emotional matters, possibly with strong ties to their mothers. Physically, they may have a round "Moon face."

Mercury ☿ in the First House

Mercury in the first house indicates mental alertness, a person who thrives on intellectual challenges, likes to travel, and enjoys meeting others. Such a person is quite the communicator and can be very eloquent. Mental initiative and higher-than-average intelligence go hand in hand with this placement.

Venus ♀ in the First House

First house Venus indicates beauty, harmony, grace, kindness, friendliness, and charm—all those wonderful Venus characteristics. A Venus in the first house cares a great deal about its appearance, and this placement also shows physical beauty and possible artistic talents. Usually with this placement, a happy childhood leads to a positive outlook on life.

Mars ♂ in the First House

Mars in the first house isn't going to take the advice of others; this placement indicates both independence and impulsiveness. A first house Mars has plenty of energy and confidence, especially when tackling new projects, but may be impatient with others who don't move as quickly, or even disregard the rights of others. This placement also indicates physical robustness and strength and people who love sports or other forms of physical exercise.

Jupiter ♃ in the First House

Generous Jupiter in the first house is honest, enthusiastic, and benevolent (although with challenging aspects, Jupiter in the first house can manifest itself as self-indulgence and an inflated sense of self-importance). With positive aspects, the person is likely to be a social, educational, or religious leader or work in some type of leadership position. These people usually have strong religious beliefs or moral ethics.

Saturn ♄ in the First House

Self-disciplined, organized, and persistent, Saturn in the first house can be quite successful. These people are likely to be very serious and hard-working, too, and might have had limitations placed on them as children. A first house Saturn person will be sensible and orderly, and, with other good factors, might be very successful in real estate. These people either readily accept major responsibilities, or may feel like they are burdened with them. They also might have several obstacles to overcome in order to become independent and free, including potential hardships or physical handicaps.

Uranus ♅ in the First House

Uranus in the first house indicates both eccentricity and inventiveness, a person whose life seems filled with the unexpected and who usually takes it all in stride. Uranus here can indicate people who are ahead of their time, and they may be geniuses or have very high intelligence. Intuition is usually strong, and they often have scientific or advanced talents. Physically these people might appear unusual in some way and have magnetic personalities.

Neptune Ψ in the First House

First house Neptune can be very sensitive, intuitive, and might be mystical or clairvoyant, too. They are so sensitive that they feel everything around them, even things at a subliminal level. They also are often very artistic and might have musical talents. In addition, they need to be very careful about using alcohol or drugs, because not only can these things leave them open to negative psychic influences, they also can be dangerous to their health. Physically, these people might appear to have a dreamy or other-worldly look to them.

Pluto ♀ in the First House

If Pluto is in your first house, your soul has a special evolutionary destiny to fulfill. To pursue this, you need plenty of independence and freedom so you can find out on your own who you are and become yourself. On the other hand, you may be too afraid or insecure to evolve beyond who you are at any point, and so you may go through periodic identity crises that force you to become involved with others. Then you can find out who you are and what your special destiny is. Your soul's intent here is to learn to develop equal relationships with others and to balance your need for freedom and independence with the needs of others. First house Plutos are often self-centered or even narcissistic in early life, but this is part of their evolutionary development. They're strong-willed, intense individuals.

North Node ☊ in the First House/South Node ☋ in the Seventh House

If your North Node is in the first house and your South Node in the seventh, you are here to learn how to establish self-identity and become a leader. Up until now, you've submerged your identity in the affairs of others and have allowed others' opinions to influence your sense of who you are. Now it's time to *become yourself* and learn to balance your own needs with those of others.

The Second House: Are You What You Own?

Your second house is where you'll find not only your money and what you own that can be easily moved (not to be confused with a home and real estate, which are part of the fourth house) but what you *will* own and value, including your income and those things you'll come to treasure. It also reveals how you feel about your possessions and will show, as well, the best ways for you to earn your living.

The second house: your possessions, earning abilities, and self-esteem.

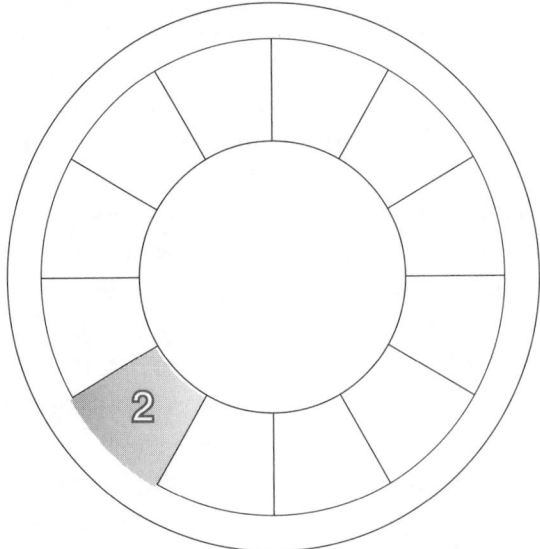

The second house also represents your self-esteem, earning abilities, and personal resources, which are interconnected, making this the house of productivity.

The natural second house cusp is ruled by Taurus ♉, the sign of self-assuredness and possessions. And the natural planet in charge is Venus ♀, whose associations are beauty, charm, values, and harmony, and the things you own.

What Do I Have in the House?

Your second house is where you develop your values, resources, and self-esteem, and so the sign on your second house cusp will describe their characteristics. Your second house ruler describes where and how you develop them. The house where the corresponding natural sign of Taurus is shows what area your values, resources, and self-esteem are tied to and where you use them to achieve the results you want. The planets in the second house give clues to all of these things: values, resources, and self-esteem.

CAUTION

Star-Crossed

Poor self-esteem might lead you to try to substitute material things for a feeling of self-worth. If there are challenging factors related to the second house, you may believe that material possessions can be substituted for inner self-worth. Or you may not feel worthy of having sufficient or plenty of money, and so manage to prevent that from happening. For that reason, it's important to truly *value yourself*. You aren't what you own!

The Sun ☉ in the Second House

A second house Sun indicates that although one will attract money, it might come and go quickly, because of a love of luxuries. The purpose of a second house Sun is to learn the correct use of material resources in ways that are beneficial to others as well as to oneself. There is a strong desire to become financially independent or at least earn a lot of money, because stability and security are very important. These people might earn money from creative talents.

The Moon ☽ in the Second House

The most important thing for a second house Moon is its strong need for emotional security, which is often tied to possessions. Establishing a strong set of values also is important. This placement indicates an ability to earn money from businesses associated with food, homes, and real estate, although one's finances may go through phases, like the Moon. This placement also can indicate gain through one's mother or spouse, or through business contacts with women.

Mercury ☿ in the Second House

Mercury in the second house means the mind and/or communication will be at work for one's earning capacity, and a second house Mercury might spend that money on travel, education, information, and time-saving gadgets. People with Mercury in the second house like to translate ideas into financial gain, and with their quick minds, might be economists, corporate planners, salespeople, writers, teachers, broadcasters, or publishers.

Venus ♀ in the Second House

A second house Venus might find financial rewards through partnership or connections and likes to spend its earnings on clothes and pleasures. People with Venus in the second house are honest and fair in their financial dealings and might pursue careers in areas that promote beauty in some way, such as the arts or interior design. Because this is one of Venus's natural residences, people with this placement are often very generous; they also might seek wealth as a means of attaining social status.

Mars ♂ in the Second House

Mars in the second house gains through its own effort and competitive spirit. Money matters, and a second house Mars will go after it. When it comes to spending, though, people with this placement are often impulsive. This placement is a good one for engineers, mechanics, career military people, government workers, those with strong initiative in business, and people who prefer to work for themselves.

Jupiter ♃ in the Second House

Lucky Jupiter has no trouble with making money in this house, but while people with Jupiter in the second house can make a great deal of money, they also might overspend it freely. People with this placement might be found in the travel business, or in banking, stocks, import/export, or insurance. Other fields for a second house Jupiter include real estate, food, education, the legal system, fundraising, and publishing. This position indicates someone with a great deal of business acumen—and expansiveness—so others are attracted to second house Jupiter's expansive ways and often benefit from this placement, too.

Saturn ♄ in the Second House

Saturn's ambition pays out in the second house, where its long-range financial planning can lead to material comfort and success. Saturn here wants to work hard to achieve financial security and may have a deep fear of poverty. Shrewd and cautious, the gain will be slow but steady. Second house Saturn might worry about money, too, even if it doesn't need to, but can do quite well with real-estate investments, government and business contracts, management, and construction—any work, in short, made for the long haul.

Uranus ♅ in the Second House

Second house Uranus might make its money in unusual ways, with opportunities that seem to literally pop up out of nowhere. There might be wild fluctuations in net worth here, which Uranus might be able to ride out. This can be anything from boom to bust, depending on the aspects and general conditions of the house. This placement indicates people who may do better with their own business and who may not "buy into" the value systems accepted by others.

Neptune ♆ in the Second House

Second house Neptune approaches making money with both intuition and imagination and might surround itself with objects valued more for their aesthetic than their material value. Second house Neptunes can be quite resourceful—or might experience financial difficulties as their finances dissolve. They have an idealistic sense about money and how to use their resources, but there may be unforeseen expenses or circumstances that make it difficult to hold on to. They may need to develop faith and a sense of flow where their resources are concerned.

Pluto ♀ in the Second House

With a second house Pluto, you have a strong survival instinct and need to develop self-reliance and self-sufficiency. Your primary identity might be focused on either (1) your sense of values, including power and possessions, or (2) your abilities, talents, and resources for earning an income. In all cases, your soul's evolutionary intent is to grow beyond the limitations of the way you've identified your self-sustenance by merging your resources, talents, or possessions with others. For example, if you've been equating material gain with self-worth or self-sustainment, you'll need to reassess this and learn about the deeper aspects of life. If, on the other hand, you're focused on your talents, earning abilities, or spiritual values, then you'll need to learn how to tie them to a social need in order to support yourself. You can be stubborn, defensive, or even lazy, but you also possess stability and inner strength, which you can use to promote self-reliance in others.

North Node ☊ in the Second House/South Node ☋ in the Eighth House

A second house North Node/eighth house South Node indicates that you've already learned how to take on the values of others to share in their possessions and resources. You know all about secrets, and you may be so busy keeping them that you neglect your present lessons about where your values really lie. You need to discover and establish that which is truly meaningful to you and understand that you can't keep what you haven't acquired honestly. You can develop a completely new and meaningful life for yourself by establishing your own values—and living by them.

The Third House: The Street Where You Live

The third house is often called the house of communication, but this term can disguise the many areas of your life that actually reside there. Because this house contains your capacities for information gathering and sharing, its areas include your knowledge, short journeys, your brothers and sisters, and your immediate environment.

You could think of your third house as where you think, as it covers logic, memory, and manual skills. It's also about your early education: how and from whom you learned what you know.

The natural third house is ruled by Mercury ☿, of course, and its associated sign is Gemini ♊. Communication, remember, is not just about talking; it's also about listening and our perceptions, as well as the many other ways we communicate.

The third house: your knowledge, siblings, and environment.

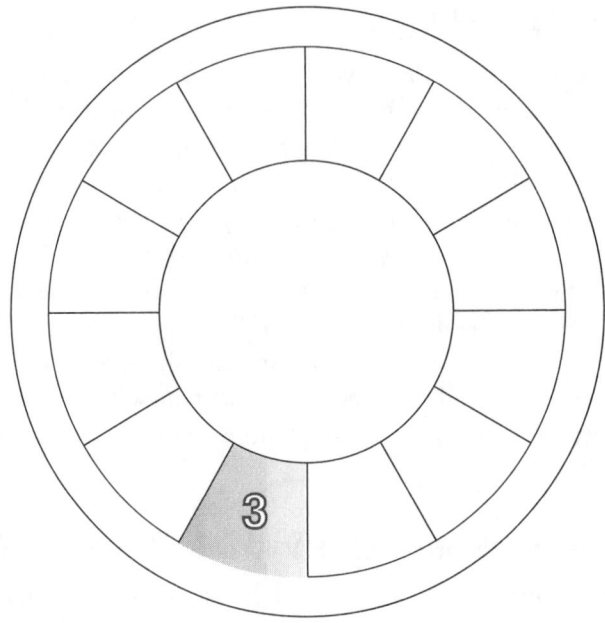

Heavenly Bodies in Your 'Hood

Because your third house accommodates the nature of your communications, perceptions, knowledge and education, and your local environment, the sign on the third house describes the traits of these areas. The landlord planet or ruler of your third house sign describes where and how you develop your ideas, communicate them to others, and how knowledge from your local environment is used. The house with Gemini on its cusp shows where you seek new knowledge and information and make mental connections with others.

> **Heaven Knows**
>
> Part of your local environment is the people you haven't "chosen," everyone from your siblings to your neighbors, in other words. The third house is the place where all these connections reside, so understanding what's in your third house can help you see why you seem to be stuck with people who drive you crazy—or why you're blessed with people you adore.

The Sun ☉ in the Third House

An active, creative Sun in the third house wants to communicate ideas and might be a leader in its field. There might be a desire to explore oneself in intellectual ways or even a driving need for intellectual distinction, as well as a knack for being in the right place at the right time. A third house Sun is a good communicator and might be active in local affairs.

The Moon ☽ in the Third House

A third house Moon cares a great deal about family and also is involved in education and travel. There's curiosity and a strong imagination here, with a primary tendency to think emotionally. This placement can be restless, because it doesn't much care for routine, but it's also a good listener with a remarkable memory for what it hears.

Mercury ☿ in the Third House

Because this is where Mercury naturally lives, this placement makes for a lively, inquisitive mind and a versatility in handling both people and projects. Mercury in the third house has a quick wit and a good sense of humor and is always eager to learn more, and third house Mercuries can be pretty smart folks. But third house Mercury also can mean restlessness, so a profession that keeps this placement on the move can work very well. These people might also be writers, speakers, reporters, or editors.

Venus ♀ in the Third House

Venus in the third house is a compromiser, always seeking harmony through communication. Charming and gentle, this placement makes communication seem effortless, and there is both charm and tact in third house Venus people. It also can indicate artistic creativity, a love of literature or poetry, and travel for pleasure.

Mars ♂ in the Third House

Third house Mars will usually speak its mind and, with its determination, often gets what it wants through its persuasive or aggressive ways with words. These people also are quick thinkers—especially in emergencies—so they have to be careful about jumping to conclusions. Often, people who deal with transportation or communication equipment will have this placement, and it also is seen in reporters or people in the political arena.

Jupiter ♃ in the Third House

Third house Jupiter often has a variety of intellectual interests and might achieve success through education, writing, or communication. Witty and optimistic, this placement is mentally expansive and philosophical as well and is well liked by others. This placement also can indicate a great deal of travel, and, because these people are usually very interested in social trends and causes, many writers with this placement pursue topics of this nature.

Saturn ♄ in the Third House

Saturn in the third house wants to learn things in order to put them to good use. This is a practical placement and can indicate a good student, as well as a strong scientific or mathematical ability. These people might work in printing, publishing, or the communications industry, and they're also good accountants, teachers, researchers, or librarians. There's a possibility that people with this placement might have had relationship difficulties with neighbors or siblings, or education problems in their early years, but they also have excellent powers of concentration and are conscientious.

Uranus ♅ in the Third House

Third house Uranus is independent and inventive and, with its unusual and intuitive mind, follows its own drummer wherever it beats. This placement might indicate genius and a keen and alert mind coupled with a love of new ideas. People with Uranus in the third house might work in communications or broadcasting. There might be unpredictable behavior with this placement or unexpected separation from brothers and sisters.

Neptune ♆ in the Third House

Third house Neptune is a daydreamer and might need to learn how to concentrate, but often has strong psychic abilities and a deep need to learn about the unexplained. This placement describes highly developed visualization abilities and a strong interest in learning or writing about mystical or occult subjects. When challenged, this placement can indicate learning difficulties, as well as confusion in communications, contracts, and traveling.

Pluto ♀ in the Third House

If Pluto's in your third house, you have strong intellectual curiosity, and your emotional security is attached to your need to understand the world within a larger framework. However, your desire to constantly take in more information leads to a quest for a deeper meaning that unifies all of this data. More facts, though, are never able to tie everything together. Your soul's evolutionary intent is to develop your intuition and understand the metaphysical significance behind the information. When this is accomplished, you must finally realize that your version of the truth is only one version. Then you can do everything from inspire and motivate to transform the mental patterns of others with your communication skills. You're intelligent, curious, and have a deep, penetrating mind.

North Node ☊ in the Third House/South Node ☋ in the Ninth House

If your North Node is in the third house and your South Node in the ninth house, you've already worked heavily to gain wisdom and understanding and now need to pay attention to communicating and disseminating information to others, and to your relationships. With this placement you must work to develop clear communications, better relationships with others, and resist the urge to sever ties whenever the going gets rough (often leaving loose ends). You're here to translate what you've already learned for society.

The Least You Need to Know

- ◆ The first three houses are the personal houses.

- ◆ Your first house represents your physical self and personality.

- ◆ Your second house symbolizes your possessions, earning abilities, self-esteem, and values.

- ◆ Your third house represents your knowledge, communications, short journeys, siblings, neighbors, and immediate surroundings.

Chapter 16

Houses in the Second Quadrant: Establishing Yourself

In This Chapter

- ◆ The second quadrant: home, creativity, and daily work
- ◆ The fourth house: it's a family affair
- ◆ The fifth house: do what you wanna do
- ◆ The sixth house: nine to five

The second quadrant houses are the areas where you connect with your immediate surroundings. Your fourth house is where you'll find your home and family; your fifth house, your pleasure and creativity; and your sixth house, your work and responsibilities. These are the houses where you'll be establishing yourself.

The Fourth House: It's a Family Affair

The fourth house is your home, the place where a house is a home, or a home is a house. But what is a home? In addition to being your domestic life, it's the place where you feel you can be yourself, with all your unconscious habits or patterns and your emotional underpinnings.

The fourth house: your home and family and the foundation of your life.

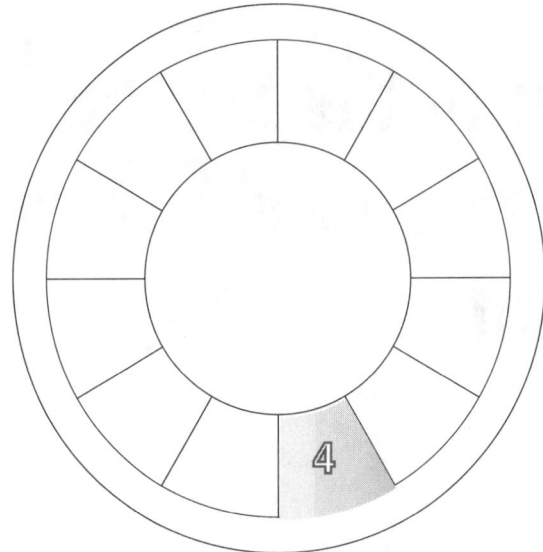

Your home is related to your insecurities or need for emotional security, so when there are lots of disruptions, renovations, or major modifications there, these needs are undergoing major changes as well.

The natural fourth house is ruled by Cancer ♋, and so there is a natural association with the Moon ☽: The fourth house is both your seclusion and your self-protection, the place you can retreat to and depend on, and the foundation of your life.

StarFacts
Your home is also where you came from—your roots and family; where you are now—your domicile and those you live with; and where you're going—the security of your old age. With the lower heaven (I.C.) as its cusp, your fourth house also indicates the point of your beginnings and psychological roots.

Who's Nesting in This House?

The sign on your fourth house describes the characteristics of your roots, inner foundations, security, and home, and its ruler shows where and how you seek to develop these things. The house where Cancer, the fourth house's natural sign, appears on your chart describes where you search for security and disclose your emotions externally.

The Sun ☉ in the Fourth House

A fourth house Sun indicates pride in the home, one or both parents strongly influencing the early life, and a strong need to establish and maintain roots. The Sun here means that the creative self will be expressed through the home, which translates to a strong attachment to family and, generally, a happy home life.

The Moon ☽ in the Fourth House

With the Moon in its natural house, there may be an overdependence on the home, but this placement can indicate both protection of and devotion to those one loves. This placement also can indicate a strong parental attachment and a person who identifies emotionally with both family and home, especially with the mother.

Mercury ☿ in the Fourth House

Fourth house Mercury might work at home, and parents and early home life often encourage this placement's curiosity to learn. There is a strong need for personal security, but people with fourth house Mercury might change residence often. In any event, their houses are places with lots of communication going on, and they might work or write in their homes.

Venus ♀ in the Fourth House

Venus in the fourth house translates to a beautiful place to live. There also will be happy memories of childhood and a strong attachment to the parents. Venus here is financially secure as well as optimistic and warm. Unless challenged, these are very pleasant people, comfortable and harmonious, who also love land, flowers, and gardening and decorate their homes as beautifully as possible.

Mars ♂ in the Fourth House

A fourth house Mars indicates a desire for independence within the home life. Because of some conflicts—especially if Mars is challenged by aspects—with the parents early in one's life, there might be questions of dominance with this placement, and Mars in the fourth house often settles far from its original home. This placement also shows strong efforts to improve the home conditions, and many of these people are "do-it-yourselfers" who fix up their homes.

Jupiter ♃ in the Fourth House

Fourth house Jupiter is generally happy and comfortable at home and takes pride in its family. There's usually a happy childhood with this placement, and there should be material comfort in later life as well. Fourth house Jupiter loves wide-open spaces and a large home, too. This is a warm and compassionate placement, which indicates people who might have many social and educational opportunities. Usually, they come from a large family circle that is financially secure, and they generally have had a strong religious or ethical upbringing as well. People with this placement might have a home in a foreign country.

Saturn ♄ in the Fourth House

Saturn in the fourth house is strongly devoted to family and might have had to assume responsibilities at an early age, perhaps because of an early loss of the father. This placement plans carefully for a more secure old age and feels very strongly about both its family and carrying on family traditions. These people often need more love and self-esteem than others. If challenged by aspects, there might be difficulties in the relationship with the parents.

Uranus ♅ in the Fourth House

Fourth house Uranus is independent and unusual, and may have had an unusual home or childhood as well. This person's life might take a sudden turn in an unexpected direction later years. There might be sudden and drastic changes in the home arena throughout life. This placement also indicates a person who might be very independent or different from his or her family, social class, or ethnic group, and the home might be used for group meetings of an occult or humanitarian nature.

Neptune ♆ in the Fourth House

Fourth house Neptune people might have an idealized picture of what a home life should be like, but if challenged by aspects, the conditions of theirs might be unsettled, uncertain, confused, or chaotic. The problems might involve anything from an alcoholic parent to frequent moves. This placement also could indicate skeletons or mysteries in the family closet. This placement shows karmic or unconscious emotional ties to the family and home life, imaginative parenting, and also might indicate some self-sacrifice connected to the home. Meditation or spiritual practices might be important, too.

Pluto ♀ in the Fourth House

With a fourth house Pluto, your soul is learning how to create internal emotional security without the need for others. You might have had emotional shocks early in your family life that forced you to learn the value of internal security or many experiences in which your emotional needs were not met. Your evolutionary intent is to learn to become responsible for your own well-being, develop your own authority or individuality, find the right career or work, and become emotionally mature. After you do this, you can help others understand their emotional needs and blockages. Fourth house Pluto people can be emotionally manipulative and even vindictive if they feel they've been wounded, but they also can be sympathetic and nurturing, as well as intensely loyal to those they care about.

North Node ☊ in the Fourth House/South Node ☋ in the Tenth House

With a fourth house North Node/tenth house South Node, you might have unconscious memories of having an authoritative position and now want to achieve it again. But this time, you're here to learn that it is very important to build the foundation of your life first, and until you do so, there might be constant conflicts between your home and career. In addition, you will learn to seek achievement for the deeds you accomplish and not for having an automatic audience as an authority figure.

The Fifth House: Do What You Wanna Do

Traditionally, the fifth house is the house of creativity, and so it is only natural that this house would also encompass children, risk-taking, and romance—all creative (and risky!) endeavors. It's also the house of investments, another risky area.

The natural house ruler here, of course, is Leo ♌, and the associated planet is the Sun ☉. People who wonder if they'll ever find the right creative outlet would do well to study their fifth house: It's possible the answer is right through Door Number 5.

Heaven Knows _____

The fifth house is where you find your pleasure, fun, parties, vacations, self-indulgences—and your self-expression. It includes everything from gambling to holidays, fun to romance, and creativity to pranks. You also could think of it as the house of joy and the heart.

The fifth house: your creativity, fun, romance, risk, and children.

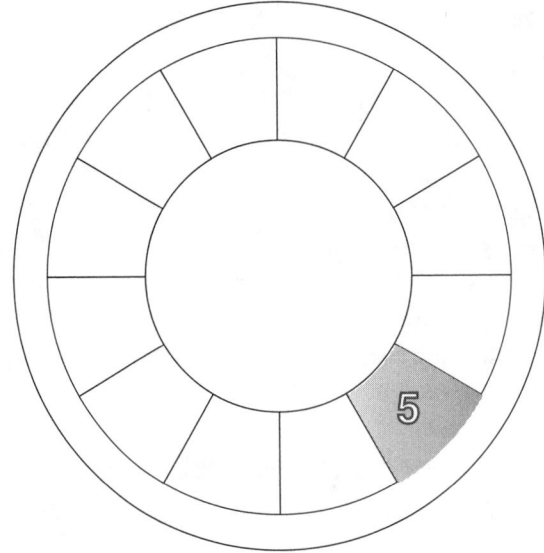

Getting Creative

Your fifth house sign describes the nature of your creativity and self-expression, and its ruler indicates how and where you develop your abilities to express yourself. The house where Leo, its corresponding natural sign, lies shows where your creativity and purpose are released and what area of your life will provide your creative potential.

The Sun ☉ in the Fifth House

Here at home, a fifth house Sun is energetic, powerfully creative, and enjoying living the good life. There's an interest in art, a desire to be with people, and a free hand with money. This placement loves a good time, and it loves children and others, too. Self-expression can be found through acting, teaching, art, sports, or other creative and artistic pursuits. People with the Sun in the fifth house are also loyal, ardent lovers. Highly competitive, they often project themselves with drama or a sense of style.

The ☽ Moon in the Fifth House

A fifth house Moon seeks out pleasure, and is both romantic and imaginatively creative. Associations with others are often intimate in some way, and there is a great desire for children. Creative, self-expressive, and romantic urges are heavily influenced by emotional needs. People with this placement might develop emotional dependencies on romantic partners—or their feelings for lovers might be very changeable.

Mercury ☿ in the Fifth House

Fifth house Mercury loves change and new people and must be intellectually stimulated to keep the good times rolling. There's a need here to give everything a personal spin, and this placement is capable of dramatic self-expression, especially in speech and writing, or can indicate a teacher, especially of the primary grades, a writer, playwright, or art critic, as well as a stock market analyst or active investor. Tricksters, the ones who like pulling pranks, are also found with this placement. In addition, people with fifth house Mercury are often attracted to intellectual or mentally stimulating romantic partners.

Venus ♀ in the Fifth House

Fifth house Venus loves the social spotlight and seems to attract romance like a moth to a flame. These people take enormous pleasure in creative work and have a flair for acting, writing, and all types of artistic pursuits. This placement is affectionate and sociable and loves to find pleasure and passion. If beneficially aspected, there can be gain through investments and speculation as well.

Mars ♂ in the Fifth House

Impulsive fifth house Mars can be impatient in love but has a personal magnetism that draws others. This Mars placement can be very competitive in sports, because these people have natural athletic skill. They also can become very impatient and jealous in romantic matters, or their strong sexual drive might lead to an urgent need for a romantic partner! When well-aspected, Mars here can work very well with children, especially as coaches or physical-education teachers, and these people know the right way to discipline, too. This placement is often found in athletes and in artists who work with tools, such as sculptors.

Jupiter ♃ in the Fifth House

Jupiter in the fifth house loves any kind of recreation, whether it's a sporting event, the theater, or another great party, and they love adventure, too. This placement indicates a tendency to take risks—and those risks often pay off. Fifth house Jupiter does just about everything in a big way and is often found in teaching, publishing, sales, the arts, the entertainment business, and in businesses related to the stock market or investments. This placement is very creative in the arts, sports, education, or anything related to children. It often inspires teachers, counselors, or advisers, especially to young people.

Saturn ♄ in the Fifth House

Disciplined fifth house Saturn needs to learn how to relax and have a good time, and for this serious, responsible planet, that's not always easy. Because of its seriousness, Saturn's fifth house creativity is often channeled into scientific discovery: This is the placement of Marie Curie, for example. But this is not the only way it manifests. People with Saturn in the fifth house also show structure and organization in art and music and an ability to be creative in politics and business management. They might work in a business associated with investments, speculation, education, places of entertainment, or the arts. It also can manifest as ambition for leadership or power in artistic areas. Usually, there are serious responsibilities concerning one's children, or, the person might not be able to have children. These people are often romantically attracted to those who are older or more mature.

Uranus ♅ in the Fifth House

Fifth house Uranus takes an inventive approach to creative expression and might make sudden changes in its direction. There's a need for self-expression and romance, but Uranus here also can be reckless, taking a few too many chances. Unusual circumstances might arise with one's children here, who might be very gifted and talented. It's also a wild ride for speculations and investments, and for sudden or unusual romantic attractions, which might break off as suddenly as they started. These people are often attracted to others who are unique, different, nomadic, or geniuses, and they like to work for themselves due to their strong independence and need for freedom.

Neptune ♆ in the Fifth House

Fifth house Neptune loves pleasure and luxury, and is drawn to anything that involves an element of fantasy. This is especially true of the movies, and Neptune's fifth house creativity is often found in this field. When challenged by aspect, this placement can indicate a childlike or naive approach to love or risks, and this, in turn, can mean people might take advantage of them. This placement also indicates idealistic and visionary potentials, and these people might create intuitively or spiritually inspired art or music. They need to be appreciated for their creative talents.

Pluto ♇ in the Fifth House

With a fifth house Pluto, you feel as though you have a special destiny to fulfill, and you'll be able to project your special abilities and creativity in any manner in which you wish to focus them. However, your soul's evolutionary purpose is to learn how to link your abilities and special destiny with the needs of others or society as a whole, and until you do, your creativity might be blocked in some way. It's not enough to just focus on yourself and your talents. Children with this placement need an insatiable amount of attention, and everyone with it can be self-centered and self-focused. You have enormous strength of will, tremendous creativity, a major need for attention, and you also can be loving, giving, and magnetic.

North Node ☊ in the Fifth House/South Node ☋ in the Eleventh House

With a fifth house North Node/eleventh house South Node, you're learning about creativity, and you're often a dreamer, apart from the crowd, watching everyone else. With this placement, you need to learn the importance of hopes or wishes and then use them to create your own destiny. Your need for friendships might dissipate your creative energies, and you must learn the self-discipline necessary to avoid this. Instead, constructively apply your hopes to creating reality.

The Sixth House: Nine to Five

Often called the house of service, the sixth house is concerned with both service and health. This is the area of your daily responsibilities and is the house of your co-workers, too. You could think of your sixth house as the work you've got to do.

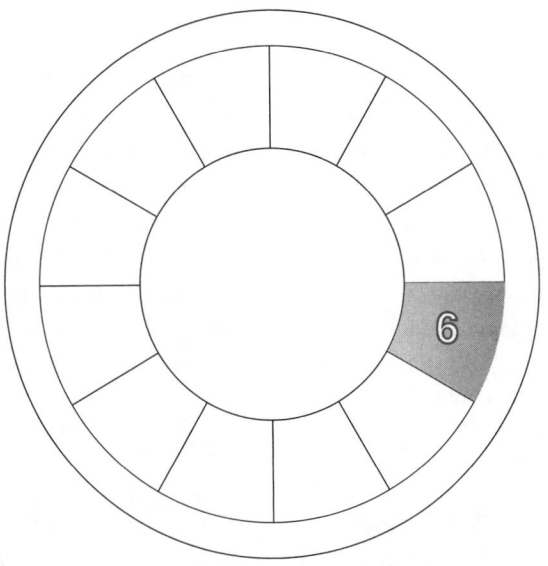

The sixth house: your personal responsibilities, health, and service to others.

The sixth house is naturally ruled by Virgo ♍, and its corresponding planet is Mercury ☿. This translates into gaining fulfillment through skills that are of value to others: If we don't develop our own special competence at doing something meaningful to us that also helps others, then we end up working at meaningless jobs.

But your sixth house is also about your responsibilities, how you help and are of service to the world. What planets reside in your sixth house can indicate whether you're an optimist or pessimist in your daily work, and the health problems you might be prone to. When people aren't fulfilled by their work, after all, they have a strong tendency to get sick.

Heavenly Bodies at Work

Your sixth house is where you will find your desire to be competent. You can be good at many things, but it's in your sixth house that you'll find meaningful responsibility—

> **Star-Crossed**
>
> Not entirely comfortable in your job? You may be good at it, but if you're not finding the meaningful responsibility of your sixth house, it's never going to fit quite right!

how the things that you're good at matter to other people, and especially to you. Your sixth house sign describes your daily responsibilities and how you prefer to be of service to others. The ruler of your sixth house shows where and how you will meet your regular obligations. The house with Virgo on its cusp, the sixth house's natural sign, describes where you apply discrimination and analysis to your duties, to get the results you desire.

The Sun ☉ in the Sixth House

A sixth house Sun takes pride in its work and is a good organizer—with a need for appreciation. If it doesn't get it, it'll often leave for a different job! This placement also requires a lot of attention to diet and personal routines to maintain good health. People with sixth house Suns are good problem solvers, and, especially if the Sun is reinforced by aspect, there can be a strong interest in health or healing careers or an intense desire to establish oneself through service to others. For an example, we need look no further than tennis star Serena Williams, whose Sun plus five planets in her sixth house (Moon ☽, Mercury ☿, Jupiter ♃, Saturn ♄, and Pluto ♇) highlight her commitment to "service." (See Serena's birth chart in Chapter 22, with transits to her 2002 win at the U.S. Open.)

The Moon ☽ in the Sixth House

The Moon in the sixth house can indicate frequent changes in jobs (unless the Moon is in a fixed sign, as discussed in Chapter 3), along with great consideration for others, including co-workers. This placement also indicates that these people's health and productivity at work tend to fluctuate with their emotions. The diet is also very important to them, and they might work in restaurants, nutrition, food preparation, or other businesses associated with food. These people like to serve others by working closely with the public. Like the Moon, their health may go through phases.

Mercury ☿ in the Sixth House

Mercury in the sixth house can be a perfectionist, but that's because this placement understands the importance of details. This natural placement of Mercury has a strong interest in matters of health and well-being as well. There can be a tendency toward unnecessary worry, but that goes with the detail-oriented territory. This placement also indicates very high intelligence and people who acquire specialized skills and knowledge for their work. Normally very systematic and efficient, they also have a strong desire to keep up with the latest research or new techniques. This is a very favorable placement for people working in healing, medicine, science, or engineering, and they'll need lots of vitamin B complex to combat their nervousness.

Venus ♀ in the Sixth House

Venus in the sixth house wants harmony and good relationships on the job. This is a good placement for counselors, arbitrators, and health-care workers, or these people might prefer to work in jobs associated with artistic pursuits or in areas that are very social. It's also found in people who work with or for women. There might be social connections—and a marriage partner—from meeting people through work. This placement indicates good health in general, but there can be a tendency to overindulge in the good stuff; these people should especially avoid sugar.

Mars ♂ in the Sixth House

Sixth house Mars wants to accomplish things, and, because it drives itself hard, expects everyone else to do the same. This placement can indicate mechanical ability but also can find it difficult to get along with co-workers. Sixth house Mars needs to beware of accidents. These people commonly use tools (especially sharp ones) and/or machinery in their work and are often mechanics, machinists, mechanical engineers, steelworkers, surgeons, or equipment operators. Their work is normally very skilled or precise, and their identity is usually tied to their work and how well they do it.

Jupiter ♃ in the Sixth House

Jupiter in the sixth house does well at work and gets along with co-workers, too. People with this placement can be very successful because of their optimism and creativity, but they need to be careful not to overindulge, as they have a tendency toward weight and liver problems. These people have a strong interest in and understanding of how the mind and emotions are connected to healing. They might pursue natural healing work, which connects with their interest in serving others in a practical way.

Saturn ♄ in the Sixth House

Sixth house Saturn is a conscientious and reliable worker, good at taking on responsibility and getting the job done, which often requires specialized skills and knowledge. Sometimes this placement can push itself too hard, resulting in chronic illness. When challenged by aspects, this placement has a tendency to do all of the work without asking for any reward, which can lead to internal problems. These people tend to work in medicine, science, engineering, food processing, or nutrition, or other areas that require specialized capabilities. Worry and anxiety tend to cause health problems here.

Uranus ♅ in the Sixth House

Those with Uranus in the sixth house bring new ideas to work, but also can be erratic or impatient; they're often people who work well alone. Because sixth house Uranus doesn't much go for routine, it might find its health difficulties are not run-of-the-mill, either. This placement also indicates that unusual or advanced methods might be employed at work, and there might be strong interest in spiritual or alternative healing practices or diets. These people might have ingenious scientific or mathematical ideas that lead to important inventions or new understandings, especially ones that have practical applications. Employment might be terminated suddenly or without notice, and illness is normally due to nervousness or irritability.

Neptune ♆ in the Sixth House

With a sixth house Neptune, people tend to be idealistic about their work and sensitive to both their surroundings and their co-workers. This placement can be highly resourceful, but these people often prefer to work alone or behind the scenes. Health problems can be difficult to pin down or might be emotionally related. These people are usually learning to view work as a means of serving others in a spiritual way, and there can be many sacrifices asked of them. They also might have an intuitive understanding regarding the most effective work methods and processes and might be interested in spiritual healing or other natural forms of healing. When ill, these people have difficulties with drugs and prescription medications but benefit from natural foods or remedies.

Pluto ♀ in the Sixth House

With Pluto in the sixth house, you're learning lessons about service to others, self-improvement, and humility. There's a powerful mind at work here, leading to cycles of introspection and self-analysis and adjustments in any aspect of yourself that's not appropriate for your evolutionary intent. Your soul's evolutionary purpose is to learn appropriate relationships between yourself and others, to develop faith, and to find a sense of connection to a higher power or force. In doing so, lessons in discrimination, tolerance, and respect for human imperfections and mistakes will be learned. Sixth house Pluto people are self-effacing, with keen, critical minds. They also might be critical or forgiving, depending on circumstances, and are sometimes crisis-prone.

North Node ☊ in the Sixth House/South Node ☋ in the Twelfth House

With a sixth house North Node and a twelfth house South Node, you're someone who spends a lot of time deep in thought. Your tendency to live your life based on fears and imagination can undermine your confidence, and those close to you might think you avoid what's real. You are here to live a life of sacrifice and service to others, so what you really need to do is learn about responsibility and trust, and develop faith in the Universe. After you do this, you will serve others with your past compassion and take great pleasure in helping them.

The Least You Need to Know

- ◆ The second quadrant houses are the areas of your home, creativity, and daily work.

- ◆ Your fourth house represents your home, emotional security, and inner foundations for your life.

- ◆ Your fifth house symbolizes your creativity, joy, children, risk-taking, and romance.

- ◆ Your sixth house contains your responsibilities, health, and meaningful service to others, including your co-workers.

Chapter 17

Houses in the Third Quadrant: Out in the World

In This Chapter

- The third quadrant houses: connecting to your outer world
- The seventh house: forever yours
- The eighth house: sex, money, and other, equally important matters
- The ninth house: don't know much about history …

In the third quadrant houses, you move from your personal world into the larger one. The seventh house is concerned with your relationships and connections with others; the eighth house with your ways of coping with everything from money to death; and the ninth house is the area of your social and moral belief systems. These houses, in other words, are the areas where your tools for navigating your world come into play.

The Seventh House: Forever Yours

The seventh house is traditionally the house of partnership and marriage and is ruled by the sign that appears on your *descendant*. Its natural sign (naturally enough) is Libra ♎, and its associated planet is Venus ♀.

The seventh house: your primary relationships and partnerships.

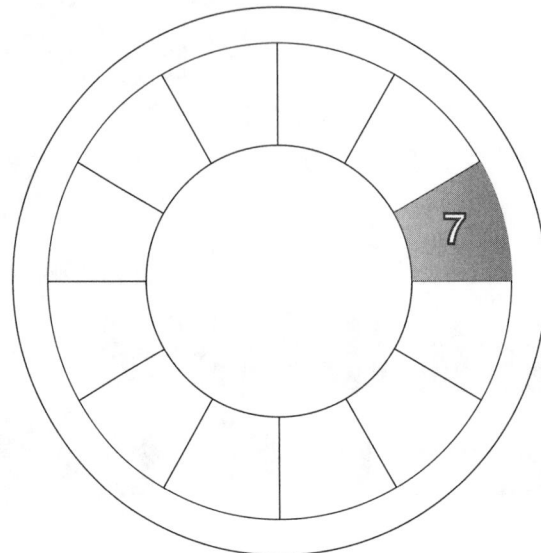

Your seventh house is the place where you learn to put your own interests aside for the sake of your primary relationships. It can indicate what kind of mate and marriage you'll have, but it also indicates other kinds of partnerships, too: important friends and associates, your business partnerships, and your legal affairs and agreements.

Successful navigation of your seventh house means that you understand shared goals and commitment. This is the house of your primary relationships, after all, and that can include everything from your soul mate to the way relationships change. Most of all, your seventh house is the place *where you cooperate and share with others*.

Star-Crossed

Your seventh house also can house your adversaries—the people or things that stand between you and your shared goals, your open enemies. Enemies in this house are people you know are your enemies, but that doesn't make it any easier to deal with them!

Heavenly Connections

Your seventh house sign describes your relationships and how you connect with others; the ruler of your seventh house describes where and how your relationships are developed. The house where Libra, the corresponding natural sign, is shows where you learn to relate to others and share your values.

And don't forget: If there are no planets in a house, the ruler and its association with other planets show what's happening in that area of your life.

The Sun ☉ in the Seventh House

A seventh house Sun expresses its creative power through relationships, for better or worse. These people's self-expression and willpower are most often shown through their major relationships. If challenged by aspect, they need to learn to respect the rights of others and cooperate. This placement also indicates people who work best with others, but at the same time they must learn to value their partner's needs and goals as much as their own. A seventh house Sun is all about the use of social ties for self-expression.

The Moon ☽ in the Seventh House

A seventh house Moon is concerned with emotional and domestic security in both marriage and relationships, and this placement can indicate marriage to a parent figure. A seventh house Moon is usually popular with others, largely because these people are very sensitive and responsive to the needs of others. They might marry early in life, and their marriage or business partners might be moody, sensitive, or emotionally changeable. Like the Moon, their relationships might go through phases.

Mercury ☿ in the Seventh House

A seventh house Mercury seeks intellectual compatibility in both marriage and partnerships, and loves a lot of verbal give and take. In particular, law, literary, or communications partnerships can benefit from this placement, as might salespeople and public relations experts, counselors, arbitrators, or mediators. This placement is a very sociable one, but when challenged by aspect, a seventh house Mercury can have relationship problems because of misunderstandings or unfulfilled agreements. These people tend to marry highly intellectual and well-educated people, because they want mental companionship from others.

Venus ♀ in the Seventh House

A seventh house Venus seeks harmony and fulfillment in its primary relationships and is able to create the harmonious environment to achieve these goals. This placement can be very successful in legal matters and, with its refined social graces, gets along well with everyone. Seventh house Venus *needs* to be socially active. This placement also shows good ability to deal with the public and works well in sales, psychology, any of the performing arts, or public relations.

Mars ♂ in the Seventh House

A seventh house Mars remains highly independent, even in its relationships, and it is usually the one to impulsively—and aggressively—begin those relationships. This placement, when challenged, might indicate more than one marriage or more than one business partnership. Seventh house Mars can be quarrelsome, largely because it likes to have its own way, or its marriage or business partners might be very aggressive or impulsive, because this energy can come out through the partners as well. When Mars is well aspected in this house, there can be a great deal of cooperative spirit and energy put into major relationships, and these people might do very well in sales or working with the public.

Jupiter ♃ in the Seventh House

Jupiter in the seventh house usually indicates success in both marriage and partnerships, although it also can indicate that one will marry more than once and/or benefit philosophically from it. This placement can mean that one's enemies will later become one's associates or, at the very least, that one will have a fortuitous partnership of some sort. Jupiter in the seventh house indicates a very affectionate and optimistic spouse, too. This placement shows someone honest and fair in dealings with others, who expects the same in return. If challenged by aspect, though, they might expect too much from others.

Saturn ♄ in the Seventh House

Saturn in the seventh house is cautious about all of its relationships, but it also shows a strong sense of responsibility and fairness in its dealings with others. This is a good placement for working in the legal system or business management. Unless challenged by aspect, these people keep their agreements and improve their lives by working with others, and will often delay involvement until they're absolutely certain of the other's commitment. Seventh house Saturn people take relationships very seriously; they might marry someone with a significant age difference. There can be difficulties relating to others with this placement, but this is largely because of their caution.

Uranus ♅ in the Seventh House

A seventh house Uranus might find sudden marriage or partnership and is often drawn to unusual people. A seventh house Uranus and his or her spouse might draw others' attention because they are both so unusual. On the other hand, there might be sudden divorce and remarriage; there's a certain lack of permanence in relationships here. The main characteristic of this placement is that these people need a lot of independence and freedom in their relationships.

Neptune Ψ in the Seventh House

Seventh house Neptune seeks others with common goals, dreams, and/or visions and will have a sensitive, intuitive, and responsive partner. This placement also can indicate a love of foreigners and foreign travel, as well as a capacity for helping those less fortunate. This placement can be truly giving—or quite deceptive and confused. These people might have karmic ties to their major relationships, and they might have to make a lot of sacrifices for their relationships. Ideally, they're seeking their spiritual mate. If challenged by aspect, they could be misled by or deceive others.

Pluto ♀ in the Seventh House

If you have a seventh house Pluto, you're learning how to participate in relationships. Your soul is now ready to relate with others on an equal basis so that neither person in the relationship *needs* or *controls* the other. The evolutionary intent for your soul is to learn how to launch your own life changes and make your own decisions, without depending on others for advice, approval, or their opinions. You need to minimize your dependence on others, learn how to trust yourself, and likewise respect the decisions and paths of others.

North Node ☊ in the Seventh House/South Node ☋ in the First House

With a seventh house North Node and a first house South Node, you're learning about cooperation with others, because you've already developed yourself as a strong individual. Now you will learn to give and sacrifice for the sake of relationships, develop consideration for others, and ultimately detach from the self and the ego-centered ideas that governed you in the past. This life is an opportunity to share your strength with others by helping them see their own self-worth.

The Eighth House: Sex, Money, and Other Equally Important Matters

The eighth house is the second of the three so-called "mystical" houses, or houses of endings (the others are the fourth and the twelfth). This house is about shared resources, and that includes everything from taxes, insurance, and business mergers to inheritances and marrying for money. The eighth house is also known as the house of death and regeneration, because it is related to transformation *and* physical death and deals with transforming physical things back into energy.

The eighth house: your joint resources, sex, death, and rebirth.

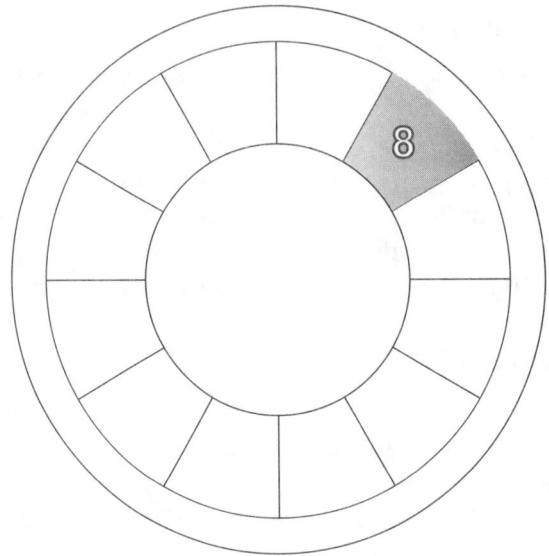

Regeneration is about more than death, too: It's also about individual transformation, whether emotional, physical, mental, or spiritual. For this reason, the eighth house includes the life forces, which are concerned with sex, birth, and the afterlife, as well as death. Here is where you'll find your instinctive desire to reproduce, as well as how you cope with and understand the "mysteries" of life. It's also where marriage is consummated, and all forms of intimacy are found.

Your eighth house also seems to unveil a bit of the mystery surrounding your death (although when it will occur can never be found in your chart, at least not by Western astrologers), and it also is the house of psychic powers, occult mysteries, and occult knowledge.

Heaven Knows

Part of understanding the mystery of one's life is one's intense experiences, whether they be the survival of consciousness after death, merging with another person via sex (orgasm is called *petit mort*—"the little death"—by the French), merging with the God of your understanding (or the Source), or birth. The way you cope with the mysteries of life and death can be found in your eighth house, and all those mysteries or secrets you unearth can be found there, too.

The eighth house is naturally ruled by Scorpio ♏, and its associated planets are Mars ♂ and Pluto ♀, so it's also associated with all forms of subtle energies. For this reason, it's related to higher mathematics, atomic energy, and sciences that deal with complex energies, such as physics. In addition, the eighth house is the area of corporate or political resources and some people with strong eighth houses might be active in one of these areas.

Who's in the Bedroom?

Your eighth house sign describes how you make your life changes, and what attitudes or areas you need to transform. Your eighth house ruler describes where and how you encounter areas of your life that need to be transformed. The house where Scorpio, the corresponding natural sign, lies reveals what areas of your life need to be regenerated and where you need to merge your energies with others.

The Sun ☉ in the Eighth House

People with an eighth house Sun constantly seek self-improvement or regeneration, and they do so by applying their willpower. Because these people are both intensely interested in deep mysteries and magnetic, they can often attract the support of others to their causes. This placement also can indicate an inheritance, or the managing of other people's money, and, while there might have been early life difficulties, there might be late fame or fortune as well—possibly even after the person's death. People with the Sun in the eighth house are primarily concerned with the need to transform and regenerate, deep mysteries of life, and mysteries in general. Vocationally, they might deal with matters of the dead, such as insurance or funerals, or they might be psychologists or sex therapists.

The Moon ☽ in the Eighth House

An eighth house Moon has a deep-seated need for security and is very interested in questions about death and the afterlife. There might be a psychic ability here, and an inheritance, especially through the mother. This placement also indicates an instinctive understanding of others' needs and wants, and these people often have changeable circumstances involving intimate relationships and shared resources.

Mercury ☿ in the Eighth House

With its penetrating mind, eighth house Mercury has a talent for research and analysis. There's an attraction to the occult with this placement, too, and people with eighth house Mercury might be intuitive, secretive, and psychic. This placement also might indicate the death of someone very close, a neighbor, or co-worker, that greatly influences the person's life, or they might get money from someone else (or both!). In addition, they have penetrating insight into sciences that deal with energy, occult mysteries, and life in general. These people are likely to understand the true motivations of others and so are able to ferret out secrets. They might work in corporate finance, taxes, insurance, research, or write about mysteries or occult topics. They shouldn't smoke if a long life is desired (but, then, who should?).

Venus ♀ in the Eighth House

Venus in the eighth house looks for and finds sexual fulfillment, often inherits money from a loved one, and is generally promised a peaceful death (we'd probably all like to move our Venuses here!). The sexual and creative potential of this placement can be helpful to other people as well. When challenged by aspect, this placement might show either an overemphasis on sex, or the possibility of marrying for money. It might also indicate intense emotions, jealousy, or possessiveness.

Mars ♂ in the Eighth House

Eighth house Mars, because of its natural placement, is passionate about life and sex and is attracted to medicine and the healing arts, as well as to research in a variety of areas. There's a possibility of family conflict over inheritances or shared resources here, and it's also possible that an eighth house Mars might have a sudden death or come into contact with death through war or violence. This placement shows intense energy, persistence, and strong desires, especially when it comes to meeting goals and wants through the use of corporate or shared resources. These people also can be very interested in psychic or occult forces.

Jupiter ♃ in the Eighth House

Jupiter in the eighth house indicates an optimistic and healthy attitude toward life, death, and sex, and this placement can inspire others as well. Eighth house Jupiter indicates financial gain through inheritance or marriage and an ability to handle money well. Like magicians, these people also are talented in creating and regenerating their deepest realities. The conditions at death will likely be easy and peaceful, and death will usually come only after a long and healthy life. This placement also can show a strong sex drive or even an overemphasis on sex, and if challenged by aspect, these people might overspend their shared resources.

Saturn ♄ in the Eighth House

Eighth house Saturn often takes responsibility for the affairs of others and is prudent about putting money away for loved ones. People with this placement either have or need to develop appropriate stewardship for material resources, because they are often accountable for other people's money or taxes. This placement can indicate sexual inhibition of some kind, or difficulty in expressing oneself emotionally. When well-aspected, eighth house Saturns usually live to a ripe old age.

Uranus ♅ in the Eighth House

Uranus in the eighth house is interested in unusual ideas about life, sex, and death and is unconventional in its approach to any or all of them. They might have sudden financial gain from unexpected sources, unreciprocated love, and/or prescient dreams. Eighth house Uranus is often highly psychic and intuitive. These people also are very interested in occult topics, telepathy, or the survival of consciousness after death. Sudden death is a possibility here, and it might come from an accident, so it's best for these people not to drive or work with dangerous equipment when they're angry.

Neptune ♆ in the Eighth House

Neptune in the eighth house can be visionary and charismatic, with strongly developed ESP and psychic abilities, as well as an idealistic desire to help others. There might be a partner whose extravagance leads to financial difficulties. This placement can indicate confusion, difficulties, or deception concerning the partner's money, taxes, or insurance. Strong interests in spiritualism also might lead to an ability to contact the dead. Eighth house Neptune might indicate a death while asleep.

Pluto ♀ in the Eighth House

With Pluto in the eighth house, you come face-to-face with the limits and parameters of who you are, as opposed to whom or what you are not. You have a strong need to not only eliminate, but also to transform, all your limitations. To do so, you might be intensely drawn to "taboo" experiences, sex, money, relationships, rituals, status, magic, meditation, or in-depth knowledge as ways of overcoming your limitations. By merging with your chosen symbol, you become whatever you were seeking, and you might gain power by doing so. But the evolutionary intent of your soul is to learn self-reliance and how to identify internal values and resources in order to sustain yourself. What you are *really* searching for is *within yourself*.

North Node ☊ in the Eighth House/South Node ☋ in the Second House

With an eighth house North Node and a second house South Node, you're learning to overcome possessiveness and learn about self-control in terms of money and possessions. It's time to move beyond self-values and what you have to a point where you integrate with the values of others. You might have a symbolic rebirth after pushing yourself beyond your limits from excessive behaviors. This is a particularly difficult lesson, because you might seem to be starting over again, but the main lesson here is about faith, and not looking back at your old ways.

The Ninth House: Don't Know Much About History

Your ninth house is where everything from higher education to philosophy and religion, from law to travel and foreign concerns reside. It also includes the medical system and politics, and all areas of collective thought structures. In addition, it's the area involved in the development of a social conscience. In other words, it's the house of your social areas.

The ninth house: higher education, philosophy, religion, law, and travel.

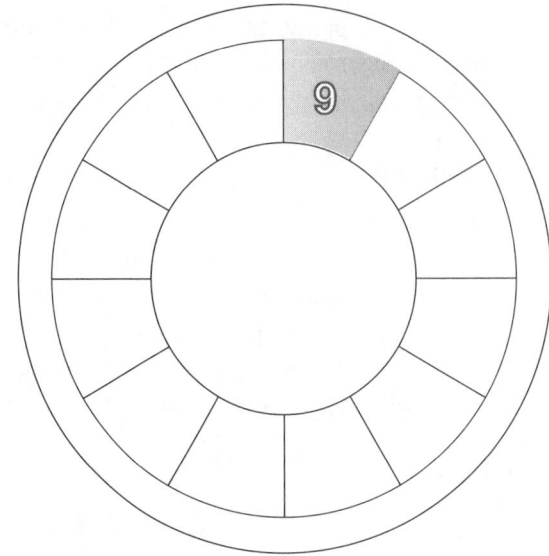

This is the house of mental exploration and long-distance travel, and it is traditionally the house of long journeys over water. We love the sound of that, and seeing new cultures and more of the world is one way to gain a new perspective of the world in general.

Your ninth house also is the place where you'll find your patterns of behavior—and how you break them. This is where you'll confront the tendency of your life to become routine as well as where you'll encounter the unpredictable that break up that routine, primarily because it's our beliefs, religion, and philosophical systems that are behind everything we do.

You could think of your ninth house as your mental "model of the universe," but remember, *your* model is but one of many. Unsuccessfully navigated, your ninth house can become a place where you mistake that model for the real world. Successfully navigated, it's the place where you'll make room in your life for miracles.

In addition to being where your cultural customs and beliefs exist, this house also is where you'll find how you publicly convey your ideas and beliefs. And the ninth house also is considered the house of publishing and teaching.

Naturally associated with Sagittarius ♐ on its cusp, the ninth house is the house of the higher mind and exploration, especially of philosophical subjects. The planet that naturally rules the ninth house is Jupiter ♃, the planet of abundance, or, when overdone, misfortune.

What's Behind Your Beliefs?

Your ninth house sign describes your beliefs, philosophies, and how you seek opportunities for expansion. Your ninth house ruler describes where and how you expand your mind and experiences and develop your understanding of life. The house where Sagittarius, the corresponding natural sign, is shows what areas of your life can provide you with growth experiences, which lead to a greater understanding of life.

The Sun ☉ in the Ninth House

A ninth house Sun pursues philosophical or religious ideas through one of the areas described by this house: higher education, publishing, or foreign affairs, for example. There's a need for truth here and so, of course, a tendency to stick to one's word. These people are both philosophical and full of optimism, mainly due to their great faith and strong moral convictions. This placement could indicate a great deal of foreign travel, as well as the pursuit of higher education, and ninth house Suns are often successful in law, travel, medicine, publishing, or religion. If this placement is challenged, though, there can be dogmatic tendencies, as well as an inclination to force their ideas and beliefs on others.

The Moon ☽ in the Ninth House

The primary factor for a ninth house Moon is that the person's religious and philosophical beliefs and views of reality are emotionally tied to the past and early home or parental conditioning. Great happiness can come from traveling, and journeys or broadening experiences can create further development of their beliefs and views of reality. This placement has an imaginative and receptive mind, and there's a high consciousness of the supernatural. These people can be natural teachers, putting their imaginative tendencies to practical use. They also tend to learn in a holistic way.

Mercury ☿ in the Ninth House

Mercury in the ninth house is both adaptable and exploratory, eager to gain further knowledge and meet new people. There can be a great deal of travel with this placement, as well as interest in everything from higher education to foreign cultures. This placement often wants to understand the development of social ideas and attitudes over time, because attitudes determine how and what facts people will integrate. Ninth house Mercury can be intuitive and philosophical, and if challenged by aspects, there might be intellectual snobbery or dogmatic beliefs.

Venus ♀ in the Ninth House

Venus in the ninth house has high ideals and an appreciation for high culture. There will be a great understanding of foreign people and places. This placement indicates one might marry a foreigner or spend much of one's life abroad. People with Venus here also might marry someone they meet at an educational institution or church, and there could be some benefits from in-laws. They might be very well-educated in artistic or cultural subjects, or religious music and art.

Mars ♂ in the Ninth House

A ninth house Mars indicates beliefs translated into action and an active enjoyment of travel and adventure. This placement seeks out new experiences and often finds gain through higher education. There also can be fervent religiosity in this placement (this is the placement of a crusader for religious, philosophical, social, legal, or educational causes) or a great restlessness that requires constant travel, sports, or outdoor activities. When challenged by aspects, this placement can lead to impatience and intolerance concerning the views of others.

Jupiter ♃ in the Ninth House

In its natural home here, Jupiter is adventurous and optimistic, and travel and education promise great rewards. The primary distinguishing trait of this placement is the meaningful pursuit of philosophy, religion, or higher education, and many of these people pursue careers as teachers or find their calling in religious occupations. They might have a flair for foreign languages, and foreigners might contribute to a ninth house Jupiter's success. This placement can indicate success in writing or publishing as well, or if in business, people who lecture or travel.

Saturn ♄ in the Ninth House

With Saturn in the ninth house, a person has a great desire to learn, and carefully explores philosophy or religion. There's an inherent distrust of new ideas, because ninth house Saturns are interested in social stability, but there's also a desire to know about everything. There can be a tendency toward fanaticism here, but these people often mellow with age, as wisdom develops. Ninth house Saturns often seek positions of authority or status in education, religious institutions, or in businesses that deal with publishing, law, politics, or international affairs. They also might be university professors or public officials.

Uranus ♅ in the Ninth House

Ninth house Uranus always seeks to expand its intellectual horizons and can often be found traveling at the drop of a hat. This placement might have unusual experiences during its travels and also might have a unique approach to religion, philosophy, or their beliefs. People with Uranus here can be unusually gifted in their understanding of religious or metaphysical concepts, with advanced ideas in philosophy, religion, or education. If they teach, they use technological tools, such as computers or audio/visual equipment, to create stimulating classes. They often study unusual systems of thought, such as astrology, reincarnation, or occult subjects. When challenged by aspect, this placement might become fanatical about religious cults, politics, or social issues.

Neptune ♆ in the Ninth House

Neptune in the ninth house is both imaginative and insightful (and might be prophetically visionary) and is often drawn to philosophical questions that are not easily answered. This placement is often associated with mystical forms of religion, meditation, cults, or yoga. With their capacity for tolerance and love of travel, people with Neptune here relate well to foreigners. They're also interested in social reform. They have very strongly intuitive minds. But if challenged by aspect, there can be problems from following misguided spiritual leaders or neglecting to pursue higher education.

Pluto ♇ in the Ninth House

With Pluto in the ninth house, you want to understand life in its broadest possible sense and to explain its connection to the universe as well. Because your emotional security is based on your beliefs, you want to get in touch with larger forces and even tell others about your beliefs. You might try to convert

> **StarFacts**
>
> Ninth house Plutos who sought greater truths include poet Kahlil Gibran, prophet Nostradamus, artist Michelangelo, former President John F. Kennedy, and, quite possibly, Jesus.

others to your ideas because this reinforces your sense of security and the feeling that you're right. However, the evolutionary intent of your soul is to learn that truth is relative, and that the path to truth is ultimately an individual one. Ninth house Pluto people are intuitive, conceptual thinkers and are above all concerned with truth.

North Node ☋ in the Ninth House/South Node ☊ in the Third House

With a ninth house North Node and a third house South Node, you are constantly getting entangled with others on the road to freedom. You like to listen to other people's problems and to give them advice, but you need to learn that truth is much larger than these day-to-day issues and the stored knowledge in your head. Your greatest growth will occur when you make the transition from lower to higher mind and open your eyes to the broader horizons before you. You're here to develop faith, intuition, and live a life of spiritual growth.

The Least You Need to Know

- ◆ Your third quadrant houses connect you to your world.

- ◆ Your seventh house is where you'll find your partnerships and relationships.

- ◆ In your eighth house you'll find your shared resources, intimate relationships, the deeper aspects of life, and transformation.

- ◆ Your ninth house contains your higher education, philosophies, and beliefs.

Chapter **18**

Houses in the Fourth Quadrant: Wishin' and Hopin'

In This Chapter

◆ The fourth quadrant houses are where you'll make your mark

◆ The tenth house: they say the neon lights are bright

◆ The eleventh house: when you wish upon a star

◆ The twelfth house: secret agent

The last three houses are the stuff of dreams—and of ambitions, reputations, interests, and goals. There are secrets here, too, but if you unlock the doors they're behind, you might find greater fulfillment. The tenth house is the area of your reputation and career; the eleventh house, your long-term dreams and goals; and the twelfth house is where you'll find your secrets, including those you're keeping from yourself.

The Tenth House: They Say the Neon Lights Are Bright

Your tenth house is the house of your reputation and your career—your own personal Broadway, in other words. Just as the fourth house is where you'll find your home, the tenth house, its opposite, is where you'll find everything outside your home: your profession, your community standing, social role, and what others think of you.

The tenth house: your reputation, career, and social responsibilities.

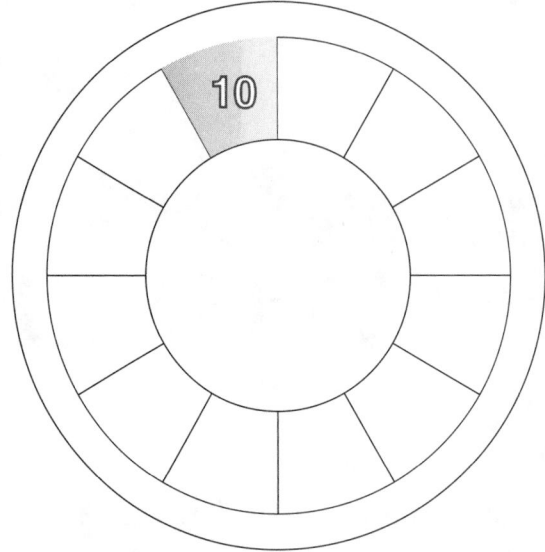

Some call this the house of ambition, aspiration, and attainment, and so it's interesting to note that it's also the house where you'll find your dominant parent. Still, this house is where you'll achieve success through your own efforts. It's a reflection of your image and achievements as shown by the rewards that you receive for your position in life.

Heaven Knows

Your tenth house represents your public identity, and at its best, it will match your needs and desires and reflect who you are as a person. Developing your social identity, after all, should be based on who you are, but accepting a role someone else gives you is what can happen when you don't get the tenth house right.

Just as your fourth house cusp is your lower heaven, or I.C., your tenth house cusp is your midheaven, or M.C. This means that this house contains things so obvious about you that they can be seen from a distance. Successfully navigated, your tenth house will give you a sense of fulfilling your destiny and an enormous sense of personal satisfaction as well.

Your tenth house is naturally associated with goal-oriented Capricorn ♑ on its cusp, and its planetary ruler is serious, responsible Saturn ♄, so naturally, the tenth house also represents positions of power and authority, and especially high government posts.

Your Supporting Cast

Your tenth house sign describes your ambitions and how you express yourself socially through your profession and community standing. Your tenth house ruler describes where and how you build your social reputation and position. The location of Capricorn, the corresponding natural sign in your chart, shows what areas of your life give you your greatest responsibilities and a need for respect from others.

The Sun ☉ in the Tenth House

A tenth house Sun indicates a strong sense of self and a will to succeed. Tenth house Suns couple ambition with power, and this is a good placement for someone interested in politics. There's both drive and leadership here, as well as the desire for social position. Although this placement needs power, there might not be the ability to handle it appropriately. If challenged by aspects, these people might use unethical methods to gain their power or position (this might sound familiar when you think of some politicians). In general, these people usually come from good homes, and if aspects are well placed, they are careful not to taint their respectability or dignity.

The Moon ☽ in the Tenth House

A tenth house Moon indicates that women will be connected to one's work in some way, and this is a good placement for "lunar" occupations, such as marketing, commodities, or shipping by water. Reputation matters to tenth house Moons, and there can be a tendency to sacrifice one's private life for the attainment of success. These people also are favored by the public and are often successful in politics or other careers that deal with the public. Usually, the mother has a strong career or reputation and sets the stage for this person's drive for achievement. Their feelings might be strongly linked to their desire for success, and until their success becomes linked to the welfare of the public, their career might go through "phases."

Mercury ☿ in the Tenth House

Mercury in the tenth house has no trouble communicating ideas to others and can often do so in a variety of ways. These people have intellectually stimulating careers and might be found in writing or communications. They tend to get an education so they can achieve significant social positions. They also can be associated with high-level political leaders and might become speech writers or political strategists. Politicians with this placement become known for their intelligent ideas. There might be travel involved in the career, or there might be more than one job.

Venus ♀ in the Tenth House

Tenth house Venus might have a career involved in the arts or in cultural work and is likely to enjoy social success and prosperity from the career. There's a natural diplomacy at work here, as well as an ability to use one's social charisma and magnetism to achieve public success. Counseling, negotiating, or diplomatic relations also might be indicated as possible careers, and these people could marry others with wealth and status.

Mars ♂ in the Tenth House

Mars in the tenth house has intense energy, initiative, and drive in its career, and will want to be the one in charge. This is a very competitive placement, but there's self-reliance, too, which means these people do very well in any executive position. They also can do well in the military or in engineering, and they make effective political leaders. This placement also can indicate some problem with the father, especially when challenged by aspects.

Jupiter ♃ in the Tenth House

Tenth house Jupiter works very well with others and has a natural ability to lead and inspire. There's a strong sense of justice here, and this placement can do well in law or politics, as well as business. Tenth house Jupiter has high moral standards, broad vision, and with its ambition and pride will achieve a good reputation. In the latter part of a tenth house Jupiter's life, there's likely to be renown or high standing in the profession. This also is an excellent position for a career in medicine, healing, religion, or social reform.

Saturn ♄ in the Tenth House

Saturn in its home, the tenth house, is determined, disciplined, self-reliant, and very likely to achieve success, because most of all, these people have extremely strong career ambitions and drive. This placement likes and needs responsibility and so is excellent in business and politics. When well aspected, this position leads to authority, high position, and high pay. But when this placement is challenged by aspect, there can be a fall from position after compromising values to achieve goals. It's important for these people to focus their ambition on serving others, instead of just seeking personal gain. There might have been early problems with the father, too, but this can translate into a strong sense of responsibility toward one's own family.

Uranus ♅ in the Tenth House

Tenth house Uranus needs its freedom and will find its career success in unusual ways. This placement is found in engineers, scientists, social reformers, astrologers, broadcasters, people in electronics or mathematics, or in those who work in humanitarian fields. But it's also an excellent placement for changing the old ways; the originality, insight, and altruism here can make tenth house Uranus a visionary leader. There might also be difficulty getting along with authority figures, so these people might prefer to work for themselves. When this placement is challenged, there can be sudden changes in career, or career disappointments.

Neptune ♆ in the Tenth House

Tenth house Neptune translates into a career that involves creativity, intuition, and imagination, and these people also might serve humanity in some way while having an unusual career at the same time. This placement is often found in actors, artists, musicians, and television personalities, and the world sees these people as glamorous and exciting. They achieve their success on their own, without much help from at least one of their parents (the other parent might compensate for this). This placement also is good for ministers, astrologers, psychics, psychologists, psychiatrists, or people who work in institutions, medical missions, humanitarian efforts, or who serve the God of their understanding. When poorly aspected, it can indicate confusion, changing career goals, or a lack of ambition.

Pluto ♀ in the Tenth House

With a tenth house Pluto, your soul is learning the lesson of how to establish your individuality and authority within your culture. This is all about laws and customs and a need to learn how to integrate your own identity into the larger framework of the social order. There is a primary need for discipline and sustained effort to achieve a major commitment or goal. Your soul's evolutionary intent here, though, is to develop internal security, personal fulfillment, and to see one's self *without* the trappings of the social role. You might be forced into a deep self-examination of your inner emotions in order to make this transformation, but this process will ultimately provide a real sense of internal security.

North Node ☊ in the Tenth House/South Node ☋ in the Fourth House

With a tenth house North Node and fourth house South Node, you're learning about the demands of family and the conflict between doing what you want to do for yourself and your career versus what you must do for your loved ones. The lesson here is to learn how to mature and rise above family problems to arrive at your own self-dignity.

After you learn this lesson, you will move away from self-interest to sharing with others joyously. This placement is all about leaving behind emotional immaturity, developing responsibility, and, in the process, reaping the benefits of sharing.

The Eleventh House: When You Wish Upon a Star

Living in your eleventh house are the groups who will help you achieve your goals and your group involvements. This is traditionally the house of friends, hopes, and wishes, and it is concerned with long-term dreams and goals, as well as with the people who share your interests and objectives. It's where you'll find your sense of future direction and purpose, your plans and goals, your hopes and dreams, and the people that can help you get there.

The eleventh house: your goals, groups, and friends.

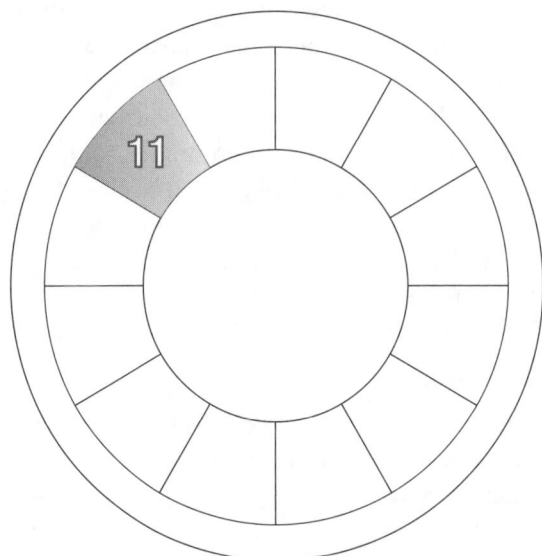

Your eleventh house also is the house of your idealism and vision, because it's where your ideas and intellectual growth for collective good reside. This house is naturally ruled by Aquarius ♒ on its cusp, and its associated planet is Uranus ♅, with Saturn ♄ as its co-ruler.

Your eleventh house identifies you with other people and with the goals of those people that parallel and assist your own. Unlike your seventh house primary relationships, these are the friends whose goals and desires parallel your desires, so it's a place where you give and take in your journey toward your future.

Social goals or reform and the need to contribute to larger goals take a front seat here: This house is associated with social contributions and accomplishments, after all. Successfully navigated, your eleventh house can provide you with strategy and direction. Unsuccessfully navigated, you'll seem to drift through your life, with no purpose, unable to make commitments or decisions, and perhaps, lonely as well.

Reaching for the Stars

Your eleventh house sign describes your group involvements and goals and how you express your sense of direction for the future. Your eleventh house ruler describes where and how your hopes and dreams are developed, along with your group contributions. The house where Aquarius, the corresponding natural sign, is shows what your group involvements are tied to, and where you share your unique ideas for the benefit of groups or social goals.

The Sun ☉ in the Eleventh House

Often socially popular and active, an eleventh house Sun indicates someone who needs to integrate personal goals, creativity, and willpower into the larger collective or social order. For this reason there is a strong desire to accomplish something important that will benefit others. These people are often helped by friends and associates in positions of power or influence. They often have humanitarian goals, and/or they seek to achieve distinction by accomplishing unique or innovative goals. The Sun in the eleventh house might be a leader or inspire others in some new field, especially one that encompasses both idealism and innovation.

The Moon ☽ in the Eleventh House

The Moon in the eleventh house is emotionally intuitive when it comes to people, and its charm can attract many admirers. These people might use their homes for group meetings or activities, and often join up with a variety of causes, which might change over time. These are primarily people who need to develop their goals and future through a constantly growing and changing social sphere. There is also an emotional need for friendships and association with others. These people might have many female friends and associates, or they might meet other people primarily through their family members.

Mercury ☿ in the Eleventh House

Eleventh house Mercury has a wide variety of friends, often based on intellectual connections, and is socially minded as well. This placement is very good at thinking of the best ways to achieve goals and is idealistic and original, bringing a lively mind to group enterprises. People with Mercury in the eleventh house are interested in communications or open exchanges of information with others. They're often dedicated to or interested in sciences, humanitarian causes, astrology, or occult subjects. They also might need to develop persistence in attaining their goals.

Venus ♀ in the Eleventh House

Venus in the eleventh house has lots of friends and benefits from its associations with people, both socially and financially. This placement indicates an idealism and interest in social values, which can lead to involvement with philanthropy or other charitable causes. People with Venus in the eleventh house might have musicians or artists as friends, or they might be involved in artistic associations. Their cooperative spirit makes them excellent team players.

Mars ♂ in the Eleventh House

An eleventh house Mars is often the leader in its circle of friends and actively pursues its well-defined goals. There's energy to spare with this placement, and eleventh house Mars makes friends quickly—although he or she might also lose them quickly by pushing them to keep up. People with an eleventh house Mars have friends or are aligned with groups that might be aggressive or masculine, and they often achieve their personal goals through such people. If heavily challenged by aspects, they can become dissatisfied with the present social order and might have revolutionary tendencies.

Jupiter ♃ in the Eleventh House

Jupiter in the eleventh house is popular and successful through groups and friends, and often benefits and grows from its associations with others. This placement does particularly well in large organizations and, if well aspected, has good judgment and intuition. People with Jupiter in the eleventh house are usually successful in very large projects, which might be associated with humanitarian, religious, educational, or charity efforts. In business pursuits, group activities are often related to the sciences, engineering, new inventions, or organizational pursuits. Eleventh house Jupiters also might benefit through travel.

Saturn ♄ in the Eleventh House

An eleventh house Saturn has a few strong and meaningful friendships and avoids any superficial relationships. There are high hopes here, but there can be delays and obstacles before one achieves them, and, although there might be inner insecurities, there is also strong loyalty to friends and family. Older people are often very helpful to these people. This placement can add structure to ideas and ideals, turning them into practical inventions, uses, or applications. There also can be strong organizational ability, because this is one of Saturn's "home" houses.

Uranus ♅ in the Eleventh House

Eleventh house Uranus people are often associated with humanitarian, astrological, scientific, broadcast, electronics, or technical groups. Remember, this is Uranus's home house, so it's very happy here. These people will have unusual goals and generally aren't concerned with approval or traditions. This placement often gives strong intuition and the ability to perceive universal laws or principles. For this reason, people with this placement often develop strong interests in humanitarian concerns, the occult, or astrology, as well as new inventions or the natural sciences. Eleventh house Uranuses also might change their goals unexpectedly, sometimes more than once during their life, before finding their path. They also might have more than one set of friends—one set of eccentrics and another set of "normals"—because both Uranus and Saturn are associated with this house.

Neptune ♆ in the Eleventh House

Neptune in the eleventh house is drawn to artistic, spiritual, or humanitarian people and often shares common goals with them. This placement indicates people who join organizations with idealistic, mystical, secret, spiritual, or visionary aims, because they're so sensitive to the needs of mankind. If well aspected, these people might receive intuitive or spiritual advice from others that benefits them. If challenged by aspect, though, they might be misled by friends or unreliable associates. It's important for people with eleventh house Neptune to exercise care in choosing friends and to avoid unrealistic expectations about them.

Pluto ♀ in the Eleventh House

If you have an eleventh house Pluto, your evolutionary purpose is to move away from old ideas about self-definition into new, uncharted areas. You don't like to be defined by situations, others, or anything external; you want to define yourself outside the mainstream, and outside of any cultural identity. The evolutionary intent of your soul is to take your ideas about yourself and use them to visualize and plan your future, and then, most importantly, to act on them. It's vital that you learn not to wait for approval or support from others before pursuing your life directions and goals. You are here to be an innovative and creative agent for change in whatever area of life is most appropriate for you. Your power here lies in understanding that it's okay to be different.

North Node ☊ in the Eleventh House/South Node ☋ in the Fifth House

With an eleventh house North Node and a fifth house South Node, you're learning to move beyond being a sole creator to create for a more global community. You need to trust your big dreams and learn the value of friendship and the greater good. In the process, you need to let go of pride and self-consciousness and become a part of the collective ego. Your past creativity and love are needed for larger purposes in this lifetime, and once you develop objectivity, you'll be able to achieve them.

CAUTION **Star-Crossed**

Among the many things lurking in the closet of your twelfth house are your secret enemies. These are the people who smile to your face, then stab you in the back. Look more closely, though, and you may discover these are your own energies projected onto someone else. Be aware of what you're hiding from yourself in your twelfth house, and you'll get your enemies out of your closet.

The twelfth house: your sub-conscious, privacy, and past karma.

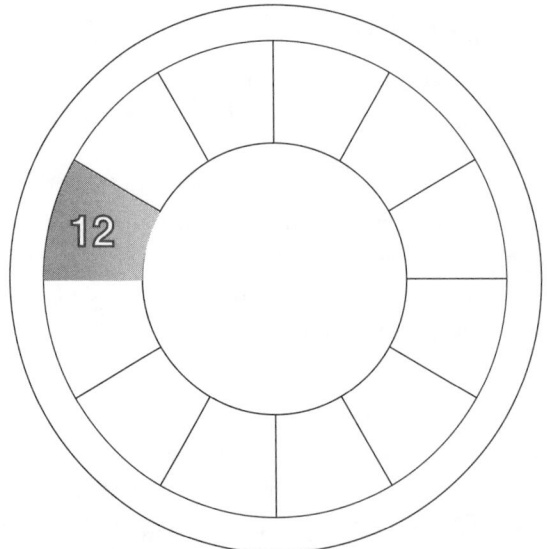

The Twelfth House: Secret Agent

The twelfth house gets a bad rap in many astrology books, particularly the older ones. Sometimes it's called the house of secrets; others call it the house of self-undoing, or the house of sorrows. Because one of us has five planets in her twelfth house, we know there's more to it than all these challenging vibes. But let's take a moment to look at where this tarnished reputation came from.

The twelfth house is certainly the most mystical of the houses: It's where you'll find your subconscious and the unknown, after all. Like most fields, though, astrology until recently had a patriarchal bend, which meant that "feminine" signs like Cancer ♋ and Pisces ♓ were called "emotional" and "weepy," and the mystical houses like the fourth, eighth, and twelfth were called "disappointing" or "irrational."

Well, it can be scary for some behind-the-times guys to get in touch with things like intuition and secrets and dreams: They operate in what they want to be a rational, ordered world. Except that we all know the world isn't always as rational or ordered as we'd like. There's even a theory for this lack of rationality now; it's called "chaos theory."

Astrologer Steven Forrest calls the twelfth house the house of troubles, but also makes it clear that it's consciousness itself that resides here. This is the point at which self meets soul, where ego can merge into spirit.

Successfully navigate your twelfth house and you'll transcend your everyday worries. Planets in this house also can help you to learn lessons that free you from past destructive patterns. Unsuccessfully navigate it, and your self-image will be blurry. You might self-destruct through alcohol, drugs, or the wrong people, or seem to have chronic "bad luck."

Your twelfth house can lead to self-transcendence, moving beyond the ego to what's beyond the self. It's here you'll find your higher consciousness, your unconscious, and what you don't yet know. Poorly aspected, though, it can be your undoing. How you navigate your twelfth house is up to you. Its ruler is Pisces ♓, and its associated planets are Neptune ♆ and Jupiter ♃: Neptune, the mystical, and Jupiter, the fortunate, or when overdone, the unfortunate.

Skeletons in Your Closet

Your twelfth house sign describes your past, the types of social services you might perform, and how you express (or don't express) your unconscious. Your twelfth house ruler describes where and how you can develop beyond your self and serve the larger collective. The house where Pisces, the corresponding natural sign, is shows where you need to be of service to others and in what areas of your life you have great potential to develop your unconscious.

The Sun ☉ in the Twelfth House

A twelfth house Sun has a strong desire for solitude, peace, and quiet and might be close to only a few carefully chosen people. There may be success later in life, and deep spiritual understanding. This placement also can be both resourceful and self-expressive. The essence of this placement is a person who works behind the scenes, instead of in the public eye. These people are here to serve others, instead of themselves, and often have profound inner lives. Many can be found working for large companies or institutions, such as hospitals and prisons or places of spiritual retreat. This is a good position for medical researchers, doctors, or people who work with the disabled or disadvantaged.

The Moon ☽ in the Twelfth House

The Moon in the twelfth house is sensitive, receptive, and intuitive, almost as if it's got radar, but it also can be easily hurt and might hide its true feelings. There will be a need for alone time or seclusion to process these feelings, meditate, or pursue spiritual teachings. If they don't get this, these people might feel pressured and will need to escape, either by "zoning out," or through fantasy. Twelfth house Moons also have a creative imagination, and so this placement is commonly found in writers. These people also make good counselors because they're so sensitive to the feelings of others. This placement primarily indicates people whose feelings and emotional responses are heavily tied to their subconscious or past lives, and for this reason they might not understand why they feel the way they do.

Mercury ☿ in the Twelfth House

Twelfth house Mercury is contemplative, and these people work things out for themselves; they might also be very reluctant to share what they think. Mercury here is subtle, but good at analyzing other people's problems, and might base its decisions on feelings rather than reason. This is because twelfth house Mercuries' thinking is heavily influenced by past experiences, unconscious memories, or the subconscious. Close to the ascendant, this Mercury might behave more like a first house Mercury and be more communicative. If Mercury is well aspected, and especially if it's aspected to any of the outer three planets, these people might gain important knowledge through their intuitive or psychic abilities.

Venus ♀ in the Twelfth House

Venus in the twelfth house is both artistic and creative and prefers a private, secluded life. This is a compassionate and sympathetic placement, because Venus is extremely happy here and has a great desire to serve others in some way. People with Venus in the twelfth house also like to look at life's deeper meanings and might find a good outlet through their devotion to the God of their understanding or an ideal. Worldly success is not as important to them as what they can contribute to help others. For this reason, they might also pursue a spiritual life. Often noted for secretive love affairs or personal contacts, this position is primarily distinguished by its artistic and strong emotional ties to the subconscious, which can result in deeply inspired art.

Mars ♂ in the Twelfth House

Twelfth house Mars people have strong feelings but prefer to keep them secret from everyone else because their desires, anger, or feelings are connected to past experiences or their subconscious, so they might not understand them. People with Mars in the twelfth house have an active imagination, and so might fight for those less fortunate. These people can be good strategists, planning things behind the scenes. This placement is also very self-motivated and able to work independently without supervision. Primarily they need *not* to be discouraged by others, which is why they might unconsciously decide to work behind the scenes to accomplish their purposes. They might appear to be mild-mannered, but when pushed to their limits and forced to release their suppressed anger, they will fight back like a caged tiger, and so make formidable foes. These people also might have a partially hidden identity that is not shared with others.

Jupiter ♃ in the Twelfth House

Jupiter in the twelfth house is kind, compassionate, and charitable and is often found helping others in some way. These people have a strong religious or philosophical faith or are likely to pursue an inner spiritual path. In fact, some have called a twelfth house Jupiter "an angel on your shoulder." This is because people with this placement are often benefited by others anonymously, just as they often help people in need the same way. It's a reward for "good behavior." This is one of Jupiter's home houses, because it co-rules Pisces, so it's very happy here, and these people are often very intuitive. If challenged by aspects, however, they might fall into impractical idealism, overindulgence, or neglect to develop their creative abilities to help others.

Saturn ♄ in the Twelfth House

Twelfth house Saturn is reserved and cautious, preferring to work alone. This placement can be lonely or afraid, especially because these people won't share their feelings with others for fear they'll be used against them. But this also can be a very good placement for those who require seclusion for their work. This placement might have unconscious, or what seem to be unfounded, fears about their own worth or about the structures of their world dissolving before them. Normally these fears are either imaginary or linked to past-life memories. It's often wise for these people to develop practical ways to help others, which they are talented at doing and which help them get past focusing on their fears and insecurities. This placement is often found in people who work in large companies, institutions, or for the government. They also might work for charitable foundations or in psychology.

Uranus ♅ in the Twelfth House

A twelfth house Uranus indicates compassion and intuition, and although people with this placement want to free themselves from society's constraints, they are the ones who hold themselves back due to their fears. They have a particular enchantment with the mysterious and romantic, but this also is an intellectual placement, with people who not only want to work in unusual ways, but who will. This placement is good for researchers or those who work behind the scenes alone. People with Uranus here might also be loners, feeling too different to make strong connections with others. Although they're very intuitive, they might not listen to their higher Self, and so might ignore information.

Neptune ♆ in the Twelfth House

Neptune in the twelfth house prefers to work in a quiet place that allows his or her creativity to flow. This placement can indicate an almost other-worldly type of person, who is also very helpful to others and finely tuned to his or her own subconscious. Because this is Neptune's home house and it's very happy here, this placement can be a strong source of wisdom. These people are highly intuitive and might be in touch with the collective mind, which could be thought of as a pool of ideas we're all plugged into. If Neptune's well aspected, those with this placement also might be artistic, musical, or poetic and could have a strong talent for psychology, psychic abilities, or healing. Their search for an inner spiritual path is important, and until they find it, their lives can be "in a fog" or isolated. Their strong ability to absorb other people's feelings and energies makes it difficult for them to be around negative people.

Pluto ♀ in the Twelfth House

If you have Pluto in the twelfth house, you have the potential to spiritualize all aspects of your life, and your unconscious intention is to merge or identify with the Source, God of your understanding, or a higher power. To do this, you are trying to dissolve any and all blockages you have to this, whether emotional, mental, physical, or spiritual. This is naturally a frightening prospect for anyone used to a concept of "self" (and that's all of us humans), and avoidance behaviors, such as living out dreams and illusions, or compulsive actions might manifest because of this. The lesson here is faith, and what you're willing to take on faith, to find the ultimate meaning of life. The evolutionary intent of your soul is to develop specific, useful methods for learning to analyze yourself and hone transcendental meditation techniques that enable you to experience the Source so that you find your blockages and eliminate them. In addition, you need to perform some type of "right work," which helps or serves others. You need to learn to believe in your own intuitive abilities, develop faith, and, in the process, let go of the idea of self. This is particularly hard for people from western civilizations to do.

North Node ☊ in the Twelfth House/South Node ☋ in the Sixth House

With a twelfth house North Node and a sixth house South Node, you're learning to move beyond yourself, but it's a tough lesson, and you might spend far too much time either wallowing in self-pity or criticizing everyone else. You need to learn not only to see yourself as part of a larger whole, but to see that the whole universe is also contained in you. When you learn this, you'll see the greater harmony and synchronicity of all things. This is an opportunity to find all the answers you need within yourself, serve others, and become part of a higher cause or purpose.

The Least You Need to Know

- ◆ The fourth quadrant houses your dreams and ambitions.

- ◆ It's your tenth house that holds your reputation, social role, and career.

- ◆ Your eleventh house is where you'll find the groups that help you achieve your goals and desires.

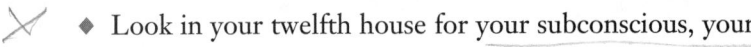 ◆ Look in your twelfth house for your subconscious, your past, and the unknown.

Part 5

Getting and Interpreting Your Birth Chart

Don't skip this part! Besides seeing how a computer calculates your birth chart, you'll learn many other useful chart basics, such as aspects, transits, and progressions. You'll also find out how to interpret your astrological signature, and determine if you're reaping or sowing in this lifetime.

Did you know that you can use astrology as a personal map to make informed choices about your life decisions? Indeed you can. In the pages that follow, you'll see just how to make the most of both the opportunities and challenges that await you.

Chapter 19

Getting Started

In This Chapter

◆ How easy is it to do your own birth chart? (It's not)

◆ Your vital statistics

◆ Supplies you'll need (and where to get them)

◆ Getting your birth chart done for you

Instead of wasting your time and ours discussing manual calculations nobody uses any more, in this chapter we're going to walk you through the steps a computer program takes when it calculates your birth chart. We'll be referring to some of the books that used to do it "the old-fashioned way," but we know you're no idiot and will have your chart done in the most efficient manner.

How Easy Is It to Do Your Own Birth Chart? (It's Not)

Lucky for Steven Spielberg, whose birth chart we'll be featuring here and in the next few chapters, Madeline cast his chart. Otherwise, he'd be spending a lot of his time and money to do his own chart, which would be a waste of both. And it would be for you, too, if you chose to calculate your chart manually.

Steven Spielberg's birth chart.

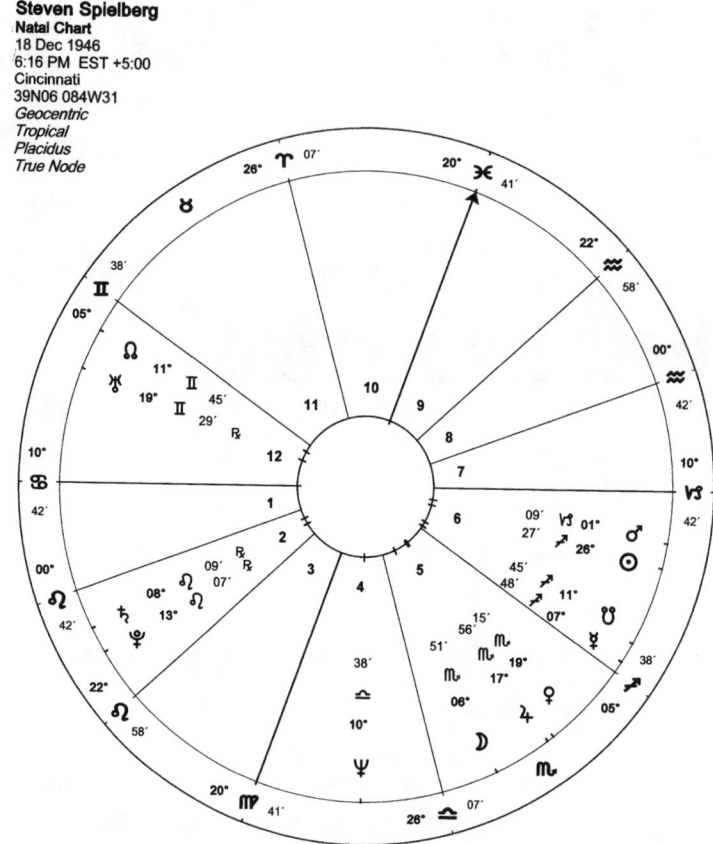

Steven Spielberg
Natal Chart
18 Dec 1946
6:16 PM EST +5:00
Cincinnati
39N06 084W31
Geocentric
Tropical
Placidus
True Node

What we're going to do here is learn something about how birth charts are done and what's behind those calculations. Then we'll show you some of the science and math behind astrology in Chapter 20. If you're saying, "Yeah!" these two chapters are for you.

Your Vital Statistics

The first things you need for creating your birth chart are probably the easiest. Plus, they're probably free (there are exceptions, but we'll get to that). What are they? Three simple numbers:

- ◆ Your date of birth
- ◆ Your time of birth
- ◆ Your place of birth

Now this sounds pretty easy, right? We all know the stories of our births ("Oh, I was in labor for two days with you, and I thought you'd never come out"), and we all, of course, know our birthdays (although, depending on our ages, we might be trying to forget them). But it may be a little harder to find out your birth time.

Okay, go ask your mother. She'll say, "Let's see, we'd just fallen asleep, and I woke up and said to Daddy, 'Something's funny, Honey,' and next thing I knew, we were off to the hospital, and then you were born." "What time, Ma?" you ask. "Oh, it must have been around three or four. Somewhere in the middle of the night. I'm just not really sure."

Heaven Knows _____

With the advent of computers, even astrologers don't calculate charts manually anymore. When a chart was done the old-fashioned way, human error often meant incorrect calculations, which made the possibility of a chart being wrong far more likely.

Not even your own mother remembers! And although you were there, you didn't yet know how to tell time.

Obviously, you could check your birth certificate. But not all birth certificates have times, at least not until more recently. And if you were born outside the United States, getting your birth certificate could take a lot of time and expense.

Well, isn't "around three or four" good enough? The answer is, it's not. And in a moment, we'll tell you why.

Your Most Important Day

Happy birthday! As you already know, your birthday determines your Sun ☉ sign. But it's also the first number you need to start your astrological birth chart, the number that would tell you which pages of the reference books would be used to find the numbers to calculate your chart (if you were doing manual calculation), or the first number you'll punch into the computer for your personal chart calculation.

So let's do that: Either write it down, or enter it into your computer program at the prompt: MM/DD/YYYY (month/day/year). There! You've taken the first step toward doing your own birth chart.

We've done this for Steven Spielberg: 12/18/1946.

Star-Crossed _____

Your midheaven changes degrees at least every four minutes, and depending on your birth chart, it could be even more often. Because the interpretation of a chart can't be more accurate than the information used to calculate it, it's worth doing some research to get your birth time right, such as sending away for your birth certificate. Otherwise, you might end up with a birth chart that's not entirely accurate.

The Time of Your Life

As we've already mentioned, the time you were born can be harder to find. Lots of people know that they were born "around 10 A.M." But the minute astrologers see a rounded number like that, they begin to think it's approximate rather than exact. Even a few minutes can mean the difference between a planet appearing in one sign or another, or in one house or another. Your ascendant or midheaven could change as well. As we've already discovered, these are *important* differences.

But the big question remains: If your mother can't remember, and it's not on your birth certificate, how do you determine your birth time? Astrologers, for a fee, will do a *rectification* for your birth time. This is a consultation where you tell the astrologer about important things that have happened in your life and how you behave in various situations, much as you might tell a therapist. The astrologer will then determine your birth time by using this information. It's kind of like finding your birth time by doing your chart, instead of the other way around.

Of course, if you don't want to pay for a rectification, you can always ask the astrologer to use a noon chart. Less accurate than a chart with your specific birth time, especially when it comes to your Moon placement and ascendant, a noon chart will nonetheless give you an overview of your planetary placements. Your noon chart will help give the astrologer an "eagle eye" view of your natal planets and how they were placed in the sky. The astrologer can view the cycles that your birth planets have and derive helpful trends in your life.

AstroLingo _____

If you don't know your birth time, **rectification** is a method used by astrologers to determine it, based on things that have happened in your life.

If you know it, let's write down or enter this number, too: time of birth. We've done this for Steven Spielberg: 6:16 P.M. EST. That takes care of step two.

Where Did You Come From?

The last number you need comes from a place: where you were born. Every place on the planet Earth can be translated into its latitude and longitude, which are written in degrees.

Latitude measures the distance north or south of the equator. 00 degrees *is* the equator, and places to the north are shown in degrees and minutes as 00N00, and places to the south are shown in degrees and minutes as 00S00.

Longitude is the distance east or west of the Greenwich Meridian. Places east of the Greenwich Meridian are shown as 00E00, and places west are shown as 00W00.

To give you an example, Aspen, Colorado, has a latitude of 39N11 and a longitude of 106W49. This means that Aspen is 39 degrees, 11 minutes north of the equator, and 106 degrees, 49 minutes west of the Greenwich Meridian.

It's pretty unlikely that you'll know the latitude and the longitude for the place that you were born. But never fear! The computer program calculating your birth chart does all the work for you.

So write down your place of birth. We've done this for Steven Spielberg: Cincinnati, Ohio.

Resources Your Computer's Replaced (Just to Give You an Idea)

Even though the computer's doing the work, we thought you might be interested in knowing just how many books and calculations it's replacing. These include, for starters, an ephemeris, a table of houses, an atlas, and a book of time zone changes, and a lot of other books we don't mention here. Let's look at what some of these books include to help you understand how your chart's being calculated.

Ephemeris

An *ephemeris* (the plural is *ephemerides*—it's Greek) is a book that shows where the planets are at noon or midnight *Greenwich mean time* every day of every year. Your computer looks up the planetary positions that are contained in an ephemeris for you. In Chapter 20, we'll show how you can do this yourself, if you want.

AstroLingo

An **ephemeris** is a book that shows where the planets are at noon or midnight Greenwich Mean Time every day of each year for the time period covered. **Greenwich mean time (GMT)** is the time standard used in astronomy for locations at 0 degrees longitude or meridian. It's four hours later than Eastern Daylight Time and five hours later than Eastern Standard Time.

Table of Houses

You find your ascendant, midheaven, and house cusps with a *table of houses*. These charts are arranged in one-degree increments of *longitude*, but amazingly enough, most people were born in between two of these. The latitudes along the side of the column are also in one-degree increments, so most people also live in between those.

AstroLingo

A **table of houses** shows you how to find your ascendant, midheaven, and house cusps.

Based on the birth information you provide, the computer program calculates the actual house positions; it's got a built-in table of houses to save you all the trouble.

Atlas

An *atlas* shows both latitude and longitude and is used to find the specific latitude and longitude for your place of birth. Almost all atlases show latitude and longitude to the minute (the Four Corners of Arizona, Colorado, New Mexico, and Utah, for example, are 37N00 and 109W00), and many show the seconds as well. In addition, *The American Atlas* shows both locations *and* the time zone changes, as well as seconds.

There are three ways the person doing your chart might use an atlas. Nearly all chart-creation programs have built-in atlases, where you or the astrologer enters the name of the place and the computer does the rest. A few use a separate atlas program to do this.

You can to do this the old-fashioned way, of course, and actually look up the latitude and longitude for your birthplace. The important thing is to enter accurate information, no matter how it's obtained.

Book of Time Zone Changes

Now, don't forget, we've also got that pesky daylight saving time to contend with. You know, that "fall back, spring ahead" deal, which we never seem to get straight no matter how many years we've been setting those clocks back and forth.

A *book of time zone changes* makes all this simple. It tells you when and if the place you were born switches to daylight saving time, and when it switches back. In the past, something called war time was also used. All places have undergone time changes at one time or another. These books include all time changes for the past, present, and future. Maybe we should all have one of these—whether we're doing our charts or not! Of course, this is one more thing your computer program will do automatically.

> **StarFacts**
>
> Some states, like Arizona, don't use daylight saving time. Others, like Indiana, allow counties to decide whether to use it or not, so driving across Indiana during the summer is like driving across a checkerboard of time (we're not making this up).

Getting Your Birth Chart Done for You

You can spend the hundred-plus bucks to buy your own chart-calculation program. The chart program used to generate the birth charts in this book is Solar Fire, published by Astrolabe, Inc. Solar Fire is available in both beginner and advanced versions. But if all you want to do is generate your own birth chart, there are several quick and inexpensive ways you can do this.

Sound simple? It is. Here's the deal. You know your birth date, your birth time, and your birth place. The easiest and most-often used method (we'll call this Plan A) is to go online. Type in "free birth chart" and you'll be inundated with choices. Click any of them, enter your birth date, birth time, and place of birth, and in seconds (depending on the speed of your connection, of course) you'll have a ready-to-print birth chart.

If you're one of the few people on the planet who doesn't yet have an Internet connection, here's Plan B: Call your local metaphysical bookstore (you can find them in the Yellow Pages under "Metaphysical Bookstores and Supplies," or possibly under "Books, New").

"Hi," you say. "What do you charge to do a chart?"

"Three dollars," they say. Or maybe they'll say, "Five." Or, if you live in one of those high-priced places, maybe it'll be six dollars. That's it. We're not kidding.

Plan C involves looking in the Yellow Pages under "Astrologers." Didn't know there was a Yellow Pages heading called "Astrologers"? Check it out. Lisa found 5 in the most recent Albuquerque Metropolitan Area yellow phone book; there were 18 in Madeline's Seattle phone book.

When you start calling those astrologers, what should you ask? You could start by asking how much they charge to just run your birth chart. Those numbers will be close to the ones listed previously. Or you can ask for a *consultation*. A consultation with an astrologer means the astrologer will run your chart, study it prior to meeting with you, and then spend the consultation time explaining just what your chart reveals about you. The astrologer might also run more charts, such as progressed charts or charts with transits, that answer more specific questions you might have about the conditions surrounding your life right now, or about the timing of a future event you are planning. The cost of a consultation will vary depending on the astrologer's hourly rate, so be sure to ask what that is. We think it's well worth the price, and we'll bet you will, too.

There's even a Plan D: You can get an online consultation. In Appendix A, we've listed some cool websites for you to check out. An online consultation will be similar to an in-person consultation, but for starters, you (obviously) won't be sitting face-to-face with the astrologer. Because most astrologers talk faster than they can type, you might get more info when you get a consultation either in person or on the telephone.

Still, this can be an attractive option if you live in a rural area, but don't rule it out if you live in a big city. Look for a licensed, certified astrologer with good credentials, years of experience, and who comes with solid recommendations from other clients. Some of the best astrologers in the country are now online, so you can choose from among them for your own private consultation. It's kind of like picking Carl Jung as your personal therapist. It could be worth it, you know?

The Least You Need to Know

- Getting your birth chart calculated by computer takes just a few minutes and can be free or cost just a few bucks.

- You'll need to know your birth date, birth time, and birth place.

- If you absolutely can't find your birth time, you can generate a birth chart with a noon birth time.

- You can combine getting your birth chart done with a professional consultation with an astrologer who will interpret your chart for you.

Chapter 20

Lost in Space: How a Computer Calculates a Birth Chart

In This Chapter

- ◆ It's about time; it's about space
- ◆ To boldly seek those planetary positions
- ◆ Houses, houses, and more houses
- ◆ Putting it all together

In this chapter, you'll see what's behind the calculations a computer makes to create a birth chart, and we're going to use Steven Spielberg as our guinea pig. It's always nice to know what's behind those numbers, after all.

First we're going to talk about time. Then we're going to talk about calculating the position of the planets. Then we'll talk about time some more and connect it to house calculation.

It's About Time; It's About Space

One of the most important things to understand about chart calculation is that it's all about time—three kinds of time, to be exact: Greenwich mean time (GMT), sidereal time (or star time; there's an explanation coming up later), and local time. We'll talk about each time at a particular point in the chart calculation process, and we'll tell you some of the astronomy behind time as well.

Working in Base 60

There are 60 seconds in a minute and 60 minutes in an hour. This is called *Base 60*—quite simply, a system that uses 60 as its basis rather than 10. Geographical distances also are calculated using this system and are measured in degrees, minutes, and seconds. All calculations for your birth chart are done in hours or degrees, minutes, and seconds, and it's important you keep these three things separate, for example 7 hours, 29 minutes, 13 seconds. This also can be written 07:29:13.

AstroLingo

Base 60 is used to calculate clock time or distance: There are 60 seconds in a minute, and 60 minutes in an hour or a degree.

Sixty seconds converts to 1 minute, and 60 minutes is either 1 hour or 1 degree, depending on whether we're measuring time or distance. Also, remember that if you subtract and need to borrow a minute, you're borrowing 60 seconds. Or if you borrow an hour, you're borrowing 60 minutes. We're starting with this so you understand the measurement system that's behind what the computer's going to do.

Converting to GMT

The first thing the computer is going to calculate is your Greenwich mean time (GMT), based on the time zone in which you were born. The person doing your chart will have checked a time changes book first to make sure the time zone he or she enters into the computer is correct. Nowadays, though, time zone changes are already programmed into most computer programs.

GMT is the time for which the ephemeris is set up, with the position of the planets calculated for midnight or noon. If a person was born anywhere other than in England or the other locations that lie within GMT, the computer will have to convert the birth time to GMT, which will in turn be used to calculate the actual position of the planets.

The conversion to GMT (for the Western Hemisphere, anyway) is made by adding to your birth time the difference in hours between the time zone where you were born and GMT. GMT is later than time in the United States, and the computer calculates this using a look-up table similar to the following table. This is such an easy calculation, though, anyone could do it!

If a person was born during daylight saving or war time, the computer would add one less hour than when converting to GMT from a standard time zone. It's easy to determine whether a person was born during daylight saving or war time by using a time changes book or a computer with such changes programmed into it.

Converting to Greenwich Mean Time (United States)	
Time Zone	**Add**
Eastern Standard	Five hours
Central Standard	Six hours
Mountain Standard	Seven hours
Pacific Standard	Eight hours
Saving or War Time Zone	**Add**
Eastern Daylight	Four hours
Central Daylight	Five hours
Mountain Daylight	Six hours
Pacific Daylight	Seven hours

StarFacts

There's a possibility that one's Greenwich mean time of birth is on a different day than the actual date of birth at the birth location. If you were using a midnight ephemeris, for example, and were born on August 1 at 8 P.M. Central Daylight Time, you'd add 5 hours, which would equal 1 A.M. GMT. That, of course, will be the next day! So you'd be looking for your planets on August 2 rather than August 1.

Using Steven Spielberg's chart as an example, we note that he was born at 6:16 P.M. EST. To change this to GMT, the computer first converts this to the 24-hour system (by adding 12 hours because he has a P.M. birth) to come up with 18:16. Then it adds five hours (to convert from Eastern Standard Time) to get a GMT time of 23:16.

To Boldly Seek Those Planetary Positions

Let's begin our mission by looking at an ephemeris page for December 1946, the month of Steven Spielberg's birth. We're going to be using a midnight ephemeris throughout the rest of this chapter, so all of our references and examples will be for a midnight ephemeris instead of a noon one.

Looking at the sample page in the following figure, let's find the date, December 18, for Spielberg's planets. The first thing you're going to see is that next to the date is a sidereal time (abbreviated SID time). We're not going to use that here, but we'll come back to it when we calculate the houses. For now, just note where it is.

A page from the ephemeris for December 1946.

(Illustration from The American Ephemeris for the 20th Century, *used by permission. Copyright ACS Publications, 5521 Ruffin Road, San Diego, CA 92123-1314. Call 1-800-888-9983 to place orders.)*

DECEMBER 1946 **LONGITUDE**

Day	Sid.Time	☉	0 hr ☽	Noon ☽	True ☊	☿	♀	♂	♃	♄	♅	♆	♇
1 Su	4 36 59	8♐11 39	27♒39 39	3♓56 1	11♊45.0	21♏ 9.4	18♏14.6	17♐41.3	14♏18.0	8♌47.4	20♊14.8	10♎18.0	13♌18.6
2 M	4 40 56	9 12 29	10♓17 28	16 44 32	11R45.0	21D 13.5	17R57.6	18 25.8	14 30.5	8R46.1	20R12.3	10 19.4	13R18.2
3 Tu	4 44 52	10 13 20	23 17 37	29 57 7	11 45.0	21 27.6	17 43.0	19 10.4	14 43.0	8 44.8	20 9.8	10 20.7	13 17.7
4 W	4 48 49	11 14 11	6♈43 19	13♈36 23	11D44.9	21 50.9	17 30.9	19 55.0	14 55.5	8 43.4	20 7.3	10 22.0	13 17.2
5 Th	4 52 45	12 15 3	20 36 23	27 43 12	11 44.9	22 22.4	17 21.2	20 39.6	15 8.0	8 41.8	20 4.8	10 23.3	13 16.6
6 F	4 56 42	13 15 57	4♉56 35	12♉16 3	11 45.0	23 1.3	17 14.0	21 24.3	15 20.3	8 40.2	20 2.3	10 24.6	13 16.1
7 Sa	5 0 39	14 16 51	19 40 59	27 10 35	11 45.2	23 46.9	17 9.3	22 9.1	15 32.7	8 38.4	19 59.7	10 25.8	13 15.5
8 Su	5 4 35	15 17 45	4♊43 51	12♊19 42	11R45.3	24 38.2	17D 7.1	22 53.9	15 45.0	8 36.6	19 57.2	10 27.0	13 14.9
9 M	5 8 32	16 18 41	19 56 56	27 34 18	11 45.3	25 34.7	17 7.4	23 38.7	15 57.2	8 34.6	19 54.6	10 28.1	13 14.3
10 Tu	5 12 28	17 19 38	5♋10 31	12♋44 25	11 45.1	26 35.6	17 10.1	24 23.6	16 9.4	8 32.5	19 52.1	10 29.3	13 13.6
11 W	5 16 25	18 20 36	20 14 51	27 40 51	11 44.5	27 40.5	17 15.1	25 8.6	16 21.6	8 30.4	19 49.5	10 30.4	13 12.9
12 Th	5 20 21	19 21 35	5♌ 1 35	12♌16 25	11 43.6	28 48.7	17 22.6	25 53.6	16 33.6	8 28.1	19 47.0	10 31.5	13 12.2
13 F	5 24 18	20 22 35	19 24 51	26 26 37	11 42.7	29 59.9	17 32.3	26 38.6	16 45.7	8 25.7	19 44.4	10 32.5	13 11.5
14 Sa	5 28 14	21 23 36	3♍21 35	10♍ 9 49	11 41.9	1♐13.6	17 44.3	27 23.8	16 57.6	8 23.2	19 41.9	10 33.5	13 10.7
15 Su	5 32 11	22 24 37	16 51 27	23 26 46	11D41.4	2 29.6	17 58.4	28 8.9	17 9.6	8 20.7	19 39.3	10 34.5	13 10.0
16 M	5 36 8	23 25 40	29 56 8	6♎19 58	11 41.4	3 47.5	18 14.7	28 54.1	17 21.4	8 18.0	19 36.7	10 35.4	13 9.2
17 Tu	5 40 4	24 26 44	12♎38 43	18 52 54	11 42.0	5 7.1	18 33.0	29 39.4	17 33.2	8 15.2	19 34.2	10 36.3	13 8.3
18 W	5 44 1	25 27 49	25 2 59	1♏ 9 30	11 43.1	6 28.2	18 53.3	0♑24.7	17 44.9	8 12.4	19 31.6	10 37.2	13 7.5
19 Th	5 47 57	26 28 54	7♏12 56	13 13 45	11 44.5	7 50.6	19 15.6	1 10.0	17 56.6	8 9.4	19 29.1	10 38.1	13 6.6
20 F	5 51 54	27 30 1	19 12 24	25 9 19	11 45.8	9 14.1	19 39.7	1 55.5	18 8.2	8 6.3	19 26.6	10 38.9	13 5.7
21 Sa	5 55 50	28 31 8	1♐ 4 53	6♐59 27	11R46.9	10 38.6	20 5.5	2 40.9	18 19.7	8 3.2	19 24.0	10 39.7	13 4.8
22 Su	5 59 47	29 32 16	12 53 23	18 46 59	11 47.2	12 4.0	20 33.1	3 26.4	18 31.2	7 60.0	19 21.5	10 40.4	13 3.9
23 M	6 3 43	0♑33 24	24 40 33	0♑34 19	11 46.6	13 30.2	21 2.4	4 12.0	18 42.6	7 56.7	19 19.0	10 41.2	13 2.9
24 Tu	6 7 40	1 34 33	6♑28 34	12 23 33	11 45.0	14 57.0	21 33.2	4 57.6	18 53.9	7 53.3	19 16.5	10 41.8	13 2.0
25 W	6 11 37	2 35 42	18 19 30	24 16 38	11 42.3	16 24.5	22 5.6	5 43.2	19 5.2	7 49.8	19 14.1	10 42.5	13 1.0
26 Th	6 15 33	3 36 52	0♒15 14	6♒15 32	11 38.7	17 52.6	22 39.5	6 28.9	19 16.3	7 46.2	19 11.6	10 43.1	12 60.0
27 F	6 19 30	4 38 1	12 17 49	18 22 22	11 34.7	19 21.1	23 14.7	7 14.6	19 27.4	7 42.5	19 9.2	10 43.7	12 58.9
28 Sa	6 23 26	5 39 11	24 29 30	0♓39 33	11 30.7	20 50.2	23 51.4	8 0.4	19 38.4	7 38.8	19 6.7	10 44.3	12 57.9
29 Su	6 27 23	6 40 21	6♓52 52	13 9 49	11 27.1	22 19.7	24 29.3	8 46.2	19 49.3	7 35.0	19 4.3	10 44.8	12 56.8
30 M	6 31 19	7 41 30	19 30 47	25 56 10	11 24.6	23 49.6	25 8.5	9 32.0	20 0.2	7 31.1	19 1.9	10 45.2	12 55.7
31 Tu	6 35 16	8 42 40	2♈26 21	9♈ 1 42	11D23.3	25 19.9	25 48.9	10 17.9	20 10.9	7 27.2	18 59.5	10 45.7	12 54.6

What you need to notice now is that the positions that are given for each planet for each day are accurate only for midnight. So the computer needs to calculate the distance traveled from the *start time* (midnight in our case) in the ephemeris to the time Spielberg was born.

AstroLingo

The **start time,** or reference time, will be either midnight or noon for a given date, depending on the ephemeris. The computer uses this to determine the daily travel of the planets.

Find the sign a planet is in by looking *up* to the nearest sign shown in the column; or, if there is a new sign change on that day, you might use that one: It all depends on whether the planet changed signs after or before the person was born. If a planet hasn't changed signs during that month, though, then it will be the sign shown at the top of the column.

Daily Travel

To calculate the distance from the start time, the computer's going to find out how far each planet traveled between the start time and the next day's position. Then it's going to calculate how much of that distance was traveled by the planet at the time Spielberg was born. Remember that we have to use the GMT here, not the birth time.

Let's use Spielberg's birth data—December 18, 1946, at 23:16 GMT—as an example. The computer is going to subtract the position shown for the planets on December 18 at midnight from the position of the planets shown for midnight on December 19. This will show you that planet's *daily travel*.

AstroLingo

Daily travel is the distance a planet moves in a 24-hour period.

Next, the computer calculates how much time elapsed between midnight and when Spielberg was born. Using his GMT of 23:16, this is calculated as follows: 23:00 is 23 hours past midnight, and 16 minutes divided by 60 minutes = .26 hours. So 23.26 hours divided by 24 hours = .9691666. In this case, each planet will have traveled 23.26 hours, or .9691666 of a day from the position shown at midnight.

Now the computer multiplies this number (.9691666) by the amount of daily travel for each of the planets that day. The Sun ☉, for example, travels about a degree per day. And on the day that Spielberg was born, it traveled a total distance of 1 degree, 1 minute, 5 seconds. So its travel until Spielberg was born would be .9691666 times the Sun's total travel for that day of 1 degree, 1 minute, and 5 seconds. (Aren't we lucky that the computer, not us, gets to figure this stuff out?)

The Sun's travel also can be expressed as 61 minutes and 5 seconds (or a total of 3,665 seconds). So .9691666 times that equals 59 minutes and 2 seconds. The computer then adds this amount to the December 18 position shown in the ephemeris (25 degrees, 27 minutes, 49 seconds) to arrive at the position for Spielberg's Sun. Adding 59 minutes, 2 seconds gives a final position of 26 degrees, 26 minutes, and 51 seconds. The computer rounds this to 26 degrees, 27 minutes of Sagittarius ♐, which is what is shown on the chart. Then the computer does the same thing to find all of Spielberg's other planets' positions, plus his North Node.

What About Retrogrades?

Now, if a planet is retrograde, or appears to be moving backward, the computer is going to work in the opposite direction. You can see for yourself when you look at the ephemeris that some of Spielberg's planets are losing ground, so you'll know right away that they're retrograde. The computer knows this, too. There's also an "R" in the column above, on the date when the planet went retrograde, or, if it started the month in retrograde motion, this will be shown on the second day for the month, as it is for Venus ♀, Saturn ♄, Uranus ♅, and Pluto ♇ in the sample ephemeris page.

What the computer does in this case will be exactly the reverse of what we've just shown you above. Because the second entry's going to be smaller than the first entry, the computer is going to *subtract* it from the first position, instead of vice versa.

In our example, this means the computer would subtract the December 19 position for Saturn from its position on December 18. Then it calculates how far it traveled until Spielberg was born and *subtracts* it from the December 18 position, because Saturn ♄ is retrograding.

A Wrinkle in Sidereal, or Star, Time

Sidereal time is time as measured by the heavens, and a sidereal day is the length of time it takes Earth to rotate on its axis once, relative to the fixed stars. On the other hand, our calendar or mean (average) solar day is the length of time it takes Earth to rotate on its axis relative to the Sun. (This also is sometimes referred to as the apparent movement of the Sun because to us, the Sun appears to move around Earth.) The mean solar day is slightly longer than the sidereal day, because while Earth is rotating on its axis, it's also moving in orbit around the Sun.

Earth gets back to the same place it started, in relation to the fixed stars, about four minutes earlier than it does in relation to the Sun. So by our clock time, the sidereal time is about four minutes later at the beginning of each new day. You can see this in the ephemeris under the column for sidereal time.

The local sidereal time tells you which degree of the zodiac is on the midheaven. This is the starting point for calculating the houses, which we'll explain later in this chapter.

AstroLingo

Sidereal time, or star time, is based on the actual amount of time it takes Earth to rotate once on its axis in relation to the fixed stars. While clock time measures a day as 24 hours based on the apparent movement of the Sun, sidereal time measures it at its astronomical, or star, speed, about four minutes less.

But let's make this a little simpler by giving you an example. Imagine a line extending directly over your head into the heavens. That's your *local zenith*. If you went outside at the same sidereal time every night, you would find the same fixed stars crossing your local zenith at that moment. You could also call this *star time*. Because it takes a little less time for Earth to get back to its initial position, relative to the stars—by about four minutes—our clock day is actually a little bit longer than the real star time, or sidereal time.

We need to convert everything into sidereal time in order to calculate a birth chart so that we can determine the ascendant, midheaven, and houses by star time.

Calculating Sidereal Time

Let's go to our example to see how this works. On the sample ephemeris page, look up the sidereal time for Spielberg's birth date, December 18, 1946. Keep in mind that the start time of our sample ephemeris page is midnight.

You'll find the sidereal time next to the date. Did you find it? It's 5 44 1. The computer will update it to the time Spielberg was born. To do this, the computer looks up the sidereal reference time for the date and year of birth. Then it adds (at least in North America) the true local time (also known as local mean time) of birth—as hours, minutes, and seconds—to the reference time of the ephemeris. Then it adds an acceleration factor based on the *time* of birth to correct for the four-minute difference between our clock time and sidereal time. And finally, it adds another acceleration correction factor for the four-minute difference, based on the *location* of the birth.

All of those factors added together give the computer the sidereal time of the birth. For you hard-core math whizzes, we're going to show you how Spielberg's sidereal time was calculated by the computer. If you're not interested in these details, of course, you can go ahead and move along to "Desperately Seeking House Cusps," later in this chapter.

First, the computer looks up Spielberg's date and year of birth in the ephemeris to get the sidereal time: In this case it's 5 hours, 44 minutes, and 1 second at midnight on December 18, 1946. Then the computer calculates the true local time, or the amount of time that passed between the reference or start time in the ephemeris and the exact time of birth.

Remember that the reference time for our ephemeris is midnight Greenwich mean time. So we have to make a few corrections to find out how many hours and minutes it was past that time when Spielberg was born in Cincinnati, Ohio. And this leads us to another discussion of time, in this case, true local time.

Will the True Local Time Please Stand Up?

Now, really, there isn't a false local time. But there *is* a true local time, and this is based on where the Sun actually is, instead of our clock time conventions. The Sun appears to move 60 miles every 4 minutes, which is the same as moving 1 degree in longitude every 4 minutes. This is why the time zones around the world change by 1 hour for every 15 degrees of longitude around the world.

Only at the primary meridians (every 15 degrees from Greenwich) does the clock time equal the Sun time. Everywhere else it's either earlier or later by actual local or solar time. So unless a person was born directly on one of the primary meridians—

in the case of North America, at 60W00, 75W00, 90W00, 105W00, or 120W00—the computer makes a correction of four minutes of time for each degree of difference in longitude for the birth location.

Imagine, for example, that the birth location is three degrees to the east of the prime meridian 75W00, at 72W00. The Sun has already reached this area and passed over it before it reached the 75W00 meridian. Basically, it's later in this location by Sun time than at the primary meridian by 3 degrees times 4 minutes, which equals 12 minutes. And because it's later in time at 72W00 than at 75W00, the 12 minutes is *added* to get the correct local time.

At 78W00, this is 3 degrees past the primary meridian of 75W00, and so the computer corrects for those 3 extra degrees and *subtracts* 12 minutes from the time for the primary meridian to get the local time. In essence, it's earlier at 78W00 than it is at 75W00, as the Sun reaches it later.

Calculating True Local Time

Now that you understand what local time is, we're going to walk you through what the computer is going to calculate for Spielberg's local time. First of all, it's going to determine if he was born during daylight saving, war, or standard time. If he had been born during either daylight saving or war time, the computer would have subtracted one hour from his birth time. But because it was an Eastern Standard Time birth, no changes were made at this step.

Next, his birth location is Cincinnati, Ohio, which has a longitude of 84W31. This is 9 degrees, 31 minutes west of the 75W00 primary meridian. The clock time when he was born was 6:16 P.M. EST, but that was accurate only at the 75W00. In Cincinnati, the solar time was a little bit earlier. So the computer multiplies the difference in longitude by 4 minutes and gets 36 minutes and 124 seconds, which converts to 38 minutes and 4 seconds.

Because Cincinnati is west of the 75W00 meridian and it's earlier there, the computer subtracts this amount from the time of 6:16 P.M. to get 5 hours, 37 minutes, and 56 seconds as his true local time. But to keep this in a 24-hour clock system, so we don't confuse A.M. and P.M., 12 hours are added and his true local time is shown as 17 hours, 37 minutes, and 56 seconds (17:37:56). This is what the computer adds to the sidereal time shown in the midnight ephemeris, as this is the real difference in time between the start, or reference, time shown there.

If Spielberg had been born somewhere east of England, such as Europe or Asia, of course, calculating the true local time would be a slightly different process from what we've used, because the time there is later than in Greenwich.

So far, we have the sidereal time and the true local time, which will be added together as follows (in a 24-hour system):

Sidereal time shown in ephemeris:	5 hours	44 minutes	1 sec
+ True local time (past midnight):	17 hours	37 minutes	56 sec

But there are still a few minor corrections to make before the computer has the final calculated sidereal time.

Acceleration

Next, the computer adds something called *acceleration*. This is how we compensate for the four-minute difference between the solar day and star time. This is added at a rate of 10 seconds for every hour from the start or reference time in the ephemeris—midnight in our case—to the true local time for North American births.

This equals 10 seconds of time for each hour after midnight that Spielberg was born. The computer uses the true local time, which, for this step, can be rounded to 17 hours and 38 minutes. So the computer multiplies 17 hours and 38 minutes past midnight by 10 seconds per hour, which equals 170 seconds plus about 6 more seconds for the 38 minutes. This adds up to 176 seconds, or 2 minutes and 56 seconds.

AstroLingo

Acceleration is a correction factor to compensate for the difference of about four minutes between a solar day and sidereal time. Acceleration is calculated for both the time of birth and place of birth.

So the computer adds 2 minutes and 56 seconds for the acceleration part of the formula based on his birth time. In our example so far, the computer has the following:

Sidereal time shown in ephemeris:	5 hours	44 minutes	1 sec
+ True local time (past midnight):	17 hours	37 minutes	56 sec
Acceleration (based on time of birth):		2 minutes	56 sec

Correction for Place of Birth

There's still *one more* minor correction for the computer to make! The computer already corrected for the difference of four minutes between sidereal time and a solar day if you were born in Greenwich, England. But because most of us are born else-where, the computer corrects for these four minutes again, based on our location. In essence, this is a correction for the place of birth, and, if we remember that distance equals time, this makes sense.

To calculate this, the computer is going to add 10 seconds for every 15 degrees of west longitude. Spielberg was born at 84W31, so for the first 75 degrees of west lon-gitude, it adds 50 seconds. That leaves another 9 degrees and 31 minutes to correct for, which is about 6 seconds, for a total correction of 56 seconds. The computer then adds the 56 seconds to the rest of the corrections and adds them all up to get the actual sidereal time for Spielberg's birth. So now we have:

Sidereal time shown in ephemeris:	5 hours	44 minutes	1 sec
True local time (past midnight):	17 hours	37 minutes	56 sec
Acceleration (based on time of birth):		2 minutes	56 sec
Acceleration (based on place of birth):			56 sec
Actual calculated sidereal time:	22 hours	83 minutes	169 sec

This converts to *23 hours, 25 minutes, 49 seconds, which is the final sidereal time for Spielberg*. Hooray! We finally have the number we need!

The computer also knows that once the sidereal clock reaches 24 hours, it starts counting over again beginning at 0. So it checks to make sure that the final sidereal time is within 24 hours. If it's not, it subtracts 24 hours from the total to get the correct sidereal time. In Spielberg's case, this wasn't necessary.

Let's summarize the corrections the computer makes for North American charts, using a midnight ephemeris in order to arrive at sidereal time:

1. The computer starts with the reference sidereal time in the ephemeris for the date and year of birth.

2. Then it calculates the true local time for the birth place. It then expresses that birth time in a 24-hour system (adding 12 hours for P.M. birth times), and adds that to the sidereal time it found in the midnight ephemeris.

3. Now it calculates and adds the acceleration factor to compensate for the difference of four minutes per day between sidereal time and regular clock time, based on the birth time.

4. The computer calculates the acceleration factor again to compensate for the birth location and adds this, too.

5. Last, the computer adds all of these and converts it to within 24 hours to get the final calculated sidereal time.

Houses, Houses, and More Houses!

It's time to talk about house systems, which are very technical. There are lots of different ways to divide space to come up with houses. One of the most commonly used house systems is Placidus; this might be because for a long time it was the only one available in reference books.

Now that there are computers, though, a wide variety of house systems are available. There are lots of technical differences between them, which we aren't going to cover, and different astrologers like different house systems. For example, some astrologers prefer Koch houses for far northern latitudes.

For the purposes of this book, though, we use the Placidus house system. It's certainly a good system to start with, and many astrologers still prefer to use it today.

Desperately Seeking House Cusps

As you might recall, house cusps are the places where the houses begin. If you look at Spielberg's chart, you'll see these lines, with a sign and degrees on each, dividing the houses.

Now that the computer has Spielberg's sidereal time, it's going to "look up" the houses in a table similar to the one shown here. This is a page from the *AFA Table of Houses, Placidus System.*

A page from the AFA Table of Houses.

(Excerpts from the AFA Table of Houses, Placidus System *are reproduced with the permission of Gregg Howe of Astro Numeric Service and the American Federation of Astrologers, Inc. Copyright 1988 by the American Federation of Astrologers, Inc.)*

23ʰ 24ᵐ 0ˢ — MC — 351° 0' 0" — ♓ 20° 12' 19"

N LAT	11	12	Ascendant	2	3
0	♈22 42.3	♉23 23.4	♊21 43.9	♋19 24.1	♌18 34.0
5	22 59.0	24 30.5	23 43.1	20 39.5	19 1.5
10	23 16.5	25 40.6	25 45.1	21 54.9	19 29.0
15	23 34.9	26 55.1	27 51.5	23 11.4	19 56.8
16	23 38.8	27 10.7	28 17.5	23 26.9	20 2.4
17	23 42.7	27 26.5	28 43.8	23 42.5	20 8.1
18	23 46.6	27 42.6	29 10.4	23 58.3	20 13.8
19	23 50.6	27 59.0	29 37.2	24 14.1	20 19.6
20	23 54.7	28 15.7	♊0 4.4	24 30.1	20 25.4
21	23 58.9	28 32.7	0 32.0	24 46.3	20 31.2
22	24 3.2	28 50.1	0 59.9	25 2.6	20 37.1
23	24 7.5	29 7.8	1 28.2	25 19.0	20 43.1
24	24 12.0	29 26.0	1 56.9	25 35.7	20 49.2
25	24 16.5	29 44.5	2 26.1	25 52.5	20 55.3
26	24 21.1	♋0 3.5	2 55.7	26 9.6	21 1.5
27	24 25.9	0 23.0	3 25.7	26 26.9	21 7.8
28	24 30.7	0 42.9	3 56.3	26 44.4	21 14.1
29	24 35.7	1 3.4	4 27.5	27 2.1	21 20.6
30	24 40.8	1 24.5	4 59.1	27 20.2	21 27.1
31	24 46.1	1 46.1	5 31.4	27 38.5	21 33.8
32	24 51.5	2 8.4	6 4.3	27 57.1	21 40.6
33	24 57.0	2 31.4	6 37.9	28 16.0	21 47.5
34	25 2.8	2 55.1	7 12.1	28 35.3	21 54.5
35	25 8.7	3 19.6	7 47.1	28 54.9	22 1.6
36	25 14.8	3 44.9	8 22.9	29 15.0	22 9.0
37	25 21.1	4 11.2	8 59.4	29 35.4	22 16.4
38	25 27.7	4 38.4	9 36.8	29 56.2	22 24.0
39	25 34.5	5 6.6	10 15.1	♋0 17.5	22 31.8
40	25 41.5	5 36.0	10 54.3	0 39.3	22 39.8
41	25 48.9	6 6.6	11 34.5	1 1.6	22 48.0
42	25 56.5	6 38.4	12 15.8	1 24.5	22 56.4
43	26 4.5	7 11.7	12 58.1	1 47.9	23 5.0
44	26 12.8	7 46.5	13 41.6	2 12.0	23 13.8

23ʰ 28ᵐ 0ˢ — MC — 352° 0' 0" — ♓ 21° 17' 27"

11	12	Ascendant	2	3	N LAT
♈23 46.0	♉24 22.0	♊22 39.2	♋20 20.3	♌19 35.0	0
24 3.5	25 29.8	24 38.5	21 35.3	20 2.0	5
24 21.7	26 40.7	26 40.5	22 50.3	20 28.9	10
24 40.9	27 55.9	28 46.8	24 6.2	20 56.1	15
24 45.0	28 11.6	29 12.8	24 21.6	21 1.6	16
24 49.0	28 27.5	29 39.0	24 37.2	21 7.2	17
24 53.1	28 43.8	♊0 5.5	24 52.8	21 12.8	18
24 57.3	29 0.3	0 32.3	25 8.5	21 18.5	19
25 1.6	29 17.1	0 59.4	25 24.4	21 24.2	20
25 6.0	29 34.3	1 26.9	25 40.4	21 29.9	21
25 10.4	29 51.8	1 54.7	25 56.6	21 35.7	22
25 14.9	♊0 9.7	2 22.9	26 12.9	21 41.6	23
25 19.6	0 27.9	2 51.5	26 29.4	21 47.5	24
25 24.3	0 46.6	3 20.5	26 46.1	21 53.5	25
25 29.1	1 5.7	3 50.0	27 3.0	21 59.5	26
25 34.0	1 25.3	4 19.9	27 20.2	22 5.7	27
25 39.1	1 45.4	4 50.4	27 37.5	22 11.9	28
25 44.3	2 6.0	5 21.3	27 55.1	22 18.2	29
25 49.6	2 27.2	5 52.9	28 13.0	22 24.7	30
25 55.1	2 49.0	6 25.0	28 31.1	22 31.2	31
26 0.7	3 11.4	6 57.7	28 49.5	22 37.8	32
26 6.5	3 34.5	7 31.0	29 8.3	22 44.6	33
26 12.5	3 58.3	8 5.0	29 27.4	22 51.4	34
26 18.7	4 22.9	8 39.8	29 46.8	22 58.4	35
26 25.1	4 48.4	9 15.3	♋0 6.6	23 5.6	36
26 31.6	5 14.7	9 51.5	0 26.8	23 12.9	37
26 38.5	5 42.1	10 28.6	0 47.4	23 20.3	38
26 45.5	6 10.4	11 6.6	1 8.5	23 28.0	39
26 52.9	6 39.9	11 45.5	1 30.0	23 35.8	40
27 0.5	7 10.5	12 25.4	1 52.1	23 43.7	41
27 8.5	7 42.5	13 6.3	2 14.7	23 51.9	42
27 16.7	8 15.8	13 48.2	2 37.8	24 0.4	43
27 25.4	8 50.7	14 31.3	3 1.6	24 9.0	44

The computer is going to look up the sidereal time closest to Spielberg's calculated sidereal time. Because it's very important to have the right sidereal time before going on to this step, it's a good thing we've got computers to do this for us!

Notice the sidereal times in the top left-hand corner of each box and you'll see that the table on the left is for 23 hours, 24 minutes, 0 seconds. The table on the right is for the sidereal time of 23 hours, 28 minutes, 0 seconds.

AstroLingo

Interpolating the houses means finding the correct positions between two sidereal times for them.

You can see that Spielberg's sidereal time of 23 hours, 25 minutes, 49 seconds is *between* those two sidereal times. So the computer knows that it's going to have to *interpolate* between these house tables to get the right houses for Spielberg. Lucky for us, we don't have to know what those steps are! But there are a few things we *can* understand easily.

The Search for Midheaven

Notice the M.C. notations in the middle of the two headers? An M.C. is the same as the midheaven or tenth house cusp for the chart. You can look at Spielberg's chart to determine that his midheaven is at ♓20°41'.

The two M.C.s shown on the previous two tables are ♓20°12'19'' (20 degrees Pisces, 12 minutes, and 19 seconds) and ♓21°17'27''. So we know the computer has calculated the correct sidereal time, as Spielberg's midheaven lies in between these two M.C.s. And when the computer is done interpolating for his correct longitude, it will have Spielberg's midheaven as well, which is 20 degrees Pisces and 41 minutes (written as ♓20°41').

> **Star-Crossed**
>
> Correcting for latitude can make an enormous difference. In Spielberg's case, most of his house cusps are about 35 to 45 minutes later than shown in the table of houses. That's not a big difference, but in some charts, this is enough for a planet to move to a different house, or for an ascendant, or M.C., to change signs—and we all know how star-crossed that could be!

Calculating the Other Houses

Now the computer needs to know Spielberg's latitude in order to find the rest of the houses. Because he was born in North America, he has a northern latitude, and the computer knows to look for it on this chart. It's 39N06, or 39 degrees and 6 minutes north of the equator. That's very close to the house cusps shown for the latitude of 39N00.

Now look at the left table with the sidereal time of 23 hours, 24 minutes, and 0 seconds, and notice the column of northern latitudes next to it. Look at the ones shown for the latitude of 39 degrees and compare them to the house cusps on Spielberg's chart. They're pretty close, but the computer goes the extra step and interpolates them for latitude corrections, too.

> **Heaven Knows**
>
> A good way to check the computer's work (if you're inclined in that direction!) is the following: If the person was born around sunrise, the Sun ☉ should be in the first house, or perhaps just into the twelfth. A noon birth means the Sun will be in the ninth or tenth house. Sunset births occur in the seventh or sixth house, or right on the descendant. And midnight births can be found in the third or fourth house.

You will see the house cusps listed for the eleventh house, twelfth house, ascendant, second house, and third house for that latitude. The other house cusps aren't listed, because they're exactly opposite the ones shown, in the opposite sign.

In general, house systems operate the same way, so that the house opposite will have the same degrees, minutes, and seconds, but the opposite sign. Using Spielberg's midheaven as an example, it is $\mathcal{H}$20°41', and the I.C. (or the fourth house cusp) will equal $\mathfrak{M}$20°41' (20 degrees Virgo, 41 minutes), the sign opposite Pisces.

It's like this for every house. In this table of houses, we know the eleventh (fifth), twelfth (sixth), ascendant (descendant—seventh), second (eighth), and third (ninth). And, of course, we already know the midheaven and I.C., too.

Putting It All Together

Finally! The computer puts this all together in a chart. It has the planets' positions, and now it has the house cusps. It puts the calculated houses in the appropriate places and then adds the planets in there, too. Thus we have Spielberg's (or your) birth chart!

Aren't we lucky computers can calculate all this for us? It not only saves us all this time-consuming work; it avoids all sorts of possible mistakes. It's good to know precisely what the computer's doing, but we can let it do all the dirty work for us.

The Least You Need to Know

- Base 60, instead of base 10, is used to calculate time and distance. For example, there are 60 minutes in an hour, or one degree.

- All birth times need to be converted to Greenwich mean time (GMT) in order to calculate the positions of the planets.

- Sidereal time is the true astronomical time, used to calculate the houses.

- Birth times need to be converted to true local time as part of the process of finding the house cusps.

- Acceleration is a correction factor to compensate for the difference of about four minutes between clock time and star time. Acceleration is calculated for both the time and place of birth.

- With a correct sidereal time, house cusps can be located in a table of houses, but to get accurate ones requires interpolation for both longitude and latitude.

Chapter 21

All About Me: Interpreting Your Birth Chart

In This Chapter

- ◆ Chart basics: it's all Greek to me
- ◆ Aspects: specifics on experience
- ◆ Chart interpretations even idiots can make
- ◆ A sample birth chart interpreted
- ◆ When you need to know more: getting a professional reading

It's time to start putting together all you've learned to interpret your birth chart. But first we need to cover one more aspect of your birth chart—aspects. In this chapter, we'll look at how these planetary relationships flavor your birth chart and unlock more secrets about why you behave the way you do.

Chart Basics: It's All Greek to Me

Well, okay, so it's not Greek. But it sure looks like a foreign language. In fact, those symbols on your birth chart *are* another language, a powerful symbolic one.

The language of astrology uses symbols for signs, planets, and houses, and to show the various relationships among them. If your child were to draw a picture of your family standing in front of your house, the stick person with the longer hair would be Mom, the one with the glasses would be Dad, and the short one would be Junior (or may be Spot, if your kid's got some Picasso tendencies).

Just as Mom, Dad, Junior, and Spot are much more than "Mom," "Dad," "Junior," and "Spot," astrological symbols represent much more than "Aries," "Mercury," "the first house," or a "sextile." For example, Aries ♈, the first sign of the zodiac, is ruled by Mars ♂, a cardinal Fire sign, and has a *yang* energy. All that should come immediately to mind when you see the symbol ♈.

In turn, each of these symbols represents a larger meaning as well. Cardinal signs, for example, like to lead, to get things started, though they aren't always around to see things through to completion. By using the symbol for Aries, ♈, these concepts are part of what's represented, too, plus a whole lot more.

Astrological Symbols

Sign	Symbol	Planet	Symbol
Aries	♈	Sun	☉
Taurus	♉	Moon	☽
Gemini	♊	Mercury	☿
Cancer	♋	Venus	♀
Leo	♌	Mars	♂
Virgo	♍	Saturn	♄
Libra	♎	Uranus	♅
Scorpio	♏	Neptune	♆
Sagittarius	♐	Pluto	♇
Capricorn	♑	North Node	☊
Aquarius	♒	South Node	☋
Pisces	♓		
Aspect	**Symbol**	**Other**	**Symbol**
Conjunction	☌	Retrograde	℞
Sextile	✶		
Square	□		
Trine	△		
Opposition	☍		
Quincunx	⚻		

Aspects: Specifics on Experience

You probably remember *aspects* from walking through the houses in Part 4. There we mentioned that a planet's aspects could determine how its energies would manifest in a certain house.

Looking at aspects means answering the question, "How do these planets get along?" There are five major aspects and many more minor aspects. Most planets can form any aspect to another, except for Mercury ☿, which is never more than 28 degrees from the Sun ☉, and Venus ♀, which is never farther than 48 degrees from the Sun ☉.

AstroLingo

In astrology, **aspect** has a technical meaning. When two planets are in aspect to each other, they are related by one of a set of geometric angles between them, some of which are beneficial, and others that are challenging.

The following are the major aspects:

◆ **Conjunctions** ☌, which are the strongest aspects

◆ **Squares** □, which are considered to be challenging, and their tension provides dynamic action in your life

◆ **Oppositions** ☍, which show a need for balance between two competing or different energies or needs

◆ **Trines** △, which are considered the most favorable aspects, as their signs usually share the same element

◆ **Sextiles** ⚹, which are harmonious, bringing opportunity and attraction

Before we walk through the aspects, it's important to understand precisely what aspects are and how they're determined. Remember those numbers before and after each sign next to the planets of your birth chart? Those are the *degrees* of each planet at your birth, and they take on prime importance when we begin aspecting. The number of degrees one planet is from another determines its aspect to that planet.

AstroLingo

Planetary **degrees** show the position of the planets in the signs. **Orbs** are the variances in degree allowed in determining aspects.

Most astrologers agree that aspects occur within *orbs*, rather than just those that create exact angles. For example, while an exact square is 90 degrees, angles from 83 to 97 degrees are commonly considered to be squares; but even these orbs of 7 degrees depend on the planets involved. Exact aspects, of course, create the strongest connections, but wider orbs cannot be ignored. Some astrologers don't take orbs beyond 6 degrees, while others will go as high as 10 degrees.

In general, different orbs are allowed for different types of aspects. This is based on the planets involved—the Sun ☉ and Moon ☽ often get 10-degree orbs—and the type of aspect. Conjunctions ☌ get more of an orb than a sextile ✶, for example, as a conjunction is a stronger aspect. We'll explain exactly what conjunctions and sextiles—and all the other major aspects—are in the next section of this chapter.

To explain this concept a little more, a conjunction is two planets within, say, 7 to 10 degrees of each other (out of 360 degrees), so the percentage of variance is small. Ten degrees out of 360 is $\frac{1}{36}$ or 2.7 percent, after all.

On the other hand, if a sextile ✶, which is only 60 degrees to begin with, had a 10-degree orb, that would be a nearly 17 percent variance. So orbs for an aspect such as a sextile ✶ are smaller than orbs for something like a conjunction ☌ or opposition ☍.

One helpful way to determine aspects is to recognize what part of a circle a particular angle represents (and you thought your geometry days were over!). We've provided a list for you.

Aspects Are Angles of the Circle

Portion of Circle	Angle	Aspect Name (* Major Aspect)
$\frac{1}{2}$	180°	Opposition*
$\frac{1}{3}$	120°	Trine*
$\frac{1}{4}$	90°	Square*
$\frac{1}{5}$	72°	Quintile
$\frac{1}{6}$	60°	Sextile*
$\frac{1}{7}$	51½°	Septile
$\frac{1}{8}$	45°	Semi-square
$\frac{1}{9}$	40°	Novile
$\frac{1}{10}$	36°	Semi-quintile
$\frac{1}{12}$	30°	Semi-sextile

Note that the major aspects are the opposition ☍, trine △, square □, and sextile ✶. There's also the *conjunction*, which isn't listed above because it's not an angle; planets in conjunction are in the same area. All the other aspects are considered minor, though some might not be *quite* as minor as once thought.

In addition, all the major aspects are essentially same-degree aspects, so planets in different signs will share the same degree. Most minor aspects involve aspects that are not the same degree.

Another way to determine aspects is to remember which signs are which quality, element, and/or energy. As a rule (there are exceptions), sextiles ✶ and trines △ are formed by signs with the same element or energy, and squares □ and oppositions ☍ are formed by signs of the same quality.

AstroLingo

A **conjunction** ☌ occurs when two planets are in the same area of the birth chart.

The New Math: From Conjunctions ☌ to Sextiles ✶

We're going to concentrate on the major aspects here, with one exception. Astrologers have recently found that *quincunxes* ⚻, or angles of 150 degrees, have far more importance than had been previously thought. Astrologers have come to recognize the quincunx as a "crisis" aspect. This aspect signals an internal need to change an old pattern or accommodate a new routine he or she hadn't planned on.

Like so many things in astrology, aspects used to be characterized as good or bad. These days, astrologers (and psychologists) recognize that we need our challenges to make the most of our lives, so aspects that used to be called "bad" are now viewed in a new light. And aspects that were called "good" in the past can sometimes make you too complacent.

Let's start at the very beginning, though.

Aspect: Conjunction ☌ 0°

Conjunctions ☌ are the strongest aspects in astrology. The two (or more) planets involved are a focal point of the chart, and their meaning is emphasized. They can be either easy or challenging, depending on which planets are involved and other aspects in the chart.

Aspect: Sextile ✶ 60°

Sextiles ✶ are considered quite favorable, as their signs usually share the same energy. They do require some effort on your part, though, unlike easy trines. Sextiles are like development opportunities, so if you don't take action to develop them, you can miss out.

Aspect: Square □ 90°

Squares □ are considered to be challenging, and their tension can provide dynamic action in your life and development. Most of us would never do anything without being motivated by squares (or oppositions)!

Aspect: Trine △ 120°

A trine △ is considered the most favorable aspect, as its signs will usually share the same element and energy. These are well-developed skills and strengths, which many people fail to recognize within themselves, because they do it so well. In fact, too many trines can make you weak or lazy, because there's no resistance here at all, just an easy flow of energy between the two planets involved.

Aspect: Opposition ☍ 180°

Oppositions ☍ are considered challenging, especially in areas of growth and achievement. They also can show a need for balancing opposite needs and/or energies, such as career versus home, or self versus others.

Aspect: Quincunx ⚻ 150°

In a quincunx ⚻ or inconjunct, there is no relationship between the signs involved—neither quality, element, nor energy. This aspect indicates a need to adjust in some way, whether it be a change in attitude, habit, or behavior.

Some planets or energies get along well together, whereas others are uncomfortable with one another. When two planets are in aspect to each other, they're essentially talking and communicating, and it's the slower planet that's telling the faster planet how to behave, think, and act. This is because the slower planet takes longer to move, so it's going to have a greater impact. In other words, Pluto's ♇ aspects have more far-reaching effects than the Moon's ☽, which we feel in a more fast-paced way.

Planets, Fast to Slow

Moon	☽
Mercury	☿

Venus	♀
Sun	☉
Mars	♂
Jupiter	♃
Saturn	♄
Uranus	♅
Neptune	♆
Pluto	♇

Getting Along: Venus/Jupiter Aspects

While we haven't got the time or the room to take you through all the aspects, we thought we could at least illustrate how aspects work by showing you two planetary relationships through each of the major aspects. First, we have charismatic Venus ♀ and expansive Jupiter ♃. These two planets get along quite well, because Jupiter, the slower planet, expands Venus's function, so there'll be more money, more love, and more relationships.

Venus Conjunct Jupiter ♀ ☌ ♃

People with this conjunction love a good time and are charming, generous, and popular. Honest and helpful, they're inclined to help those less fortunate. They've also got artistic ability and might be talented as peacemakers as well.

Venus Sextile Jupiter ♀ ⚹ ♃

Jupiter's expansiveness enhances Venus's charisma with this aspect, making these people graceful, charitable, outgoing, and affectionate. This is a highly favorable aspect, often considered good luck.

Venus Square Jupiter ♀ □ ♃

This more challenging aspect can make people vain, lazy, extravagant, or ostentatious. This is the aspect of someone who might blow his or her money on luxury items. Used constructively, this aspect can lead to success in public relations, counseling, or the media.

Venus Trine Jupiter ♀ △ ♃

There's a great deal of grace and elegance with this aspect, plus there's a knack for making big money, having successful partnerships—and enjoying lots of love affairs! This aspect indicates success in music and the arts, and harmony in marital and domestic affairs.

Venus Opposition Jupiter ♀ ☍ ♃

This aspect is extravagant like the square, and in addition is often found in social climbers, who acquire and discard friends in a never-ending pursuit of the "in crowd." Navigated well, this aspect can learn to relate well to others—but it's a major challenge.

Venus Quincunx Jupiter ♀ ⚻ ♃

This aspect needs to learn self-respect rather than rely so much on what others think. These people lack faith in themselves, which can make them defensive, or others might walk all over them. Growth with this quincunx comes when these people truly understand that the greatest approval comes from within.

A Harder Row to Hoe: Sun/Saturn Aspects

In the second pairing we'll look at, strict Saturn ♄ gives just about everybody a hard time. The Sun ☉ is about creativity, a person's vitality, and his or her sense of self; Saturn is about structure, limitations, losses, or responsibilities, and there's no exception here.

Saturn is the slower planet, so it's the one in charge here. People with this combination might find it hard to enjoy life, or might end up censoring themselves, even when Saturn and the Sun are in good aspect to each other. There might be problems with authority figures or the father, especially when the two planets are in challenging aspects to each other. Even in its more favorable aspects, Sun/Saturn aspects make for a no-nonsense, hardworking relationship.

Sun Conjunct Saturn ☉ ☌ ♄

People with this aspect will have material success because they are hardworking and single-minded. A Sun-Saturn conjunction means these people take their lives very seriously and learn from their experiences, but they should also learn to find some easy-going friends to offset the demands they make on themselves.

Sun Sextile Saturn ☉⚹♄

This aspect means a long, well-ordered, successful life, and these people will joyfully accept all duties and responsibilities that come their way. Working together, the Sun and Saturn lead to good common sense and solid self-confidence.

Sun Square Saturn ☉□♄

There's a major challenge at work here, and these people have to work very hard to achieve what they desire. There can be a feeling of underachievement, or internal insecurity, and these people want to make certain that they hang on to any position they have.

Sun Trine Saturn ☉△♄

Success with this aspect comes through one's own efforts and powers of concentration, and these people not only grow easily but prosper as well. Accepting responsibility comes naturally to people with this aspect, and so they might be managers or supervisors.

Sun Opposition Saturn ☉☍♄

This challenging aspect can actually cause people to fight against themselves, or refuse to accept the obstacles in front of them. The lesson with this aspect is to learn to work with limits and conform to structures and limitations, a hard thing for a strong Sun to do.

Sun Quincunx Saturn ☉⚻♄

People with this quincunx often have authority issues and can become self-righteous if challenged. They might let others take advantage of them, or simply ignore others' wishes. The lesson for people with this aspect is to learn to relax, and to learn to live and work constructively with other people.

Aspect Grid

When your birth chart is created, an *aspect grid* is created at the same time. This is a set of boxes, with the planets listed across the top and down the side, showing the various aspects those planets make. To illustrate, we will show you Steven Spielberg's aspect grid.

Your birth chart also might show aspects at its center, represented as lines, with the type of aspect shown on each line. Lots of astrologers either use a color printer or colored highlighter to differentiate between the aspects on a birth chart.

> **AstroLingo**
>
> An **aspect grid** is a chart showing the relationships among planets on a birth chart.

Chart Interpretations Even Idiots Can Make

One easy way to start making chart interpretations that include the aspects is to think of aspects as planetary relationships. Ask the question, "How do these planets get along?"

For example, we noted earlier that charismatic Venus ♀ and expansive Jupiter ♃ get along quite well, and that Jupiter, the slower planet, expands Venus's function, so there'll be more money, more love, and more relationships.

We also said that the Sun ☉ is about creativity, a person's vitality, and his or her sense of self, but Saturn ♄ is about structure, limitations, losses, or responsibilities. Knowing this, we can see why this is going to be a more challenging relationship.

Steven Spielberg's aspect grid.

Steven Spielberg
Natal Chart
18 Dec 1946
6:16 PM EST +5:00
Cincinnati
39N06 084W31
Geocentric
Tropical
Placidus
True Node

	☽	☉	☿	♀	♂	♃	♄	♅	Ψ	♇	☊	☋	As	Mc
☽														
☉						∥ 0°49		# 0°16		# 0°01	# 1°11	∥ 1°11	# 0°23	
☿							# 1°43				# 1°45	∥ 1°45		
♀					∥ 1°41									
♂		☌ 4A41						# 1°06		# 0°48			# 1°12	
♃				☌ 1S18										
♄	□ 1A18		△ 0A21											
♅		☍ 6S57								∥ 0°18	∥ 0°54	# 0°54	∥ 0°06	
Ψ		⚹ 2A49				⚹ 2S28								∥ 0°50
♇	□ 6A15	△ 5A18	□ 6S08		□ 4S49	☌ 4S57		⚹ 2A28			∥ 1°13	# 1°13	∥ 0°24	
☊		☌ 3A57						☌ 7A43	△ 1S07	⚹ 1A21			∥ 0°48	
☋		☌ 3A57						△ 3S36	☍ 7A43	⚹ 1S07	△ 1A21		# 0°48	
As	△ 3A51									□ 0A04				
Mc		□ 5S45		△ 1A26	△ 2A45	□ 1S12								

It might help you to go back and look at the keyword concepts for each planet. Better yet, we've provided a quick reference for you in the following table. So now, you can use those keywords to begin answering the question about how these planets get along.

Planetary Keywords

Planet		Keywords
Sun	⊙	Purpose and self, the person's center
Moon	☽	Emotions, habits, and unconscious patterns
Mercury	☿	Thinking and communication
Venus	♀	Relationships, possessions, money, and harmony
Mars	♂	Action and independence
Jupiter	♃	Growth, optimism, success, and generosity
Saturn	♄	Responsibilities, rules, and limitations
Uranus	♅	Invention, originality, and sudden change
Neptune	♆	Spirituality, dreams, and the mystical
Pluto	♀	Renewal and transformation

Last, don't forget that the slower planet will always act on the faster planet; it's the one that will be dominating the relationship, in other words.

StarFacts

In matters of love, it takes more than a good Sun ⊙ sign aspect to make a good relationship. Matches "made in heaven" have several good aspects between other planets in their charts. For example, a good aspect between two people's Moons ☽ is very helpful because the couple will be comfortable together on a daily basis and emotionally compatible at the same time. But the best love matches have some challenging aspects between them as well because without a little challenge, the couple might never get together because they'd have nothing to learn from each other! We'll be looking at using astrology to chart your relationships in Chapter 23.

Your Astrological Signature

Your astrological signature is determined by counting up all the planets you have in each element. How many planets are in Earth signs, for example? Air signs? Fire signs? Water signs?

You'll be using only planets, not Nodes ☋☊, or angles in the chart, at least to start. In the same way, you'll then count up how many planets are in each quality: How many are in cardinal signs? Fixed signs? Mutable signs?

Next, check to see which element and quality have the largest number of planets. Only one sign will represent each pair. That sign is your astrological signature.

For example, Spielberg has five Fire planets and five fixed planets. The fixed Fire sign is Leo ♌, so Spielberg's astrological signature is Leo, and creativity and self-expression would be extremely important to him.

The astrological signature is valuable because it gives the overall tenor or flavor of the chart. If a person has an Aries ♈ signature (that is, the majority of his or her planets were in cardinal and Fire signs), for example, but only one of his or her planets is in Aries, this emphasis won't be obvious from a first glance. Yet that person will want to lead, and start or pioneer new things; he or she will act somewhat like an Aries, in other words.

In Spielberg's chart, he has only two planets in Leo, so the fact that it's his astrological signature reveals a great deal.

What if there's a tie? Well, first look to see if the Sun ☉ or Moon ☽ are in the groups that tie. If only one or both are in the same group and neither is in the other, then that breaks the tie. But if the Sun is in one and the Moon is in the other, then you still have a tie.

That's when you add, first, the ascendant, and then, if there's still a tie, the midheaven. Usually the tie is broken by then, but not always. If it's not, it really *is* a tie.

Sowing or Reaping: Which Lifetime Are You In?

Whether you're sowing or reaping in this lifetime can be determined by counting the number of planets on the eastern half (the left half of the chart, houses 10 through 3) of your chart and then counting the number of planets on the western side (the right side of your chart, houses 4 through 9).

If there are more planets in the east than the west, then this lifetime is a *sowing lifetime* and you'll have a great deal of freedom and choices about what you do. Things won't usually fall in your lap from others, but anything you work toward consistently can work out. You'll have to put in a lot of energy to make things work, but you *will* have lots of choices as to what you work on. This time around, you're sowing your seeds and creating your own opportunities.

On the other hand, if there are more planets in the west than the east, you're in a *reaping lifetime*, and will have less freedom. However, you could say your life is set up for you to walk through, and you'll usually find that it opens up to new opportunities from others just when you need it to do so.

In essence, you're harvesting the seeds you planted in previous lives, so your life is already "in place," so to speak. You might have fewer choices, but you don't have to work so hard to get where you're going: You just reap your harvest from previous lives. If you believe this is your only lifetime, then this will still reveal whether you create your own opportunities or receive them through others.

A Sample Chart Interpreted, or Let's Be Voyeurs

Here's Steven Spielberg's chart again, but you might notice a difference this time. If so, good for you. The difference is that we've put in the aspects.

Steven Spielberg
Natal Chart
18 Dec 1946
6:16 PM EST +5:00
Cincinnati
39N06 084W31
Geocentric
Tropical
Placidus
True Node

Steven Spielberg's birth chart, with aspects.

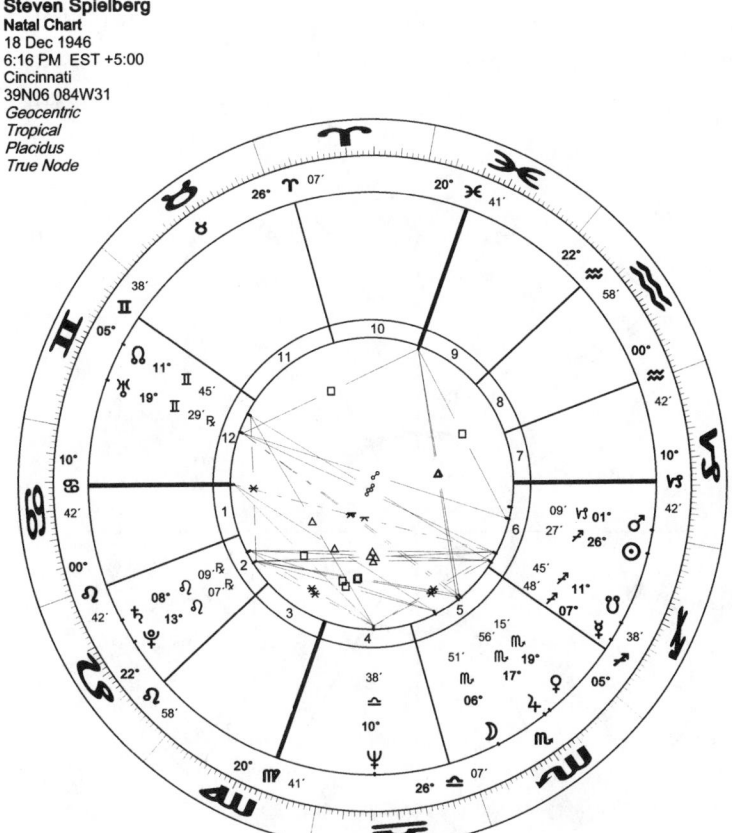

First, note that, using the preceding formula, Spielberg's in a *reaping lifetime*. He's a great example of that type of life, and, as a young director, he was taken under an older, wiser director's wing, a major opportunity for him. Next, let's look at some of the aspects in Spielberg's chart and apply them to what we've just learned so that we can see what else we can discover about him.

Spielberg's chart has lots of trines △. Eight trines △ appear, to be exact. Trines can be charms for the easy life—too easy, sometimes, but this preponderance is set off by the eight squares □ that are also formed by Spielberg's planets. Squares □, remember, are challenging, so they provide dynamic action as well.

No planet forms more aspects on Spielberg's chart, though, than Pluto ♀, which appears at 13♌07R in his second house. Pluto ♀ squares Spielberg's fifth house Moon ☽, Venus ♀, and Jupiter ♃ (all in Scorpio ♏), trines △ his sixth house Mercury ☿ and South Node ☋ (in Sagittarius ♐), is conjunct ☌ to his second house Saturn ♄, and is sextile ✶ to his fourth house Neptune ♆ (in Libra ♎).

All these aspects to Pluto ♀ show how important power, regeneration, and transformation are to Spielberg's life. He'll also have an intensity about him that few others can match. Life is serious and important to him, not just a time to have fun.

As we continue to take a peek into Spielberg's chart, let's review the houses and their areas of influence.

The houses and their areas of influence.

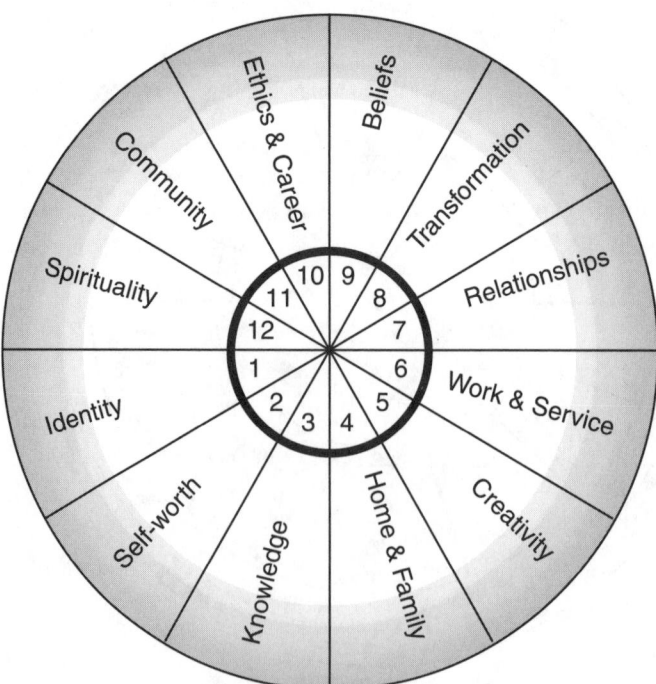

Here Comes the Sun ☉

Before we get into more specific aspects of Spielberg's chart, though, we need to get a general feel for him. We notice his Sun ☉ is in Sagittarius conjunct Mars ☉☌♂, and remember that this Sun sign is here to seek truth, wisdom, knowledge, and understanding. This is a sign that likes both freedom and adventure.

With his Sun close to Mars, Spielberg's trailblazer tendencies are even more pronounced, as Mars is also an independent influence. But noting that Mars ♂ is in Capricorn ♑ instead of Sagittarius ♐, we realize that whatever vision or truth he's seeking, he wants to use his energies (Mars) to build something long-lasting (Capricorn) that will influence others for many years to come. Because his Sun ☉ and Mars ♂ are in the sixth house, we would expect these pursuits to be part of his day-to-day work.

Next, we look across the chart and see that Uranus is opposite his Sun ♅☍☉. This is *another* influence showing Spielberg's need for freedom and independence, but this time, it shrieks of someone unusual, different, and possibly too rebellious or willful to work for someone else. He might also dislike authority, routine, and doing the same thing day after day. This aspect suggests that he prefers to do whatever he wants on his own terms, and whatever he does will be uniquely and authentically him.

Now, notice that both Spielberg's Sun ☉ and Uranus ♅ are square □ to the midheaven, the symbol for his career. This aspect indicates that he needs plenty of freedom and independence to make choices in his career. Working for someone else would probably not be his preference. In addition, he wants to be known for projects the establishment wouldn't do, ones that are daring, different, and authentically him.

When we look at the sign on his midheaven, we see that it's Pisces ♓, the sign associated with film, movies, photography, spiritual pursuits, being of service, and inspiring others. In his unique way, Spielberg brings his vision and truth to others in his films, and inspires our world in original ways (Uranus square midheaven).

Interestingly, Spielberg's Sun ☉ and Uranus ♅ both rule two houses. The Sun is in charge of the second and third houses, while Uranus is in charge of the eighth and ninth. This gives these planets more emphasis than normal, with two kingdoms instead of the usual one.

Having Leo ♌ in both the second and third houses, Spielberg is being challenged to use his creative and self-expressive talents (Leo, second house resources) to acquire new, self-expressive abilities and information, and to form creative (Leo) associations with others in his community (third house). In his case, it's not enough to just get rich, as his self-worth (second house) is tied to his mental and intellectual achievements (third house).

Moon River (a.k.a. Moon ☽ in Scorpio ♏)

Now that we've looked briefly at his Sun ☉, we'll move on to Spielberg's Moon ☽, the second part of the important triad. We notice his Moon is in Scorpio ♏ in the fifth house, which tells us that this is someone with very powerful emotions. He might not always share them with others, but it is definitely part of his strong, creative drive. Additionally, because Scorpio is a fixed sign, he never gives up, no matter what the odds.

Notice that the sign of Scorpio doesn't have a house cusp. This is called an *interception*, and it shows an area of his life that he needs to develop on his own, outside of his local environment, because others might not understand his true needs or respond in ways that are supportive.

In Spielberg's case, because the Moon ☽ is intercepted, his emotional needs might not be understood by others, so he may be less likely to express them. Or they might run rampant when he's upset. (Note that Venus ♀ and Jupiter ♃ are in the same boat, so he might have been forced to develop his values and beliefs on his own terms for similar reasons.) With his Moon ☽ in Scorpio ♏ *and* intercepted, his vulnerability may be so great that he could take special precautions to prevent others from getting too close.

AstroLingo

An **interception** means that a sign doesn't appear on a house cusp. Instead, it appears totally within a particular house, with the sign before it beginning the house and the sign after it ending the house. Intercepted signs represent areas that the person will need to develop on his or her own, because others won't be aware of those needs.

We also notice that the Moon is square to Saturn ☽□♄ in the second house and realize that he tries to keep his emotions under a tight rein, while channeling those strong feelings into his creative, fifth house endeavors. However, too much internalizing of his emotions could lead to difficulties with depression or despondency.

In any case, Spielberg's emotional nature (Moon ☽) is very intense (Scorpio ♏), and it's very much behind his powerful success. According to distinguished astrologer Noel Tyl, who wrote the foreword to this book, Spielberg's Moon ☽ in the fifth house also shows his "incredible imagination in his films, appealing not just to children but to the fanciful child in every adult."

And He's Got Personality!

Looking beyond, we notice Spielberg's ascendant is Cancer ♋. Now this is an interesting piece of information, and one we might not expect. From this we realize he's here to learn about responsible nurturing, and his personality is adaptable, or able to sense the moods and feelings of others.

We know Cancer ♋ is an emotional sign, so we might be tempted to assume that Spielberg would wear his feelings on his sleeve. But we already know the ruler or landlord of this house, the Moon ☽, is more likely to keep them under wraps in his case, due to his strong vulnerability. So although Spielberg exhibits some of the characteristics of a Cancer rising, he could be cautious about revealing his feelings. On the other hand, we see his Moon trining △ his ascendant and realize that when he does express his feelings, he does so constructively.

Now notice that his ascendant is exactly square □ to Neptune ♆, showing some confusion regarding his identity or personality, especially when he was young. He may have had difficulties expressing himself as a child, or lived in his own fantasy world. Because Neptune is in the fourth house, his family might have had shifting circumstances, or there might have been something confusing or uncertain about his home life.

Happy Trails to You!

Finally, we note that Spielberg's Neptune is trine with the North Node ♆△☊, the path of his future development and greatest growth. He had the option of channeling all this uncertainty, fantasy, or confusion into his path for the future. His North Node ☊ is in Gemini ♊, the sign of ideas and mental pursuits. Because Neptune ♆ is the ruler of Pisces ♓, the sign associated with films, photography, magic, and such, his home influences somehow led him to his path.

We need to keep in mind that we still have a trailblazer here, seeking his grail, truth, or vision, and that all of these parts of his chart are like different internal parts of himself. We don't have enough space to tell you everything about Spielberg's chart or life, but you can see from this short demonstration that there's a *lot* to anyone's chart—including, of course, your own.

When You Need to Know More: Professional Readings

Just as with everything in astrology, reading and interpreting a birth chart takes years and years of training, as well as an intuitive sense of what it all means. This is just one reason you might choose to get a professional reading. But there are other reasons as well. Let's say, for example, you have specific questions: When should I start my business? Is there a good time soon for me to propose to my sweetie?

A professional reading can help you answer those questions, as well as give you a comprehensive overview of why you behave and/or react the way you do.

The Least You Need to Know

- ◆ The language of astrology uses symbols for signs, planets, and houses, and shows the various relationships among them.

- ◆ When two planets are in aspect to each other, they are related by one of a set of geometric angles between them.

- ◆ You are either reaping or sowing in this lifetime.

Chapter **22**

Using Astrology to Map Your Life

In This Chapter

♦ Progressions, or I can't stand still

♦ Transits, or planetary triggers

♦ Astrology is your compass

♦ Windows of opportunity

With progressions and transits, we begin to explore how the movement of the planets interconnects with what's happening in your life *now*. Understanding transits and progressions can give you the foresight to take advantage of your life's favorable times, and not let the less favorable ones get you down.

What Transits and Progressions Have to Do with You

Progressions contain the primary timing for your development and growth and show how you evolve and grow. They are generally felt internally. You might make external changes based on them, but they are like the unfolding of your astrological DNA. The timing for all of these changes is very personal, based solely on your own chart. Because evolution is slow, these are slow changes.

> **AstroLingo**
>
> **Progressions** show how you and your chart progress throughout your life and contain the timing for your development and growth. **Transits** occur when the present positions of planets overhead aspect their various positions in your birth chart. You could think of them as triggers for events in your life and the development shown by progressions.

Transits, on the other hand, are based on the movement of the planets overhead in comparison to the position of the planets in your chart. They're much faster than progressions and often act as triggers or release points for whatever themes of development your progressions are suggesting.

Transits can also appear to us as events, external matters, or issues with our environment and the people around us. Until we learn to recognize our external circumstances as metaphors for our internal self, challenging transits can feel like someone hitting us with obstacles and problems.

Progressions, or I Can't Stand Still

You might have been born with your Sun ☉ in Libra ♎ and your Venus ♀ in Scorpio ♏, but as you progress through your life, so do your planets. How your planets progress as you age is what progressions are all about.

A *progressed chart* moves each planet by however far it moves in one day for each year of life. The Sun ☉, for example, moves about one degree per day, so in a progressed chart, the Sun would move about one degree per *year*. The slowness of this process means that only the inner planets (Sun ☉, Moon ☽, Mercury ☿, Venus ♀, and Mars ♂) are going to move significantly within a lifetime. The outer planets might progress into an exact aspect or placement and then get your attention, but generally it's the inner planets and the angles (ascendant and midheaven) of the chart that evolve over time.

> **AstroLingo**
>
> Your **progressed chart** is different from your birth chart in that it moves each planet by its amount of daily travel for each year of life after the person is born. Progressions show how you evolve and develop over time.

To look at your progressions, you've got to use a double astrological wheel with your birth chart on the inside, and your progressed chart on the outside. When you look at these two charts, you see how your birth planets are evolving over time.

Basically, your progressions move all your planets by one day for each year of life after birth. So you can look up your birth date in an ephemeris and find (roughly) that the planetary positions each day after your birth are going to represent the way your chart unfolds year by year. (You'll remember from Chapter 19 that an *ephemeris* is a book showing where the planets are at noon or midnight Greenwich mean time.)

There are some more technicalities to finding your progressions than what we're going to cover, but the "formula"—one day for each year—gives you the general idea. You can see, then, that progressions and the unfolding of your development are individually determined by your chart alone.

The Moon ☽, for example, moves about 13 degrees a day, which translates in a progressed chart to about 13 degrees a year. Because each sign covers 30 degrees, this means that about every two and a half years, your progressed Moon moves into a new sign. It also means that approximately every 28 years, you will have a progressed lunar return, where the Moon returns by progression to its original position in your chart.

Themes for Personal Change

Progressions signal the themes and changes in your chart that are waiting to unfold over time. They are often felt internally before they manifest as external changes. As an example, one of us became an author when her Sun ☉ and Mercury ☿ both moved into her third house, the house of communications. Before this change occurred on an external level though, it was first experienced as an internal need or desire to start writing about important experiences and ideas.

The changes in you represented by progressions can appear as a planet that …

- Changes signs or houses.
- "Changes direction" (goes retrograde or goes direct).
- Makes an aspect to a natal planet.
- Makes an aspect to another progressed planet.

Each of these can unlock a different type of change in you as you progress through your life.

When progressed planets make aspects to your natal planets, they're only allowed very tight orbs because they take such a long time to move. A one-degree orb is allowed for both before and after the aspect is exact. Yet even with that, except for the Moon, it normally takes a few years for a progressed planet to move out of aspect with a birth planet.

Knowing what your progressions are and when they'll occur can help you unlock the potentials of these cycles. But even if you don't know what's happening and when, you'll evolve anyway, according to the timing of your astrological schedule.

Who, Me? Evolve?

Yes, you. It takes the Sun ☉ about 30 years to move through a sign, so depending on the degree at which your Sun began, you either have already moved into a new Sun sign, or will someday. A 39-year-old with a 16Ⅱ03 Sun, for example, progressed into a Cancer ♋ Sun at about age 14, and at age 44 will move into a Leo ♌ Sun.

Notice how slowly this change takes place, every *30 years* after the first one. Sun ☉ sign changes are *major* changes in how you behave, and this includes your interests, attitudes, and outlook, too. Of course, a progressed Sun never gets around the entire zodiac, because it only moves about one degree per year.

Some of the progressed Sun aspects you can expect include a helpful sextile ✶ to your natal, or birth, Sun from your progressed Sun when you're about 60. At 45, there will be a less-helpful semi-square, and, when you're 90, you'll get a square □. Unless you're as old as Methuselah, though, your progressed Sun never gets much more than a quarter of the way around your chart. Still, your progressed Sun can be busy aspecting any of your other planets while it's progressing through your chart.

Your Moon ☽ evolves as well, in a very different way. It takes the Moon about two and a half years to move into a new sign, and about 28 years to return to its original sign. When this happens, the area of life with Cancer ♋ on the cusp (that is, the house ruled by the Moon ☽) might have significant changes. Also, this progression occurs near another important transit at age 29, so there can be major issues coming up at this time.

How Your Chart Evolves

Let's introduce Rosa Parks's birth chart, progressed to the day she refused to move to the back of that bus in Montgomery, Alabama, December 1, 1955. We don't know the exact time of Parks's birth on February 4, 1913, so we've generated a birth chart for her with a noon birth time. A noon chart places the Sun ☉ on the midheaven. Although casting any birth chart without a precise birth time introduces some imprecision (for example, the ascendant sign changes every two hours), a noon chart allows a method for casting a chart that anyone can use when the birth time is unknown. It is altogether possible that Rosa herself, along with many people born nearly a century ago, does not know her precise birth time. A professional astrologer has more sophisticated methods to rectify a birth chart when the precise birth time is not known.

Parks's birth chart shown in the inner wheel represents the foundation or the blueprint of her life, and here we see the basics of who she is already there. She is the humanitarian through her Aquarius ♒ Sun ☉. She is hard-working, persevering, and serious about life through her Capricorn ♑ Moon ☽. She is a steadfast study of human nature,

articulate, aware, and constantly asking the
question "why" through her ascendant
Gemini ♊. And her strong natal *stellium* in
Aquarius ♒ is certain to evolve into a rebel
with a cause, a humanitarian seeker of truth,
someone who will cut away the dead wood
along her path in life.

AstroLingo

A **stellium** of planets in
a birth chart represents a star-like
focal point because of the many
planets and the aspects these
planets form.

Inner Wheel
Rosa Parks
Natal Chart
Feb 4 1913
12:00 pm CST +6:00
Tuskegee, AL
32°N25'26" 085°W41'30"
Geocentric
Tropical
Placidus
True Node

Outer Wheel
Rosa Parks
Sec.Prog. SA in Long
Dec 1 1955
5:00 pm CST +6:00
Montgomery, AL
32°N22' 086°W18'
Geocentric
Tropical
Placidus
True Node

*Rosa Parks's progressed birth
chart.*

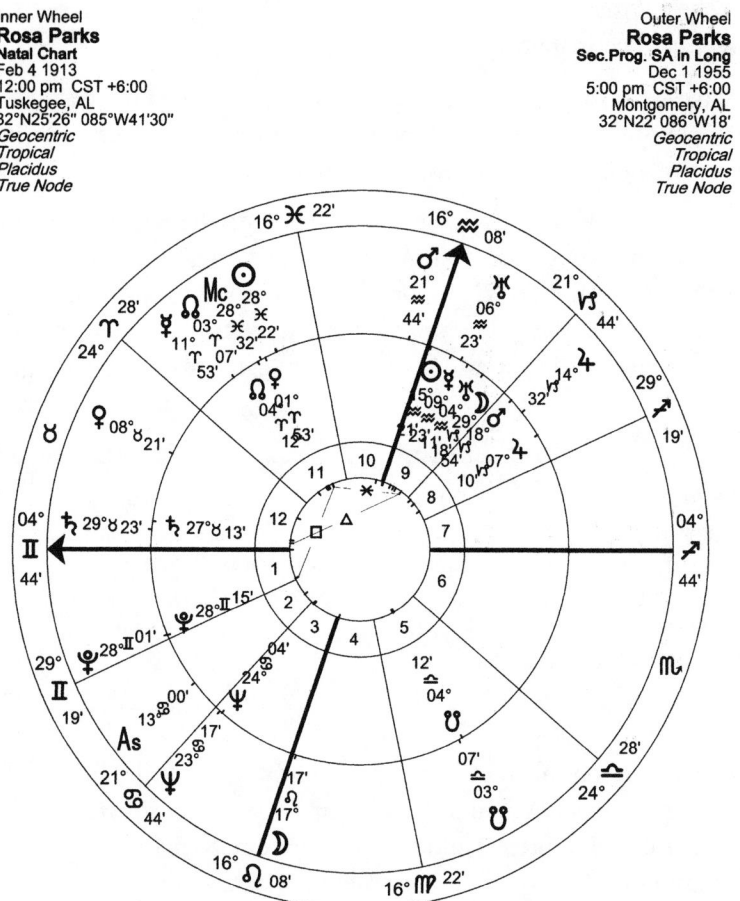

In progressions, the Moon ☽ is often the "timer," because it moves faster than any
other planet. In this case, it's pointing to an important social achievement for Parks.
Her progressed Moon is in the fixed Fire sign of Leo ♌. Because Aquarius ♒ is in
opposition ☍ to the progressed Moon ☽, Parks would evolve into someone who

needed to express an emotional concern. To put it another way, she would become the opposition herself. Plus, this suggests that exactly two months before her famous bus ride, she was thinking and planning something to make a point.

Parks's desire to create awareness was also evident in this progression. Her inner self would have been struggling with her outer image. Chances are, she had been mulling some kind of statement for a while, and no one who has this type of opposition from her progressed chart to her birth chart could keep quiet for too long. Because Parks has this opposition from the fourth house of her roots, beliefs, and home, she would want to extend that to the opposite house and her natal Sun ☉ in the tenth house of public recognition, career, and contributions to society.

As amazing as it must have been to watch this woman do what most would fear, the fixed Aquarius ♒–Leo ♌ opposition, as with all fixed signs interacting together through their aspects, would result in an event that would be lasting.

Parks's progressed Saturn ♄ is at 29 degrees of Taurus ♉, signaling the ending of a crisis. In her twelfth house of karmic duty and destiny, we find her progressed Saturn ♄ trine △ her natal Moon ☽ at 29 degrees of Capricorn ♑. This indicates that she was bound and determined to enlighten the public on injustices done to the group consciousness. It was about her, yes, but it was also about changing an existing attitude.

Heaven Knows _____

At this point in time, Parks didn't care about the cost to her or her future. She was "pushed" by a strong obligation to "do something," almost as if she were being compelled by a debt to society. In other words, she did what she felt was obligatory to her world. Parks's chart indicates that she had a debt to pay to her culture and country, that she was here to enlighten *all* of society, and that she would choose an unusual and even unpredictable way to effect this change. Pretty cool, huh?

Throughout the next year, Parks continued to have the Moon ☽ in Leo ♌. By the time November 1956 came, her progressed Moon in Leo had made an exact square □ to her natal Saturn ♄ at 27 degrees of Taurus ♉ and then *another* exact square □ to progressed Saturn ♄ at 29 degrees of Taurus ♉. Because these are again fixed signs, the squares *forced* Parks to work through a difficult legal process, one which would ultimately generate a wide range of changes in the law. The squares □ these two planets made reflected the public attention and conflict.

Three to four years after this moment, Parks's progressed Sun ☉ in 28 degrees of Pisces ♓ conjuncted ☌ her natal Venus ♀ at 1 degrees of Aries ♈. This is when her life would become increasingly public, including public speaking and writing as well as invitations to continue what she began.

Rosa Parks's noon birth chart and progressed birth chart show a gentle rebel with a cause. And aren't we all the more fortunate because of it!

Just as with Park's, your birth chart progresses in its own way, with your progressed planets aspecting your natal or birth planets. As your progressed planets move through the signs, they show how and when you develop and evolve.

Transits, or Planetary Triggers

You could think of transiting planets as being part of a cosmic transit system, moving around overhead on a regular schedule (better than most earthly transit systems!). This is one way to keep in mind that these planets are always on the move, changing positions at the rate of their daily travel. It's another kind of transit system—one we can predict and plan by.

Transits are concerned with particular moments in time. Even your birth chart is a transit, one that was frozen in time when you were born. Transits are also concerned with the relationships that occur when the present positions of the planets aspect your natal planets. Like a progressed chart, a transit chart looks like a double wheel: Your birth chart is on the inside, and *the moment's chart*, or transit chart, is on the outside.

Here, for example, we have Serena Williams's birth chart, with transits, for her U.S. Open win on September 7, 2002.

Transits are like triggers—they pop the cork right off the bottle. They're quicker—and happen faster—than progressions, and most of them are specific to each person. At the same time, though, there are transits that are aspects between the same natal and transiting planet that occur at the same ages for everyone. We'll look at those in more detail later in this chapter.

Serena's transiting Sun ☉ and Moon ☽ were both in the sign of Virgo ♍ going over her natal Moon ☽ in her sixth house of work and service. These triggers reveal that she was in top form on that day because the planets aligned over her natal Moon created a supercharged energy for her win.

The triggers of planetary transits show us potential strengths and weaknesses. Serena Williams's chart for this day provides a perfect example of how transits conjuncting ☌ natal planets can create a day of particular personal power. The conjunction is considered the strongest power point, or, to put it another way, "Everything is a go!" Not only was Serena's energy at this moment powerful, her focus and concentration were perfect, and her passion and desire positively surreal.

Serena Williams's birth chart, with transits, for September 7, 2002.

Inner Wheel
Serena Williams
Natal Chart
Sep 26 1981
8:28 pm EDT +4:00
Saginaw, MI
43°N25'10" 083°W57'03"
Geocentric
Tropical
Placidus
True Node

Outer Wheel
Transits US Open WIN
Natal Chart
Sep 7 2002
12:00 pm EDT +4:00
New York, NY
40°N42'51" 074°W00'23"
Geocentric
Tropical
Placidus
True Node

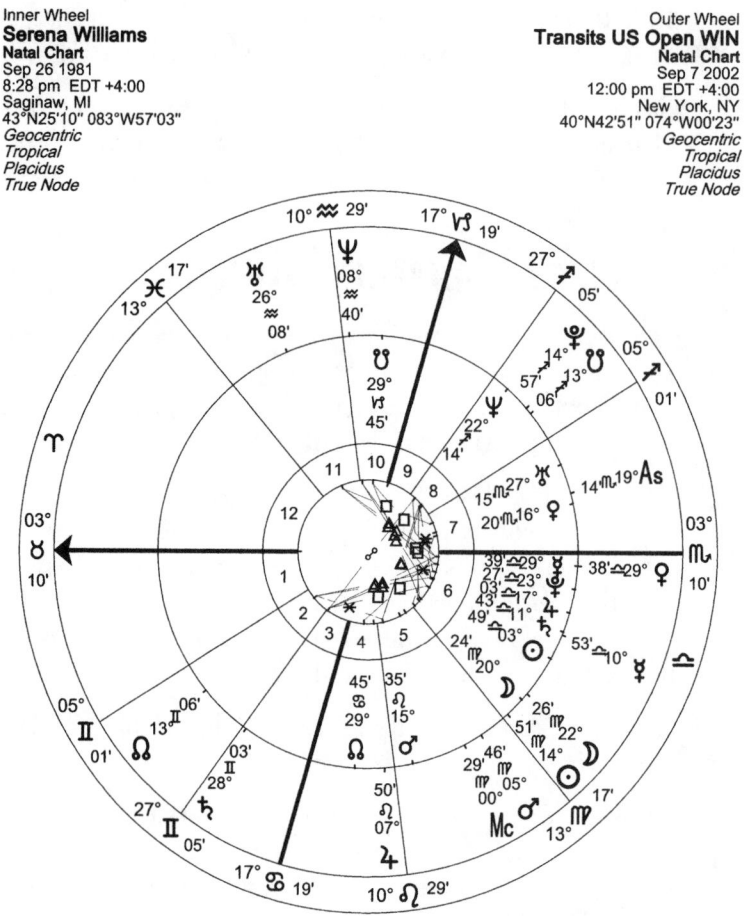

And there are still more conjunctions here: Transiting Mercury in Libra was conjunct her natal Saturn in Libra ☿♂♄, giving her not only stamina but balance via internal discipline, and transiting Venus in Libra was conjunct her natal Mercury in Libra ♀♂☿!

In addition to this incredible focus of power points, transiting Mars ♂ in Virgo ♍ was trine △ Serena's natal ascendant Taurus, which gave her the physical power and extra stamina to maintain strength for the day, and Saturn ♄, the planet of discipline and concentration, was transiting in Serena's chart to make a trine △ to both Pluto ♀ and Mercury ☿ in Libra ♎.

This combination of aspects literally pointed Serena to one of her greatest moments. From an astrologer's viewpoint, the many conjunctions suggest that Serena was intensely focused on her goal, aided by the ability to control her own power and be her greatest self, and abetted by the discipline and focus of the Saturn ♄ trines △.

Finally, the day itself had a *grand trine* in Air signs, helping Serena's own Air sign planets— the Sun ☉, Saturn ♄, Jupiter ♃, Pluto ♇, and Mercury ☿, all in Libra ♎—to manifest at their highest harmonics. It's unusual to see so many aspects so perfectly aligned. In astro-logical terms, not only was Serena as ready as she would ever be—she was destined to shine that day!

AstroLingo

A **grand trine** occurs when three or more planets aim their energy toward one focal point. In the zodiacal sky, these planets form a 120° triangle.

Serena's shining moment was enhanced by the triggers of the transits that we see here. So focused are these transits that from this moment on, Serena's career would generate further recognition and public admiration—as we've seen!

Remember: Transits focus on a moment in a time; progressions show how your per-sonal planets move over time. Transits show the actual position of the planets at a given moment; progressions show how you progress personally as you grow older.

Outer and Social Planet Transits

Astrologers look at the transits that the outer planets make more closely than those of the inner planets because they move more slowly and so have a much more powerful effect on our lives.

Pluto's ♇ motto is "Change or be transformed!" Its transits always pressure you to transform some aspect of your life that isn't authentically you. Generally, with a Pluto transit you will be forced to change the area ruled by the planet that Pluto contacts. Most people find it *very* painful not to cooperate with Pluto transits.

Neptune ♆ transits encourage us to view old problems from a spiritual or transcend-ing perspective, and to let go and move on. Neptune's unpredictable, though, and its transits can either unleash psychic or imaginative powers—or lead to confusion, self-doubt, escapism, irresponsibility, or even self-destruction.

Uranus ♅ transits are associated with innovation, rebellion, and unexpected change. A Uranus transit makes you see things in a new way. Once you do, you can never go back to the old way of seeing things.

While **Saturn** ♄ is associated with limitation, its transits also can herald movement to a higher level of responsibility and to rewards for a job well done. If there's still work to be done, though, these transits can make you sit down, reassess, and seek the right path.

Heaven Knows

We can't stop the planets in their cycles—or our own growth, which they represent—but we can be aware of those cycles and plan our lives accordingly. Knowing that you've got a Saturn ♄ transit going on, for example, can help you to know that it's time to reassess and restructure.

Jupiter ♃ transits often involve broadening your horizons in some way, either through travel, social contacts, or physically, philosophically, or intellectually. Jupiter, remember, is the planet of expansion, and the house it's transiting will determine in what area of your life the expansion is occurring.

The inner planets transit far more quickly, so their effects are not as profound as those of the outer and social planets. In fact, often when an astrologer looks at the transiting cycles for a client's chart, he or she only checks the major ones shown by the outer and social planets.

From the Terrible Twos to the Midlife Crisis and Beyond

These are the cycles, or passages, that are common to everyone, and that occur at about the same age for everyone, too. They're timed by transits of planets that aspect themselves, such as Saturn ♄ to Saturn ♄. Because the planet is aspecting itself, and each planet moves at a certain rate, these always occur at about the same age for everyone.

Let's start by looking at the terrible twos. This is the point at which Mars ♂ comes around and conjuncts itself for the first time. The terrible twos are the equivalent of a person's first taste of independence and assertion. Mars returns occur every two years, so we get more accustomed to them as we get older. But this first time is a lulu—as any parent can tell you!

Next, there's the Jupiter ♃ cycle, which is a 12-year growth cycle. Every 12 years, when transiting Jupiter comes around to conjunct your natal Jupiter, you start a new growth cycle, learning completely new things, and expanding your mind and self in new ways.

Another transit that has a marked effect is when Uranus ♅ is sextile ⚹ itself for the first time during the teen years. This is when people get their first need for independence, to separate from their parents and become their own person. We're all familiar with this cycle—either from our own experience or that of our children—and we all know it can be a very chaotic period!

Between ages 28 and 30, people experience their first Saturn ♄ return. This is a major transit: "Grow up," it says, and, if you're not yet on the right path, you'll have a strong feeling of apprehension. All sorts of major changes might occur at a Saturn return if you haven't been on *your* path, but instead have been meeting other people's expectations. You might even quit your job or get divorced!

However, if you're doing what you're supposed to be doing, then you won't have challenges. You might be rewarded with a promotion for good work, or similar "prize." You could think of a Saturn return as a time to clean up the inappropriate parts of your life and to ensure that you're on the right path for you (or reassess your path) instead of worrying about what others think.

The second Saturn return, which occurs between the ages of 58 and 60, is also a major transit. Business people might be made chair of the board or achieve an important goal. A human life is roughly two-thirds over at this point, and, interestingly, statistics indicate that people who feel unhappy with their lives, are depressed, or feel like a failure in some way might end up using this as their exit point from the planet.

The Midlife Crisis

The midlife crisis used to occur at age 42. This cycle coincides with when transiting Uranus comes opposite natal Uranus ♅☍♅, transiting Neptune squares itself ♆□♆, and shortly afterward, when transiting Saturn opposes itself ♄☍♄. However, because some of the outer planets are in the faster portions of their orbits right now, this has been happening during baby boomers' late 30s. In addition, another planet has gotten into the fray.

Because of its erratic orbit, Pluto ♇ is moving through the signs faster than its average. For this reason, transiting Pluto is currently squaring personal Pluto ♇□♇ at age 36 or 37, well before the midlife crisis. (We're speaking here about people who have Pluto ♇ in Virgo ♍; those with Pluto ♇ in Leo ♌ experienced this right *during* their midlife crisis, at around 39 to 40 years old.) Transiting Pluto square natal Pluto signals general transformation. This square used to appear late in people's lives (one hundred years ago the average lifespan in the United States wasn't much over 40!), so there is a major evolution in the meaning of this aspect for our, and future, generations.

Preparing for the latter part of your life (and eventually death) is a big step, but it isn't one that's necessary when this aspect occurs in midlife. Instead, this transit's intensity should be focused on changing one's life for the better, giving up whatever is being brought up from the past that isn't appropriate or authentic.

People who successfully make it through this series of "midlife" transits develop a new maturity to become their true selves. The purpose of the midlife crisis is to reorient themselves away from just meeting external demands toward more internal needs that give real meaning to their lives.

Before we discuss the specifics of the midlife transits, let's look at the transiting Pluto square natal Pluto ♇□♇ in more detail.

Oh, What Fun It Is to Transform Ourselves!

General transformation is a period when past issues that are no longer relevant are dug up and eliminated. This can include aspects of yourself that have been forgotten or repressed for so long, you no longer remember them.

The Pluto square natal Pluto transit lasts almost two years, and by the time it ends, a person's life and consciousness are quite changed. Sometimes a person's life is completely rebuilt after this occurs. It's better to cooperate with the changes that need to happen to you during this period than resist them, because the consequences of resistance can be quite destructive.

Transiting Pluto square natal Pluto ♀□♀ is happening to many people who are still young, people who have half their lives to live at this higher level of consciousness.

StarFacts

Pluto ♀ transits are just too demanding to ignore. People find they can't hang on to their old behavior patterns during these periods in their lives, and so they give up and make the change!

This unusual situation is one indicator of the High Renaissance period the earth is experiencing now, a time of rapid and profound change, growth, and transformation.

This early Pluto transit is going to happen, at least during this period in time, *before or during* the midlife crisis. So by the time the midlife crisis is over, the men are separated from the boys and the women from the girls!

Uranus ♅ and Neptune Ψ and Saturn ♄—Oh My!

Yes, indeed! The midlife crisis can be a lot like encountering lions and tigers and bears! And with Neptune Ψ in the act, even if these aren't real dangers, you might *believe* they exist. Here's an up-close and personal look at these midlife transits.

When transiting Uranus opposes natal Uranus ♅☌♅, its purpose is to reorient you to doing things with personal meaning. At this point in your life, you've spent most of it trying to have an impact on the external world and meeting the expectations of others. Now it's time to shift toward doing the things that have *internal* meaning for you.

For people who've been doing what they were "supposed" to be doing, this period is often an epiphany. For those who've gotten into premature ruts or who've stopped growing along the way, though, there's a sudden "last chance" feeling about it that sends some people off on radical changes quite unlike their normal selves. This could mean a career change (this happened to both of us), or, more negatively, leaving one's spouse for someone younger, buying a snazzy sports car, or seeking new adventures.

The most appropriate response to this transit is to withdraw internally and figure out *what you really want to do with the rest of your life*. If you don't take the time to examine what you want and then make the needed changes, you might find yourself living a hollow life later and never understand why.

When transiting Neptune squares natal Neptune ♆□♆, you can expect another period of intense questioning of yourself, your ideals, and how well you've lived up to them. But because it's Neptune, it's difficult to see where you're really going during this period—and if it's even worth going there.

This is a lot like driving a twisty road in heavy fog and not being able to see well. While you may decide you should make some changes in your life, you may *not* understand which ones to make. Instead of actually making these changes during this time, it's best to consider which course to take until the fog clears. This period or transit takes almost three years.

When transiting Saturn is opposite natal Saturn ♄☍♄, it can mean either a successful culmination of your effort and work, or it can be a time when old patterns that weren't cleared out earlier challenge your career and relationships. Once again, it's a time for reassessment and refocusing. This transit occurs a little later than the Uranus ♅ and Neptune ♆ transits, but in past times, all three used to happen together.

This entire process is geared toward questioning your present life and yourself. If you ever thought you knew yourself, this period may prove otherwise. But instead of responding with an intense desire to recapture your youth, it's best to find out what in life really has meaning for you, and then find a way to refocus your life on that.

Unlocking Personal Transits

Personal transits are cycles whose timing is based on the placement of your own planets. Unlike the cycles that occur at specific ages when a planet aspects itself, these transits can occur at any age. For example, transiting Saturn will conjunct each person's Sun at a different age ♄☌☉, and the timing of that will depend upon what sign your Sun is in and where Saturn was when you were born.

CAUTION

Star-Crossed

If a person has taken shortcuts to his or her achievements, then the Saturn ♄ transit across the midheaven can unravel it all, which is what happened to Richard Nixon during Watergate! If a person's well prepared for it, though, this transit will culminate in success.

For example, if your Sun ☉ is in Cancer ♋ and Saturn ♄ was in Gemini ♊ when you were born, then this transit would have happened for the first time when you were a young child. But if Saturn ♄ was in Leo ♌ when you were born (and you have a Cancer Sun ♋☉), then you would have been in your mid-20s before this occurred for the first time.

In general, you can look at your birth chart and the current planetary positions to see what's happening for you at any given moment in time.

Astrology Is Your Compass

Now that you understand how your chart unfolds with progressions and transits, you can see how astrology can be used to look ahead into your life.

It's always a good idea to check out your progressions and transits regularly, and it's also good to know three to five years in advance what's coming down the pike in the way of major changes. You can anticipate and plan for everything, from job or career changes to financial difficulties, having children, or even relocating. Looking ahead gives you the room to plan what responses you might choose and to accept responsibility for what the changes end up being.

Relationship issues might come up, too. If you know a troubling time is approaching, you can understand what the likely issues are and learn appropriate ways to handle and deal with them. Then when it actually arrives, it's not a cataclysmic period, but one of growth and understanding of how you and your relationships are changing. We'll be looking at this more closely in the next chapter.

Astrology can be used as a compass because you can see not only the kinds of events or changes that are going to unfold, but also how you're evolving and growing during your life. Knowing that gives you a road map for your life and a more conscious approach for dealing with it. After all, wouldn't you rather know where you're headed on your life's journey than move ahead blindly?

Heaven Knows

If you're trying to make a career change, it's best to look for trines △ or sextiles ✳ with planets to the midheaven, tenth house ruler, or the planets in the tenth house, to initiate that change. Why make things harder for you than they need to be? Make the most of your windows of opportunity and your career will be rewarded accordingly.

Windows of Opportunity

Windows of opportunity are periods where your progressions and transits are beneficial: good times to make changes, progress, and develop things easily. These progressions and transits are usually trines △ and sextiles ✳ (sometimes conjunctions ☌), and they're just waiting for you to take advantage of them.

Often, though, when these periods hit, there's a tendency to sit back and take it easy, so it's important to use them to your advantage and not squander them.

But you won't know there's an opportune period unless you're looking at your progressions and transits to determine when they are. So look: Do it yourself, or visit an astrologer at least once a year. It's a good investment!

Jump or Be Pushed, Your Choice

Unlike a trine △ or sextile ✶, when squares □ or oppositions ☍ come up by transit or progression, you'll be *forced* to do something. Either you'll take matters into your own hands and take action or an external action will *force* you to do something.

Some of these squares □ from outer planets, like Neptune ♆ or Pluto ♀, can take a couple years to get through. If you don't consciously understand what's happening and, as a consequence, respond inappropriately, you can end up projecting the energy outward, and it will come back to you as difficult external events.

Anything that's blocking positive growth, be it a job, a relationship, or personal property, will be removed to ensure that the needed growth occurs. Some of these external events can be cataclysmic—a serious accident, a severe illness, or even a death in the family— and *force* you to make the change. But challenging progressions and transits can trigger internal desire for change, too. The important thing is to notice them.

Star-Crossed

Ignoring the signals that challenging progressions or transits put out can lead to cataclysmic or life-changing events. So it's best to pay attention!

Let's take an example. Suppose that you feel that you're in the wrong job but you don't do anything about it. Rather than take the cues you're getting and act when you have control over the situation, you decide to just "wait and see." Eventually, you might get fired, or the company might go bankrupt. Then you'll be forced to act. Progressions and transits are the blueprints for what's happening in your life, but what you choose to do with them is up to you. Remember, astrologically, there are no accidents, just misdirected energy.

Obviously, it's best to take the appropriate action before a catastrophe occurs. Serious accidents, something terrible happening in one's career, or a major blow-up in a relationship are all manifestations of a "jump-or-be-pushed" aspect. Something's gotta blow to send you in the direction that you must go. If you get to that point without doing anything constructive, you'll be pushed.

If You Want to Know More

Because this is a beginners' book, we can't really cover all the transits and progressions in detail. If you're interested in learning more about them, we'd suggest Robert Hand's *Planets in Transit*, which is the bible on transits. Another is *The Eagle and the Rose*, by Bernadette Brady, which has a much more in-depth discussion of both transits and progressions. Our intention was to introduce you to these concepts so you'd understand how they work—and, of course, to pique your curiosity!

The Least You Need to Know

- ◆ Progressions signal the themes and changes in your chart that are waiting to unfold over time.

- ◆ Transits occur when the planets' present positions overhead aspect your birth-chart planets or move into new houses.

- ◆ You can use astrology as a compass to navigate through your life.

- ◆ Windows of opportunity are times when it's easy for you to accomplish things.

- ◆ Squares □ or oppositions ☍ force you to act or make a change, whether you want to or not.

Part 6

You've Done Your Chart, Now You Want More

Astrological matchmaking? Astrological business decisions? You bet! You can use astrology to plan your whole life—and you'll benefit in the process. Learn how to use your and your partner's Moon ☽ signs, ascendants, the signs and planets in your houses, and aspects to find out if your relationship is a match made in heaven.

You'll also meet the asteroids, Ceres, Juno, Pallas Athene, and Vesta, as well as Chiron, and learn their astrological meanings. You'll find out why you feel differently, depending on the Moon's phase as we explain why the Moon really *is* a monitor for Earthly moods.

Next, we'll look at astrology and business—Madeline's specialty—and show you how astrological timing can help you achieve success. And finally, we'll take a look at some of the major astrological cycles for the next 100 years, and what they predict about our future.

Chapter **23**

Relationship Astrology: Love Matches Made in Heaven, or in ...?

In This Chapter

◆ Using relationship astrology to chart your love life

◆ Beyond the signs—planets, houses, and aspects

◆ Michael and Catherine in love

◆ Matches made in heaven

You've seen the love sign books. You may even own one. And yet, it doesn't seem to fit. You're a Pisces ♓ and she's a Capricorn ♑, and, though your book says that mixing Water and Earth signs makes mud, you think you've got something better going. What gives?

As you might have suspected, there's more to relationship astrology than just your Sun ☉ signs. You'll want to look at your Moon ☽ signs, too, for starters, where you'll find your emotional makeups, and you'll want to check out the matches of your other planets and your ascendants, as well as what houses your signs and planets are in. Last, you'll want to look at how your charts aspect each other—that's the real key to a match made in heaven.

Relationship Astrology and You

You can approach relationship astrology from two different angles:

◆ Confirming what you already know by comparing your charts

◆ Comparing your charts before you get in too deep

If you're already in a relationship, there are most likely certain things you know about each other and how you interact. Chances are, for example, one of you is the "controller," while the other is the "agree-er." One of you might have a shorter fuse than the other, or one of you might want to make love every night, while the other would rather wait for Saturday—or Christmas!

If you're considering a relationship and know the person's birth date, birth place, and birth time, you can get their chart and do a little detective work to see if this will be a match made in heaven. If you've both got Aries ♈ at your midheaven, you'll be constantly butting heads—and you may want to avoid all that confrontation. Then again, as Aries midheavens, you may not! Confrontation is part of who you are, after all.

Charting Your Relationships

Once you have both charts in hand, the fun can begin. In a few pages, we're going to illustrate this by looking at the birth charts of actors and lovers Michael Douglas and Catherine Zeta-Jones, but before we do, we want to show you the steps you can take to chart your own relationships. You might want to return to Chapter 3 to find out which signs represent which qualities and elements. We've provided a quickie reminder chart for the energies, *yin* and *yang*.

The Signs and Their Energies

Yang	*Yin*
Aries ♈	Taurus ♉
Gemini ♊	Cancer ♋
Leo ♌	Virgo ♍
Libra ♎	Scorpio ♏
Sagittarius ♐	Capricorn ♑
Aquarius ♒	Pisces ♓

Got those charts in hand? Good. Let's start with the obvious: your Sun ☉ signs.

	Person 1	Person 2
Sun signs:	_____	_____
Are your Sun signs *yin* or *yang?*	_____	_____
How about the quality of your Sun signs: cardinal, fixed, or mutable?	_____	_____
Next, note the element of each Sun sign: Fire, Earth, Air, or Water?	_____	_____

Now, you'll want to do the same for each of your ascendants.

	Person 1	Person 2
Ascendants:	_____	_____
Are your ascendants *yin* or *yang?*	_____	_____
How about the quality of ascendants: cardinal, fixed, or mutable?	_____	_____
Next, note the element of each ascendant:Fire, Earth, Air, or Water?	_____	_____

Now that you've written it all down, let's see what these match-ups say about your relationship.

Energies. If one of you has a *yin* Sun sign or rising sign and one of you has a *yang*, it's a good beginning. It means that you're two halves of the same whole. But two *yins* don't make a wrong, nor do two *yangs*. If you're both *yin*, you might need a third party to get things going, while if you're both *yang*, there may be arguments about where to go for dinner. But remember, this is just the

Heaven Knows _____

There's no need to limit relationship charting to your love life. You can use these steps to see why you and your mother seem to fight about everything, or why you felt an instant affinity for someone who's now a good friend. All you need is both your charts.

tip of the iceberg; there's a lot more to relationship astrology than just the energy of your Sun signs and ascendants.

Qualities. If your relationship got out of the gate quickly, it's likely because you both have cardinal Sun signs or ascendants. It's probable that at least one of you does. If you're looking for staying power, a fixed Sun sign or rising sign person is usually in it for the long haul, but if you want to play the field, a mutable Sun sign or ascendant might be "ISO" the same thing.

Elements. Remember that Pisces ♓ and Capricorn ♑/Earth-and-Water example we gave at the beginning of this chapter? Earth and water *do* make mud—but sometimes a soothing mud bath is just what a relationship needs. Down-to-earth Earth signs and intuitive Water signs can actually make a good match, just as any of the elements can combine in interesting ways. The important thing is to be aware of these combinations and their permutations. Here are some of our takes—all in fun, of course.

Combination	Permutation
Fire + Fire	Quick-burning, but nothing to feed it
Fire + Earth	Earth slows down the fire, longer lasting heat
Fire + Air	Air feeds fire, fire needs air
Fire + Water	Steam heat! Passion and fire
Earth + Earth	Slow and steady; progressive
Earth + Air	Slow, but heady
Earth + Water	Optimum for growth
Air + Air	Nowhere to go but up
Air + Water	A light, misting rain and champagne, too
Water + Water	A downpour—lots of love, lots of emotion!

Signposts

The next thing to look for is the placement of each of the signs. Recall our example of the two Aries' midheavens earlier? That's just one signpost to note. You'll want to have the sign and house for each of your planets on hand. Here's a worksheet to do just that.

Note the sign and house for each planet.

	Person 1		Person 2	
	Sign	*House*	*Sign*	*House*
Sun ☉	_____	_____	_____	_____
Moon ☽	_____	_____	_____	_____
Mercury ☿	_____	_____	_____	_____
Venus ♀	_____	_____	_____	_____
Mars ♂	_____	_____	_____	_____
Jupiter ♃	_____	_____	_____	_____
Saturn ♄	_____	_____	_____	_____
Uranus ♅	_____	_____	_____	_____
Neptune ♆	_____	_____	_____	_____
Pluto ♇	_____	_____	_____	_____
North Node ☊	_____	_____	_____	_____
South Node ☋	_____	_____	_____	_____

Planet Placings

Look to the Moon ☽! That's the first rule of thumb when it comes to looking at your planet placings to see how your relationship will fare. You can use the preceding chart to see which sign each of your Moons is in. Both at home in Cancer ♋? Be sure to keep tissues in every room! A big-hearted Leo Moon ♌☽ plus a detached Aquarius Moon ♒☽? Could mean emotional misunderstandings because a Leo Moon is all about ego and pride while Aquarius, its opposite, is about the *lack* of ego and pride.

Star-Crossed

Remember the adage "Opposites attract"? The same holds true when it comes to astrological match-ups. Sure, we give the example of a big-hearted Leo Moon ♌☽ and a detached Aquarius Moon ♒☽ meaning emotional misunderstandings, but Aquarius's emotional detachment may be just what exuberant Leo needs. At the same time, Leo can inject a shot of cheeriness into the life of a sometimes too serious Aquarius Moon.

You can review the Moon in each zodiac sign section in Chapter 10. For easy reference, here's a chart of how each Moon sign feels. You can use this chart to see how each of you feels, which can help you understand why one of you cries at dog food commercials while the other didn't even cry at birth!

Moon Sign	How It Feels
Aries ♈	With its *head*
Taurus ♉	With its *senses*
Gemini ♊	With its *mind*
Cancer ♋	With its *feelings*
Leo ♌	With its *heart*
Virgo ♍	With its *logic*
Libra ♎	Through *others*
Scorpio ♏	With intense *emotions*
Sagittarius ♐	Through its *experiences*
Capricorn ♑	Through *perseverance*
Aquarius ♒	Through its *individuality*
Pisces ♓	Through its *imagination*

House Hunting

Using your signpost exercise, you can now see which signs are in which houses. We introduced you to the houses in Part 4, and we discussed each house in depth in Chapters 15 through 18. For a quick review of the area of each house, simply look at the reverse of the tear-out reference card inside the front cover of this book.

But there's much more to house hunting than just which signs are in which houses—and this is where the fun really begins. Set your charts next to each other, and spend some time looking at the signs and planets, house by house. Here are some easy connections you can make.

Aspects, Heart to Heart

Because they reveal planetary relationships, aspects are the heart and soul of relationship astrology. One Cancer ♋ woman we know, for example, is married to a Gemini ♊ man—but there's nothing typically Gemini about him: He's quiet, thoughtful, and takes his time making decisions. While she has many planets in Cancer, her twelfth house, where these planets reside, is ruled by Mercury ☿ because Gemini ♊ is on its cusp. There's our first "aha."

The second "aha" occurs when we look at their Venus ♀ placements:

His	Hers
07 Taurus ♉ 05 in the twelfth house	18 Cancer ♋ 01 in the twelfth house

While this isn't a conjunction, both have Venus ♀ in the twelfth house, so they prefer privacy and are deeply creative.

Aspecting your relationships is where you really get down to the nitty-gritty. One simple way to do this is to look at your aspect grids. When this couple looked at their aspect grids, they immediately noted that both their Neptunes were sextile their Plutos ♆✶♇, and both their Neptunes ♆ were in Leo ♌, too. Dreamy Neptune sextile transformer Pluto means they both can transform their dreams into reality—something both of these creative people do on a daily basis—in their studies at opposite ends of the house!

The branch of astrology concerned with relationships is called *synastry*. Using synastry, astrologers can quickly note the relationships between the two people's signs and planets, and in turn make some educated statements about their relationship.

> **AstroLingo**
>
> **Synastry** is the branch of astrology that looks specifically at relationships. A **synastry grid** combines two aspect grids into one to easily analyze a relationship.

Study these two aspect grids and see what connections you can make.

Another way to look at two aspect grids is to set up a *synastry grid*, which combines the two grids into one easy-to-read grid. We'll do that next for Michael Douglas and Catherine Zeta-Jones.

Stars by the Stars: The Relationship Charts of Michael Douglas and Catherine Zeta-Jones

To illustrate how looking at a couple's birth charts and synastry grid represent a "map" of their relationship, we've chosen Hollywood couple Michael Douglas and Catherine Zeta-Jones. Before we begin our analysis, there are a few steps we like to take to get us started.

In this synastry grid for Michael Douglas and Catherine Zeta-Jones, Michael's aspects are read across and Catherine's are read down.

Across
Michael Douglas
Natal Chart
Sep 25 1944
10:30 am EWT +4:00
New Brunswick, NJ
40°N29'10" 074°W27'08"
Geocentric
Tropical
Placidus
True Node

Down
Catherine Zeta-Jones
Natal Chart
Sep 25 1969
2:40 pm CET −1:00
Swansea, WALES
51°N38' 003°W57'
Geocentric
Tropical
Placidus
True Node

Synastry Grid

	☽	☉	☿	♀	♂	♃	♄	♅	♆	♇	☊	☋	As	Mc
☽	□ 4A55	☍ 3A42							☍ 5A15		△ 3S36			
☉	□ 1A17	☌ 0A05							☌ 1A37					
☿	□ 6A38	☌ 7A50						□ 0A08	△ 2S54	☌ 6A18	✶ 0A26			
♀	△ 0A39													
♂	☌ 0A55	□ 0S17							☍ 7A25	□ 1A15				
♃				☌ 4A41					□ 3S14	△ 0S12				
♄	△ 4A18								△ 5S16	✶ 2S12		□ 1S54		
♅	□ 0S40	☌ 1S53							□ 5A49	☌ 0S21				
♆											△ 1S30	✶ 1S30		□ 1S31
♇		☌ 7A11								☌ 8A43	✶ 0S08	△ 0S08		
☊		☍ 6A10			☍ 7A59						△ 3S56		△ 5A54	
☋		☌ 6A10			☌ 7A59							△ 3S56		
As														△ 2A04
Mc				☌ 0A28							□ 2A08	□ 2A08	✶ 2A09	

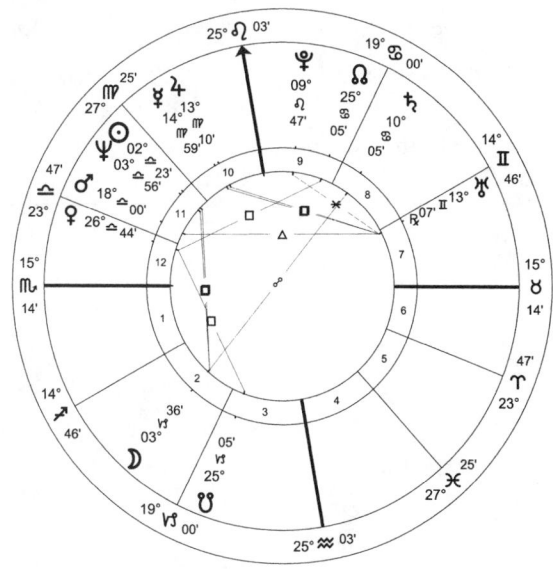

Michael Douglas's birth chart.

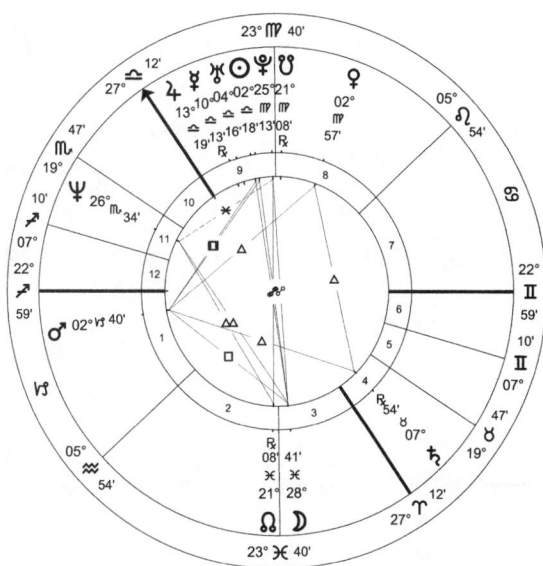

Catherine Zeta-Jones's birth chart.

Here are the breakdowns of Michael and Catherine's Sun ☉ signs and ascendants:

	Michael	Catherine
Sun ☉ signs:	Libra ♎	Libra ♎
Are their Sun signs *yin* or *yang?*	*Yang*	*Yang*
How about the quality of their Sun signs: cardinal, fixed, or mutable?	Cardinal	Cardinal
Next, note the element of each Sun sign: Fire, Earth, Air, or Water?	Air	Air

Now, you'll want to do the same for each of their ascendants.

	Michael	Catherine
Ascendants:	Scorpio ♏	Sagittarius ♐
Are their ascendants *yin* or *yang?*	*Yin*	*Yang*
How about the quality of ascendants: cardinal, fixed, or mutable?	Fixed	Mutable
Next, note the element of each ascendant: Fire, Earth, Air, or Water?	Water	Fire

Finally, note the sign and house for each planet.

	Michael		Catherine	
	Sign	*House*	*Sign*	*House*
Sun ☉	Libra	11th	Libra	9th
Moon ☽	Capricorn	2nd	Pisces	3rd
Mercury ☿	Virgo	10th	Libra	9th
Venus ♀	Libra	12th	Virgo	8th
Mars ♂	Libra	11th	Capricorn	1st
Jupiter ♃	Virgo	10th	Libra	9th
Saturn ♄	Cancer	8th	Taurus	4th
Uranus ♅	Gemini	7th	Libra	9th
Neptune ♆	Libra	11th	Scorpio	11th
Pluto ♇	Leo	9th	Virgo	9th

First, we see that Michael and Catherine's Libra ♎ Suns ☉ are exactly conjunct ☌. It's as if they're looking at opposite sex versions of themselves, mirror images that complement the other as no other can.

Next, we note that Michael's Sun ☉ in Libra ♎ and Moon ☽ in Capricorn ♑ are aspected by many of Catherine's personal planets: her Libra ♎ Sun ☉, Pisces ♓ Moon ☽, Libra ♎ Mercury ☿, and Capricorn ♑ Mars ♂. This shows that she is able to understand him in every aspect of his persona. She knows her partner intimately, and by this we mean his *real* self, when he is at home.

While the age difference between these two may be a matter of some discussion, in astrology, the 25 years between them are actually complementary because they represent a strong generational connection.

Karmic connections are strong because of this age difference, too. Let's take a look at Michael and Catherine's Saturns ♄ and Nodes ☊☋, both in their charts and in their synastry grid, to see how this works.

Planet	Michael's Sign	House	Catherine's Sign	House
Saturn ♄	Cancer ♋	8th	Taurus ♉	4th
North Node ☊	Cancer ♋	9th	Pisces ♓	2nd
South Node ☋	Capricorn ♑	3rd	Virgo ♍	8th

Saturn ♄ relates to endurance, and the responsible and consistent flow of lessons and experiences for both. Saturn is the teacher who enlightens via duty and responsibility, including karmic debts and rewards. Catherine's retrograde Saturn ♄ is trine △ Michael's Moon ☽ in Capricorn ♑, and his Jupiter ♃ in Virgo ♍. These aspects allow for a flow of communication and understanding even in stressful times. Not only do these two tolerate each other's different opinions, they give each other strength when the other is down.

Michael's Saturn ♄ in Cancer ♋ is square ☐ Catherine's Mercury ☿ in Libra ♎, her Jupiter ♃ in Libra ♎, and her Uranus ♅ in Libra ♎. This suggests that both as a teacher and by simple encouragement, he can help her make forays into areas that she had previously considered but felt challenged to try without his support. In many ways, he is a father figure to her, someone who wants to create business ventures with her as well as encourage her own independent career ventures.

The North and South Nodes ☊☋ of both are amazingly strong in many aspects. Michael's North and South Nodes, for example, are trine △ and sextile ✳ to Catherine's Moon ☽, Neptune ♆, and Pluto ♀. This suggests that he not only encourages her in both her personal and career goals, but feels it's his duty to get her to her best level.

Catherine's retrograde North and South Nodes ☊☋ are making oppositions ☍ and conjunctions ☌ to Michael's Mercury ☿ and Jupiter ♃ in Virgo ♍. This suggests that she is watchful of his well-being, making sure he stays mentally and physically healthy so that he is ready for new accomplishments. She also supports his every career move with pride. There's so much pride in each other, we see a clear karmic obligation here. Together, they will likely become known for community service as well as through their creative work.

Finally, Michael's midheaven and Catherine's midheaven are sextile ✶, affording them the opportunity to leave a legacy of inspiration in their respective careers. Together, they're even more powerful: Through community service, work on behalf of children, and in education, their combined zodiacal strength will ultimately make a world of difference.

Matches Made in Heaven

Is there such a thing as a soul mate? And if there is, can you find it in your charts? The answer to both questions is "Yes." You'll find a wealth of information about soul mates in *The Complete Idiot's Guide to Reincarnation*, by David Hammerman and your co-author, Lisa Lenard. But let's look at the idea astrologically for now.

As you'll recall from Chapter 13, many astrologers believe that your South Node ☋ reveals your past lives and your North Node ☊ reveals your destiny. These signposts are one way to see if you've been together before—and if you're destined to be together again.

> **CAUTION**
>
> **Star-Crossed**
>
> In any lifetime, you'll have more than one soul mate, and not all your soul mates are your lovers—or even your best friends. Soul mate relationships present both challenges and opportunities, and when you understand what the soul mate dance is all about, you can work with it instead of against it.

But, as we did for Michael Douglas and Catherine Zeta-Jones earlier in the chapter, there are other things to look for as well. Parallel paths can be found in conjunctions between either your houses or signs—and especially when both occur. Trines △ and sextiles ✶ can indicate that your relationship will be a good one this time around, while an opposition ☍ can indicate stormier weather, or that the present relationship has had many challenges in past lives that need to be overcome—if not in this life, then in a future one!

Two more places that reveal whether you're soul mates:

♦ Saturn ♄ has a lot to do with past lives. You'll want to check out how your Saturn aspects pair up.

♦ Your twelfth house also reveals a great deal about your recent past lives. If you—or your partner—has any planets or Nodes there, you'll want to search both your souls for the lessons they're suggesting.

By now, it's clear that there's a whole lot more to relationship astrology than just your Sun ☉ signs. So, happy hunting—and happy relationships!

The Least You Need to Know

♦ Relationship astrology, or synastry, looks to much more than just your Sun ☉ signs.

♦ Examine what energies, qualities, and elements you share—and don't share.

♦ Explore what houses your signs and planets are in—and how they aspect each other.

♦ Signs that you're soul mates can be found in your astrological birth charts.

Chapter 24

Other Heavenly Influences: The Asteroids and Chiron

In This Chapter

- ◆ Meet the asteroids
- ◆ Goddesses in your everyday life
- ◆ Chiron ⚷: astrology meets shamanism
- ◆ Every Chiron ⚷ tells a story
- ◆ But seriously, folks: the asteroids and Chiron in Jay Leno's birth chart

There is a group of heavenly bodies astrologers can also show on your birth chart and synastry grid that we haven't yet mentioned. That's because we've saved this intriguing band of asteroids and the planetoid/comet Chiron until now. Let's see what astrology has to say about what these heavenly bodies reveal.

The asteroids—Ceres ⚳, Juno ⚵, Pallas Athene ⚴, and Vesta ⚶—are connected with realms that are traditionally female, and the planetoid/comet Chiron ⚷ invites you to change your perceptions in ways you might have not consciously considered. We'll be looking at a few Chiron cycles to show you just how this wounded healer can manifest in your birth chart.

Goddesses in Your Everyday Life

Even if you're not familiar with Greek or Roman mythology, the names of the *asteroids* probably sound familiar. That's because the asteroids have been named after goddesses. Not surprisingly, each is concerned with an area generally considered to be a female realm.

The following table introduces you to each asteroid's realm, and the specific areas for which she is responsible.

Asteroid	Realm	Areas of Responsibility
Ceres ⚷	Motherhood	Fertility, parent/child relationships, crops, natural cycles
Juno ⚵	Marriage	Partnerships, contracts, social obligations
Pallas Athene ⚴	Wisdom	Knowledge, justice, understanding
Vesta ⚶	Power	Devotion, sexuality, health, service to others

In addition to her own realm, each asteroid is associated with both signs and planets, connections that will likely seem natural to you as you learn more about the asteroids.

AstroLingo

The **asteroids**—Ceres, Juno, Pallas Athene, and Vesta—refer to a belt of planetoids that orbit as a group between Mars ♂ and Jupiter ♃. Astrologically, each asteroid is concerned with a specific area of womanhood.

Ceres ⚷: Mom, With or Without the Apple Pie

Ceres (Demeter in Greek) is the goddess of fertility. Her realm—fertility, parent/child relationships, crops, and natural cycles—covers everything that grows. Ceres in your chart shows your unique approach to mothering.

Ceres ⚷ is associated with the sign Cancer ♋ and with the planet the Moon ☽. Locate Ceres on your birth chart. Then, join us for a quick tour of Ceres through the signs.

Ceres ⚷ Through the Signs

Sign	Your Approach to Mothering
Aries ♈	Enthusiastic
Taurus ♉	Steadfast

Sign	Your Approach to Mothering
Gemini ♊	Communicative
Cancer ♋	Nurturing
Leo ♌	Generous
Virgo ♍	Devoted
Libra ♎	Judicious
Scorpio ♏	Intense
Sagittarius ♐	Adventurous
Capricorn ♑	Cautious
Aquarius ♒	Inventive
Pisces ♓	Unconditional

StarFacts

As you may recall, according to myth, when Ceres's daughter Proserpina (Persephone) was abducted by Hades (Pluto) to be his wife, Ceres became so depressed that all things on Earth ceased to grow. Only when a bargain was struck allowing Persephone to spend six months with her mother and six months with her husband did the terrible drought end—but only for the six months that Proserpina was in the world of the living, which became spring and summer. The six months she spent in the Underworld became autumn and winter, when the world lay cold and fallow.

Juno ⚹: The Queen of All Wives

Juno (Hera in Greek) is the goddess of marriage and partnership, and so her realm covers all the areas associated with social responsibilities and the home. As the wife of Jupiter (Zeus in Greek), Juno is often portrayed as jealous and vengeful, but today we note that her power to destroy her spouse's paramours was the best way Juno had to protect her home and her role.

Juno is associated with the signs Taurus ♉ (the home) and Libra ♎ (partnerships), as well as the planet Venus ♀. Locate Juno on your birth chart. Your Juno placement reveals your own unique approach to partnership, and the following table shows you what Juno reveals in each astrological sign.

Juno ⚵ Through the Signs

Sign	Your Approach to Partnership
Aries ♈	Impulsive and fiery
Taurus ♉	Committed and secure
Gemini ♊	Casual and mentally agile
Cancer ♋	Cautious and tenacious
Leo ♌	Dramatic and adored
Virgo ♍	Practical and devoted
Libra ♎	Romantic and balanced
Scorpio ♏	Powerful and magnetic
Sagittarius ♐	Adventurous and exciting
Capricorn ♑	Steady and cautious
Aquarius ♒	Inventive and unusual
Pisces ♓	Idealistic and intuitive

Pallas Athene ⚴: Wise Woman and Warrior

Pallas Athene is the goddess of justice and wisdom, and so her realm is diplomacy—knowledge, empathy, and understanding. Pallas Athene's ⚴ placement in your birth chart shows how you approach decisions, and where your potential for diplomatic resolution lies. We like to think of Pallas Athene as the United Nations of the zodiac!

This asteroid is associated with the humanitarian sign Aquarius ♒ and the quicksilver planets Mercury ☿ and Uranus ♅. Find your own Pallas Athene ⚴ placement on your birth chart. Here's a quick guide to Pallas Athene through the signs.

Pallas Athene ⚴ Through the Signs

Sign	Your Approach to Decision-Making
Aries ♈	Taking the lead
Taurus ♉	Building consensus
Gemini ♊	Forging communication
Cancer ♋	Listening closely
Leo ♌	Creating coalitions
Virgo ♍	Organizing the ideas

Sign	Your Approach to Decision-Making
Libra ♎	Weighing the issues
Scorpio ♏	Seizing control
Sagittarius ♐	Forging ahead
Capricorn ♑	Managing cautiously
Aquarius ♒	Coming from right field
Pisces ♓	From the heart

Vesta ⚶: The Importance of Being Devoted

The last of the asteroids is Vesta (Hestia in Greek), who according to myth is responsible for protecting the hearth and family. Your Vesta ⚶ placement on your birth chart shows your unique approach to giving. Find Vesta ⚶ on your birth chart.

The signs associated with Vesta ⚶ are service-oriented Virgo ♍ and powerful Scorpio ♏, and her planet is transformational Pluto ♇. The following table illustrates how Vesta manifests in each of the signs.

Vesta ⚶ Through the Signs

Sign	Your Approach to Giving
Aries ♈	Impulsive
Taurus ♉	Generous
Gemini ♊	Witty
Cancer ♋	Empathetic
Leo ♌	Heart-centered
Virgo ♍	Sensible
Libra ♎	Harmonious
Scorpio ♏	Passionate
Sagittarius ♐	Spontaneous
Capricorn ♑	Careful
Aquarius ♒	Unusual
Pisces ♓	Compassionate

We'll return to the asteroids at the end of this chapter, when we show what their placement, and the placement of Chiron ⚷, reveals in the birth chart of *Tonight Show* host Jay Leno.

Chiron: Astrology Meets Shamanism

Chiron ⚷, the wounded healer of astrology, has long been considered the astrological link to *shamanism*, an ancient practice of using intuition to heal. Chiron is located between Saturn ♄ and Uranus ♅, and follows the same orbital plane as the planets. It is named after a mythical centaur who was a gifted warrior, teacher, and shamanic healer. Chiron is officially classified astronomically as both a minor planet and a comet, according to the International Astronomical Union's Minor Planet Center at the Smithsonian Astrophysical Observatory.

AstroLingo

Shamanism is the belief that a tribe's priests, or shamans, are in touch with, and can help others get in touch with, the spirit world.

Astrologically, Chiron is studied as both symbolic shaman and wounded healer. Astrologers study Chiron's cycles to note both universal and personal healing patterns.

When astrologers look at Chiron cycles, they're using an ancient art with a modern twist. Chiron is a recent discovery, and adding it to the astrological dance provides new insight into global affairs. Each Chiron cycle with an outer planet invites us to make symbolic shifts of consciousness.

Heaven Knows

You can find Chiron on your astrological chart. Its symbol is ⚷. Like the planets and Nodes ☊☋, Chiron can be found in a sign and house, and aspects other planets as well.

Chiron's cycles with Uranus ♅, Neptune ♆, and Pluto ♇ are of particular interest because, as you'll recall from Chapter 22, these are slower-moving planets and so form aspects with longer and stronger impacts.

Ancient Art Meets Modern Mastery

With Chiron ⚷ identified as the Shaman, let's add a few more symbolic characters to our shamanic mix:

♦ Uranus ♅, the Revolutionary

♦ Neptune ♆, the Mystic

♦ Pluto ♇, the Transformer

> **CAUTION**
>
> **Star-Crossed** _____
>
> The wounded side of Pluto ♀ is the vengeful destroyer. This alter-ego was evident at the beginning of our current Chiron-Pluto cycle in 1941, when Hitler's army invaded Russia, Italy and Germany invaded Egypt, the Japanese attacked Pearl Harbor, and the United States entered World War II. A meeting of these two is always explosive, but this conjunction ♂ was unusually so, because it was in Leo ♌.

Each of these planetary pairs has a cycle of its own which invites a symbolic shift of consciousness. Let's look at some of the most recent cycles for each of these pairs.

A **Chiron-Uranus** ⚷♅ cycle invites a dialogue between the Shaman and the Revolutionary. The current Chiron-Uranus cycle began in 1898, when Chiron joined Uranus in the sign of Sagittarius ♐. This beginning beckons us to open to radical new ways in order to shift our consciousness about the nature of reality, and so heal old wounds.

A **Chiron-Neptune** ⚷♆ cycle tracks the dance between the Shaman and the Mystic. The current Chiron-Neptune cycle began in August 1945, when Chiron was conjunct Neptune ⚷♂♆ in Libra ♎. That conjunction began the process of healing unfair religious and spiritual beliefs, as well as a focus on traditional marriages and partnerships.

A **Chiron-Pluto** ⚷♀ cycle promises that when the Shaman meets the Transformer we will use our power wisely by cleaning up hidden manipulative patterns. The cycle before the current one began in July 1941, with a conjunction ♂ in the sign of Leo ♌.

A new Chiron-Pluto cycle in Sagittarius ♐ began on December 30, 1999. This cycle promises that the meeting of the Shaman and Transformer will seek out new truths and greater understanding (Sagittarius). In this cycle, we'll examine the wounds inflicted by our dogmatic belief systems, and begin to heal them as well.

Heal Thyself

Finding Chiron ⚷ in your own chart is like finding a personal invitation to heal your wounds. Take a moment to locate your Chiron now.

Just as Chiron is the symbolic shaman, each sign has a symbolic role as well. By locating your Chiron, you've taken the first step toward healing yourself. In the following chart, we've provided both the psychic wound and the healing potential for Chiron in each sign.

Chiron Sign	Psychic Wound	Healed By
Chiron in Aries ♈	Impatience	Patience
Chiron in Taurus ♉	Doubt	Understanding
Chiron in Gemini ♊	Self-distrust	Wisdom
Chiron in Cancer ♋	Indifference	Gentleness
Chiron in Leo ♌	Overenthusiasm	Tolerance
Chiron in Virgo ♍	Servility	Strength
Chiron in Libra ♎	Indecision	Steadfastness
Chiron in Scorpio ♏	Possessiveness	Selfless love
Chiron in Sagittarius ♐	Restlessness	Inner peace
Chiron in Capricorn ♑	Fear	Courage
Chiron in Aquarius ♒	Aloofness	Sharing
Chiron in Pisces ♓	Paranoia	Self-transcendence

By knowing what heals the negative side revealed by your Chiron, you can begin your own healing process, too.

But Seriously, Folks: The Asteroids and Chiron in Jay Leno's Birth Chart

We thought it would be fun to see how the asteroids and Chiron manifest in a man's chart, so we picked *Tonight Show* host Jay Leno for this serious task. Take a moment to study Leno's birth chart and note the placement of his Ceres ⚳, Juno ⚵, Pallas Athene ⚴, Vesta ⚶, and Chiron ⚷ before we begin our analysis.

First, let's list where each of the asteroids and Chiron ⚷ are placed in Leno's chart.

Asteroid	Direct/Retrograde	Sign	House
Ceres ⚳	Retrograde ℞	Sagittarius ♐	10th
Juno ⚵	Retrograde ℞	Virgo ♍	7th
Pallas Athene ⚴	Retrograde ℞	Scorpio rade ♏	8th
Vesta ⚶	Direct	Aries ♈	1st
Chiron ⚷	Retrograde ℞	Sagittarius ♐	10th

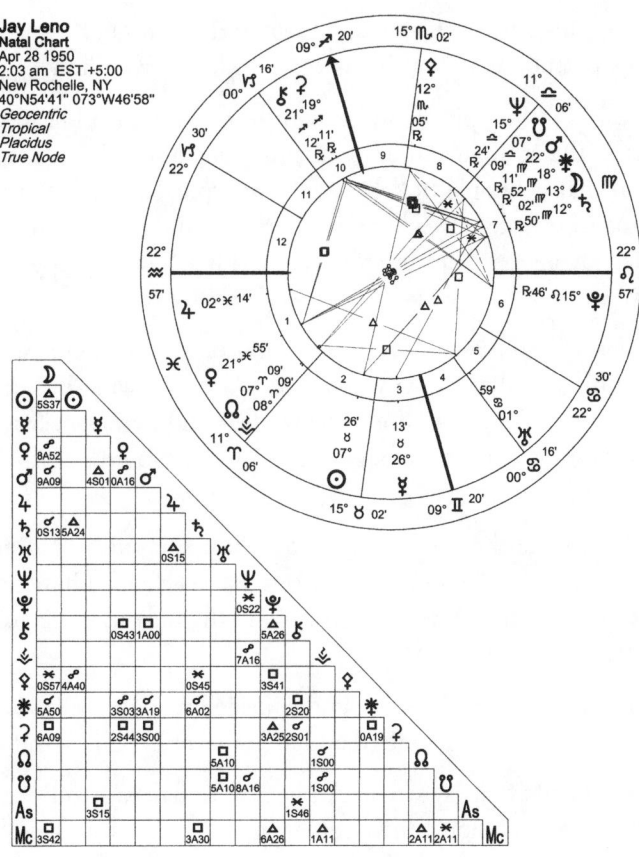

Jay Leno
Natal Chart
Apr 28 1950
2:03 am EST +5:00
New Rochelle, NY
40°N54'41" 073°W46'58"
Geocentric
Tropical
Placidus
True Node

The birth chart for Jay Leno.

Just for fun, before we give you our analysis, see if you can use the keywords we provided for each of the asteroids plus the house keywords from the tearcard at the front of this book to see what you can discover about the asteroid and Chiron placements in Leno's chart. An exercise like this will help you practice finding your own astrological insights.

Now let's start with Leno's Ceres ⚷, which we find in Sagittarius ♐ in his tenth house of career and public contributions. Ceres ⚷ in Sagittarius ♐ in the tenth house indicates a desire to develop and "grow" his career in an expansive manner. Jay will likely want to be independent in how he deals with career development and how he relates to the public. There is an adventurous approach, and possibly even risk-taking where his career is concerned. This is our first glimpse at Jay's focus on career and his ability to venture where no man or woman has gone before—taking over a spot held by the venerated Johnny Carson. Quite a feat—but Jay pulled it off.

Next we look at Jay's Juno ⚴ in Virgo ♍ in his seventh house of marriage and partnership. The asteroid of marriage in the marriage house—what a perfect placement! It indicates that Jay is devoted and loyal to all marriage, partnership, and contractual agreements he has made. He is traditional in his approach to marriage and yet with

Juno there he is proud that his wife is also independent and can do her own thing. He encourages growth in his partner as well as being open to learn from her.

Jay Leno's Pallas Athene ⚴ is in Scorpio ♏ in his eighth house. This indicates that he wants to try to understand the strange and unusual situations of our lives. He has a great curiosity as to what makes people tick, because a Scorpio ♏ Pallas ⚴ wants to know not only the depths of people's lives but *why* they have the habits and beliefs they have. This is what makes Jay an excellent interviewer, and his "Jay Walking" technique applies wonderfully here as well.

When we look at Jay's Vesta ⚶ in Aries ♈ in his first house, we find someone who's studied both himself and his world and is now devoted to sharing what he's discovered about them. This placement shows a devotion to new ideas and new concepts, as well as someone who enjoys sharing his distinctive perspective. As Jay would put it, "When you thought you heard everything!"

This placement also indicates that he is often amazed at how the public and he get along, but it's his personal drive and devotion to his work that has helped him get here. Leno's Vesta reveals just how much he loves his work—and the nurturing he gets from it. Jay Leno needs his public for his creativity.

Last, but not least, we find Jay's Chiron ⚷, the wounded healer, in Sagittarius ♐ in his tenth house of career. This suggests that Jay is one of a kind, a maverick, and a trendsetter.

Chiron in his 10th house suggests that Jay would not be able to have a traditional career. With this placement, he needs the unique, the unusual, and the offbeat to help him feel he is contributing something to society. With Chiron in his house of career, he needs to become his own authority figure. Rather than follow the path his family desired, Jay branched out and created a unique, unusual career. Mom and Dad should be proud. Of course, with his Taurus ♉ Sun ☉ and Sagittarius ♐ Chiron ⚷, he's outstanding in his field!

See how it works? Now, look for the placement of the asteroids and Chiron in your own birth chart.

The Least You Need to Know

- ◆ The asteroids represent specific areas of womanhood.
- ◆ Ceres ⚳ represents mothering, Juno ⚵ partnering, Pallas Athene ⚴ diplomacy, and Vesta ⚶ giving.
- ◆ Chiron's ⚷ cycles invite symbolic shifts in consciousness.
- ◆ Your Chiron's ⚷ placement can show both your psychic wound and your potential for healing.
- ◆ The asteroids and Chiron add extra meaning to your birth chart.

Chapter **25**

Moon ☽ Phases: Our Unconscious Collective Mood Monitor

In This Chapter

◆ What are moon phases?

◆ The tides affect us all

◆ Our monthly highs and lows

◆ How do moon phases affect the way we do things?

Chances are you're already aware of the Moon's *phases*, even if you've never paid them much attention. In its 29½-day cycle, the Moon ☽ moves through four major phases: the New Moon ●, the First Quarter Moon ☽, the Full Moon ○, and the Last Quarter Moon ☾.

In this chapter, we'll explore just how the Moon ☽ affects everything and everyone here on Earth.

What Are Moon Phases?

How much of the Moon is illuminated—and, therefore, the phase we see—depends upon its angle to the Sun. The Moon begins waxing, or growing in light, at the New Moon until it's a Full Moon. Then the Moon begins to wane, or decrease in light, at the Full Moon until the next New Moon.

AstroLingo

Moon phases are the names for the eight parts of the Moon's 29½-day cycle. They are: the New Moon, Crescent Moon, First Quarter Moon, Gibbous Moon, Full Moon, Disseminating Moon, Last Quarter Moon, and the Balsamic Moon.

Here on Earth, we see these changes in the Moon's appearance. As it moves through these *phases*, the Moon is moving through the signs as well, spending about two and a half days in each sign.

The Moon travels about 1 degree every 2 hours (sometimes faster or slower), which translates into crossing a sign about every 60 hours. And as you might recall from Chapter 10, the Moon's energies are manifested differently in each of the signs.

The 29½-day cycle of the Moon ☽—from New Moon to New Moon—is how we got our month. And Monday is named for the Moon, too!

Flavors of the Day: Every Day Tells a Story

We like to think of the way a day feels as that particular day's flavor. A day in an Aries Moon will feel like a good day to start things, for example, while a day in a Pisces ♓ Moon ☽ will feel like a good day to imagine them.

Armed with a Moon ☽ sign calendar, you can know the feel of a day without an intuitive nudge. But why not see if your intuition "tells" you what sign the Moon is in on any given day? Here's a key to the Flavors of the Day, by the Moon signs.

Moon ☽ In	Flavors of the Day
Aries ♈	Beginnings/pushiness
Taurus ♉	Steady course/getting bogged down
Gemini ♊	Communication/lack of listening
Cancer ♋	Sensitivity/moodiness
Leo ♌	Exuberance/boisterousness
Virgo ♍	Organization/nitpicking
Libra ♎	Equilibrium/indecision

Moon ☽ In	Flavors of the Day
Scorpio ♏	Power/possessiveness
Sagittarius ♐	Enjoyment/restlessness
Capricorn ♑	Control/challenges
Aquarius ♒	Independence/detachment
Pisces ♓	Dreaminess/over imagination

Void, of Course

When the Moon ☽ is *void of course*, it has made its last major aspect to other planets until it moves into the next sign. This is a period when it's best not to begin things: Purchases can turn out to be mistakes or bad investments, decisions can be the wrong ones, and new starts or actions taken tend to come to nothing. Although you can't always delay decisions, it's best to be aware of these periods in order to avoid what could be costly mistakes. We'll discuss void of course Moons in more detail in Chapter 26.

AstroLingo

When the Moon ☽ is **void of course,** its energy is spent, and this is a time of gestation, research, or rest. Either nothing will come of decisions made during this time, or there will be unexpected problems that can prevent a successful completion. The Vietnam Peace Accord is an example of a treaty signed during a void of course Moon ☽.

In and Out with the Tide

The Moon affects all liquids on Earth, from the tides to our bodily fluids. The Moon's cycles were originally noted in ancient times, in fact, precisely because their effect on everything from the tides, to growing things, to human nature, was quite apparent.

Tidal charts help fishermen and marine biologists follow the rhythm of the tides and of marine life. And they can help us determine the general mood of humanity as well. The lunar cycle is one of the three primary biorhythmic cycles, which measure the cyclical changes inside your body, using your birth date as a starting point. The 3 major biorhythms are the 23-day physical cycle, the 29-day emotional cycle, and the 33-day intellectual cycle.

The oceans' tides are directly affected by the position of the Moon. When the Moon's at its highest point (about once a day), the tides at that point—and at the point on Earth exactly opposite it—are at their highest. When the Moon is at its exact opposite point, the tides are at their lowest. So each day there are two high tides and two low tides.

We humans tend to retain more water during the Full Moon each month, and because the skull can't really expand when its fluid pressure increases, we sometimes see the excess water there manifested in "Full Moon Madness." Hospitals have also noted there's more likelihood of hemorrhage during a Full Moon, again, due to an increase in fluid. And it's been proven that more bleeding occurs with surgeries performed during a Full Moon as well.

Lunar cycles—and the Moon's sign—also affect the best times to plant, water, weed, and harvest. It's best to plant during certain signs and harvest during others. Here's a quick guide to lunar gardening.

Gardening by the Signs

Activity	Moon Signs for Best Results
Planting and fertilizing	Fruitful signs: Cancer ♋, Scorpio ♏, Pisces ♓
Harvesting	Dry signs: Aries ♈, Leo ♌, Sagittarius ♐, Gemini ♊, Aquarius ♒
Irrigation	Water signs: Cancer ♋, Scorpio ♏, Pisces ♓
Weeding and pest control	Barren signs: Aries ♈, Gemini ♊, Leo ♌, Virgo ♍, Sagittarius ♐, Aquarius ♒

Everybody Feels the Pull

Thousands of years of lunar observation and recording of that data have indicated the same results over and over: begin in a New Moon; nurture in a First Quarter (Wax) Moon; harvest in a Full Moon; review in a Third Quarter (Wane) Moon. Many proverbs also allude to this idea:

AstroLingo

Your **lunar high** (or personal new Moon) occurs when the Moon ☽ is in the same sign as your natal Sun ☉ sign. Your **lunar low** occurs when the Moon ☽ is in the sign opposite your natal Sun ☉ sign.

Tell your troubles to the Waning Moon
And they'll be gone in the morning
Tell your wishes to the Waxing Moon
And they'll be there when day is dawning.

You "feel" the pull of the Moon just as the tides do, and your *lunar high*, or personal New Moon, occurs when the Moon is in the same sign as your natal Sun sign. So if your Sun ☉ sign is Gemini ♊, you're going to feel your best when the Moon ☽ is in

Gemini ♊. This is a good time for you to start new projects, and you will feel your best, both emotionally and intellectually.

Your *lunar low* occurs when the Moon is in the sign opposite your natal Sun. In the example above, Gemini's ♊ opposing sign is Sagittarius ♐. During your lunar low, it's best not to make any decisions, and you may run into obstacles in projects already begun.

How Moon Phases Affect the Way We Do Things

Understanding the Moon's phases and their effect on our daily lives can help us work with these energies rather than against them. Let's take a walk through each to see exactly what this means.

A New Moon ● begins in darkness and will slowly emerge as a crescent that appears to us like the curve of the letter D. This is the Moon that is full of possibilities, the Moon of beginnings, as well as a period when people have a natural urge to start something.

The First Quarter, or Waxing, Moon ◑ is also known as the Half Moon and appears to us as a filled-in "D." This is the Moon that will see projects through, the Moon of action and independence. It also can bring external challenges to light, and in fact, the astrological definition of a First Quarter Moon is "crisis in action." It's typically a period when a lot is happening, and when there's often a crisis or challenge associated with whatever was started at the time of the New Moon.

The Moon is always exactly opposite the Sun when it is Full ○, which is why you see it rise at the moment the Sun sets. It's at this point that activities are brought to fruition, like a blossoming flower: Whatever was being developed comes to light at this time. Everything's visible during a Full Moon, when it truly has become a "full circle."

The Third Quarter, or Wane, Moon ◐ looks like a filled-in "C," and is the midpoint of the Moon's waning phase. It's a time to assess, to look over what's been accomplished, to learn from one's mistakes, and to wind down and prepare for the next cycle.

During the Moon's dark night, which is called a Balsamic Moon, before it once again begins its next cycle, psychic energy is at its peak. It's time to retreat, reflect, and get ready to begin again.

> **StarFacts**
>
> What's a Blue Moon? And why do things only happen "once in a Blue Moon"? Well, there are usually 13 Full Moons each year, and, while the lunar cycle is about 29½ days, months are anywhere from 28 to 31 days. Once in a Blue Moon, there are two Full Moons during one month, and that second Full Moon is called the "Blue Moon."

Using Moon Signs to Guide You

Annual Moon sign guides, like *Llewellyn's Moon Sign Book*, show the best times for activities as diverse as getting your hair cut, borrowing money, having your teeth filled, getting married, and buying a house. Some of these guides list the best and worst times for more than 100 activities.

Basically, Moon ☽ sign guides will tell you things like the best time to buy a house is when the Moon ☽ is in a fixed sign (Taurus ♉, Leo ♌, Scorpio ♏, or Aquarius ♒), or that the best time to go fishing is when the Moon ☽ is in a Water sign (Cancer ♋, Scorpio ♏, or Pisces ♓). If you've been paying attention as we've gone along, you'll soon be making these connections on your own.

> **Heaven Knows**
>
> A Moon ☽ cycle, also known as a goddess cycle, can be viewed at its literal level, a woman's natural 28-day menstrual cycle. Or it can be taken to a more metaphoric level, such as birth–growth, aging–death–rebirth. Viewed metaphorically, we can see why the Moon rules everything from gardens to growth and from banquets to bath water.

When we learn to associate the Moon's natural cycles—both through its phases and through the signs—with our own, we can plan our lives to move *with* these rhythms rather than *against* them. And don't forget—the Moon has been a woman for as long as anyone can remember. With the recent resurgence of interest in goddesses and goddess cycles, the phases of the Moon have reclaimed their ancient stories as well. We'll share a few of these with you as we look at the Moon's phases in more detail.

Beginnings and the New Moon ●

The New Moon is the very beginning of everything, when a seed first germinates and comes out of its seed capsule and the first green shoots appear. This is life at its most basic, with only instinct to guide it, the starting point for all ventures. The Sun and Moon are conjunct, or in the same place, during a New Moon, so they'll have the same sign.

The New Moon is the most masculine form of the Moon's feminine energy, because this is its most active, primitive, and impulsive phase. This is a good time to begin new projects, or to set the plans you've made in motion. It's a good time to plant anything that you hope to see succeed. The New Moon is the planted seed, the first of the elemental powers of fertility and nurturing. This Moon represents gestation, the first step toward birth. Aries ♈ is the sign associated with this Moon.

First Quarter Moon: External Challenges ◐

During the First Quarter Moon, you'll begin to see a seedling's stem with its first pair of leaves, and it will have started to establish its root system. In the next phase, Gibbous

Moon, it will make its first buds. This is the time to make sure that everything continues to go smoothly. Here is where you'll meet your challenges; in the case of that seedling, a late spring frost could threaten it, and in the case of a project, someone in power might question your direction or motive.

During this phase, the Moon is 90 degrees ahead of the Sun, or square to it, so it's a time of challenges and, hence a good time to seek guidance. A seedling might flounder in the hot sun or strong wind, and you may need to stake it or give it more water. Or that project, gathering its own momentum, may run into the first bureaucratic snafu.

The key during a First Quarter Moon is to know that challenges will appear so that you can anticipate them, prepare for them, and meet them.

People born during a First Quarter Moon become very experienced and are capable of meeting crisis after crisis. They have an instinctive understanding of what actions to take to resolve issues and get things back on track. Some of these First Quarter people get an adrenaline rush from doing this, because they're so competent at it, and they might actually create crises in order to get their "fix," or energy high! This Moon is associated with Cancer ♋, because nurturing is required to further programs, projects, and efforts.

Full Moon: The Better to See What's Happening ○

When the Moon is full, it's exactly opposite the Sun, and in this bright glare, all activities reach their harvesting stage. This is the time when the flower blooms and you see the results of your efforts. If things haven't gone quite according to plan, everything that's wrong will suddenly be seen quite clearly, but if they have, it will be the time to gather your rewards.

This is the Moon of high energy, the Moon's highest peak before it begins its waning phase. Crazy things happen during Full Moons, often because all that energy hasn't been channeled during the earlier phases.

A Full Moon can be a time of grand achievement or great disillusionment. If you followed the Moon's phases in your planning and development up to this point, you're probably enjoying the fruits of your labors.

The Full Moon is the romantic lover, the fulfillment of a child, and also the beginning of the separation from the child. This is the Moon most closely associated with Libra ♎, or seeing things from other people's points of view. This is also why this period is associated with rewards or disappointments, as this is when others become aware of what you're doing.

Third Quarter Moon: Internal Challenges ◑

Just because the Moon is continuing to wane doesn't mean its energies aren't at work; they're just moving in a different direction. Once again the Moon is 90 degrees from the Sun, though on the other side of the circle, and so the Third Quarter Moon is assessment time, when we look back at what we've done and see where we can make improvements. We'll also note what we did right, of course. But rather than bask in our glory, as we did during the Full Moon, it's best to use this time to diagnose and correct.

All this assessment can lead to disappointment or a resolve to improve or do better, both of which can in turn lead to internal challenges as we question whether we should have tackled something like this in the first place. And sometimes the Third Quarter Moon means we have to go back to square one and start all over again.

This is a good time to remember that mistakes are lessons, not reprimands. If you learn from your errors and don't repeat them, then you should congratulate yourself. And learning from your errors is what this Third Quarter Moon is all about. The Third Quarter Moon is the Wise Woman, whose knowledge of the mystical and unknown can help us arrive at greater understanding. This is the Moon associated with Scorpio ♏.

Finally, there's the Balsamic cycle, part of the Last Quarter cycle, the dark Moon when the plant releases its seed to start the next generation—the plants that will be born at the beginning of the next New Moon phase. This is the period that bridges the ending of the last cycle with the beginning of the one to come.

Just like life itself, the phases of the Moon wax and wane. Planning your life by the Moon's cycles can help you achieve better results—and save you lots of heartache.

The Least You Need to Know

◆ Approximately every 29½ days, the Moon ☽ moves through four major phases. Every two and a half days, the Moon changes signs.

◆ When a Moon ☽ is no longer forming major aspects to other planets while it's in a sign, it is said to be "void of course," a time when no new actions should be begun.

◆ The New Moon is the time to plant, a time of beginnings.

◆ The First Quarter Moon is the time of growth, when challenges are discovered and overcome.

◆ The Full Moon is the time of fruition and things coming to light.

◆ The Third Quarter Moon is the time for retreat and review.

Chapter **26**

The Best Timing for Better Business

In This Chapter

- ◆ Working with cycles, not against them
- ◆ Time Outs: don't do it!
- ◆ Gearing up and reaching out
- ◆ Communications, travel, and computers
- ◆ Getting to "yes" and signing on the dotted line

There's a popular myth that says that each day has the same potential as every other day. If you think about this long enough, common sense will tell you that this just isn't so. Everyone has good days and bad days, and plenty of in-between days. And it's not just a matter of attitudes going into it, as others around us often have the same type of day.

Now imagine you could know ahead of time which days were going to be good, neutral, or challenging. In business, you would know when to promote or introduce new products, sign contracts, or start new projects, companies, or divisions. And perhaps, even more important, you would know when *not* to take action or make decisions.

Using astrology, you can know ahead of time what the cycles or transits for each day are and plan your schedule accordingly. And lucky for us, business astrology is Madeline's specialty. Read on to hear what she has to say about the best timing for better business.

Working with Cycles, Not Against Them

In our fast-paced new millennium world, we're often asked to work harder, longer, and faster, and be more productive than we've been in the past, even though we might have already been giving 120 percent! If we understand cycles and work with them, we can be more productive, simply by being in harmony with the universal energies occurring at any time.

StarFacts
J. P. Morgan was a wealthy American financier at the turn of the century who used astrology for business-timing purposes. He financed such companies as U.S. Steel Corporation and the Great Northern & Pacific Railroad, as well as the Boer War. His use of astrology for business made him a billionaire, back in the early part of the last century when a million dollars was a vast fortune!

Time Outs: Don't Do It!

The Wall Street Journal once published an article about 1,400 businesses that all started under the same astrological cycle, one that "randomly" occurs 2 to 3 times per week, and lasts anywhere from minutes or hours to 2 days. The essential meaning of this cycle is "nothing will come of it," and all of these 1,400 businesses went bankrupt! This cycle is not actually random, but it's not "visible" in the usual sense either; if you're aware of when it occurs, you can plan accordingly. What's this cycle called? It's the void of course Moon, a cosmic Time Out. When the Moon ☽ is void of course, its energy is spent, and this is a time for gestation, research, or rest. Either nothing will come of decisions made during this time, or there will be unexpected problems that can prevent a successful completion.

When the Moon ☽ is void of course, it's best not to take any action. You may recall from Chapter 25 that void of course Moons, or cosmic Time Outs, are periods when the Moon is no longer making major aspects (conjunction ☌, sextile ✶, square □, trine △, or opposition ☍) to the other planets, and last until it enters the next sign. These times are designed for gestation, regrouping, and internal processing, but not for taking action.

In addition, the last aspect the Moon ☽ makes before it goes void determines the final outcome of an event. This means, for example, if you begin a new venture while the Moon is in Leo ♌, then the last aspect the Moon makes while it's in Leo is what the final outcome of your venture will be—even if the final aspect is a day or two away. So it pays you handsomely to know what the Moon is doing and to adjust your schedule to be in tune with it.

Star-Crossed

Presidential candidates Dewey, Nixon (versus Kennedy in 1960), Goldwater, and McGovern were all nominated during void of course Moons ☽ and so lost their elections. In 1972, Nixon was elected under this cycle (the term he resigned), and President Ford, a lame-duck president, was sworn in under it.

Swimming Against the Tide

When decisions are made or actions taken during these Time Out periods, either nothing comes of them or there are unexpected difficulties. Meetings convened often fail to come to any decisions, because the key information required is usually missing, or the person with the best understanding of it or the power needed to implement it isn't present. When decisions are made anyway, they're plagued by false starts, mistakes, and difficulties. Frequently remaking the decision becomes necessary later. This often means changing course after spending valuable resources on an erroneous path.

Time Outs, or void of course Moons ☽, are gestation periods that are better used for rest and regrouping. These times are good for research, information gathering, brainstorming, catching up on paperwork, filing, writing status reports, cleaning, reading, or reviewing ideas, meditation, introspection, and getting centered. These times also are perfect for just enjoying yourself!

Other typical business examples that have been observed under this cycle include proposed new products that are approved by management but don't make it to market. Purchases made often have quality or delivery problems or parts missing. Sales calls and presentations fizzle, as customers aren't ready to make a decision, and when they are, they don't choose the product presented during the Time Out. Investments made go nowhere, and contracts and other legal matters signed go astray or come to nothing.

A Message from the Universe: Relax!

In essence, the Universe is asking us to use this time to slow down. It wants us to recognize that the creative process of life includes time for regrouping, gestating our ideas, and collecting our thoughts or data.

Nothing in nature demands constant progress and action, except humans! There's often a clear reason not to push forward during these times, and when we do so anyway, we're disregarding our better senses and the Universe's plan.

A better scenario would be to make and implement important decisions only during action cycles, when the Moon ☽ is still making aspects. Imagine not wasting time in meetings that will come to nothing anyway and not expending resources going down the wrong path. Plenty of increased productivity could result from just following this one cycle.

Gearing Up and Reaching Out

Every business has times when it's ready to launch an important product or service, start a new ad campaign, begin a new group, development team, or division within the company, or merge with another company. In manufacturing companies, a new line might be created for a new product. In some cases, facilities changes might be needed, either to increase sales in a retail operation or to restructure an organization.

All these various activities have one thing in common: In some way, they are all new starts. In astrology, these types of activities are primarily under the leadership of Mars ♂ and, again, the Moon ☽. Remember from Chapter 25 that the phases of the Moon give us key signals for when to start things (with a Waxing or New Moon) and when it's time to reorient ourselves (during a Waning or Last Quarter Moon) before the next push. Mars ♂, however, is the planet we call on when it's time to take action, be decisive, or make a new start.

Listening to Mars ♂

Mars ♂ is an extremely important planet to business cycles, as businesses are built on action. Nothing happens until a sale is made through a promotional effort, a product ships, or a service is provided. Action is the essence of business!

When Mars ♂ has beneficial aspects to other planets and its motion is direct or forward, then our urges to make progress are strong, and our efforts are generally successful. When Mars ♂ has challenging aspects (but is still moving forward), one of two things happens: We either get a surge of energy to push past the challenge that comes up, or we get frustrated or angry because we meet resistance.

But because it moves relatively fast, even when Mars ♂ gets into challenging situations with other planets, it usually manages to rally quickly and find support by moving into beneficial aspects with other planets. The real difficulty for businesses hits when Mars goes retrograde.

Warning: Mars Retrograde ♂ ℞

During Mars retrograde ♂℞, or the period when we perceive Mars to be moving backward, business activity decreases or companies often run into serious obstacles. The purpose of this cycle is to reconsider our motivations, actions, and the company's activities.

While this biennial, 10-week cycle seems very inconvenient, when used appropriately it can save companies from throwing a lot of money at bad ideas. Often, it coincides with the time companies are about to make major mistakes in their directions, activities, or new products. Serious disputes can occur between people who want to continue pushing forward and those who recognize the need to reconsider goals and directions.

Introducing products during Mars retrograde is like launching battleships to go to war without ammunition and weapons—very unsuccessful! Because this is not a time for new beginnings, products and services introduced during this period aren't well-received. Actual sales for new products can be as low as 15 percent of the forecast.

What Goes Wrong

It's not that introducing a new product under Mars retrograde actually *causes* it to fail. Instead, whatever is being introduced has one or more of the following problems:

- The product or service isn't ready for the market or vice versa.

- The promotion isn't adequate to create desire for the product, so sales don't materialize.

- There are mechanical or quality issues with the product or service, leading to unsatisfied customers.

In addition, products can suffer from serious mechanical failures during this period, as Boeing's new 777 jet did when it lost oxygen on its test flight in early 1995. Because Mars ♂ is associated with heat and mechanical processes, it's also common to encounter soldering problems, injection molding, or engine failures during this period.

Worse yet, cost-cutting manufacturing changes to products under this cycle can later result in product recalls. Mars retrograde is suggesting that more testing is needed to prevent these problems, instead of prematurely implementing changes or starting new product lines.

All these difficulties are well suited to further research, or beta testing, which is ideal to do during a Mars retrograde.

And Still More Problems!

Stock prices can also go down during Mars retrograde, especially if a company continues down the wrong path or chooses inappropriate goals. This cycle is even harder on stocks that are expected to continue rising in price. Momentum is not viewed as a good excuse by the universe for continuing down a wrong course, and the consequences can be serious! During Mars retrograde, companies might need to stop and reconsider actions, motives, and directions before proceeding. Failing to do so could invite dire consequences. Remember, the Enron collapse occurred during a Mars retrograde.

What to Do, What Not to Do

Every two years when Mars goes retrograde for 9 to 10 weeks, the universe asks us not to start anything new, and to reconsider our direction and goals. "What an inconvenience!" you say? Yes, indeed, but it's even more inconvenient to fail.

The universe believes that every two years we need to take stock of what we're doing, and make sure we're still on the right path, or determine where we should be headed instead. We need to reassess our goals, discover our true motives, and become clear about how we're using our energies. Once we do so, we're ready to set our course for the next two years!

Communications, Travel, and Computers: Mercury ☿

Three times each year for three and a half weeks, the Universe believes we need a period of time to catch up. Now most of us, if we stopped to consider this idea seriously, would realize that we *need* to stop and catch our breath periodically. We really do need to find all the things that slipped through the cracks, get some things redone correctly, clean up, and correct all the wrong assumptions we made earlier. This is the essence of Mercury retrograde ☿℞.

Mercury ☿ is another important business planet, because it's associated with communications, travel, computers, and all forms of transportation. When it's moving forward and making beneficial aspects to other planets, we're doing well in all these areas.

There are times when Mercury runs into challenging aspects with other planets, but as long as it's moving forward, these times are generally resolved fairly quickly when Mercury gets to a good aspect again. Because Mercury is very speedy (it's the messenger after all), this usually doesn't take too long.

But when Mercury slows down and seems to stop then "turn around and move backward," this is our cue to do the same. Because Mercury is associated with thinking, analysis, and communications, we're being asked to rethink, replan, reconsider, recommunicate, and redo whatever fell through the cracks. If only we humans would schedule catch-up time, our experience of this period would be a lot better!

Ignoring the Messenger

Because we're always pushing forward, with little time for these important activities, we often experience the following: Communications become miscommunications and misunderstandings. Transportation becomes difficult, with more delays and accidents than usual. Computers and other electronic equipment break down frequently, and our mistakes come to light. Appointments are missed or rescheduled and, in general, we're frustrated!

Business-wise, this is a terrible time to sign contracts of any kind. One or both parties might misinterpret the agreement or wish they hadn't signed it, and contracts often have mistakes in them. Contract discussions announced or initiated during this cycle are fraught with schedule difficulties and misunderstandings, and they often fall apart. This is definitely not the time to start new projects, because the purpose of this cycle is to catch up.

Products and services introduced or promoted under Mercury retrograde are unsuccessful, in terms of actual sales versus forecasts. Why? Customers misunderstand what's being offered or miss the offer and fail to buy it. Equally often, the product is incomplete or ineffective, especially in terms of documentation or software. The promotion might also "miss the boat" and fail to create desire for the product.

Heaven Knows _____

America Online once unsuccessfully tried to upgrade some of its software during one of these periods, only to be offline for about 15 hours! Computer hardware or software purchased or installed during Mercury retrograde is very likely not going to work, or it will be a nightmare before it finally does. Basically, if your computer is working fine, it's best not to do *anything* to it until the retrograde is over.

Don't Rush!

Generally, when we look back at these situations, we see that we rushed to market, or to complete our project, in time to fail. We took shortcuts that didn't work or refused to reconsider previous decisions, even when we were warned otherwise. In short, we used the period inappropriately and paid the price. Sometimes we pay dearly.

Business travel during this cycle can be difficult. Missed plane connections, lost luggage, and hotel rooms or cars that were never booked, or given away, are much more frequent. Flights might leave very late or not take off at all. Miscommunications, or nonworking electronic equipment (phones, computers, copiers), make matters worse. Appointments and calls are missed. Messages are lost or misinterpreted. Contracts and negotiations can turn sour. In short, it's best to stay home and catch up.

As you might imagine, because Mercury is associated with computers, during Mercury's retrograde period there are lots of computer failures, glitches, and complete power overloads from too much computer usage. Companies that try to switch to new computer programs or upgrade their hardware under this cycle are asking for major problems! In fact it's best to do all your preventive maintenance *before* the retrograde starts.

Working with Mercury ☿

Once we understand all of the potential glitches that lie in wait for us during each Mercury retrograde period, it's easy to see how all the schedule delays occur. This is just the Universe's way of encouraging us to go back and correct what needs to be redone. And when we cooperate and do this, we find that whatever changes we made to our new product, project, or activity helped it become more successful than it was before.

We also realize that there's never going to be a major project without necessary changes or corrections. And when we truly understand that, we can plan for them during the Mercury retrograde periods. But if we don't volunteer to redo what needs to be redone, then circumstances will prevent us from making any progress until we do.

Imagine working in a company where every fourth month was scheduled for catch-up and rethinking! Impossible, you say? Imagine saving thousands and millions of dollars by not pushing forward when you're supposed to be catching your mistakes! Imagine missing costly schedule delays and hassles, because you're fixing your old problems and not making new ones! Now, imagine success, because you're not spitting into the cosmic wind.

Getting to "Yes" and Signing on the Dotted Line

Contracts, negotiations, financial issues, and legal issues are all associated with Venus and Saturn. This includes all relationships with suppliers, vendors, business partners, and banks or financial institutions. It also includes general relationships with employees and managers. As long as Venus and Saturn are making beneficial aspects to other planets and moving forward, these areas flow well.

When challenging aspects come up, though, we may run into difficulties. While Venus ♀ usually moves out of problems and back into positive relationships with the other planets fairly quickly, her speed can keep her moving back and forth between easy and challenging situations.

Saturn ♄, on the other hand, can take much longer to get out of difficulties, especially if it's on troublesome terms with any of the outer planets. If that's not the case, though, challenging aspects to Saturn can be resolved in a few weeks, usually when the other planet moves out of a difficult aspect to it.

Periodically, we encounter a period of about six weeks in which these areas can meet obstacle after obstacle. Venus retrogrades for about 6 weeks out of every 19 to 20 months. When it does, it's time to reconsider our values, along with contracts, finances, pricing, and relationship needs.

The Venus ♀ Bottom Line

In company charts, Venus ♀ represents assets and credit, the ability to partner or create business alliances, purchasing, and the company's contract negotiations. It also represents how well the products and services are approved or accepted by customers. When Venus retrogrades, or appears to move backward, all of these areas should be reconsidered. Moving forward in these areas during this cycle can result in difficult consequences.

For example, products introduced during this period are much less likely to be accepted by customers. This is generally because customers question the value of the product or service and might not purchase it due to price or quality issues.

Partnerships, supplier relations, and major business alliances often need to be reevaluated, especially the ones with strained situations. This is often the time when difficult partnerships or vendor relationships are terminated or else set straight.

False Starts

Venus retrograde is also an unfavorable time to start a new company, because the company's assets may be less than adequate. Taking on debt should definitely be avoided. Financing for business activities or new ventures may not be available under this cycle, and assets may be revalued downward. It's not the time to seek new financial backing, loans, or credit, either. Even if credit's available, there will probably be a major string attached to it!

Legal and purchasing contracts signed under this cycle can also have unpleasant consequences. Contract negotiations can be difficult, and this is a very unfavorable time to buy a new company, division, or rights to a product. A company might pay too much under these circumstances, but it's not likely to be discovered until it's too late and the deal is closed. Or there might be major disputes regarding the price, and then the negotiations fall apart completely. It's best to wait until after this cycle is over before signing any important contracts.

> **StarFacts**
>
> The word *consider* originally meant *con*, or "with," and *sider*, from the word *sidereal*—"to look at the movement of the heavens first to be sure you're in alignment with the stars." Thus, when a person considered something, he or she checked it out with the planets before making a final decision. The word *disaster* originally meant "against (*dis*) the stars (*aster*)." Going against the stars was considered to be a disaster.

About every 19 to 20 months, the universe thinks we need to reconsider our values, money, what we need or want, any legal issues, and how well our relationships are working in general and in business.

If we do these things instead of signing contracts, pursuing legal or financial issues, or ignoring our business relationship needs, we can ensure these important areas continue to meet our needs. If we ignore them, though, we run a major risk of failing in these areas either then or in the near future.

It's clear that steering your business and financial decisions by the planets will save you both time and money. Why not follow the example of J. P. Morgan and use good timing to *your* advantage, too?

The Least You Need to Know

- Using astrology, we can know what the cycles for each day are ahead of time and plan our schedules to work *with* them instead of against them.

- Avoid taking action and making decisions during a void of course Moon. These are gestation periods, and usually nothing good will come of anything begun during these times.

- During Mars ♂ retrograde ℞, business activity decreases or companies often run into serious obstacles. The purpose of this period is to reconsider our actions, goals, motives, and the path we are on to determine if they're still appropriate for us.

- When Mercury ☿ is retrograde ℞, we're being asked to rethink, replan, reconsider, recommunicate, and redo whatever fell through the cracks.

- Contracts, negotiations, and financial and legal issues are all associated with Venus ♀ and Saturn ♄. When Venus retrogrades ♀℞, all these areas should be reconsidered.

- Steering your business and financial decisions by the planets can save you both time and money.

Chapter **27**

Larger Astrological Cycles and the Next 100 Years

In This Chapter

- ◆ How the position of the heavens reflects our global experience
- ◆ Where the heavens are now: the age of Aquarius
- ◆ As above, so below
- ◆ Saturn ♄-Jupiter ♃ challenges and opportunities

Astrology is about more than fixed moments in time; it's a study of cycles—the cycles of the planets and the cycles of events, cultures, and societies and how they interweave with each other. Every planetary cycle corresponds to cycles of human consciousness and is revealed in everything from political and sociological structures to science, religion, philosophy, myth, music, and art.

A glimpse at this interaction between the heavens and everything on Earth is, appropriately enough, the grand finale, so to speak, of this book. We finish our exploration of astrology by looking at the big picture and our future.

How the Heavens Reflect Our Global Experience

By now, it should be clear that the timing of events in the world is tied to the movement of the planets. This makes it possible for us to preview social, political, business, and even personal trends ahead of time by checking what will be happening in the heavens at a particular time in the future.

One branch of astrology, called *mundane astrology*, devotes itself to studying what's happening in the world rather than to individuals.

AstroLingo

Mundane astrology examines what is happening not to individuals but rather to the bigger picture of societies, countries, and cultures.

Beyond mundane astrology, the daily cycles of planets in both aspects and signs are related to what we all experience at any given moment as well as to the world around us. Whether it's more global events like changing social trends or political alliances or more personal ones such as the moment you meet the love of your life or get your raise, astrologers can likely locate it by looking at where the planets are at that particular moment in time.

Where the Heavens Are Now: The Age of Aquarius

Once you begin to study the relationship between global events and planetary cycles, it soon becomes clear that there *is* a relationship. For starters, *astrological ages*—the approximately 2,160 years it takes the vernal equinox to move from one constellation to the next—always herald enormous changes for humankind.

Astrological ages occur because over a span of many hundreds of years the earth's slight rotation "wobble" changes the apparent location of the Sun ☉ at the time of the spring equinox. At present, instead of the Sun entering into the area with the constellation of Aries ♈ at the spring equinox, the Sun ☉ is shifting from Pisces ♓ into Aquarius ♒. This backward shift through the signs continues over time and is called the *precession of the equinox*. It takes approximately 2,160 years per sign, which means that it takes 25,920 to get through all the signs!

The Age of Pisces, which began at approximately the same time as the birth of Christ, has been the age of Christianity. Pisces ♓, after all, is about sacrifice and compassion for others—but it's also prone to blind faith. The various problems of the Catholic Church as the age of Pisces draws to a close likely mark a new era for Christianity—or a more Aquarian religion—as well.

No one really knows the exact date the Age of Aquarius starts (or if it has already started), and astrologers still debate this both astronomically and astrologically. No matter when it does begin, however, everyone agrees that it takes at least 250 to 300 years to transition to a new age, and the changes that occur during a new age take hundreds and hundreds of years. In other words, we're not going to wake up one day and find a completely new world (at least, we hope not!). Transformation takes time—and the consciousness and cooperation of everyone.

So what about this Age of Aquarius? For starters, unlike the Age of Pisces, the Age of Aquarius will be concerned with the projection of social ambitions and ideals. Aquarius ♒, remember, is the sign of humanitarianism, of making plans and structuring ideas, and it's especially noted for its inventiveness and ability to communicate.

It's generally agreed that one of the manifestations of this "inventive communication" will be a much wider acceptance of New Age ideas like intuition and dreams as tools for personal and global discovery. Humans are fonts of untapped potential, and during the Aquarian Age, we'll begin to tap into them.

Some astrologers believe (and hope) that the Age of Aquarius will herald the dissolution of nation-states, as humans join together and truly become "one people." It's something to pray for, isn't it?

Leo ♌, Aquarius's ♒ opposite, indicates that people will want to learn how to use their creative abilities (Leo) to achieve their humanitarian (Aquarius) goals. Remember, a sign's opposite always indicates the goals and ideals to which it wants to apply its energies.

The Age of Aquarius could be the age of universal harmony, but there are enormous hurdles for humankind to cross before we get there. If any age can generate creative solutions to these problems, though, it's the Age of Aquarius, which offers hope for a brighter future.

> **StarFacts**
>
> Think about how much more accepted eastern and holistic medical practices have been by western physicians over the past 10 years, and you get a taste of what the Age of Aquarius will be like in all areas of our lives.

A Study of Cycles: As Above, So Below

As much as it is a study of fixed moments in time, astrology is also a study of cycles, whether of planets, societies, or individual lives. We like to think of planetary cycles as corresponding to cycles of human consciousness. When astrologers look at these cycles, they look especially closely at the synchronistic link between what the planets were doing "above" and important personal and collective human events "below."

Just as each planet has its own timetable to complete one orbit around the Sun, each set of planetary pairs has its own timeline for completing its particular cycle. Jupiter ♃ and Saturn ♄, for example, come together in the same place in the sky to form a conjunction about every 20 years.

By tracking how the various paired planetary cycles correspond to historic events here on Earth, astrologers can interpret how the relationship between the two planets corresponds to our consciousness on Earth for a given moment. Armed with this information, we can learn how the invitations from the planetary archetypes for us to evolve and transform also affect us both collectively and personally.

Saturn ♄-Jupiter ♃ Challenges and Opportunities

It takes 20 years for the social planets Jupiter ♃ and Saturn ♄ to complete one cycle and return to a seed point of conjunction. In their cycle, Jupiter, the expanding Philosopher, dances with Saturn, the grounded Builder, to explore personal and collective processes of growth and contraction. During the 20 years of their cycle, they invite us to change our patterns of socialization with one another and our world. The sign in which the conjunction ♂ occurs is like the sound of a tuning fork that keeps us in tune with our current tasks of balancing between give and take.

There are five Jupiter-Saturn conjunctions ♂ of the twenty-first century, and we're currently moving from a cycle of conjunctions occurring in an Earth element to conjunctions in an Air element. This means that as a global community, we're leaving behind the growth and stabilization of government and personal security systems as we explore more equal and experimental social systems.

How does this planetary dance affect *you* in the first century of the new millennium? Let's explore the key challenges of the five Jupiter-Saturn conjunctions as they impact each of the Sun signs.

2000 to 2020: Aries ♈ to Pisces ♓

The most recent Jupiter-Saturn conjunction occurred at 23 degrees of Taurus on May 28, 2000. This was the last conjunction to take place in the Earth sign cycle that began in 1802. The other recent conjunctions in Taurus were in 1881 and in 1940 and 1941. The key challenge of this conjunction is to both expand and stabilize with respect to the right use of personal and social resources.

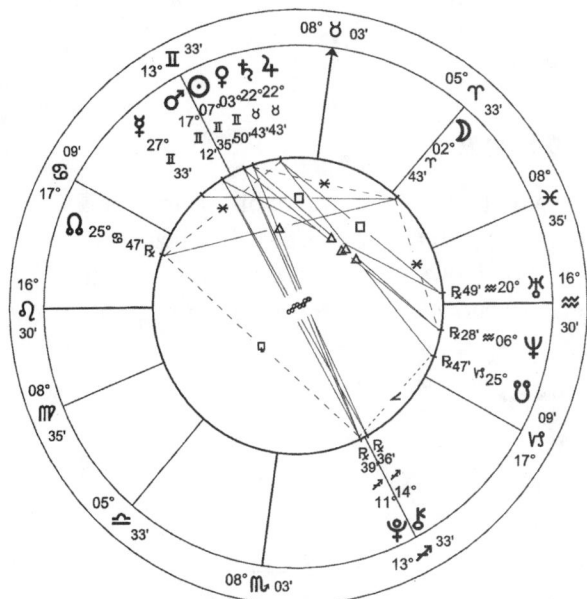

Jupiter–Saturn Conjunction
Natal Chart
May 28 2000
11:05 AM EDT +4:00
Washington DC
38N54 077W02
Geocentric
Tropical
Placidus
True Node

The Jupiter-Saturn conjunction of May 2000.

♦ The three *Fire* signs are invited to ground their fiery natures. Aries ♈ Sun signs need to slow down, get rooted, and claim ownership of their life. Leo ♌ Sun signs need to recognize their own authority and ability to maturely administrate their lives. Sagittarius ♐ Sun signs need to focus on personal health and self-care in a consistent and supportive way.

♦ The three *Earth* signs are challenged to loosen up and invest in their own creative and enthusiastic sides. Taurus ♉ Sun signs need to assess whether their possessions and resources are truly reflective of their individual natures. Virgo ♍ Sun signs need to consider their personal truths and philosophy about money and resources. Capricorn ♑ Sun signs need to invest resources in their own creative and self-expressive sides.

♦ The three *Air* signs are invited to make changes in their relationships to reflect their emotional needs. Gemini ♊ Sun signs need to address the emotional overwhelming caused by doing too many things with too many people at one time. Libra ♎ Sun signs are challenged to become more intimate and committed in their relationships. Aquarius ♒ Sun signs need to confront their fear of losing personal freedom if they say yes to settling down and growing roots.

♦ The three *Water* signs are challenged to get a more dispassionate perspective on their emotional lives. Cancer ♋ Sun signs need to explore new communities and friendships that support their value systems. Scorpio ♏ Sun signs need to embrace fairness and equality in relationships to balance out their tendency to dive in with both feet. Pisces ♓ Sun signs need to explore alternative ways to communicate their intuitive and sensitive natures.

2020 to 2040: Aries ♈ to Pisces ♓

The Jupiter-Saturn conjunction occurs at 1 degree of Aquarius on December 21, 2020. The invitation is to explore ways to create a larger global community that is humanitarian and innovative in nature. How do we collectively form societies that are diverse and open to change, yet stable enough to include and support all members of its groups?

The Jupiter-Saturn conjunction of December 2020.

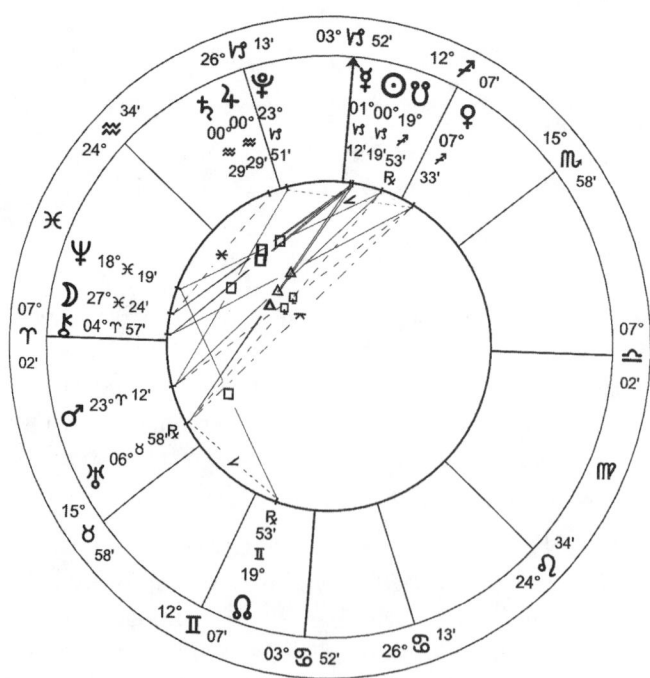

◆ The three *Fire* signs are invited to bring their fiery enthusiasm to dialogue and relate with others. Aries ♈ Sun signs need to initiate new ways to form community and take risks to manifest their dreams. Leo ♌ Sun signs need to focus on fair and equal partnerships and restoring balance to their lives. Sagittarius ♐ Sun signs need to explore new perspectives in their personal philosophy.

◆ The three *Earth* signs are encouraged to stabilize and solidify their physical structures and game plans. Taurus ♉ Sun signs need to claim their capable management skills and be willing to take charge as administrators of resources. Virgo ♍ Sun signs need to find work and service that truly uses their abundant skills and gifts in a fair and supportive way. Capricorn ♑ Sun signs need to organize their own physical resources and possessions and attune their financial situations with their value systems.

◆ The three *Air* signs are invited to get moving on manifesting and expressing their ideas and passions. Gemini ♊ Sun signs need to take some time to synthesize their ideas and vast amount of data into a more concise belief system. Libra ♎ Sun signs need to explore fun and playfulness in their relationships. Aquarius ♒ Sun signs need to actualize more of their uniqueness and take some risks to be independent and self-reliant.

◆ The three *Water* signs are challenged to explore how to deepen their own emotional expression and attune to their sensitivity in social situations. Cancer ♋ Sun signs need to become emotionally honest about the price they pay to be caretakers for others and to be willing to ask others to support them, too. Scorpio ♏ Sun signs need to release old emotional patterns from family dynamics so that they can have a more intimate experience of home. Pisces ♓ Sun signs need to recognize their intuitive and visionary natures and create ways to honor them.

2040 to 2060: Aries ♈ to Pisces ♓

The Jupiter-Saturn conjunction occurs at 18 degrees of Libra on October 31, 2040. This 20-year cycle explores social structures that are equal and balanced, yet also creative and artistic.

◆ The three *Fire* signs are challenged to mentally understand decisions before they leap into action. Aries ♈ Sun signs need to be willing to see the other guy's point of view and to explore partnerships with equals. Leo ♌ Sun signs need to share in dialogue with the world their creativity and full-heartedness and not be attached to being special. Sagittarius ♐ Sun signs need to explore communities with kindred spirits who share similar life dreams and goals.

The Jupiter–Saturn conjunction of October 2040.

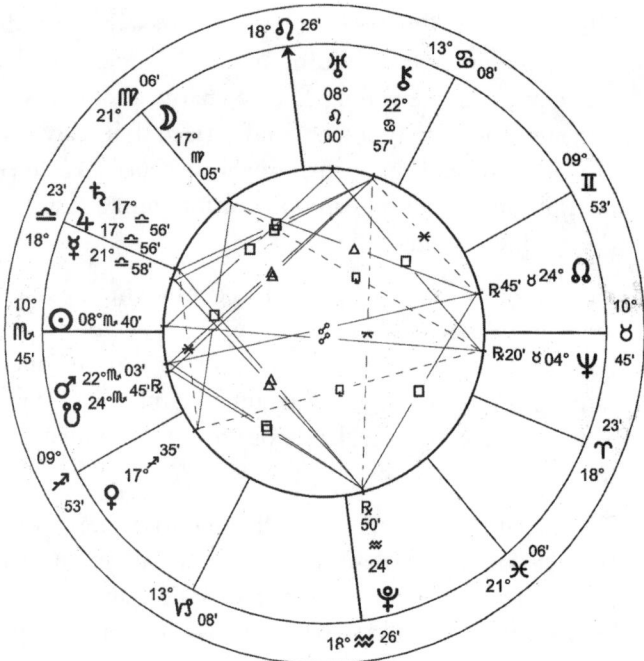

Jupiter–Saturn Conjunction
Natal Chart
Oct 31 2040
6:50 AM EST +5:00
Washington DC
38N54 077W02
Geocentric
Tropical
Placidus
True Node

◆ The three *Earth* signs are challenged to participate in relationships that are pragmatic and grounded. Taurus ♉ Sun signs need to create daily routines that are balanced with work and self-care and to explore service that is worthwhile. Virgo ♍ Sun signs need to create a functional and practical way to manage their finances. Capricorn ♑ Sun signs need to explore career paths that allow their natural leadership abilities to balance with their creative needs.

◆ The three *Air* signs are invited to become enthusiastic and fired up about their relationships. Gemini ♊ Sun signs need to discover creative ways to express their diverse interests. Libra ♎ Sun signs are challenged to become more selfish in an appropriate way and not always defer to the other guy's needs and wants. Aquarius ♒ Sun signs need to explore their personal truths and beliefs about equal relationships.

◆ The three *Water* signs are challenged to honor their authentic emotional natures in their relationships. Cancer ♋ Sun signs need to nest and create emotionally secure relationships. Scorpio ♏ Sun signs need to release their need to control and to seek the more subtle and spiritual dimensions in relationships. Pisces ♓ Sun signs need to explore the ability to establish clear emotional boundaries and dialogue about power issues in relationships.

2060 to 2080: Aries ♈ to Pisces ♓

The Jupiter-Saturn conjunction occurs at 1 degree of Gemini on April 7, 2060. This is close to the Neptune-Pluto conjunction degree of 1892, so this Jupiter-Saturn cycle links us back to the seed gate of the current civilization. This 20-year cycle invites us to explore and create new structures for using data and information.

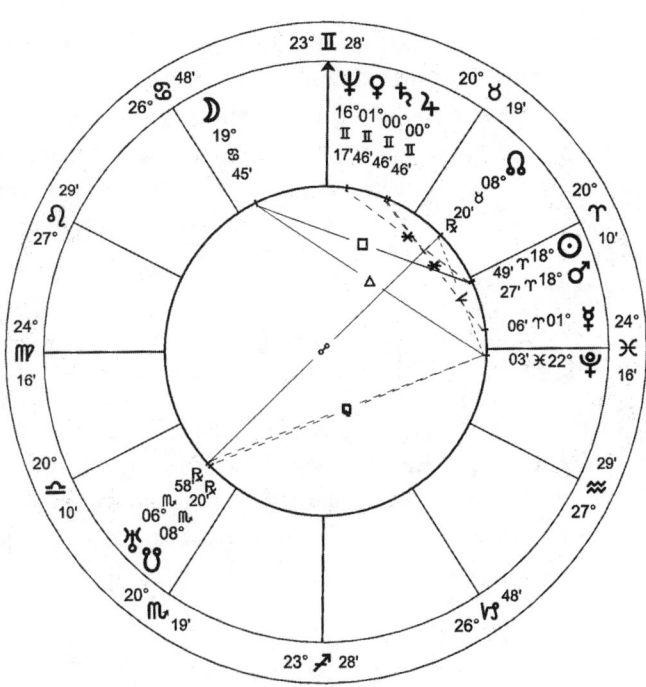

Jupiter–Saturn Conjunction
Natal Chart
Apr 7 2060
4:32 PM EST +5:00
Washington DC
38N54 077W02
Geocentric
Tropical
Placidus
True Node

The Jupiter-Saturn conjunction of April 2060.

◆ The three *Fire* signs are invited to intensify their spirited natures and develop new forms to communicate their uniqueness. Aries ♈ Sun signs need to discover how to best articulate their pioneering and courageous ideas. Leo ♌ Sun signs need to create communities and friendships in which personal creativity and skills are mutually shared. Sagittarius ♐ Sun signs need to release judgment and dogmatic stances in relationships and be willing to learn deeper truths from others.

◆ The three *Earth* signs are challenged to explore innovative new ways to manage and administrate technological and communication resources. Taurus ♉ Sun signs need to create physical and financial security through appropriate dialogue with others. Virgo ♍ Sun signs are invited to step forward with their analytical skills to help administrate and organize ways to manage resources. Capricorn ♑ Sun signs need to analyze personal and collective strategies for the healthy maintenance of whole systems.

◆ The three *Air* signs are invited to pursue their intellectual and communication gifts in new ways. Gemini ♊ Sun signs need to take risks to step out in new directions to express their ideas and knowledge. Libra ♎ Sun signs are challenged to reflect on their philosophy about relationships and to quest for greater beauty in their lives. Aquarius ♒ Sun signs need to explore playfulness and their willingness to reveal their creative gifts to others.

◆ The three *Water* signs are invited to communicate their emotional truths and to explore new paths with personal intimacy. Cancer ♋ Sun signs need to develop their intuitive and psychic natures and explore the union of spirituality with emotionality. Scorpio ♏ Sun signs need to develop the ability to share honest dialogue about issues of power and emotional intimacy with others. Pisces ♓ Sun signs need to explore how to make a safe home in the world for their mystical and sensitive natures.

2080 to 2100: Aries ♈ to Pisces ♓

The Jupiter-Saturn conjunction occurs at 12 degrees of Aquarius on March 15, 2080. As the twenty-first century comes to a close, the Jupiter-Saturn dance again occurs in Aquarius (the conjunction in 2020 was also in Aquarius). We return to the challenge of how to create an open and free, yet also stable, society that honors the uniqueness of all its members and is organized, functional, and efficient.

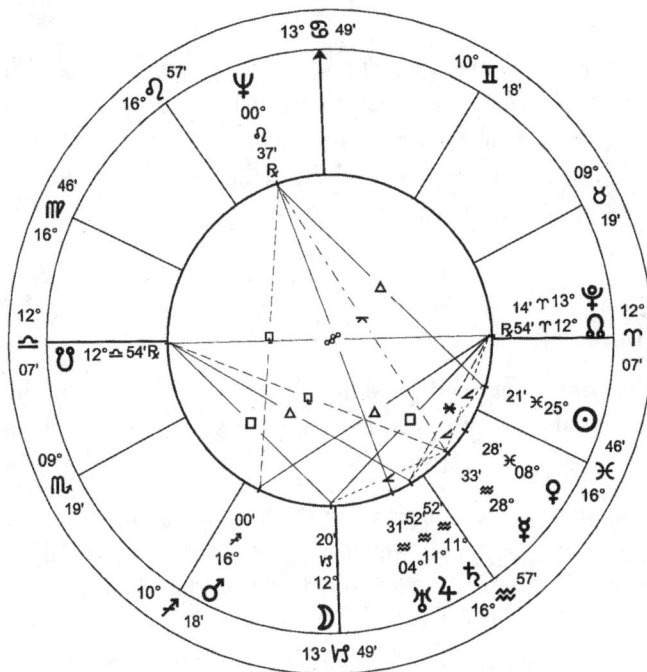

Jupiter–Saturn Conjunction
Natal Chart
Mar 14 2080
7:34 PM EST +5:00
Washington DC
38N54 077W02
Geocentric
Tropical
Placidus
True Node

The Jupiter-Saturn conjunction of March 2080.

♦ The three *Fire* signs are invited to bring their fire to their world on an intellectual and relational level with others. Aries ♈ Sun signs need to seek out friendships and group experiences that honor their courage and strong individuality. Leo ♌ Sun signs need to seek balance and harmony in their lives. Sagittarius ♐ Sun signs need to quest for new understanding about their personal truths.

♦ The three *Earth* signs are encouraged to get their lives grounded and functional in experimental new ways. Taurus ♉ Sun signs need to organize their personal resources in efficient and functional ways. Virgo ♍ Sun signs need to analyze and discern the most effective way to maintain their health and stability. Capricorn ♑ Sun signs need to clarify how best to manage their personal physical and financial resources.

◆ The three *Air* signs are called to get inspired about participation in community and group processes. Gemini ♊ Sun signs need to explore new belief systems that can assist them in communicating their wisdom. Libra ♎ Sun signs need to celebrate their special gifts of heart and creativity. Aquarius ♒ Sun signs need to follow their own drummer and to claim more fully their individual natures in the world.

◆ The three *Water* signs are challenged to express their emotional truths with friends and community. Cancer ♋ Sun signs need to explore emotional intimacy with self and others. Scorpio ♏ Sun signs need to explore new visions of family and home in which their passionate natures are honored. Pisces ♓ Sun signs need to seek spiritual and contemplative experiences with their friends and community.

A New World Awaits

We are poised on the cusp of unimagined possibilities for both humans and humanity. What we do with the potentials and energies that are represented by the planets is up to each one of us.

We can use astrology to achieve some of these unimagined opportunities, and, to that end, this book is only a beginning. It's our hope that you've found it a solid beginning, one that you'll embrace as the first step toward a future filled with wonderful possibilities for all of us.

The Least You Need to Know

◆ What's happening overhead is what's happening all around us.

◆ The precession of the ages has led to our present time, the dawning of the Age of Aquarius.

◆ By tracking paired planetary cycles, astrologers can interpret how they correspond to our consciousness on Earth for a given moment.

◆ What we do with the marvelous opportunities ahead is up to each one of us.

Online with the Heavens

The Internet is literally exploding with astrology sites. As with almost all subjects, the best way to find what you want online these days is to do a search that includes the desired topic. If you want a free birth chart, you type "astrology birth chart free" into the search line, and then choose from among your thousands of choices. If you want to find out more about your particular Saturn ♄ in Aries ♈ in your fifth house, you could type in "astrology Saturn Aries fifth house," and see what comes up.

That said, we do have a few favorites where we tend to go for quick, easy-to-find answers:

♦ At Madeline's website, www.astro-cycles.com, you can order the latest edition of Madeline's *Good Timing Guide*, find out about Madeline's current appearances, sign up for a consultation, read some of Madeline's recent articles, or find out more about Madeline's area of expertise, business astrology.

♦ You can also reach Madeline at Polaris Business Guides, www.polarisbusinessguides.com, a network of New Age specialists in fields such as astrology, coaching, numerology, and Feng Shui, that guides clients in making business decisions.

♦ Astrologer and Tarot reader Arlene Tognetti's website, www.mellinetti.com, offers up-to-the-minute astrology information, as well as an online Tarot spread to answer your questions.

♦ For birth dates of the rich and famous, you can't do better than the late Lois Rodden's website, www.astrodatabank.com. You can also order software to generate your own charts here, as well as find charts for many of today's newsmakers.

♦ Thanks to sites like astrologer Kelli Fox's www.goddess.astrology.com, information about the asteroids, as well as other aspects of feminine energy in astrology, is just a click away.

♦ At www.artcharts.com/astrology/moonvoids.html, you can download a monthly Moon void of course table to help you plan your schedule.

♦ Go to Astrolabe, Inc., www.alabe.com, for more information on their popular astrology chart software, Solar Fire, and other special astrology programs. Solar Fire software is used to generate the birth charts you see in this book.

Of course, these are but a few of the thousands upon thousands of astrological websites now available. And remember, when accessing information and services from an astrology website, be sure to check the credentials of the astrologer or organization hosting it to guarantee the best data and interpretations. Happy browsing!

Appendix **B**

Resources for the Starry-Eyed: If You Want to Find Out More

Astrology—General

Ahlquist, Cynthia, ed. *Llewellyn's Moon Sign Book 1996*. St. Paul: Llewellyn, 1995.

Birkbeck, Lyn. *Do It Yourself Astrology*. Rockport, MA: Element, 1996.

Forrest, Steven. *The Inner Sky*. San Diego: ACS Publications, 1996.

Gerwick-Brodeur, Madeline, and Lisa Lenard. *The Pocket Idiot's Guide to Horoscopes*. Indianapolis: Alpha Books, 1998.

Heindel, Max, and Augusta Foss Heindel. *The Message of the Stars*. Oceanside, CA: The Rosicrucian Fellowship.

Hickey, Isabel M. *Astrology: A Cosmic Science*. Bridgeport, CT: Altieri Press, 1970.

March, Marion D., and Joan McEvers. *The Only Way to Learn Astrology, Vol. 1: Basic Principles*. San Diego: ACS Publications, 1995.

Munkasey, Michael. *The Astrological Thesaurus. Book 1: House Keywords*. St. Paul: Llewellyn, 1992.

Oken, Alan. *Alan Oken's Complete Astrology*. New York: Bantam, 1988.

Rejali, Roxanna, and Cynthia Ahlquist, eds. *Llewellyn's Sun Sign Book 1996*. St. Paul: Llewellyn, 1995.

Sakoian, Frances, and Louis S. Acker. *The Astrologer's Handbook*. New York: Harper and Row, 1973.

Tyl, Noel. *Horoscope Construction*. St. Paul: Llewellyn, 1973.

———. *The Houses and Their Signs*. St. Paul: Llewellyn, 1974.

———. *Synthesis and Counseling in Astrology: The Professional Manual*. St. Paul: Llewellyn, 1994.

Wickenburg, Joanne. *Astrology—the Cosmic Pattern. Course 4: Basic Interpretation*. Seattle: Search, 1977.

Woolfolk, Joanna Martine. *The Only Astrology Book You'll Ever Need*. Lanham, MD: Scarborough House, 1990.

Astrology Magazine

The Mountain Astrologer
PO Box 970
Cedar Ridge, CA 95924

Astrology Audiotape

Lewis, Jim. "The Uranus-Neptune Conjunction." Lecture given June 1993 to the Washington State Astrological Association.

Astrology—Ascendants

Giamario, Daniel, with Carolyn Brent. *The Shamanic Astrology Handbook*. Tucson: JCA, Ltd., 1993.

Astrology–Business

Hawken, Paul. "Natural Capitalism." *Mother Jones*. April 1977.

McEvers, Joan, ed. *Financial Astrology*. St. Paul: Llewellyn, 1991.

Astrology–Gardening

Riotte, Louise. *Astrological Gardening*. Pownal, VT: Storey Communications, 1990.

Astrology–Health

Khan, Nancy. "Summary List of Nutrients and Their Planetary Rulers." (Class supplement). Available from Nancy Kahn at 206-284-1143.

Astrology–Natal

Hamaker-Zondag, Karen. *The Twelfth House: The Hidden Power in the Horoscope*. York Beach, ME: Samuel Weiser, 1992.

Hand, Robert. *Planets in Youth: Patterns of Early Development*. Rockport, MA: Para Research, 1977.

Lundsted, Betty. *Astrological Insights into Personality*. San Diego: Astro Computing Services, 1980.

McEvers, Joan, ed. *The Houses: Power Places of the Horoscope*. St. Paul: Llewellyn, 1989.

Astrology–Nodes

Bohannon, Cynthia. *The North and South Nodes: The Guideposts of the Spirit*. Jacksonville, FL: Arthur Publications, 1979.

Schulman, Martin. *Karmic Astrology: The Moon's Nodes and Reincarnation*. York Beach, ME: Samuel Weiserc., 1975.

Astrology–Planets

Arroyo, Stephen. *Exploring Jupiter: The Astrological Key to Progress, Prosperity and Potential.* Sebastopol, CA: CRCS Publications, 1996.

Green, Jeff. *Pluto: The Evolutionary Journey of the Soul.* St. Paul: Llewellyn, 1996.

Astrology–Retrogrades

Wickenburg, Joanne. *Your Hidden Powers: Intercepted Signs and Retrograde Planets.* Tempe, AZ: American Federation of Astrologers, 1992.

Astrology–Technical

Astro Numeric Services. *AFA Tables of Houses Placidus System.* Tempe, AZ: American Federation of Astrologers, 1977.

March, Marion D., and Joan McEvers. *The Only Way to Learn Astrology, Vol. II: Math and Interpretation Techniques.* San Diego: ACS Publications, 1981.

Michelsen, Neil F. *The American Ephemeris for the 20th Century.* San Diego: ACS Publications, 1991.

Astrology–Transits and Progressions

Brady, Bernadette. *The Eagle and the Lark: A Textbook of Predictive Astrology.* York Beach, ME: Samuel Weiser, 1992.

Forrest, Steven. *The Changing Sky.* San Diego: ACS Publications, 1989.

Hammerslough, B. F. *Forecasting Backward and Forward.* St. Paul: Llewellyn, 1994.

Hand, Robert. *Planets in Transit: Life Cycles for Living.* Gloucester, MA: Para Research, 1976.

Mason, Sophia. *Delineation of Progressions.* Tempe, AZ: American Federation of Astrologers, 1985.

Meece, E. Alan. *Horoscope for a New Millennium.* St. Paul: Llewellyn, 1997.

The Intuitive Arts

Tognetti, Arlene, and Cathy Jewell. *The Intuitive Arts on Family*. Indianapolis: Alpha Books, 2003.

Tognetti, Arlene, and Lisa Lenard. *The Intuitive Arts on Love*. Indianapolis: Alpha Books, 2003.

Tognetti, Arlene, and Deborah S. Romaine. *The Intuitive Arts on Work*. Indianapolis: Alpha Books, 2003.

Tognetti, Arlene, and Carolyn Flynn. *The Intuitive Arts on Health*. Indianapolis: Alpha Books, 2003.

Tognetti, Arlene, and Katherine A. Gleason. *The Intuitive Arts on Money*. Indianapolis: Alpha Books, 2003.

Mythology

Brown, Dee. *Folktales of the Native American*. New York: Henry Holt, 1993.

Burt, Kathleen. *Archetypes of the Zodiac*. St. Paul: Llewellyn, 1994.

Campbell, Joseph. *Myths to Live By*. New York: Bantam, 1988.

———. *The Power of Myth*. New York: Doubleday, 1988.

Cavendish, Richard, ed. *Mythology: An Illustrated Encyclopedia*. New York: Barnes & Noble, 1993.

Graves, Robert. *The White Goddess*. New York: Vintage, 1959.

Guttman, Ariel, and Kenneth Johnson. *Mythic Astrology: Archetypal Powers in the Horoscope*. St. Paul: Llewellyn, 1993.

Hamilton, Edith. *Mythology*. New York: Mentor, 1969.

Marriott, Alice, and Carol K. Rachlin. *American Indian Mythology*. New York: Mentor, 1968.

Prabhavananda, Swami, and Christopher Isherwood, trans. *Bhagavad-Gita*. New York: Mentor, 1951.

Zimmerman, J. E. *Dictionary of Classical Mythology*. New York: Bantam, 1978.

Numerology

Adrienne, Carol. *The Numerology Kit*. Forest Knolls, CA: Wink Books, 1988.

———. *Your Child's Destiny*. New York: Penguin, 1994.

Deaver, Korra. *The Master Numbers*. Alameda, CA: Hunter House, 1993.

Decoz, Hans. *Numerology: Key to Your Inner Self*. Garden City Park, NY: Avery, 1994.

DiPietro, Silvia. *Live Your Life by the Numbers*. New York: Penguin, 1991.

Hitchcock, Helen. *Helping Yourself with Numerology*. West Nyack, NY: Parker Publishing Co., 1972.

Jordan, Juno. *Numerology: The Romance in Your Name*. Marina del Rey, CA: DeVorss & Co., 1965.

———. *Your Right Action Number*. Marina del Rey, CA: DeVorss & Co., 1979.

Lagerquist, Kay, and Lisa Lenard. *The Complete Idiot's Guide to Numerology, Second Edition*. Indianapolis: Alpha Books, 2004.

Palmistry

Gile, Robin, and Lisa Lenard. *The Complete Idiot's Guide to Palmistry*. Indianapolis: Alpha Books, 1999.

Psychic Intuition

Budilovsky, Joan, and Eve Adamson. *The Complete Idiot's Guide to Meditation, Second Edition*. Indianapolis: Alpha Books, 2003.

Just, Shari L., and Marci Pliskin. *The Complete Idiot's Guide to Interpreting Your Dreams, Second Edition*. Indianapolis: Alpha Books, 2004.

Robinson, Lynn A., and LaVonne Carlson-Finnerty. *The Complete Idiot's Guide to Developing Psychic Awareness, Second Edition*. Indianapolis: Alpha Books, 2004.

Scott, Laura, and Mary Kay Linge. *The Complete Idiot's Guide to Divining the Future*. Indianapolis: Alpha Books, 2003.

Zimmermann, Denise, and Katherine A. Gleason. *The Complete Idiot's Guide to Wicca and Witchcraft, Second Edition*. Indianapolis: Alpha Books, 2003.

Reincarnation

Hammerman, David, and Lisa Lenard. *The Complete Idiot's Guide to Reincarnation*. Indianapolis: Alpha Books, 2000.

Tarot

Connolly, Eileen. *Tarot: A New Handbook for the Apprentice*. N. Hollywood, CA: Newcastle Publishing Co., 1979.

Garen, Nancy. *Tarot Made Easy*. New York: Fireside (Simon & Schuster), 1989.

Gray, Eden. *Mastering the Tarot*. New York: Penguin Books, 1988.

Greer, Mary K. "Tarot and Astrology." *The Mountain Astrologer*, vol. 10, no. 3.

Martello, Leo Louis. *Reading the Tarot*. Garden City Park, NY: Avery Publishing Group, 1990.

Tognetti, Arlene, and Lisa Lenard. *The Complete Idiot's Guide to Tarot, Second Edition*. Indianapolis: Alpha Books, 2003.

Appendix C

Glossary

acceleration   The correction factor used to compensate for the approximate four-minute difference between a solar day and sidereal time. It is used when calculating both your time of birth and place of birth.

angular houses   The first, fourth, seventh, and tenth houses are angular houses. They correspond to the natural cardinal signs and are houses with the potential for dynamic action.

anthroposophical movement   Founded by Rudolph Steiner in 1912, the anthroposophical movement incorporates mystical insight and superior speculation to arrive at a larger meaning.

archetype   A term used by psychologist/psychiatrist Carl Jung to represent patterns of the psyche, such as characters that have universal meaning. The Hero is an archetype, for example, and so is the Villain. Other archetypes include Youth, Beauty, and the Trickster.

ascendant   Your ascendant is your rising sign, the sign that has just risen over the horizon at the moment of your birth. It represents the "you" that the outside world perceives, as well as your personality traits, needs, and physical characteristics.

aspect grid   This grid shows the relationships among planets on a birth chart. *See also* synastry grid.

aspects   In technical astrological terms, when two planets are in aspect to each other, they are related by one of several geometric angles between them. Some are beneficial, and others are challenging.

asteroids   Ceres ⚳, Juno ⚵, Pallas Athene ⚴, and Vesta ⚶ refer to a belt of planetoids that orbit as a group between Mars ♂ and Jupiter ♃. Astrologically, each asteroid is concerned with a specific area of womanhood.

AstroCartoGraphy   Invented by Jim Lewis, this is a map of the world showing where your planets were rising and setting at the time of your birth. It can also help you determine what types of experiences you might have in a particular location.

Astrological Ages   A period of about 2,160 years, based on the precession of the equinoxes. Over a span of many hundreds of years, Earth's slight rotation "wobble" changes the apparent location of the Sun at the time of the spring equinox. This backward shift through the signs continues over time, and it takes 25,920 years to get through all the signs!

astrology   This science began as the study of the "wandering" stars (or planets, as we know them today). It is actually the study of planetary cycles and how the energies of these events relate to their concurrent time on Earth. Astrology uses the harmony of the universe to observe the possibilities of human behavior and experience. Astrologers analyze the position of the planets at the time and place you were born to map not only your strengths and challenges but your soul's purpose as well.

base 60   A measurement system used for calculations of time or distance: 60 seconds in a minute; 60 minutes in an hour or a degree.

biorhythmic cycles   These cycles measure the cyclical changes inside your body, using your birth date as a starting point. The three major biorhythms are the 23-day physical cycle, the 29-day emotional cycle, and the 33-day intellectual cycle.

birth chart   This is a unique map of who you are. Using the date, time, and place of your birth, it shows the positions of the planets in the signs and houses. The odds of anyone else having the same birth chart as you are astronomically small!

Book of Time Zone Changes   This guide contains all time changes for the past, present, and future for the place you were born (such as daylight saving time and, in the past, war time).

cadent houses   The cadent houses, which correspond to the mutable signs, are the most adaptable group of houses. The third, sixth, ninth, and twelfth houses are cadent, and are primarily concerned with relationships and transitional states.

cardinal signs   *See* qualities.

certified astrologer   Someone who has studied astrology and has passed the demanding professional certification tests.

conjunction of planets   When two planets appear in the same place in the sky at the same time. Conjunctions begin new cycles that reflect the planets involved.

consultation   A consultation with an astrologer is a meeting in which your birth chart is explained to you in detail.

cusp   The beginning of each house, the door to each, so to speak. Cusps also separate the houses from each other.

daily travel   This is the distance a planet moves in a 24-hour period.

descendant   Located on the cusp of your seventh house, this represents how you channel your energies through partnerships and relationships.

elements   The four elements—Fire, Earth, Air, and Water—describe the basic qualities of the signs and of life. The Fire signs are Aries ♈, Leo ♌, and Sagittarius ♐; the Earth signs are Taurus ♉, Virgo ♍, and Capricorn ♑; the Air signs are Gemini ♊, Libra ♎, and Aquarius ♒; and the Water signs are Cancer ♋, Scorpio ♏, and Pisces ♓.

energies   The energy manifested by a sign is either direct or indirect, external or internal. You'll see the energies called "feminine" and "masculine" in some books, but we prefer to call them *yang* (direct/masculine) and *yin* (indirect/feminine).

ephemeris   An ephemeris is a book that shows where the planets are at noon or midnight Greenwich mean time every day of each year for a specific time period.

financial astrology   This is the study of how and when to best invest your money and manage your finances.

fixed signs   *See* qualities.

grand trine   Occurs when three or more planets aim their energy toward one focal point, highlighting that point on a birth chart. In the zodiacal sky, these planets form a 120° triangle.

Greenwich mean time (GMT)   One of the time standards used in astronomy for locations at the zero-degree longitude or meridian, it's four hours later than Eastern Daylight Time and five hours later than Eastern Standard Time.

horizon line   This line on your birth chart divides your chart into north, which is the bottom half, and south, the upper half. It also connects your ascendant, the beginning of the first house, and your descendant, the beginning of the seventh house.

houses   These are the "where" of astrology. Each of the 12 houses encompasses a specific arena of life and is the stage where the drama of the planets unfolds.

I.C.   *See* lower heaven.

interception   An intercepted sign is a sign that doesn't appear on a house cusp. Instead, it appears totally within a particular house, with the sign before it beginning the house and the sign after it ending the house. Intercepted signs represent areas people need to develop on their own, because others won't be aware of these needs.

interpolating   Interpolating the houses means finding the correct positions between two sidereal times for them.

lower heaven   Your lower heaven, or I.C., is the cusp of the fourth house, the point on your birth chart that represents your life's foundations and psychological roots.

luminaries   The Sun ☉ and the Moon ☽, so-named because they are the planets that provide light to us here on Earth.

M.C.   *See* midheaven.

medical astrology   This study uses your chart to determine the best ways for you to stay healthy and achieve a sense of well-being. It also can be used for diagnosis.

meridian line   This is the line on your birth chart that intersects it from north to south, dividing it into left, the eastern half, and right, the western half. The line of your meridian connects your lower heaven and your midheaven.

midheaven   Your midheaven, or M.C., is the cusp of the tenth house and represents your ambition, career or social role, and public image.

Moon phases   The eight phases are the parts of the Moon's 29½-day cycle. They are the New Moon, Crescent Moon, First Quarter Moon, Gibbous Moon, Full Moon, Disseminating Moon, Last Quarter Moon, and the Balsamic Moon.

mundane astrology   This field of astrology examines what's happening to society rather than to individuals.

mutable signs   *See* qualities.

natal astrology   This is the interpretation of your birth chart based on the position of the planets at the time and place that you were born, which creates a map unique to you and your authentic self.

Nodes   The Nodes physically represent moving points that relate to the Moon's orbit around the Earth. Astrologically, the South Node ☋ represents your heredity or your past, and the North Node ☊ represents your possibilities for growth and where your future lies.

opposite signs   Also known as a polarity, opposite signs appear directly across from each other in the zodiac. Taurus ♉ and Scorpio ♏ are opposites, for example.

orbs   Orbs are the variances in degree allowed in determining aspects.

palmistry   Also called chiromancy, palmistry is the art of predicting a person's fortune by studying a person's hand.

personal planets   In astrology, the Sun ⊙, Moon ☽, Mercury ☿, Venus ♀, and Mars ♂ are called the personal planets. They manifest their energies in the ways we reveal ourselves.

personal retrograde   A planet that was retrograde at the time of your birth.

planetary degrees   This is the longitude and latitude of the position of the planets in the signs.

planetary natives   These have an astrological commonality, such as a planet in the same sign or house.

planetary rulers   The planetary rulers of signs are the "landlords" of the house with that sign on the cusp. Each planet is in charge of certain signs and shares certain characteristics of those signs.

planets   The "what" of astrology, planets represent the various energies of a person, including one's mental and emotional nature, desires, vitality, soul, will, consciousness, and subconscious, as well as the people in one's life. Throughout this book, we'll include the Sun ⊙, Moon ☽, and the North and South Nodes ☊☋, even though they aren't actually planets.

progressed chart   This chart shows how your birth planets evolve over time.

progressions   These show how you and your chart evolve through your life and contain the timing for your development and growth. Generally, progressions are felt more internally than transits.

qualities   The characteristics of different modes of activity associated with the signs. They represent different types of activities and are related to where in a season a sign falls. Cardinal signs begin each season, and so they like to begin things. Fixed signs, in the middle of each season, are preservers, keeping things as they are. Mutable signs occur as the season is changing, so they are associated with transitions.

quincunx   A quincunx is an aspect of 150 degrees and indicates a need to adjust in some way.

reaping lifetime   When the majority of the planets in a birth chart are in the fourth through ninth houses (right side of the chart), the person's opportunities come through others.

rectification   This is a method for determining your birth time based on things that have happened in your life.

relationship astrology   This is the branch of astrology that studies people's charts to determine their compatibility or incompatibility with others.

relocation astrology   This branch of astrology determines what type of experiences you will have in a particular area of the country or world.

retrograde   When planets are retrograde, they appear to be moving backward. Although this is not actually occurring (planets can only move in one direction along their orbits), this is the way it appears to look from Earth.

rising sign   *See* ascendant.

rulers   *See* planetary rulers.

sextile   A sextile is an aspect of 60 degrees and is considered an opportunity for development.

shamanism   The belief that a tribe's priests, or shamans, are in touch with, and can help others get in touch with, the spirit world.

sidereal time   Also called star time, sidereal time is based on the actual amount of time it takes the earth to rotate once on its axis in relation to the fixed stars. While clock time measures a day as 24 hours, based on the apparent movement of the Sun, sidereal time measures it at its astronomical or star speed, about four minutes less.

signs   The "how" of astrology, the signs of the zodiac are Aries ♈, Taurus ♉, Gemini ♊, Cancer ♋, Leo ♌, Virgo ♍, Libra ♎, Scorpio ♏, Sagittarius ♐, Capricorn ♑, Aquarius ♒, and Pisces ♓. The needs and styles of the planets are shown by the signs, as well as what methods could be used to achieve those needs and styles.

social planets   Jupiter ♃ and Saturn ♄ are the social planets, and they manifest their energies in our interactions with the world around us.

sowing lifetime   When the majority of the planets in the birth chart are in the tenth through third houses (left side of the chart), the person creates his or her own opportunities.

start time   Also called reference time; for an ephemeris, start time will be either midnight or noon for a given date. You use it to determine your planets' daily travel.

stellium   A stellium of planets in a birth chart represents a starlike focal point because of the many planets and the aspects these planets form.

succedent houses   These houses correspond to the natural fixed signs and are the houses that give us stability and purpose. The second, fifth, eighth, and eleventh houses are succedent.

Sun sign   A Sun ☉ sign represents the sign associated with the position of the Sun in the heavens at the moment of your birth. When someone asks you what your sign is, he or she is referring to your Sun sign.

synastry   The branch of astrology that looks specifically at relationships.

synastry grid   Also, *aspect grid*, a table that combines two aspect grids into one in order to easily analyze a relationship between two birth charts by looking at the aspects the two peoples' planets make.

synchronicity   This is the belief that everything in the Universe is interconnected, that it is a pattern of meaningful coincidences, or, as psychoanalyst Carl Jung said, that everything born or occurring at a particular time has the energies of that time.

table of houses   A reference chart that shows you how to find your ascendant, mid-heaven, and house cusps.

Tarot   This is the name for a deck of cards used for fortune telling. As the cards are dealt, the fortunes are interpreted by the dealer based on the cards' combinations.

transiting retrogrades   These retrogrades occur as the movements of the planets change and affect everybody. Unlike personal retrogrades, which happened at the moment of your birth, transiting retrogrades are related to what's happening over-head at a given moment.

transits   Transits are like triggers for events in your life and the development shown by progressions. They occur when the planets' present positions aspect their various positions in your birth chart.

transpersonal planets   Uranus ♅ , Neptune ♆, and Pluto ♇ are the transpersonal planets; they're concerned with energies beyond the self, with global universal connections.

trine   An aspect of 120 degrees, this is considered the most favorable of astrology's aspects, although too many trines may make you complacent.

vocational astrology   This is the branch of astrology that studies your potential in order to determine your career or path.

void of course   When the Moon is void of course, its energy is spent, and this is a time of gestation, research, or rest. Either nothing will come of decisions made during this time, or there will be unexpected problems, which can prevent a project's successful completion.

Waning Moon   When the Moon is waning, it's decreasing in light, moving from the Full Moon to the next New Moon.

Waxing Moon   When the Moon is waxing, it's growing in light, moving from the New Moon to the next Full Moon.

zodiac   The zodiac is the name of the elliptic pattern Earth follows in its annual revolution around the Sun. This path is always the same and always passes through the same 12 signs.

Index

A

Age of Aquarius, 352-354
aggression, association with
  Mars, 148-149
air
  houses, 129
  signs, 33-35
angular houses, 126
Aquarius
  Age of Aquarius, 352-354
  ascendants, 121
  Jupiter alignment, 156
  Mars alignment, 151
  Mercury alignment, 144
  Moon alignment, 141
  myths, 103
  Neptune alignment, 168
  North Node alignment with
    South Node in Leo, 174
  Saturn alignment, 160
  South Node alignment with
    North Node in Leo, 173
  symbols, 100
  traits, 99-104
  Uranus alignment, 165
  Venus alignment, 148
Archer symbol, 92
Aries, 55
  ascendants, 114
  Jupiter alignment, 154
  Mars alignment, 149
  Mercury alignment, 142
  Moon alignment, 138-139
  North Node alignment with
    South Node in Libra, 172
  Saturn alignment, 158
  South Node alignment with
    North Node in Libra, 173

traits, 56-59
Uranus alignment, 163
Venus alignment, 146
ascendants, 12, 39
  fall signs
    Libra, 118
    Sagittarius, 119
    Scorpio, 119
  finding your ascendant, 110,
    113-114
  spring signs
    Aries, 114
    Gemini, 115
    Taurus, 115
  summer signs
    Cancer, 116
    Leo, 117
    Virgo, 117
  winter signs
    Aquarius, 121
    Capricorn, 120-121
    Pisces, 122
aspects
  charting relationships,
    314-316
  in aspect (planets), 190
  interpreting astrological
    charts, 275-281
    circle and angle represen-
      tations, 276
    conjunctions, 277
    grids, 281
    listing of planets from fast
      to slow, 278-279
    oppositions, 278
    quincunxes, 278
    sextiles, 278
    squares, 278
    Sun/Saturn aspects,
      280-281

trines, 278
Venus/Jupiter aspects,
  279-280
relationships, 283
symbols, 274
asteroids
  Ceres, 324
  Juno, 325-326
  Pallas Athene, 326-327
  rules and responsibilities, 324
  Vesta, 327-328
Astraea, 77
astrologers
  certified astrologers, 22
  creating astrological charts,
    258
  Newton, Isaac, 10
  Nostradamus, 10
  online consultations, 258
  professional readings, 289
  Pythagoras, 10
  Three Wise Men, 9
astrological charts, 4-5, 129
  asteroids, 330-332
  Chiron, 330, 332
  creating, 252
    birth times, 254
    birthdays, 253
    computer calculations,
      260-272
    place of birth, 255
  Dalai Lama's chart, 26-27,
    190
  defining characteristics, 26
  horizon lines, 192
  houses, 130
  interpreting, 282
    aspects, 275-281
    astrological signatures, 284
    planetary keywords, 283

professional readings, 289
reaping lifetimes, 285
sowing lifetimes, 284
symbols, 274
meridian lines, 192
midheavens, 254
personal uniqueness, 38
progressions
charts, 292
evolution, 294-297
jump or be pushed aspects,
305
resources, 306
themes for personal
change, 293
windows of opportunity,
304
relationships
aspects, 314, 316
elements, 312
houses, 314
planet placing, 313-314
qualities, 312
signposts, 312-313
signs and energies, 310-312
soulmates, 320-321
resource tools
astrologers, 258
atlases, 256
book of time zone
changes, 257
computers, 257
ephemeris, 255
metaphysical bookstores,
257
online consultations, 258
table of houses, 256
samples, 48-51
transits, 297-306
cycles, 300-301
general transformations,
302
jump or be pushed aspects,
305
Neptune, 303
outer and social planet
transits, 299-300

personal transits, 303
resources, 306
Saturn, 303
Uranus, 302-303
windows of opportunity,
304
astrological signatures, 284
astrology
applications, 13-19
calendar cycles, 5-6
celestial navigations, 11
myths, 6-8
natal astrology, 11-12
scientific origins, 3
universal connections, 22-24
atlases, 256

B

Balsamic Moon, 337
Base 60, 260
birth charts,
birth charts. *See* astrological
charts
birth places
corrections, 268-269
creating astrological charts,
255
birth times
creating astrological charts,
253-254
rectification, 254
Blue Moon, 137, 337
body part representations
(zodiac signs), 17
Bohm, David, 8
book of time zone changes, 257
business astrology, working with
cycles
Mars, 344
Mars retrogrades, 345-346
Mercury retrogrades,
346-348
Venus and Saturn, 348-350
void of course Moons,
342-344

C

cadent houses, 128
calculations (creating astrologi-
cal charts)
Base 60, 260
Greenwich mean time
(GMT), 260-261
houses, 269-272
planetary positions, 261-269
calendar cycles, 5-6
Cancer
ascendants, 116
Jupiter alignment, 155
Mars alignment, 150
Mercury alignment, 143
Moon alignment, 139
Neptune alignment, 166
North Node alignment with
South Node in Capricorn,
173
Pluto alignment, 170
Saturn alignment, 158
South Node alignment with
North Node in Capricorn,
174
traits, 68-71
Uranus alignment, 163
Venus alignment, 146
Capricorn
ascendants, 120-121
Jupiter alignment, 156
Mars alignment, 151
Mercury alignment, 144
Moon alignment, 141
Neptune alignment, 168
North Node alignment with
South Node in Cancer, 174
Saturn alignment, 159
South Node alignment with
North Node in Cancer, 173
traits, 96-99
Uranus alignment, 164
Venus alignment, 148
cardinal quality signs, 32-33

careers
Aquarius, 103
Aries, 58-59
Cancer, 71
Capricorn, 99
Gemini, 66
Leo, 75
Libra, 85
Pisces, 108
Sagittarius, 93
Scorpio, 89
Taurus, 62
Virgo, 79
vocational astrology, 15-16
celestial navigation, 11
Ceres, 324
certified astrologers, 22
charts. *See* astrological charts
Chiron, 77
cycles, 328-329
Chiron-Neptune, 329
Chiron-Pluto, 329
Chiron-Uranus , 329
healing potentials, 329-330
computers
calculating astrological
charts, 260-272
creating astrological charts,
257
conjunct aspects
Sun conjunct Saturn, 280
Venus conjunct Jupiter, 279
conjunctions
aspects, 275-277
Jupiter-Saturn, 354-362
creating astrological charts,
252-258
birth times, 254
birthdays, 253
place of birth, 255
tools, 255-258
Cronus, 99
cusps, 47, 126, 270
cycles
Chiron, 328-329
Chiron-Neptune, 329
Chiron-Pluto, 329
Chiron-Uranus, 329

planetary cycles
affects on business deci-
sions, 342-350
affects on global events,
352-362
studying, 353-354
transits, 300-301

D

daily travel, 262-263
Dalai Lama's astrological chart,
26-27, 190
Dark Moon, 138
days of the week, 6
degrees (planetary), 275
Demeter. *See* Ceres
descendants, 12
Douglas, Michael, relationship
chart, 316-320
dreams, associations with
Neptune, 165-166
Dürer, Albrecht, 37

E

Eagle and the Rose, 306
early crescent moon. *See* New
Moon
Earth
houses, 129
signs, 33, 35
eighth house
elements, 129
North Node alignment, 227
planetary alignments 225-227
qualities, 128
representations, 223, 225
South Node alignment, 199
elements, 8
charting relationships, 312
house divisions, 129
Minor Arcana, 36
Sun signs, 33-35
eleventh house
elements, 129
North Node alignment, 242

planetary alignments, 239-241
qualities, 128
representations, 238-239
South Node alignment, 213
energies
charting relationships,
310-312
Minor Arcana, 36
planets, 41-42
Sun signs
yang, 30
yin, 30
ephemeris, 255
evolution (progressions), 294-297

F

fall signs
Libra
ascendants, 118
traits, 82-85
Sagittarius
ascendants, 119
symbols, 92
traits, 90-94
Scorpio
ascendants, 119
traits, 85-90
feminine side representations
(Moon), 136-138
fifth house
elements, 129
North Node alignment, 213
planetary alignments, 210-212
qualities, 128
representations, 209-210
South Node alignment, 242
financial astrology, 18
Aquarius, 104
Aries, 59
Cancer, 71
Capricorn, 99
Gemini, 66
Leo, 75
Libra, 85
Pisces, 108
Sagittarius, 93-94

Scorpio, 90
Taurus, 63
Virgo, 79
fire
    houses, 129
    signs, 33-35
first house
    elements, 129
    North Node alignment, 195
    planetary alignments, 193-195
    qualities, 127
    representations, 192-193
    South Node alignment, 223
First Quarter Moon, 137,
    337-339
fixed quality signs, 32-33
Flavors of the Day, 334-335
fourth house
    elements, 129
    North Node alignment, 209
    planetary alignments, 207-209
    qualities, 127
    representations, 206-207
    South Node alignment,
        237-238
fourth quadrant houses
    eleventh house, 238-242
    tenth house, 235-238
    twelfth house, 242-247
free will versus horoscopes, 21
Full Moon, 137, 339
future implications (Jupiter-
    Saturn conjunction), 354-362

G

gardening (lunar), 336
Gemini
    ascendants, 115
    Jupiter alignment, 155
    Mars alignment, 149
    Mercury alignment, 143
    Moon alignment, 139
    North Node alignment with
        South Node in Sagittarius,
        172-173
    Pluto alignment, 170

Saturn alignment, 158
South Node alignment with
    North Node in Sagittarius,
    174
traits, 63-66
Uranus alignment, 163
Venus alignment, 146
general transformations (tran-
    sits), 302
generational planets
    Neptune, 133
    Pluto, 133
global events, effects of plane-
    tary cycles on
    Age of Aquarius, 352-353
    Jupiter-Saturn conjunction,
        354-362
    studying cycles, 353-354
GMT (Greenwich mean time),
    256, 260-261
grids (aspects), 281

H

healing potentials (Chiron),
    329-330
health. *See also* medical astrology
    Aquarius, 102
    Aries, 58
    Cancer, 70
    Capricorn, 98
    Gemini, 65
    Leo, 74
    Libra, 84
    Pisces, 107
    Sagittarius, 92-93
    Scorpio, 88
    Taurus, 61-62
    Virgo, 78
Hera. *See* Juno
Hestia. *See* Vesta
history of planetary motion,
    175-176
home behaviors
    Aquarius, 103
    Aries, 58
    Cancer, 70

Capricorn, 98
Gemini, 66
Leo, 74
Libra, 84
Pisces, 107
Sagittarius, 93
Scorpio, 88
Taurus, 62
Virgo, 79
horizon lines, 192
horoscopes, 19-22
    sun sign horoscopes, 20-21
    telephone hot lines, 21-22
    versus free will, 21
houses, 5
    astrological charts, 129-130
    charting relationships,
        312-314
    computer calculations for
        creating astrological charts,
        269-272
        cusps, 270
        midheavens, 271
    cusps, 47, 126
    Dalai Lama's astrological
        chart, 190
    defining characteristics, 190
    determining which house
        planets are in, 130-131
    eighth house
        planetary alignments,
            225-227
        representations, 223-225
    element divisions, 129
    eleventh house
        planetary alignments,
            239-242
        representations, 238-239
    fifth house
        planetary alignments,
            210-213
        representations, 209-210
    first house
        planetary alignments,
            193-195
        representations, 192-193

fourth house
  planetary alignments, 207-209
  representations, 206-207
fourth quadrant houses, 233-247
interpolating, 270
lessons, 126
ninth house
  Pluto alignment, 231
  planetary alignments, 229-232
planetary landlords, 131-133
qualities
  angular houses, 126
  cadent houses, 128
  succedent houses, 127
representations, 45-47
second house
  planetary alignments, 197-199, 227
  representations, 195-196
second quadrant houses, 205-217
seventh house
  planetary alignments, 221-223, 195
  representations, 219
sign and planet connections, 47-48
sixth house
  planetary alignments, 214-217, 247
  representations, 213
tenth house
  planetary alignments, 235-238, 209
  representations, 233-235
third house
  planetary alignments, 200-203, 232
  representations, 199
third quadrant houses, 219-223, 226-232
twelfth house
  Pluto alignment, 246
  planetary alignments, 217, 243-247

I

I.C. (lower heaven), 27
in aspect (planets), 190
interception, 288
interpolating (houses), 270
interpreting astrological charts, 274-289
  aspects, 275-281
  astrological signatures, 284
  planetary keywords, 283
  professional readings, 289
  reaping lifetimes, 285
  sample charts, 285-289
  sowing lifetimes, 284
  symbols, 274
invention and revolution, associations with Uranus, 162

J

jump or be pushed aspects, 305
Juno, 325-326
Jupiter, 41
  associations with personal growth, 154
  eighth house alignment, 226
  eleventh house alignment, 240
  fifth house alignment, 211
  first house alignment, 194
  fourth house alignment, 208
  Jupiter-Saturn conjunctions, 354-362
  ninth house alignment, 230
  retrogrades
    personal retrogrades, 178, 182
    transiting retrogrades, 182-183
  second house alignment, 198
  seventh house alignment, 222
  sign alignments, 154-156
  sixth house alignment, 215
  tenth house alignment, 236
  third house alignment, 201
  transits, 300

twelfth house alignment, 245
Venus/Jupiter aspects, 279-280

L

Leno, Jay, astrological charts, 48-51, 330-332
Leo
  ascendants, 117
  Jupiter alignment, 155
  Mars alignment, 150
  Mercury alignment, 143
  Moon alignment, 140
  Neptune alignment, 166
  North Node alignment with South Node in Aquarius, 173
  Pluto alignment, 170
  Saturn alignment, 158
  South Node alignment with North Node in Aquarius, 174
  traits, 72-75
  Uranus alignment, 163
  Venus alignment, 147
Libra
  ascendants, 118
  Jupiter alignment, 155
  Mars alignment, 150
  Mercury alignment, 144
  Moon alignment, 140
  Neptune alignment, 167
  North Node alignment with South Node in Aries, 173
  Pluto alignment, 171
  Saturn alignment, 159
  South Node alignment with North Node in Aries, 172
  traits, 82-85
  Uranus alignment, 164
  Venus alignment, 147
love. See relationship astrology
lower heaven. See I.C.
luminaries, 41, 136
lunar highs (personal New Moon), 336-337
lunar lows, 337

M

M.C. (midheaven), 27
Major Arcana cards (Tarot), 36
Mansion of the Fathers, 137
Mars, 41
    association with assertiveness
        and aggression, 148-149
    eighth house alignment, 226
    eleventh house alignment, 240
    fifth house alignment, 211
    first house alignment, 194
    fourth house alignment, 207
    ninth house alignment, 230
    retrogrades
        personal, 181
        transiting, 181
        working with cycles (busi-
            ness astrology), 345-346
    second house alignment, 197
    seventh house alignment, 222
    sign alignments, 148-151
    sixth house alignment, 215
    tenth house alignment, 236
    third house alignment, 201
    twelfth house alignment, 245
    working with cycles (business
        astrology), 344-346
medical astrology, 16-17. *See
    also* health
Mercury, 41
    association with mental
        nature, 142
    eighth house alignment,
        225-226
    eleventh house alignment,
        239-240
    fifth house alignment, 211
    first house alignment, 193
    fourth house alignment, 207
    ninth house alignment, 230
    retrogrades
        personal, 179
        transiting, 180
        working with cycles (busi-
            ness astrology), 346-348

second house alignment, 197
seventh house alignment, 221
sign alignments, 142-144
sixth house alignment, 215
tenth house alignment, 235
third house alignment, 201
twelfth house alignment, 244
meridian lines, 192
metaphysical bookstores, 257
midheaven. *See* M.C.
mid-life crisis, 301
Minor Arcana cards (Tarot), 36
money. *See* financial astrology
Moon, 41
    Blue, 137
    Dark, 138
    eighth house alignment, 225
    eleventh house alignment,
        239
    feminine side representations,
        136-138
    fifth house alignment, 210
    first house alignment, 193
    First Quarter, 137
    fourth house alignment, 207
    Full, 137
    New, 137
    ninth house alignment, 229
    Nodes
        North, 44
        South, 44
    phases, 334-340
    second house alignment, 197
    seventh house alignment, 221
    sign alignments, 138-142
    sixth house alignment, 214
    tenth house alignment, 235
    third house alignment, 201
    Third Quarter Moon, 137
    twelfth house alignment, 244
    void of course, 342-344
Morgan, J. P., 8, 342
mundane astrology, 352
mutable quality signs, 32-33
myths, 6-8, 103

N-O

natal astrology, 11-12
natives, 166
navigation (celestial), 11
Neptune, 42
    association with dreams and
        spirituality, 165-166
    eighth house alignment, 227
    eleventh house alignment,
        241
    fifth house alignment, 212
    first house alignment, 195
    fourth house alignment, 208
    generational planets, 133
    ninth house alignment, 231
    retrogrades
        personal, 178, 184-185
        transiting, 185
    second house alignment, 198
    seventh house alignment, 223
    sign alignments, 166-168
    sixth house alignment, 216
    tenth house alignment, 237
    third house alignment, 202
    transits, 299, 303
    twelfth house alignment, 246
New Moon, 137, 337-338
Newton, Isaac, 10
ninth house
    elements, 129
    North Node alignment, 232
    planetary alignments, 229-231
    qualities, 128
    representations, 228-229
    South Node alignment, 203
Nodes, 44
    North Node. *See* North
        Node
    South Node. *See* South
        Node
North Node, 171-172
Nostradamus, 10

online consultations, 258
opposite signs, 60
opposition aspects, 275, 278
    Sun opposition Saturn, 281
    Venus opposition Jupiter,
        280
orbs, 275

P–Q

Pallas Athene, 326-327
personal growth, association
    with Jupiter, 154
personal New Moon, 336-337
personal planets, 41
personal retrogrades (planets),
    176
    Jupiter, 178, 182
    Mars, 181
    Mercury, 179
    Neptune, 178, 184-185
    Pluto, 178, 185-186
    Saturn, 178, 183
    Uranus, 178, 184
    Venus, 177, 180-181
personal transits, 303
phases (Moon)
    affects on ocean tides,
        335-336
    Blue Moon, 337
    First Quarter, 337
    First Quarter Moon, 338-339
    Flavors of the Day, 334-335
    Full Moon, 339
    gardening tips, 336
    lunar high, 336-337
    lunar lows, 337
    New Moon, 337-338
    sign guides, 338
    Third Quarter, 337
    Third Quarter Moon, 340
    void of course, 335
Pisces
    ascendants, 122
    Jupiter alignment, 156
    Mars alignment, 151
    Mercury alignment, 145

Moon alignment, 141-142
    North Node alignment with
        South Node in Virgo, 174
    Saturn alignment, 160
    South Node alignment with
        North Node in Virgo, 173
    traits, 104-108
    Uranus alignment, 165
    Venus alignment, 148
place of birth
    corrections, 268-269
    creating astrological charts,
        255
planetary natives, 166
planets, 5
    aspects. See aspects
    computer calculations for
        creating astrological
        charts, 261-269
        acceleration, 267-268
        correction for place of
            birth, 268-269
        daily travel, 262-263
        retrogrades, 263-264
        sidereal time, 264-265
        true local times, 265-267
    determining which houses
        planets are in, 130-131
    energies, 41-42
    generational planets
        Neptune, 133
        Pluto, 133
    houses. See houses
    in aspect, 190
    interpreting astrological
        charts, 283
    Jupiter. See Jupiter
    landlords, 131, 133
    listing of planets from fast
        to slow, 278-279
    Mars. See Mars
    Mercury. See Mercury
    Neptune. See Neptune
    personal planets, 41
    placings (charting relation-
        ships), 313-314

planetary cycles, 362
    affects on business deci-
        sions, 342-350
    affects on global events,
        352-362
    studying, 353-354
Pluto. See Pluto
progressions
    charts, 292
    evolution, 294-297
    jump or be pushed
        aspect, 305
    resources, 306
    themes for personal
        change, 293
    windows of opportunity,
        304
retrogrades, 133
    history of planetary
        motion, 175-176
    Mars, 181-183
    Mercury, 179-180
    Neptune, 184-185
    personal, 176-178
    Pluto, 185-186
    Saturn, 183-184
    transiting, 176-178
    Uranus, 184
    Venus, 180-181
rulership, 44-45
Saturn. See Saturn
social planets, 41
stelliums, 295
stories, 42-43
symbols, 28-29, 41-42, 274
transits, 297-306
    cycles, 300-301
    general transformations,
        302
    jump or be pushed
        aspects, 305
    Neptune, 303
    outer and social planet
        transits, 299-300
    personal transits, 303

resources, 306
Saturn, 303
Uranus, 302-303
windows of opportunity, 304
transpersonal planets, 42, 161
Uranus. *See* Uranus
Venus. *See* Venus
Planets in Transit, 306
Pluto, 42
association with the soul's journey, 169-170
eighth house alignment, 227
eleventh house alignment, 241
fifth house alignment, 212-213
first house alignment, 195
fourth house alignment, 209
generational planets, 133
ninth house alignment, 231
personal retrogrades, 178
retrogrades
personal, 185-186
transiting, 186
second house alignment, 199
seventh house alignment, 223
sign alignments, 169-171
sixth house alignment, 216-217
tenth house alignment, 237
third house alignment, 202
transits, 299
twelfth house alignment, 246
professional readings, 289
progressions
charts, 292
evolution, 294-297
jump or be pushed aspect, 305
resources, 306
themes for personal change, 293
windows of opportunity, 304
Pythagoras, 10

quincunx aspects, 278
Sun quincunx Saturn, 281
Venus quincunx Jupiter, 280

R

Reagan, Nancy, 8
realms (asteroids), 324
reaping lifetimes, 285
rectification, 254
relationship astrology
Aquarius, 101
Aries, 57-58
aspects, 283
association with Venus, 145-146
Cancer, 69-70
Capricorn, 97-98
charting relationships, 312-321
Gemini, 65
Leo, 73
Libra, 83
Pisces, 106-107
Sagittarius, 92
Scorpio, 88
Taurus, 61
Virgo, 78
relocation astrology, 19
resources
creating astrological charts, 255-258
progressions and transits, 306
retrogrades (planets), 133
computer calculations for creating astrological charts, 263-264
history of planetary motion, 175-176
Jupiter
personal, 182
transiting, 182-183
Mars
personal, 181
transiting, 181
Mercury
personal, 179
transiting, 180

Neptune
personal, 184-185
transiting, 185
personal, 176-178
Pluto
personal, 185-186
transiting, 186
Saturn
personal, 183
transiting, 183-184
symbols, 274
transiting, 176-178
Uranus
personal, 184
transiting, 184
Venus
personal, 180-181
transiting, 181
working with cycles (business astrology)
Mars, 345-346
Mercury, 346-348
Venus, 349-350
rising signs. *See* ascendants
Roddenberry, Gene, 94
rulers (planetary), 131
rulership (planetary), 44-45
rules and responsibilities, association with Saturn, 157

S

Sagittarius
ascendants, 119
Jupiter alignment, 156
Mars alignment, 151
Mercury alignment, 144
Moon alignments, 141
Neptune alignment, 168
North Node alignment with South Node in Gemini, 174
Pluto alignment, 171
Saturn alignment, 159

South Node alignment with North Node in Gemini, 172-173
traits, 90-94
Uranus alignment, 164
Venus alignment, 147
Saturn, 41
association with rules and responsibilities, 157
eighth house alignment, 226-227
eleventh house alignment, 240-241
fifth house alignment, 212
first house alignment, 194
fourth house alignment, 208
Jupiter-Saturn conjunctions, 354-362
ninth house alignment, 231
retrogrades
personal, 178, 183
transiting, 183-184
second house alignment, 198
seventh house alignment, 222
sign alignments, 158-160
sixth house alignment, 216
Sun/Saturn aspects
Sun conjunct Saturn, 280
Sun opposition Saturn, 281
Sun quincunx Saturn, 281
Sun sextile Saturn, 281
Sun square Saturn, 281
Sun trine Saturn, 281
tenth house alignment, 236
third house alignment, 202
transits, 299, 303
twelfth house alignment, 245
working with cycles (business astrology), 348-350
scientific origins, 3
Scorpio
ascendants, 119
Jupiter alignment, 156
Mars alignment, 150
Mercury alignment, 144

Moon alignment, 140
Neptune alignment, 167
North Node alignment with South Node in Taurus, 173
Pluto alignment, 171
Saturn alignment, 159
South Node alignment with North Node in Taurus, 172
traits, 85-90
Uranus alignment, 164
Venus alignment, 147
second house
elements, 129
North Node alignment, 199
planetary alignments, 197-199
qualities, 128
representations, 195-196
South Node alignment, 227
second quadrant houses
eleventh house, 213
fifth house, 209-213
fourth house, 207-209
sixth house, 213-217
tenth house, 209
seventh house
elements, 129
North Node alignment, 223
planetary alignments, 221-223
qualities, 127
representations, 219
South Node alignment, 195
sextile aspects, 275, 278
Sun sextile Saturn, 281
Venus sextile Jupiter, 279
shamanism, 328
sidereal times, 264-265
signatures (astrological), 284
signposts (charting relationships), 312-313
signs (zodiac). *See* zodiac signs
sixth house
elements, 129
North Node alignment, 217
planetary alignments, 214-217
qualities, 128
representations, 213
South Node alignment, 247

social planets, 41
Jupiter
association with personal growth, 154
sign alignments, 154-156
Saturn
association with rules and responsibilities, 157
sign alignments, 158-160
soulmates, 320-321
South Node
eighth house alignment, 199
eleventh house alignment, 213
fifth house alignment, 242
first house alignment, 223
fourth house alignment, 237-238
lessons, 171-172
ninth house alignment, 203
representations, 44
second house alignment, 227
seventh house alignment, 195
sixth house alignment, 247
tenth house alignment, 209
third house alignment, 232
twelfth house alignment, 217
sowing lifetimes, 284
Spielberg, Steven, astrological chart, 285-289
spiritual premises, 7
spirituality, association with Neptune, 165-166
spring signs
Aries, 55-56
ascendants, 114
traits, 56-59
Gemini
ascendants, 115
traits, 63-66
Taurus
ascendants, 115
traits, 59-63
square aspects, 275, 278
Sun square Saturn, 281
Venus Square Jupiter, 279
Star Wars, 23

stars (celestial navigation), 11
stelliums (planets), 295
succedent houses, 127
summer signs
  Cancer
    ascendants, 116
    traits, 68-71
  Leo
    ascendants, 117
    traits, 72-75
  Virgo
    ascendants, 117
    traits, 75-79
Sun, 41, 136
  eighth house alignment, 225
  eleventh house alignment, 239
  fifth house alignment, 210
  first house alignment, 193
  fourth house alignment, 207
  ninth house alignment, 229
  second house alignment, 197
  seventh house alignment, 221
  sixth house alignment, 214
  Sun/Saturn aspects
    Sun conjunct Saturn, 280
    Sun opposition Saturn, 281
    Sun quincunx Saturn, 281
    Sun sextile Saturn, 281
    Sun square Saturn, 281
    Sun trine Saturn, 281
  tenth house alignment, 235
  third house alignment, 200
  twelfth house alignment, 243-244
sun sign horoscopes, 20-21
sun signs. See zodiac signs
symbols
  aspects, 274
  interpreting astrological charts, 274
  planets, 28-29, 41-42, 274
  retrogrades, 274
  signs, 28, 274
synastry grids, 315
synchronicity, 7

T

table of houses, 256
Tarot cards, Major Arcana, 36
Taurus
  ascendants, 115
  Jupiter alignment, 154
  Mars alignment, 149
  Mercury alignment, 143
  Moon alignment, 139
  North Node alignment with South Node in Scorpio, 172
  Saturn alignment, 158
  South Node alignment with North Node in Scorpio, 173
  traits, 59-63
  Uranus alignment, 163
  Venus alignment, 146
telephone hot line horoscopes, 21-22
tenth house
  elements, 129
  North Node alignment, 237-238
  planetary alignments, 235-237
  qualities, 127
  representations, 233-235
  South Node alignment, 209
third house
  elements, 129
  North Node alignment, 203
  planetary alignments, 201-202
  qualities, 128
  representations, 199
  South Node alignment, 232
third quadrant houses
  eighth house, 223-227
  ninth house, 228-232
  seventh house, 219-223
Third Quarter Moon, 137, 337, 340
Three Wise Men, 9
tides, effects of Moon phases on, 335-336

time of birth
  creating astrological charts, 254
  rectification, 254
Time Out periods, 342-344
transiting retrogrades (planets), 176-178
  Jupiter, 182-183
  Mars, 181
  Mercury, 180
  Neptune, 185
  Pluto, 186
  Saturn, 183-184
  Uranus, 184
  Venus, 181
transits, 297-305
  cycles, 300-301
  general transformations, 302
  jump or be pushed aspects, 305
  Neptune, 303
  outer and social planet transits
    Jupiter, 300
    Neptune, 299
    Pluto, 299
    Saturn, 299
    Uranus, 299
  personal transits, 303
  resources, 306
  Saturn, 303
  Uranus, 302-303
  windows of opportunity, 304
transpersonal planets, 42
  Neptune
    association with dreams and spirituality, 165-166
    sign alignments, 166-168
  Pluto
    association with the soul's journey, 169-170
    sign alignments, 169-171
  Uranus
    association with invention and revolution, 162
    sign alignments, 162-165

trine aspects, 275, 278
    Sun trine Saturn, 281
    Venus trine Jupiter, 280
true local times, 265-267
twelfth house
    elements, 129
    North Node alignment, 247
    planetary alignments, 244-246
    qualities, 128
    representations, 242-243
    South Node alignment, 217

U

universal connections, 22, 24
Uranus, 42
    association with invention
        and revolution, 162
    Chiron-Neptune cycle, 329
    Chiron-Pluto cycle, 329
    Chiron-Uranus cycle, 329
    eighth house alignment, 227
    eleventh house alignment, 2
    fifth house alignment, 212
    first house alignment, 194
    fourth house alignment,
    ninth house alignment,
    retrogrades
        personal, 178, 184
        transiting, 184
    second house alignment, 198
    seventh house alignment, 222
    sign alignments, 2-165
    sixth house alignment, 216
    tenth house alignment, 237
    third house alignment, 202
    transits, 299-3
    twelfth house alignment, 246

V

Venus, 41
    eighth house alignment, 226
    eleventh house alignment, 240
    fifth house alignment, 211
    first house alignment, 194
    fourth house alignment, 207

nt, 230
ninth house
retrogrades, 180-181
    persona
    transiti ment, 197
second h gnment, 221
seventh   145-148
sign ali gnment, 215
sixth h alignment, 236
tenth alignment, 201
third se alignment, 244
twel iter aspects
Ver conjunct Jupiter, 279
    is opposition Jupiter,
    0
    nus quincunx Jupiter,
    280
    Venus sextile Jupiter, 279
    Venus square Jupiter, 279
    Venus trine Jupiter, 280
working with cycles (business
    astrology), 348-350
Vesta, 327-328
Virgo
    ascendants, 117
    Jupiter alignment, 155
    Mars alignment, 150
    Mercury alignment, 143
    Moon alignment, 140
    Neptune alignment, 167
    North Node alignment with
        South Node in Pisces, 173
    Pluto alignment, 170
    Saturn alignment, 159
    South Node alignment with
        North Node in Pisces, 174
    traits, 75-79
    Uranus alignment, 164
    Venus alignment, 147
vocational astrology, 15-16
void of course Moon, 335,
    342-344

W

Waning moon. *See* Third
    Quarter Moon

water
    houses, 129
    signs, 33, 35
Water Bearer symbol, 100
Waxing moon. *See* First
    Quarter Moon
windows of opportunity, 304
winter signs
    Aquarius
        ascendants, 121
        myths, 103
        symbols, 100
        traits, 99-104
    Capricorn
        ascendants, 120-121
        traits, 96-99
    Pisces
        ascendants, 122
        traits, 104-108

X-Y-Z

yang energies
    traits, 30
    zodiac signs, 30
yin energies
    traits, 30
    zodiac signs, 30

zodiac, 5
zodiac signs, 29, 138, 166
    Aquarius
        ascendants, 121
        Jupiter alignment, 156
        Mars alignment, 151
        Mercury alignment, 144
        Moon alignment, 141
        myths, 103
        Neptune alignment, 168
        Saturn alignment, 160
        symbols, 100
        traits, 99-104
        Uranus alignment, 165
        Venus alignment, 148
    Aries, 55
        ascendants, 114
        Jupiter alignment, 154

Mars alignment, 149
Mercury alignment, 142
Moon alignment, 138-139
Saturn alignment, 158
traits, 56-59
Uranus alignment, 163
Venus alignment, 146
ascendants, 39
Cancer
ascendants, 116
Jupiter alignment, 155
Mars alignment, 150
Mercury alignment, 143
Moon alignment, 139
Neptune alignment, 166
Pluto alignment, 170
Saturn alignment, 158
traits, 68-71
Uranus alignment, 163
Venus alignment, 146
Capricorn
ascendants, 120-121
Jupiter alignment, 156
Mars alignment, 151
Mercury alignment, 144
Moon alignments, 141
Neptune alignment, 168
Saturn alignment, 159
traits, 96-99
Uranus alignment, 164
Venus alignment, 148
elements, 33-35
energies
yang, 30
yin, 30
Gemini
ascendants, 115
Jupiter alignment, 155
Mars alignment, 149
Mercury alignment, 143
Moon alignment, 139
Pluto alignment, 170
Saturn alignment, 158
traits, 63-66
Uranus alignment, 163
Venus alignment, 146

importan___
36-38   owing signs,
intuitive co___
landlords, 1___ns, 35-36
Leo
ascendants___
Jupiter alig___ 155
Mars alignm___0
Mercury alig___ 143
Moon alignme___0
Neptune alignm___66
Pluto alignment___
Saturn alignment___
traits, 72-75
Uranus alignment,___
Venus alignment, 14___
Libra
ascendants, 118
Jupiter alignment, 155
Mars alignment, 150
Mercury alignment, 144
Moon alignment, 140
Neptune alignment, 167
Pluto alignment, 171
Saturn alignment, 159
traits, 82-85
Uranus alignment, 164
Venus alignment, 147
opposite signs, 60
Pisces
ascendants, 122
Jupiter alignment, 156
Mars alignment, 151
Mercury alignment, 145
Moon alignment, 141-142
Saturn alignment, 160
traits, 104-108
Uranus alignment, 165
Venus alignment, 148
planetary rulers, 44-45
qualities, 31-33
representation of self, 35
Sagittarius
ascendants, 119
Jupiter alignment, 156
Mars alignment, 151

Mercury alignment, 144
Moon alignments, 141
Neptune alignment, 168
Pluto alignment, 171
Saturn alignment, 159
symbol, 92
traits, 90-94
Uranus alignment, 164
Venus alignment, 147
Scorpio
ascendants, 119
Jupiter alignment, 156
Mars alignment, 150
Mercury alignment, 144
Moon alignment, 140
Neptune alignment, 167
Pluto alignment, 171
Saturn alignment, 159
traits, 85-90
Uranus alignment, 164
Venus alignment, 147
symbols, 274
Taurus
ascendants, 115
Jupiter alignment, 154
Mars alignment, 149
Mercury alignment, 143
Moon alignment, 139
Saturn alignment, 158
traits, 59-63
Uranus alignment, 163
Venus alignment, 146
Virgo
ascendants, 117
Jupiter alignment, 155
Mars alignment, 150
Mercury alignment, 143
Moon alignment, 140
Neptune alignment, 167
Pluto alignment, 170
Saturn alignment, 159
traits, 75-79
Uranus alignment, 164
Venus alignment, 147